AVANT-GARDE IN THE CORNFIELDS

AVANT-GARDE IN THE CORNFIELDS

Architecture, Landscape, and Preservation
in New Harmony

Ben Nicholson and Michelangelo Sabatino

EDITORS

University of Minnesota Press
MINNEAPOLIS
LONDON

The publication of this book was assisted with funding from Jane Blaffer Owen; the Architecture Center Houston Foundation; the Gerald D. Hines College of Architecture and Design at the University of Houston; and the Rowe Family College of Architecture Dean Endowed Chair and the John Vinci Distinguished Research Fellowship at Illinois Institute of Technology.

Every effort was made to obtain permission to reproduce material in this book. If any proper acknowledgment has not been included, we encourage copyright holders to notify the publisher.

Paul Tillich, "Estranged and Reunited: The New Being," is reprinted courtesy of Ted Farris, representative of the Estates of Paul Tillich and Hannah Tillich.

Published by the University of Minnesota Press
111 Third Avenue South, Suite 290
Minneapolis, MN 55401-2520
http://www.upress.umn.edu

Printed in Canada on acid-free paper

The University of Minnesota is an equal-opportunity educator and employer.

25 24 23 22 21 20 19   10 9 8 7 6 5 4 3 2 1

Library of Congress Cataloging-in-Publication Data
Names: Nicholson, Ben, editor. | Sabatino, Michelangelo, editor.
Title: Avant-garde in the cornfields : architecture, landscape, and preservation in New Harmony / Ben Nicholson and Michelangelo Sabatino, editors.
Description: Minneapolis : University of Minnesota Press, 2019. | Includes bibliographical references and index. | Identifiers: LCCN 2018045734 (print) | ISBN 978-1-5179-0313-8 (hc) | ISBN 978-1-5179-0314-5 (pb)
Subjects: LCSH: Midcentury modern (Architecture)—Indiana—New Harmony. | Art patronage—Indiana—New Harmony. | Cultural landscapes—Indiana—New Harmony. | Cultural property—Protection—Indiana—New Harmony. | New Harmony (Ind.)—Buildings, structures, etc.
Classification: LCC NA735.N38 A93 2019 (print) | DDC 720.9772/34—dc23
LC record available at https://lccn.loc.gov/2018045734

*This book is dedicated to Jane Blaffer Owen and Ralph Grayson Schwarz,
who each changed the face of New Harmony in the twentieth century*

The ship that Theseus and the youth of Athens returned from Crete
had thirty oars, and was preserved by the Athenians down even
to the time of Demetrius Phalereus. Over time, they took away the old planks
as they decayed, putting in new and stronger timber in their places.
This ship became a standing example among the philosophers,
for the logical question of things that grow; one side holding that the ship
remained the same, and the other contending that it was not the same.

PLUTARCH
"Theseus," *Plutarch's Lives*

CONTENTS

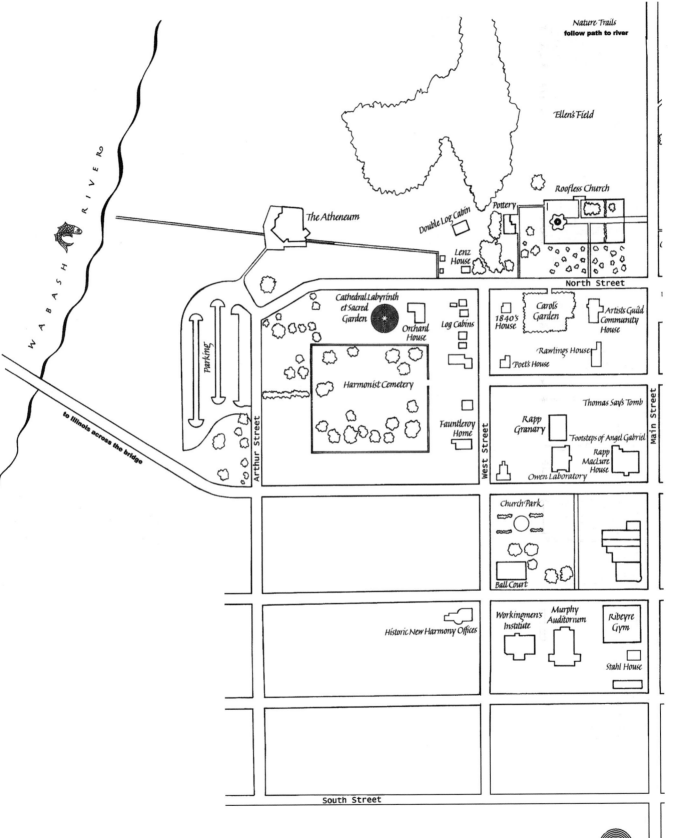

New Harmony · Indiana

Historic Buildings and Gardens

1814·2016

© Janet Lorence · 2016

New Harmony, Indiana. *Historical Buildings and Gardens, 1814–2016.* Map by Janet Lorence; copyright 2016 Janet Lorence.

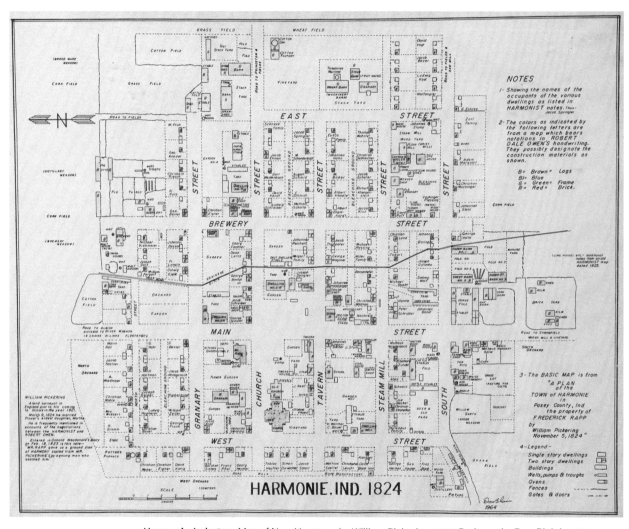

Harmonie, Ind. 1824. Map of New Harmony by William Pickering, 1824. Redrawn by Don Blair in 1964. Map courtesy of Judith Blair Nix; copyright 2017.

INTRODUCTION

Avant-Garde in the Cornfields

MICHELANGELO SABATINO

> On the banks of the Wabash River, not far from the cornfields of
> Indiana, stands a gleaming white structure that is as radical an addition
> to the rural American heartland as Le Corbusier's Villa Savoie was to
> the French countryside at Poissy half a century ago.
>
> ADA LOUISE HUXTABLE ON THE ATHENEUM,
> "A RADICAL NEW ADDITION FOR MID-AMERICA"

SINCE THE TIME OF ITS FOUNDING on the Wabash River in 1814, the town of New Harmony, Indiana, has remained an epicenter for experiments in communal living, educational reform, spirituality, and scientific research. However, despite its significance for the arts, the sciences, and society, the town's population has never exceeded one thousand.[1] Nineteenth-century utopian aspirations based on the renewal of society through faith and later science contributed to New Harmony's reputation as the progressive "wonder of the West."[2] During the second half of the twentieth century, this midwestern town underwent significant transformations, due to the vision and efforts of the Texas philanthropist Jane Blaffer Owen (1915–2010).[3] Blaffer Owen sought to reconcile the seemingly contradictory religious and secular attitudes of New Harmony's original nineteenth-century communities: the Harmonie Society that founded the town in 1814 and shaped its development until 1824 under the leadership of Georg (George) Rapp (1757–1847), a German Pietist prophet, and the Owen/Maclure community led by Robert Owen (1771–1858), a Welsh social reformer, with William Maclure (1763–1840), a Scottish geologist and cartographer.[4] Their project at New Harmony spanned five years after Owen bought the town in 1825 from Rapp.[5] Over six decades Blaffer Owen, who in 1941 married Kenneth Dale Owen (1903–2002), great-great-grandson of Robert Owen, worked to preserve and reinvent New Harmony's living traditions in the spirit of Lyndon B. Johnson's Great Society, challenging artists, architects, and landscape architects to engage New Harmony's natural and built heritage with the living memorials she commissioned.

The architects Philip Johnson, Frederick Kiesler, Richard Meier, and Evans Woollen worked alongside the artists Jacques Lipchitz, Ralph Beyer, and Stephen De Staebler and the landscape architects Thomas Kane, Robert Zion, and Harold Breen, among others, and their collective activity became the basis for renewal in the historic context of New Harmony. The experimental and "situated" works produced during this time synthesized competing and nondoctrinaire attitudes, to the extent that abstraction easily coexisted with representational art and rationalism coexisted with organicism. Amid the cornfields of Indiana, site-specific works at New Harmony challenged the midcentury tendency toward generic modernist buildings inspired by the International Style and at the same time reinvigorated America's long-standing fascination with wilderness.[6]

The built environment of New Harmony from its founding through the beginning of the twentieth century has been amply studied.[7] *Avant-Garde in the Cornfields: Architecture, Landscape, and Preservation in New Harmony* examines the reinvention of New Harmony's twentieth-century identity as a locus of spirituality through the lens of architecture, gardens, landscapes, historic preservation, and memorials undertaken there from the 1950s to the present. Works produced for New Harmony by Johnson, Lipchitz, and Meier have been analyzed in individual monographs, but rarely have they been discussed in terms of their cumulative contribution to the "new" New Harmony. In light of different generations of institutions and individuals vying to interpret the histories and meanings of New Harmony, the reader will notice that throughout the chapters there are some variations in the nomenclature of buildings and places as well as the spelling of names of individuals. Rather than eliminate this variety, the authors have endeavored to provide clarification along the way about usage. The coeditors and contributing authors contend that New Harmony occupies a distinctive place in the history of postwar culture in the United States, insofar as it provided a unique context for the realization of contemporary works that explored the realm of the spiritual against the political backdrop of the atomic age and its corollary, the Cold War.[8]

Going against the grain of technological utopianism promoted by the likes of Buckminster Fuller, Blaffer Owen's patronage embraced alternative forms of spirituality based on a dialogue with nature as a source of beauty and utility through cultivating the land.[9] As a lifelong Anglican and member of the St. Stephen's Episcopal Church in New Harmony, her spirituality was informed by her broad and voracious readings of the texts of different faiths; she was particularly interested in the writings and teachings of Paul Tillich (1886–1965), a German-born philosopher and theologian, avidly sharing his interest in art and architecture.[10] In the mid-1820s the Owen/Maclure community's adaptation of the brick cruciform Harmonist Church

Figure I.1. Architectural expressions of the first two communities of New Harmony: David Dale Owen Laboratory (1859), left center, and Rapp–Owen Granary (1818), right, which served as an early headquarters for the USCMOS Geological Survey. Courtesy of Special Collections, University of Southern Indiana.

to secular purposes signaled an abrupt change in New Harmony's leadership and, likewise, the construction in 1859 of David Dale Owen's Gothic-revival geological laboratory across the street from the church as a challenge to the authority of religious faith. Blaffer Owen brought the religious devotion of the Harmonist era into dialogue with the scientific and pedagogical legacy of the Owen/Maclure era (Plate 3).[11] She avoided ideological extremes by bridging differences rather than exacerbating them. Her fascination with multiple layers of meaning is echoed in a figurative weathervane she discovered when her husband first brought her to New Harmony in August 1941. Mounted on the turret of David Dale Owen's geological laboratory adjacent to the Rapp–Owen Granary (Plate 21), this revolving pointer combines representations of a fossilized fish (*Ictalurus*) from the Paleozoic period held up by a bryozoan (*Archimedes*) and a blastoid (*Pentremites*). New Harmony's complementary historic identities can be understood through this weathervane:

Figure I.2. New Harmony's complementary historic identities can be understood through the weathervane of the David Dale Owen Laboratory: the fish is a powerful Christian symbol and the fossil represents scientific research into natural history. Undated postcard, copyright 2018 Austrian Frederick and Lillian Kiesler Private Foundation, Vienna.

while the fish is a powerful Christian symbol, the fossil stands as a beacon of scientific research into natural history.[12]

The retreat from metropolitan centers to reap nature's bounty in the pursuit of agriculture and forestry along with various kinds of manufacturing was typical for communal utopias in the United States during the nineteenth century.[13] In the New World as well as the Old World, a widespread reaction to industrialization and urbanization led to the romantic idealization of nature and the countryside just as it was being transformed by and exploited in the name of progress and commerce.[14] Shellfish middens discovered on Indian Mound indicate that the site of New Harmony was first occupied by Native American tribes of the Wabash River Valley.[15] Although the Harmonist community transformed the Indiana wilderness into productive orchards and fields, the town's nineteenth-century reputation as a progressive seedbed is tied to the pioneering accomplishments of American natural scientists such as Thomas Say (1787–1834).[16]

From the time of its founding, New Harmony was shaped by an intermingling of faith- and science-based worldviews. The German immigrants led by Rapp had separated from the Evangelical state church of Württemberg. In America the Harmonists (or Rappites, as they were also called) founded three communities in rapid succession: Harmony, Pennsylvania (1803); New Harmony, Indiana (1814); and Economy, Pennsylvania, now known as Old Economy Village (1824).[17] Over the years these communities have been the subject of numerous representations and maps

Figure I.3. Period photograph of original Harmonist Church attributed to Frederick Rapp in 1822. During the Owen/Maclure period the church was repurposed into a dance hall, theater, and library. The building was dismantled in 1874. Courtesy of Special Collections, University of Southern Indiana.

Figure I.4. New Harmony from Indian Mound, April 22, 1906, before mature trees would obscure the view of the town. Courtesy of Special Collections, University of Southern Indiana.

that reveal slightly different aspects of the natural and built environment. Moving from the hills of western Pennsylvania, where Rapp had directed the building of Harmony in 1803, Harmonists migrated to the Midwest via the Ohio and Wabash Rivers. Rapp, engineers from Vincennes, Indiana, and laborers among his followers helped cut New Harmony's original street grid of three blocks (east–west) and five blocks (north–south) out of the lush, riparian wilderness of the lower Wabash River Valley. *New Harmony of the Wabash* (1842) by Swiss artist Karl Bodmer (1809–1893) illustrates the wilderness that greeted the settlers in 1814 (Plates 1, 2, 7).[18]

By the time Bodmer reached New Harmony with Prince Maximilian of Wied-Neuwied in 1832, the town had already been inhabited and partially abandoned by another colony of idealistic settlers including Robert Owen and William Maclure. The arrival on January 25, 1826, of Maclure with Charles-Alexandre Lesueur (1778–1846), a French naturalist, artist, and explorer; Thomas Say, a British naturalist, entomologist, malacologist, herpetologist, and carcinologist; and other enlightened passengers aboard Owen's keelboat the *Philanthropist* (informally called "The Boatload of Knowledge") signaled the eclipse of religion by science (and pedagogy) as New Harmony's overarching idea (Plate 5).[19] The members of this adventurous group were affiliated with the Academy of Natural Sciences in Philadelphia, which played a pioneering role in developing the fields of botany, zoology, and paleontology in the United States.[20] In parallel with Owen's economic investment, William Maclure, longtime president of the Academy of Natural Sciences, played a leadership role in the scientific and educational life of New Harmony, which is only now being fully acknowledged by scholars. The passengers who arrived on "The Boatload

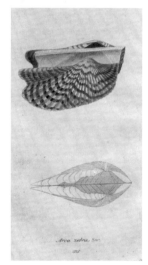

Figure I.5. *Arca zebra,* illustration by Lucy Way Sistare Say, from Thomas Say, *American Conchology: or, Descriptions of the shells of North America. Illustrated by coloured figures from original drawings executed from nature* (New Harmony, 1830). From the collections of Historic New Harmony / University of Southern Indiana.

Figure I.6. T. M. (Thaddeus Mortimer) Fowler's bird's-eye view of Harmony, Butler County, Pennsylvania (1901), first community established by the Harmonists/Rappites after their arrival in the United States from Germany. Courtesy of Library of Congress, Geography and Map Division.

of Knowledge" facilitated a considerable transfer of scientific expertise from Europe to the United States. Viewed through the initiatives of European émigrés Rapp and Owen (the former having fled religious persecution, the latter in search of a place to carry out his social experiments in education and science), the retreat to the wilderness of New Harmony exemplifies what cultural historian Leo Marx has described as a quest for a mythical "virgin continent."[21] In his study *The Machine in the Garden: Technology and the Pastoral Ideal in America*, Marx discusses "the ruling motive of the good shepherd, leading figure of the classical, Virgilian mode, [who] was to withdraw from the great world and begin a new life in a fresh, green landscape."[22] Harmonists encountered the American wilderness and left a cultivated agrarian landscape streamlined by manual production. In 1785 David Dale (1739–1806) and Richard Arkwright (1732–1792) founded New Lanark Mills along the River Clyde, twenty-five miles southeast of Glasgow, Scotland, depending on American cotton plantations to supply the raw material, and Eli Whitney's cotton gin (1794) and his subsequent contribution of the American System of interchangeable parts for mass production. With New Harmony, Robert Owen (David Dale's son-in-law) and his own sons (Robert, William, David, and Richard) and daughter (Jane Dale Owen Fauntleroy) were poised to link British industrial manufacturing systems with a new

Figure I.7. New Harmony's town grid and surrounding fields, orchards, and Wabash River looking south drawn by Charles-Alexandre Lesueur in 1834. Reproduced from E. T. Hamy, "Les voyages du Naturaliste Ch. Alex. Lesueur dans l'Amérique du Nord (1815–1837)," *Journal de la Société des Américanistes de Paris* V (1904): 54.

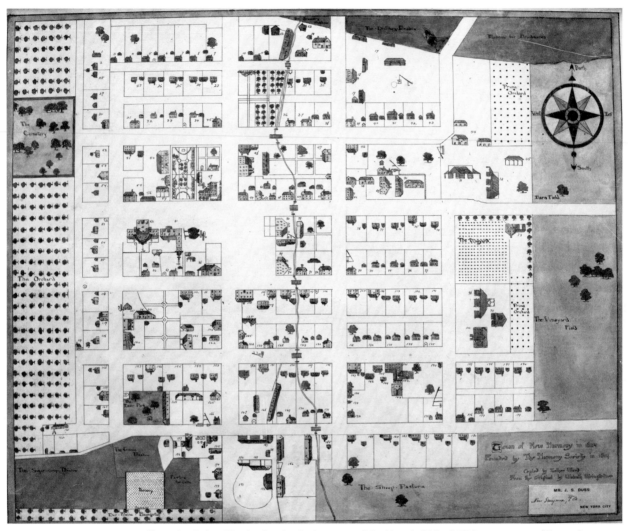

Figure I.8. Esther Wand redrawing in the 1930s of the historic Walrath Weingartner map "Town of New Harmony in 1824," showing buildings and manufacturing sites. Weingartner documented the town's assets before the time of its sale by Rapp to Owen in 1825. Illustration courtesy of Historic New Harmony / Special Collections, University of Southern Indiana.

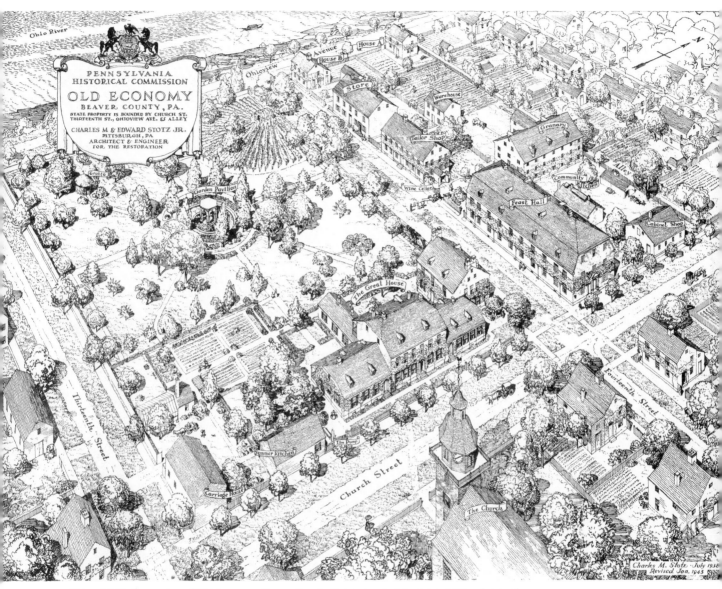

Labels within illustration: Ohio River; Avenue; House; Ohioview; House B; Store; Warehouse; Granary; Tailor Shop; Community Kitchen; Alley; Wine Cellar; Feast Hall; Cabinet Shop; Grotto; Garden Pavilion; The Great House; Summer Kitchen; The Pump; Fourteenth Street; Thirteenth Street; Carriage House; Church Street; The Church

PENNSYLVANIA
HISTORICAL COMMISSION
OLD ECONOMY
BEAVER COUNTY, PA.
STATE PROPERTY IS BOUNDED BY CHURCH ST.,
THIRTEENTH ST., OHIOVIEW AVE. & ALLEY
CHARLES M. & EDWARD STOTZ JR.
PITTSBURGH, PA
ARCHITECT & ENGINEER
FOR THE RESTORATION

Charles M. Stotz July 1938
Revised Jan. 1943

Figure I.9. Bird's-eye view of Old Economy, Beaver County, Pennsylvania, drawn July 1938 and revised January 1943 by preservation architects Charles M. Stotz and Edward Stotz Jr. Charles M. Stotz worked on the restoration of Old Economy Village for more than twenty-seven years. Courtesy of Virginia Stotz; illustration from Pennsylvania Historical and Museum Commission, Old Economy Village.

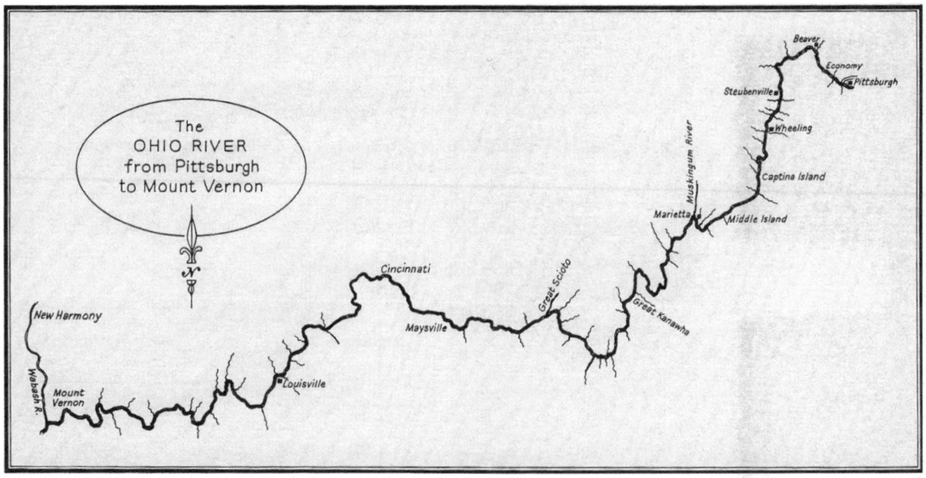

Figure I.10. "The Ohio River from Pittsburgh to Mount Vernon," drawing in Josephine M. Elliott, editor, *To Holland and to New Harmony. Robert Dale Owen's Travel Journal, 1825–1826* (Indianapolis: Indiana Historical Society, 1969), 236. Courtesy of Indiana Historical Society.

Figure I.11. Charles-Alexandre Lesueur, "Sketch of a Keelboat with nine men on its roof, Friday, January 13, 1826." The *Philanthropist* brought scientists, educators, and artists to New Harmony by way of the Ohio and Wabash Rivers in 1826. Sketch courtesy of Muséum d'histoire naturelle, Le Havre.

communal political order on the American continent. During the mid-1930s, the agrarian Midwest witnessed another wave of industrialization when hybrid corn was invented in DeKalb, Illinois. In contrast to the maize/corn grown by Native Americans, the new hybrid corn was "designed" to be machine-friendly for harvesting.[23]

While *Avant-Garde in the Cornfields* acknowledges Blaffer Owen's leading role as a protagonist, it seeks to recognize different contributions by discussing public and privately funded initiatives that defined the "new" New Harmony of the second half of the twentieth century. Blaffer Owen explains her own efforts to preserve and transform New Harmony in the posthumously published memoir *New Harmony, Indiana: Like a River, Not a Lake*.[24] *Avant-Garde in the Cornfields* assumes the position of a scholarly complement to her memoir by situating her contribution in the broader context of patronage of the arts. For example, upon her arrival in August 1941, she would have discovered that the State of Indiana had been working (through the New Harmony Memorial Commission established in 1937) to preserve the town's historic legacy at least since the 1939 project to reconstruct the

Figure I.12. Contemporary aerial view of New Lanark World Heritage Site along River Clyde in Scotland, 2013. Mill buildings Number 1, 2, 3 and Institute on left and Robert Owen's house on the right, at center. Courtesy of New Lanark Trust.

Figure I.13. Harmonist Labyrinth in New Harmony, designed by Frederick Rapp circa 1815 as monocursal, was reconstructed in 1939 as a hedge maze near the site of the first labyrinth. It returned in 2008 to the original one-path layout. Photograph courtesy of John Busch.

New Harmony Labyrinth (originally completed circa 1815 based on Frederick Rapp's design; Plate 19). The New Harmony Historic District was listed in the National Register of Historic Places in 1966. To be sure, Blaffer Owen brought her idealism to a place where the mundane realities of everyday life were inflected with aspirations of past generations. Her initiatives can be interpreted as *utopian* if one understands the term as the embrace of communitarian ideals.[25] Her spirituality and desire for community were fundamental to her efforts to reinvigorate New Harmony's built and natural environments. In parallel with the initiatives of the State of Indiana, she was to advocate for the realization of modernist works of architecture, gardens, and landscapes while simultaneously advancing preservation projects.

Nancy Mangum McCaslin's chapter "Jane Blaffer and Kenneth Dale Owen: A Family and Educational Portrait" describes their backgrounds and distinguishes between their individual attitudes toward philanthropy in the context of preserving and transforming New Harmony. Mangum McCaslin discusses the enduring influence of Robert Lee Blaffer (1876–1942), Blaffer Owen's oil-tycoon father (who introduced her as a teenager to a biography of Robert Owen), and Sarah Campbell Blaffer (1885–1975), her mother, art patron and philanthropist, who modeled the importance of supporting living artists. Just as Blaffer Owen did not conform to expectations in that domain by limiting herself to the mere accumulation of art objects, in marriage she also chose an unconventional path when she wed Kenneth Dale Owen, a petroleum geologist whose ancestry led her to New Harmony. For her part, Blaffer Owen sought to make New Harmony a spiritual and cultural destination, while her husband was focused on consolidating the Owen legacy by reassembling original land holdings and reacquiring key historic properties. Educational influences discussed in this chapter include Blaffer Owen's charismatic professors at Bryn Mawr College in Pennsylvania and later the prominent twentieth-century Protestant theologian Paul Tillich.

Stephen Fox's chapter "Patronage and Modernism" presents New Harmony as a lens through which to view the ways in which liberal-minded patrons such as Blaffer Owen shaped "imagined communities," transforming the built and natural environment by commissioning architecture, landscapes, and gardens while preserving the past. Fox positions Blaffer Owen's patronage within the broader milieu of her American peers. The patrons Fox discusses include Blaffer Owen's peers Dominique Schlumberger and John de Menil of Houston and J. Irwin Miller of Columbus, Indiana; each of these individuals occupies a significant role in post–World War II America insofar as they were invested in modern architecture as a tool with which to promote spirituality. The Rothko Chapel in Houston (1971) embodied Dominique and John de Menil's triad of "faith, activism, and aesthetics."[26] J. Irwin Miller's support of social justice initiatives, the establishment of the Architecture Program in 1960 (Cummins Foundation), and in particular his commissioning of Eliel and Eero Saarinen to design First Christian Church (1942) and Eero Saarinen to design North

Christian Church (1964) for Columbus, Indiana, demonstrate his deep commitment to modern architecture and faith.[27]

Christine Gorby's chapter "New Harmony as an Evolving Commemorative Environment" emphasizes Blaffer Owen's commitment to living memorials while discussing preservation efforts made over time by institutions such as the New Harmony Memorial Commission created by the Indiana General Assembly (legislature) as well as private individuals. Gorby distinguishes between the "revised past" of certain preservation initiatives and the "invented past" that characterized some of Blaffer Owen's interventions, including relocating the conjoined 1814 Harmonist Sadler Shop log house and mid-nineteenth-century building that she rechristened the Barrett–Gate House (just opposite the Ceremonial Gate by Jacques Lipchitz of the Roofless Church) (Plate 10). For this and several other interventions, Blaffer Owen relied on the advice of an important local engineer, (Robert) Don Blair (1909–1992), who, among his many contributions,

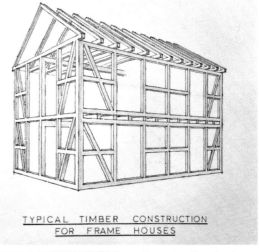

TYPICAL TIMBER CONSTRUCTION
FOR FRAME HOUSES

Figure I.15. Drawing by engineer Don Blair of typical timber construction for frame houses built in New Harmony from 1814 to 1824. Courtesy of Judith Blair Nix.

Figure I.14. The Barrett–Gate House, a two-story Harmonist log house with a mid-nineteenth-century addition, was relocated in 1959 to a new site at the intersection of Main Street and North Street, across from the Lipchitz Gate of the Roofless Church. Courtesy of Judith Blair Nix and the Robert Lee Blaffer Foundation.

Figure I.16. Rawlings House, a Harmonist-era building circa 1815, with Thomas Kane fence and landscape, was Jane Blaffer Owen's final New Harmony residence. Photograph courtesy of and copyright Darryl D. Jones.

published the only study on Harmonist timber-frame buildings.[28] Blaffer Owen's first family house (No. V) was one of these, and likewise Rawlings House (circa 1815), which she occupied afterward until the end of her life. Gorby shows how Blaffer Owen's desire to preserve New Harmony's identification with spiritual practices belongs to a feminist trajectory in the evolution of a town where women have consistently functioned as advocates of its history.[29]

As she worked to transform New Harmony into a pilgrimage site, Blaffer Owen gradually recognized the need to combine spiritual practices with heritage tourism that steadily increased during midcentury thanks to access to automobiles by America's middle class. She embraced the idea of a "living community," an idea shared and reinforced by the first president of Historic New Harmony, the historian Ralph G. Schwarz (1925–2018); at the same time she rejected the strategies of "reconstruction" and "reenactment" deployed in Colonial Williamsburg.[30] Following the advice of Schwarz, Blaffer Owen commissioned Indianapolis architect Evans Woollen (1927–2016) to design the New Harmony Inn (1974) and Conference Center

(1986), which was intended to provide accommodations for modern-day pilgrims and revitalize the local economy. Woollen's elegant yet understated New Harmony Inn thoughtfully draws on and transforms vernacular sources such as the wood- and brick-clad timber-framed Harmonist communal houses (Plate 22).[31] Shortly after completion of the New Harmony Inn and Conference Center, Blaffer Owen commissioned Robert "Bob" E. Hatch (1927–2016), a preservation architect, to relocate a historic barn and convert it into a retreat center and dormitory. The building was named the MacLeod Barn Abbey (1976) in honor of the Reverend George MacLeod, an inspirational leader of the Iona Community in Scotland with whom Blaffer Owen was associated. It is worth noting how Blaffer Owen welcomed the coexistence of architect-designed one-offs alongside utilitarian (barns) and residential buildings that were part of the vernacular fabric of New Harmony (Plate 23).

Figure I.17. Interior view of Entry House, The New Harmony Inn, Evans Woollen, Architect (Woollen Associates), 1974, New Harmony, Indiana. Courtesy of Library of Congress, Prints and Photographs Division, Balthazar Korab Archive at the Library of Congress.

Cammie McAtee argues in "'The Rib Cage of the Human Heart': Philip Johnson's Roofless Church" that this challenging commission—the first new building and landscape to be realized after Blaffer Owen established the Robert Lee Blaffer Trust in 1958 in memory of her much-loved father—enabled the architect to "explore new directions in his architectural work, but also afforded him the opportunity to realize the forms of long-held ideals" in an "out-of-the-way location." The billowing, shingle-clad dome is part of an open-air "roofless" space of worship and contemplation that blends architecture, art, and landscape (Plates 9–12). The Roofless Church (1957–60) achieves an informal and monumental quality. For this work Johnson studied the Harmonist tradition of vernacular building with bricks, timber frame, and shingles while eschewing the quality of "rusticity." For visitors, the agrarian context is framed by a classical loggia inserted into the northern perimeter wall facing the Wabash River and its floodplain (Plate 6).

A couple of years after the inauguration of the Roofless Church, Blaffer Owen

Figure I.18. Harmonist Community House No. 2 in New Harmony, March 9, 1906. The portico was added subsequently and ultimately removed. Thomas Say's tomb is visible on the far right; he was interred with members of the Maclure family. Courtesy of Special Collections, University of Southern Indiana.

Figure I.19. Roofless Church (before partial removal of limestone pavers) with view of the Atheneum and pottery house in the background. Photographer unknown. From the collections of Historic New Harmony / University of Southern Indiana.

invited Frederick Kiesler, a New York–based Austrian émigré architect and artist, to New Harmony to design a modest cave-shelter in proximity to the Roofless Church, a structure that was to house life-size sculptures of the Holy Family made by the artists Frank and Elizabeth Haines.[32] The humble sculptures hand-carved of soft wood were meant to strike a note of contrast to Lipchitz's bronze *Notre-Dame-de-Liesse* (renamed *Descent of the Holy Spirit*) and Ceremonial Gate (1946–56) for the nearby

Roofless Church. The chapter by Ben Nicholson in collaboration with the late William R. Crout, "Frederick Kiesler's Grotto: A Promethean Spirit in New Harmony," examines the unrealized project *Cave of the New Being / Grotto for Meditation* (1962–65); the cave-shelter was eventually reconceived as a memorial commissioned by Blaffer Owen in honor of her spiritual mentor Tillich, which subsequently served as the site of the interment of his ashes. Nicholson and Crout address the struggle between Kiesler and Tillich for control of this project, essentially a struggle over the symbolism of the cave/grotto and the fish (Plates 13–16). Nicholson's understanding of Kiesler's relationship to the site is fueled by the artist–architect's description of New Harmony as "beautifully magic" and a place where "primitive craftsmanship" can be observed.[33] Kiesler's practice had been occupied with a series of commissions that included the cavernous installation for Peggy Guggenheim's The Art of This Century gallery (1942–47), the *Endless House* (1947–61), and the Shrine of the Book (1965). Because Kiesler saw *Grotto for Meditation* as the de facto realization of his concept for the *Endless House*, he insisted that it be built beyond the modest scale Blaffer Owen intended, which led to a misunderstanding between them and the end of the project.

If the Roofless Church functions as an open-air precinct with a dome, and *Grotto* as an archetypal shelter, one could interpret them as Johnson's and Kiesler's personal explorations of the discursive role of the "primitive" in modern architecture.[34] Writing about notions of the "modern unhomely," Anthony Vidler discusses the

Figure I.20. The dedication ceremony of the gates designed by Jacques Lipchitz occurred in 1962, two years after the opening of the Roofless Church. Photographer unknown. From the collections of Historic New Harmony / University of Southern Indiana.

surrealist artist Tristan Tzara's fascination with "uterine" constructions exemplified by the cave, grotto, and tent.[35] Tzara, who was a friend of Kiesler, identified the cave as an "intermediary form between the grotto and the tent."[36] In the spirit of German expressionist architecture, Kiesler challenged "pseudo-functionalism" with his concept of "magic architecture" developed after 1940.[37] His desire to transcend "pseudo-functionalism" found expression in his *Grotto for Meditation,* for which a compelling archetype may have been the New Harmony Labyrinth built by the Harmonists with a circular stone building at its center. It was often referred to as a "grotto," and Kiesler is likely to have visited it.[38]

Although Kiesler's *Grotto for Meditation* remained unbuilt, its intended site was reshaped with evocative earthen berms (likely inspired by archetypal mounds) planted with Norwegian spruce and hemlock trees, both used by Robert Zion and Harold Breen in their design for Paul Tillich Memorial Park in 1965–66 (Plate 18).[39] Working with the firm of Zion & Breen, Blaffer Owen chose to remind visitors of the difficulties inherent in reconciling nature with twentieth-century life. A number of small granite boulders were installed along the park's internal pathways, with inscriptions incised by Ralph Beyer, a German sculptor and letter-cutter.[40] The dedication stone, unveiled by Blaffer Owen in the presence of Tillich, was incised with the title of his dedication address: "Estranged and Reunited: The New Being, Pentecost, June 2, 1963."[41] The remaining boulders are inscribed with quotations from Tillich's sermons, such as "Man and nature belong together in their created glory—in their tragedy and in their salvation."[42] Tillich's ashes are interred in the park named after him, next to a memorial stone marked with the dates of his birth and death. Poignantly, Tillich's ashes were buried on land that had once been plowed by German immigrants who had fled religious persecution in Germany just as Tillich had.

The Roofless Church and *Grotto for Meditation* emerged during a period of renewed interest in the modernist religious building, especially around the time the Second Vatican Council concluded in 1965.[43] In the decade following the end of World War II, the university chapel became a prominent site of experimentation for modernist religious architecture in the United States, especially at universities associated with the type of scientific and technological research that had made much nuclear warfare possible.[44] At the Illinois Institute of Technology (IIT) in Chicago, Ludwig Mies van der Rohe realized the Robert F. Carr Memorial Chapel of St. Savior (1949–52), and in Cambridge, Massachusetts, the Massachusetts Institute of Technology (MIT) dedicated Eero Saarinen's MIT Chapel (1950–55). These two chapels, both modest in size and restrained in character, aimed to minister to a new brand of "moral scientist" who would question the ethical implications of scientific discoveries and use science and technology responsibly.[45] The chapels at IIT and MIT are self-contained buildings, but the Roofless Church eschews conventional forms of enclosure in order to meld architecture and landscape.

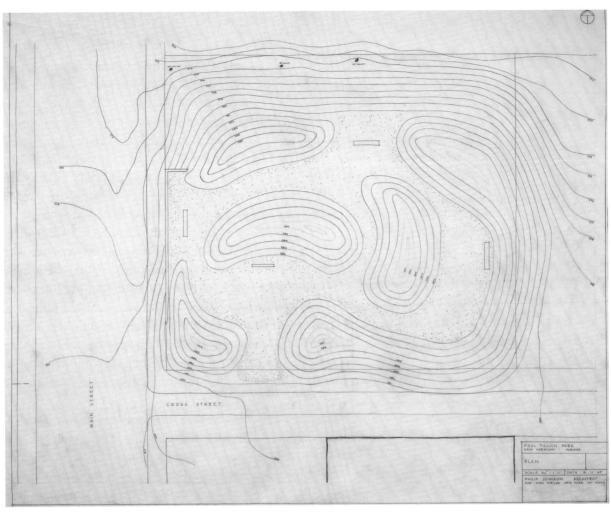

Figure I.21. Landscape drawing with earthen berms for Paul Tillich Memorial Park, prepared by Robert Zion (and Harold Breen) for Philip Johnson, Architect, 1965. Drawing courtesy of Philip Johnson architectural drawings, 1943–94, Avery Architectural and Fine Arts Library, Columbia University. Architectural design copyright the Estate of Philip Johnson; courtesy of the Glass House, a site of The National Trust for Historic Preservation.

The site of the Roofless Church is one of four garden landscapes discussed by Christine Gorby in "The New Harmony Gardens of Jane Blaffer Owen." Gorby analyzes the role that gardens, such as Carol's Garden (1982) and the Cathedral Labyrinth and Sacred Garden (1997), play in creating spaces for "monastic" meditation and prayer for residents as well as visitors to the agrarian town and surveys significant garden commissions where she argues that place-based historical consciousness and the realm of the unconscious meet (Plates 17, 20). In New Harmony the archetype of a walled garden reappears in the low-lying perimeter brick walls of the Harmonist cemetery (1874) as well as the architectural utopia conceived by Stedman Whitwell (circa 1824) on behalf of Robert Owen (Plates 4, 8). Gorby's two chapters, one on

Figure I.22. Tillich quotation stone from his sermon "Nature Mourns for a Lost God," in *The Shaking of the Foundations,* 1948. Ralph Beyer, letterer; Robert Zion (and Harold Breen) for Philip Johnson, Paul Tillich Memorial Park, 1965–66, New Harmony, Indiana. Photograph courtesy of Michelangelo Sabatino, 2015.

preservation and one on gardens, demonstrate the degree to which the passage from Tillich's *The Religious Situation* (1932) summarizes Blaffer Owen's understanding of the relationship between the present and future: "To understand the present means to see it in its inner tension toward the future."

Ben Nicholson's chapter "The New Harmony Atheneum: White Collage" delves deeply into Richard Meier's design process to demonstrate how the architect's use of collage allowed him to project an entirely new vision of space while echoing the historic dimension of the site. Despite Meier's rotation of the plan five degrees out of alignment with New Harmony's street grid, the Atheneum (1975–79) is more responsive to context than it first appears to be, especially in terms of its engagement with neighboring buildings, including the Roofless Church and the Rapp–Owen Granary (1818). Meier's Atheneum was conceived as an entrance pavilion meant to serve an educational mission for visitors to New Harmony. An archival photograph of Meier leaning against a split-rail fence, an element that embodies agrarian materiality, with the "high-tech" porcelain panel–clad Atheneum in the background speaks to a strategy of coexistence between past and future.

It is not surprising that as an advocate of a "living community" that both revises and invents the past, Ralph G. Schwarz was instrumental in the decision to commission Meier, at the time an emerging architect who had designed several award-winning houses but had little experience with large-scale public buildings.

With the objective of including a selection of primary sources that informed the research and writing of the chapters in this book, the coeditors have added "Three Voices in New Harmony," texts authored by key figures: Tillich's dedicatory address in 1963 of the park named in his honor, Schwarz's reflection about his work, and Kenneth A. Schuette Jr.'s description of his recently completed Jane Blaffer Owen Sanctuary Plan (2013).

The Atheneum—replete with an auditorium that hosts an educational film especially created for New Harmony visitors—extends the traditional uses associated with this type of building in America during the nineteenth century.[46] Although the Atheneum was not commissioned or financed by Blaffer Owen, she was instrumental in bringing Schwarz to Indiana, and his unconventional approach to the commemoration of New Harmony's past was as innovative as the Atheneum's architecture would be.[47] As Ada Louise Huxtable noted, Meier's selection as architect of the Atheneum qualified New Harmony as a "very special kind of American town."[48]

Blaffer Owen's sixty years of involvement with New Harmony outlasted the ten-year experiment of the Harmonists on the Wabash, the five-year Owen/Maclure period, and the several decades that followed, when Robert Owen's children and their New Harmony contemporaries were alive. But this third communal experiment is also a story of waxing and waning, of decline and rebirth. New Harmony's cultural singularity declined after the Civil War, only to be replaced by more conventional patterns associated with its role as a market town in agricultural Posey County. This role was manifested in the cluster of civic and commercial buildings erected between the mid-nineteenth and first half of the twentieth century, including the cast-iron and plate-glass storefronts on Main Street fabricated by George L. Mesker & Co. Iron Works of Evansville, Indiana (1860s and 1880s), the Richardsonian Romanesque Working Men's Institute (George O. Gannser, 1894), the classical Murphy Auditorium (John W. Gaddis, 1914), the Ribeyre Gymnasium (Harry E. Boyle & Co. Architects, 1924), and the Harmony Way Bridge (Parsons, Klapp, Brinckerhoff & Douglas, 1930).[49]

New Harmony's singularity was revalued when faith in the American city faltered during the Great Depression and again during the Cold War. By the 1950s the rural American countryside began to assume a new role in the large-scale migration from city to suburb, as large swaths of territory surrounding metropolitan areas were claimed for residential development and formerly pastoral landscapes were transformed into a sea of "little boxes all the same."[50] The postwar years during which Blaffer Owen was active in New Harmony witnessed the subsequent transformation and destruction of vast agrarian landscapes of the United States, largely due to another machine other than the train invading the garden: the automobile, which became crucial for reaching the suburbs then being developed at the edges of cities across the country. During these years, when such places as Eliel Saarinen's Cranbrook Academy of Art, Black Mountain College, and Walter P. Paepcke's Aspen Institute for Humanistic Studies functioned as sites of intellectual and cultural engagement, New Harmony reemerged as a place in which exiles and émigrés from Europe mingled with American architects and academics to leave a distinctive mark on its historic landscape.[51]

Twentieth-century New Harmony was the seedbed for Jane Blaffer Owen's communal and utopian mission to encourage a dialogue between spirituality and enlightened secular ideals. Building on the legacy of the Rapp and the Owen/Maclure communities—colorfully represented by Harry Hayden Hawkins's painting *George Rapp Deeding the Present Site of New Harmony to Robert Owen* (1907)—Blaffer Owen's

Figure I.23. From right to left, Working Men's Institute, Murphy Auditorium, and Ribeyre Gymnasium, as seen in the early 1920s. Photographer unknown. Courtesy of Special Collections, University of Southern Indiana.

Figure I.24. Harmony Way Bridge over the Wabash River, connecting southwestern Indiana with southeastern Illinois, 1930. Photographer unknown. Courtesy of Special Collections, University of Southern Indiana.

philanthropic contributions complemented other public and private initiatives. Yet, through her singular efforts to bring together artists and architects of different faiths and professional persuasion, Blaffer Owen cultivated a serene and congenial community that countered the secular bravado and anxiety of the postwar era. Public and private initiatives thus created a preservation-oriented historic town in the cornfields of Indiana that also became a place to observe avant-garde art, architecture, and landscape architecture. Yet, just as utopias are never complete, so too *Avant-Garde in the Cornfields,* by focusing on buildings and landscapes, lays the groundwork for further studies about the myriad of complementary cultural activities that contributed to New Harmony's twentieth-century renaissance.

Figure I.25. *George Rapp Deeding the Present Site of New Harmony to Robert Owen,* painted in 1907 by Harry Hayden Hawkins (1885–1973). The painting represents a transaction in 1825 between the first two founding communities that laid the foundations on which Jane Blaffer Owen built her "new" New Harmony. Painting courtesy of Ann Hawkins Luce, Harriet Hawkins Adams, and Jane Hawkins Bynum. From the Collection of the Working Men's Institute, New Harmony. Image courtesy of Zachary Straw Photography.

Notes

1. According to the 2010 U.S. Census, New Harmony has a population of 789.

2. For reference to "wonder of the West," see Donald E. Pitzer and Connie A. Weinzapfel, "Utopia on the Wabash: The History of Preservation in New Harmony," *Cultural Resource Management* 9 (2001): 18–20. See also Ray E. Boomhower, "Destination Indiana: New Harmony: Home to Indiana's Communal Societies," in *Traces of Indiana and Midwestern History: A Publication of the Indiana Historical Society* 14 (Fall 2002): 36–37.

3. For a brief overview of Blaffer Owen's contributions, see Stephen Fox, "A Life of Harmony—Jane Blaffer Owen, 1915–2010," *Cite: The Architecture and Design Review of Houston* (Fall 2010): 8–9; and Blaffer Owen, *New Harmony, Indiana: Like a River, Not a Lake: A Memoir* (Bloomington: Indiana University Press, 2015). See also William R. Crout, "Jane Blaffer Owen: A Personal Tribute," *Bulletin of the North American Paul Tillich Society*, 36, no. 3 (2010): 3–4.

4. For an overview of the Harmonist/Rappite and Owen/Maclure communal experience, see William Edward Wilson, *The Angel and the Serpent: The Story of New Harmony* (Bloomington: Indiana University Press, 1964). See also Anne Taylor, *Visions of Harmony: A Study of Nineteenth-Century Millenarianism* (New York: Oxford University Press, 1987); Arthur Bestor, *Backwoods Utopias: The Sectarian Origins and the Owenite Phase of Communitarian Socialism in America: 1663–1829,* 2nd ed. (Philadelphia: University of Pennsylvania Press, 1970); the 2012 reprint features a new introduction by Donald E. Pitzer.

5. A painting representing the sale, *George Rapp Deeding the Present Site of New Harmony to Robert Owen* (1907), was produced by New Harmony native Harry Hayden Hawkins (1885–1973) and is currently on display in the hall as part of the Collection of the Working Men's Institute Museum and Library, New Harmony. See Mary Quick Burnet, *Art and Artists of Indiana* (New York: Century Company, 1921); Joel Willis Hiatt, "The Workingmen's Institute," in *History of Posey County, Indiana,* edited by John C. Leffel (Chicago: Standard Publishing, 1913), 105–10.

6. Morton White and Lucia White, *The Intellectual versus the City, from Thomas Jefferson to Frank Lloyd Wright* (Cambridge, Mass.: Harvard University Press, 1962); Roderick Nash, *Wilderness and the American Mind,* 3rd ed. (New Haven, Conn.: Yale University Press, 1982).

7. See, e.g., Paul Douglas, *Architecture, Artifacts, and Arts in the Harmony Society of George Rapp: The Material Culture of a Nineteenth-Century American Utopian Community* (Lewiston, Me.: Edwin Mellen, 2008). The most comprehensive study to date addressing the built environments of communitarian utopias in the United States from the late eighteenth century to the 1970s (including, albeit briefly, New Harmony) is Dolores Hayden, *Seven American Utopias: The Architecture of Communitarian Socialism, 1790–1975* (Cambridge, Mass.: MIT Press, 1976). John W. Reps dedicates a chapter to the "cities of Zion," with brief commentary on Rapp and Owen, in *The Making of Urban America: A History of City Planning in the United States* (Princeton, N.J.: Princeton University Press, 1965), 453–57.

8. For an insightful overview of American culture and society since World War II, see Peter Bacon Hales, *Outside the Gates of Eden: The Dream of America From Hiroshima to Now* (Chicago: University of Chicago Press, 2014).

9. Howard P. Segal, *Technological Utopianism in American Culture* (Syracuse, N.Y.: Syracuse University Press, 2005).

10. Paul Tillich, *On Art and Architecture,* edited by John Dillenberger in collaboration with Jane Dillenberger (New York: Crossroad, 1987).

11. On David Dale Owen's geological laboratory and other nineteenth-century buildings in New

Harmony, see Nora C. Fretageot and William V. Mangrum, *Historic New Harmony: Official Guide* (Evansville, Ind.: Keller Crescent Company, 1914). On Robert Owen, see Donald F. Carmony and Josephine M. Elliott, "New Harmony, Indiana: Robert Owen's Seedbed for Utopia," *Indiana Magazine of History* 76, no. 3 (1980): 161–261; Dame Margaret Cole et al., *Robert Owen: Industrialist, Reformer, Visionary, 1771–1858: Four Essays* (London: Robert Owen Bicentenary Association, 1971); and *Selected Works of Robert Owen,* edited by Gregory Claeys (London: Pickering, 1993). On William Maclure, see Leonard Warren, *Maclure of New Harmony: Scientist, Progressive Educator, Radical Philanthropist* (Bloomington: Indiana University Press, 2009); and *The European Journals of William Maclure*, edited with notes and introduction by John S. Doskey (Philadelphia: American Philosophical Society, 1988). See also *Partnership for Posterity: The Correspondence of William Maclure and Marie Duclos Fretageot: 1820–1833,* edited by Josephine Mirabella Elliott (Indianapolis: Indiana Historical Society, 1994).

12. A wartime article titled "Life Visits New Harmony," written shortly after Marguerite Young's pioneering account *Angel in the Forest, a Fairy Tale of Two Utopias* about historic New Harmony, featured a photograph by Kosti Ruohomaa of the weathervane atop of the laboratory. See *Life*, September 17, 1945, 133–36, 139. This photograph appears in this book in the chapter written by Nancy Mangum McCaslin.

13. The literature on communal utopias in the United States is extensive. For a historical account, see John Humphrey Noyes, *Strange Cults and Utopias of Nineteenth-Century America* (New York: Dover, 1969), originally published as *History of American Socialisms* (Philadelphia: J. B. Lippincott, 1870); see also Paul Kagan, *New World Utopias: A Photographic History of the Search for Community* (New York: Penguin Books, 1975); and *America's Communal Utopias,* edited by Donald E. Pitzer (Chapel Hill: University of North Carolina Press, 1997). In 1976 Donald E. Pitzer established the Center for Communal Studies at the University of Southern Indiana.

14. For a fascinating study on the changing relationship between nature and the built environment in Europe, see David S. Landes, *The Unbound Prometheus: Technological Change and Industrial Development in Western Europe from 1750 to the Present,* 2nd ed. (Cambridge: Cambridge University Press, 2003).

15. Hiram Williams Beckwith, *History of Wabash Valley, Indiana–Illinois: Gleaned from early authors, old maps and manuscripts, private and official correspondence, and other authentic, though, for the most part, out-of-the-way sources* (Chicago: H. H. Hill and N. Iddings, 1880); see reprint edition (Knightstown, Ind.: The Bookmark, 1977).

16. Thomas Say, *American Conchology; or, Descriptions of the shells of North America. Illustrated by coloured figures from original drawings executed from nature* (New Harmony, Ind.: School Press, 1830). *American Conchology* was illustrated in part by Lucy Way Sistare Say (1801–1886). See Jordan D. Marché and Theresa A. Marché, "A 'Distinct Contribution': Gender, Art, and Scientific Illustration in Antebellum America," *Knowledge and Society* 12 (2000): 77–106. After the death of Thomas Say, Sistare Say returned to Philadelphia, where she became the first woman to be elected a member of the Academy of Natural Sciences of Philadelphia.

17. The term *Harmonists* is used in this book to maintain consistency, even though earlier studies tended to refer to members of the community as Rappites. For a recently published historical overview of New Harmony, see Donald E. Pitzer, *New Harmony Then and Now* (Bloomington: Quarry Books, 2012). Michael J. Lewis's *City of Refuge: Separatists and Utopian Town Planning* (Princeton, N.J.: Princeton University Press, 2016) includes chapters on the settlements of Harmony and Economy. See *Harmony on the Connoquenessing, 1803–1815: George Rapp's First American Harmony: A Documentary History,* compiled and edited by Karl J. R. Arndt (Worcester, Mass.: Harmony Society Press, 1980); *George Rapp's Separatists, 1700–1803: The German Prelude to Rapp's American Harmony Society: A Documentary History,* compiled and edited by Karl J. R. Arndt (Worcester, Mass.: Harmony Society

Press, 1980); and Charles Morse Stotz, "Threshold of the Golden Kingdom: The Village of Economy and Its Restoration," *Winterthur Portfolio* 8 (1973): 133–69.

18. *Karl Bodmer's America,* edited by David C. Hunt and Marsha V. Gallagher, introduction by William H. Goetzmann, exhibition catalog (Lincoln: Joslyn Art Museum, University of Nebraska Press, 1984), 81. Maximilian zu Wied-Neuwied and Bodmer sojourned in New Harmony from October 20, 1832, until March 15, 1833. See *The North American Journals of Prince Maximilian of Wied: May 1832–April 1833,* edited by Stephen S. Witte and Marsha V. Gallagher, 3 vols. (Norman: University of Oklahoma Press, 2008–12), 1:204–332. Bodmer's interests included landscape and Native American culture, history, and society. See Christian F. Feest, *Indians and Europe: An Interdisciplinary Collection of Essays* (Lincoln: University of Nebraska Press, 1999), 405, 486, 541, 611.

19. On "The Boatload of Knowledge," see Donald E. Pitzer, "The Original Boatload of Knowledge Down the Ohio River: William Maclure's and Robert Owen's Transfer of Science and Education to the Midwest, 1825–1826," *Ohio Journal of Science* 89, no. 5 (1989): 128–42; and Pitzer, "William Maclure's Boatload of Knowledge: Science and Education into the Midwest," *Indiana Magazine of History* 94, no. 2 (1998): 110–37. See also Patricia Tyson Stroud, *Thomas Say: New World Naturalist* (Philadelphia: University of Pennsylvania Press, 1992), 167–82; Robert William Glenroie, *The American Sketchbooks of Charles Alexandre Lesueur, 1816–1837* (Worcester, Mass.: The Society, 1938); Ernest Théodore Hamy, *The Travels of the Naturalist Charles A. Lesueur in North America, 1815–1837* (Kent, Ohio: Kent State University Press, 1968); and Josephine M. Elliott and Jane Thompson Johansen, *Charles-Alexandre Lesueur: Premier Naturalist and Artist* (New Harmony, Ind.: [s.n.], 1999); Ritsert Rinsma, *Alexandre Lesueur. Tome 1, Un explorateur et artiste français au pays de Thomas Jefferson* (Le Havre: Éd. Du Havre de grâce, 2007). See the forthcoming study by Ritsert Rinsma, *Eyewitness to Utopia: Sketches of a Brave New World by C.-A. Lesueur, 1816–1837.*

20. Robert McCracken Peck and Patricia Tyson Stroud, *A Glorious Enterprise: The Academy of Natural Sciences of Philadelphia and the Making of American Science* (Philadelphia: University of Pennsylvania Press, 2012); see also Amy R. W. Meyers, *Knowing Nature: Art and Science in Philadelphia, 1740–1840* (New Haven, Conn.: Yale University Press, 2011).

21. Leo Marx, *The Machine in the Garden: Technology and the Pastoral Ideal in America,* 2nd ed. (New York: Oxford University Press, 2000), 3.

22. Ibid.

23. John C. Hudson, *Making the Corn Belt: A Geographical History of Middle-Western Agriculture* (Bloomington: Indiana University Press, 1994).

24. Blaffer Owen, *New Harmony, Indiana.*

25. For a broad discussion of utopia, see Gregory Claeys, *Searching for Utopia: The History of an Idea* (London: Thames and Hudson, 2011); and *Earth Perfect? Nature, Utopia, and the Garden,* edited by Annette Giesecke and Naomi Jacobs (London: Black Dog, 2012). See also Howard P. Segal, *Utopias: A Brief History from Ancient Writings to Virtual Communities* (Chichester, U.K.: Wiley-Blackwell, 2012). For an overview of utopia as it relates to architecture, see Nathaniel Coleman, *Utopias and Architecture* (London: Routledge, 2005); Robert Fishman, *Urban Utopias in the Twentieth Century* (Cambridge, Mass.: MIT Press, 1982); and Franco Borsi, *Architecture and Utopia* (Paris: Hazan, 1997).

26. Pamela G. Smart, *Sacred Modern: Faith, Activism, and Aesthetics in the Menil Collection* (Austin: University of Texas Press, 2010); Susan J. Barnes, *The Rothko Chapel: An Act of Faith* (Houston: Rothko Chapel and University of Texas Press, 1989). On Blaffer Owen's friendship with the Menils, see *Jane Blaffer Owen,* Menil House Seminar 3363 (Houston: Menil Archives, The Menil Collection, April 16, 2010), DVD. On the architecture of the Rothko Chapel, see Frank D. Welch, *Philip Johnson and Texas* (Austin: University of Texas Press, 2000), 66–68; Stephen Fox, "Howard Barnstone, 1923–1987," *Cite:*

The Architecture and Design Review of Houston (Fall 1987): 18–21. For original documentary footage of the dedication, see *The Rothko Chapel*, directed by J. Michaels and Francois de Menil, music by Morton Feldman, edited by J. Michaels and Anita Thatcher (San Francisco: Microcinema International, 2011).

27. J. Irwin Miller sponsored the March on Washington led by Dr. Martin Luther King Jr. in 1963. See Will Miller, "Joseph Irwin Miller—Biographical Memoirs," *Proceedings of the American Philosophical Society* 150, no. 3 (September 2006): 493–97. For an overview of J. Irwin Miller's views on architecture, see his speech "The Art of Architecture," May 20, 1994, Indianapolis Museum of Art Columbus Gallery, Columbus, Indiana (Item ID: M1003, box 545, folder 21; Indiana Historical Society, Irwin–Sweeney–Miller Family Collection, 1790–2008). For a comprehensive overview of Miller's contributions, see *Columbus, Indiana: A Look at Modern Architecture and Art* (Columbus, Ind.: Visitors Center, 2012).

28. Don Blair, *Harmonist Construction, Principally as Found in the Two-Storey Houses Built in Harmonie, Indiana, 1814–1824* (Indianapolis: Indiana Historical Society, 1964).

29. See Rüdiger Reitz, *Paul Tillich und New Harmony* (Stuttgart: Evangelisches Verlagswerk, 1970), where he writes: "For New Harmony it was above all a woman who began to disclose the hidden meaning of New Harmony for our time. This woman is Jane Blaffer, daughter of Robert Lee Blaffer, a founding member of 'Humble Oil and Refining Company' in Houston, Texas" (63–66). On New Harmony's female protagonists, see Caroline Dale Snedeker, *The Town of the Fearless* (Garden City, N.Y.: Doubleday, Doran, 1931). Abolitionist and social reformer Frances Wright (1795–1852), for example, delivered her first public lecture in New Harmony. See Celia Morris, *Fanny Wright, Rebel in America* (Cambridge, Mass.: Harvard University Press, 1984); and Carol A. Kolmerten, *Women in Utopia: The Ideology of Gender in the American Owenite Communities* (Bloomington: Indiana University Press, 1990). Marguerite Young's *Angel in the Forest, a Fairy Tale of Two Utopias* (New York: Reynal and Hitchcock, 1945) did much to bring New Harmony's history to the attention of a lay audience.

30. Richard Handler, *The New History of an Old Museum: Creating the Past at Colonial Williamsburg* (Durham, N.C.: Duke University Press, 1997).

31. Gerald Allen, "The New Harmony Inn: A Triumph of Modesty," *Architectural Record* 159, no. 4 (1976): 101–6. The New Harmony Inn is discussed by Evans Woollen, Gerald Allen, David Lewis, and Jane Blaffer Owen in a documentary about Woollen that was partially funded by Blaffer Owen, *Building for Meaning: The Architecture of Evans Woollen* (Indianapolis: Spellbound Productions, 1994).

32. On the Philadelphia-based puppet artists Frank and Elizabeth Haines, see Bobbie Marcroft, "Frank and Elizabeth Haines—of Marionettes and Brides," *Scene Magazine,* August 1976, 4–8, 21–22.

33. See Frederick Kiesler's Composition Book and notes dated October 18, 1962; a facsimile is held in the Tillich Archive of the Robert Lee Blaffer Foundation, New Harmony; the original is held by the Frederick and Lillian Kiesler Private Foundation, Vienna.

34. For an in-depth account, see my "Remoteness and Presentness: The Primitive in Modernist Architecture," in "Taboo," edited by John Capen Brough, Seher Erdogan, and Parsa Khalili, special issue, *Perspecta* 43 (Fall 2010): 139–44.

35. Vidler writes in the chapter "Homes for Cyborgs": "Against the horizontal extensions and the dissolution of the barriers between public and private implied by the Domino model, Tzara posed the maternal and sheltering images of 'uterine' constructions which, from the cave to the grotto and the tent, comprised the fundamental forms of human habitation: 'From the cave (for man inhabits the earth, 'the mother'), through the Eskimo yurt, the intermediary form between the grotto and the tent (remarkable example of uterine construction which one enters through cavities with vaginal forms), through to the conical or half-spherical hut furnished at its entrance with a post of sacred character, the dwelling symbolizes prenatal comfort'" (*The Architectural Uncanny: Essays in the Modern Unhomely* [Cambridge, Mass.: MIT Press, 1992], 151).

36. Ibid.

37. Fredrick Kiesler, "Pseudo-Functionalism in Modern Architecture," *Partisan Review,* July 1949, 733–42, reprinted in *Friedrich Kiesler: Endless House* (Ostfildern-Ruit: Verlag Gerd Hatje, 2003), 29–49. See also Kiesler, "Magic Architecture," in *Frederick J. Kiesler—Selected Writings,* edited by Siegfried Gohr and Gunda Luyken (Ostfildern-Ruit: Verlag Gerd Hatje, 1996), 34.

38. Ross F. Lockridge, *The Labyrinth: A History of the New Harmony Labyrinth, Including Some Special Study of the Spiritual and Mystical Life of Its Builders, the Rappites, and a Brief Survey of Labyrinths Generally* (Westport, Conn.: Hyperion, 1975).

39. "Robert Zion: A Profile in Landscape Architecture," *Process: Architecture* 94 (February 1991): 6–150. In Paul Tillich Memorial Park, Tillich's ashes were interred beneath an epitaph stone in 1966. Wallace K. Harrison deployed allusions to the Christian symbol of the fish for his First Presbyterian Church for Stamford, Connecticut, inaugurated in 1958; see also Victoria Newhouse, "Small Buildings," in *Wallace K. Harrison, Architect* (New York: Rizzoli, 1989), 166–85. Kiesler viewed the dolphin as a variation on the fish. See Ben Nicholson's chapter in this book, "Frederick Kiesler's Grotto: A Promethean Spirit in New Harmony."

40. For Blaffer Owen's reaction to the charred Coventry cross, see *New Harmony, Indiana,* 242. Beyer met Nicholas Pevsner, an architectural historian, in a British internment camp for Germans. It was likely Pevsner who introduced him to Sir Basil Spence. Coventry's tablet lettering was inspired by early Christian catacomb carvings. The cathedral (and the town) were rebuilt after the German Luftwaffe heavily bombed Coventry on November 14, 1940. That a German would be asked to participate in the rebuilding of the cathedral as part of an act of reconciliation would not have escaped Blaffer Owen. The Ralph Beyer Archive at the Craft Study Centre of the University for the Creative Arts holds stone inscriptions, drawings, rubbings, and prints related to Beyer's Coventry and New Harmony commissions. Ralph Beyer's signed and dated original drawings of his lettering for some stones in Tillich Park were returned to the Robert Lee Blaffer Foundation archives in February 2018 by the Reverend Arthur Hadley, then rector of St. Stephen's Episcopal Church in New Harmony, to whom Beyer had given them at the time the stones were carved on the rectory's screened porch. On Coventry, see Sir Basil Spence, *Phoenix at Coventry: The Building of a Cathedral* (New York: Harper and Row, 1962); and Louise Campbell, *Coventry Cathedral: Art and Architecture in Post-War Britain* (Oxford: Clarendon, 1996).

41. The original dedication stone was replaced by one incised by Beyer before being placed in its current location at the entrance to the park.

42. Paul Tillich, "Nature, Also, Mourns for a Lost God," in *The Shaking of the Foundations* (New York: C. Scribner's Sons, 1948), 83.

43. The Council adopted the Constitution on Sacred Liturgy, *Sacrosanctum Concilium,* which permitted priests to celebrate the mass in "vernacular" languages instead of Latin. This and the emphasis on "active participation" affected both the tone and the program of modern architecture. See Peter Hammond, *Liturgy and Architecture* (London: Barrie and Rockliff, 1960); Hammond, ed., *Towards a Church Architecture* (London: Architectural Press, 1962); Albert Christ-Janer and Mary Mix Foley, *Modern Church Architecture: A Guide to the Form and Spirit of Twentieth Century Religious Buildings* (New York: McGraw-Hill, 1962); G. E. Kidder Smith, *The New Churches of Europe* (New York: Holt, Rinehart and Winston, 1963); Sep Ruf, *German Church Architecture of the Twentieth Century* (Bonn: Kulturabteilung des Auswärtigen Amtes, 1964); Robert Maguire and Keith Murray, *Modern Churches of the World* (New York: Dutton, 1965). See also Richard Kieckhefer, "Modernism and the Concept of Reform: Liturgy and Liturgical Architecture," in *Sanctioning Modernism: Architecture and the Making of Postwar Identities,* edited by Vladimir Kulić, Timothy Parker, and Monica Penick (Austin: University

of Texas Press, 2014), 169–80; and Richard Kieckhefer, *Theology in Stone: Church Architecture from Byzantium to Berkeley* (Oxford: Oxford University Press, 2004).

44. Margaret M. Grubiak, *White Elephants on Campus: The Decline of Religious Architecture in the American University, 1920–1960* (South Bend, Ind.: University of Notre Dame Press, 2014). See also Jay M. Price, *Temples for a Modern God: Religious Architecture in Postwar America* (New York: Oxford University Press, 2013).

45. Margaret M. Grubiak, "Educating the Moral Scientist: The Chapels at I.I.T. and M.I.T.," *ARRIS: Journal of the Southeast Chapter of the Society of Architectural Historians* 18 (2007): 1–14.

46. For a discussion of the role played by the Atheneum in nineteenth-century America, see *America's Membership Libraries,* edited by Richard Wendorf (New Castle, Del.: Oak Knoll, 2007).

47. It is worth comparing New Harmony's Atheneum with the visitor center in Old Economy Village in Ambridge, just outside Pittsburgh, the last of the Harmonist settlements in the United States. Inaugurated in 2003 and designed by Susan Maxman & Partners Architects (with Gillan & Harmann, Inc.), the visitor center's volume and material palette attempts to imitate rather than reinvigorate the identity of the historic town.

48. Ada Louise Huxtable, "A Radical New Addition for Mid-America," *New York Times,* September 30, 1979, reprinted in Ada Louise Huxtable, *Architecture, Anyone?* (Berkeley: University of California Press, 1986), 75–86.

49. Nora C. Fretageot and W. V. Mangrum, *Historic New Harmony: Official Guide—Centennial Edition* (Evansville, Ind.: Keller-Crescent, 1914; 2nd ed., 1923; 3rd ed., 1934); Lee Burns, *Early Architects and Builders of Indiana* (Indianapolis: Indiana Historical Society, 1935); Coppa and Avery Consultants, *Architecture and Preservation in Indiana: A Guide to Historic Sites, Homes, and Churches* (Monticello, Ill.: Vance Bibliographies, 1981).

50. See Malvina Reynold's lyrics for the song "Little Boxes" (1962).

51. On these educational institutions, see, e.g., Robert Judson Clark et al., *Design in America: The Cranbrook Vision, 1925–1950* (New York: Abrams, 1983); Martin B. Duberman, *Black Mountain: An Exploration in Community* (Evanston, Ill.: Northwestern University Press, 2009); *Black Mountain College: Experiment in Art,* edited by Vincent Katz (Cambridge, Mass.: MIT Press, 2003); *The Aspen Papers: Twenty Years of Design Theory from the International Design Conference in Aspen,* edited by Reyner Banham (New York: Praeger, 1974); and James Sloan Allen, *The Romance of Commerce and Culture: Capitalism, Modernism, and the Chicago–Aspen Crusade for Cultural Reform* (Boulder: University Press of Colorado, 2002).

Figure 1.1. Jane Blaffer and Kenneth Dale "K. D." Owen, July 12, 1941. They exchanged vows outdoors on the verdant grounds of the Blaffer estate and summer home, Ste. Anne, near Grafton, Ontario. The newlyweds visited New Harmony on their return to Houston, Texas. Courtesy of the Kenneth Dale and Jane Blaffer Owen Family.

1

Jane Blaffer and Kenneth Dale Owen

A Family and Educational Portrait

NANCY MANGUM MCCASLIN

JANE BLAFFER OWEN, CBE (1915–2010), devoted six decades to revitalizing New Harmony, the ancestral hometown of her husband, Kenneth Dale "K. D." Owen (1903–2002). Beginning with her initial visit in 1941, she became intrigued with the town's history as the site of two important communal experiments, the religious Harmonie Society, led by George Rapp, and the scientific and educational Owen/Maclure community, founded by Kenneth's great-great-grandfather Robert Owen together with William Maclure. She reveals how and why New Harmony became the recipient of her philanthropy in *New Harmony, Indiana: Like a River, Not a Lake: A Memoir,* which she began writing in her late eighties.[1] Blaffer Owen's objective in the book is to communicate her personal story about the influence of the town's history on her life. She describes her contributions to the town's built environment and historic preservation through selective narrative, which includes her perspective of her husband's involvement.

Jane and Kenneth Owen adopted differing but complementary approaches to preserving New Harmony's heritage. His focus was to restore the accomplishments of early Owen ancestors. Her focus began in the context of marriage at a time when a woman's identity was often subordinated: "As a young bride, I had changed my name, and as a social malcontent, I had yearned for a new country and a new way of life."[2] New Harmony liberated her from the expectations of being a Blaffer in Houston, where the couple would reside primarily. As Mrs. Kenneth Owen, she would merge her family's history with his tie to the town for their descendants. However, her mission expanded beyond the historic preservation that the couple pursued initially. She also endeavored to honor the spiritual legacy of the Harmonists and to revive the intellectual imprint on the town from the Owen/Maclure experiment's scientists, naturalists, educators, and artists represented by "The Boatload of Knowledge."[3] The distinctive communities—one spiritual and the other intellectual—presented a challenge to her imagination, because she believed that both attributes were compatible rather than mutually exclusive. In her mind there was much to preserve, not only the natural and built environment but also an intellectual legacy.

Blaffer Owen's achievements were formally acknowledged throughout the years and culminated with the National Trust for Historic Preservation's 2008 Louise du Pont Crowninshield Award, "for life-long dedication to preservation in New Harmony, Indiana."[4] Little wonder that hagiographic terms describe Jane Owen as New Harmony's champion, legend, visionary, patron saint, godmother, and angel.[5] The preservationist, philanthropist, and arts patron often ceded the spotlight or responded with self-deprecating humor. When the then governor Mitch Daniels presented her with the State of Indiana's highest honor, the 2007 Sachem Award, for her work in the National Historic Landmark town, at a ceremony in the state house rotunda, he said, "Jane Owen is a gift beyond description. She has lived a truly unique life of virtue and goodness that has blessed Indiana in so many ways."[6] From the podium she countered, "I really have to meet this person they are describing. I really don't know who she is."[7]

Attempts to communicate Blaffer Owen's personality prove challenging. Howard Barnstone, a Houston-based architect, once replied when asked about her: "Jane is magic."[8] Others describe a soft-spoken charisma. The Reverend John Philip Newell identifies an essential attraction: "It was the way she embodied vision that drew most of us to her."[9] Over six decades, Jane Owen inspired some of the twentieth century's notables in their respective fields to participate in her quest to transform New Harmony.

The Newlyweds in New Harmony

Jane and Kenneth married on July 12, 1941, in Canada at the Blaffer summer home and estate named Ste. Anne, in honor of the Cathedral and Shrine Sainte-Anne-de-Beaupré's association with divine healing.[10] Sarah Campbell Blaffer (1885–1975), Jane's mother, had discovered the old stone farmhouse near Grafton, which featured a beautiful view of Lake Ontario, and purchased it as a summer home in 1939, when the rumblings of war inhibited the family's customary travel to Europe. By autumn of that year, Mrs. Blaffer had set plans in motion with Frank Abbott, a New York architect and artist, who had a summer home in Cobourg, to begin a rehabilitation that would bring modern conveniences and expand the house. Sarah Blaffer had demonstrated sensitivity to the historical integrity of the structure. The exterior masonry was pink-hued rose quartz. Even though it had seemed impossible to duplicate the house's large, rectangular-cut stones, she had recruited locals to find matching fieldstones and reclaim cut stones from abandoned structures of the same vintage in the area.

When Jane and Kenneth became engaged, her mother added "the wedding room" for dancing. The summer ceremony took place outdoors. Pastel shades of the bridesmaids' dresses mirrored the blooming petunias; even the planting of buckwheat was

Figure 1.2. Sarah Campbell Blaffer's rehabilitation of Ste. Anne began in 1939 with New York architect Frank Abbott. The "wedding room" addition for dancing (far right) used reclaimed cut stones of pink-hued rose quartz and fieldstones. Jane and K. D. witnessed an adaptive approach to restoration that would influence their New Harmony projects. Courtesy of the Kenneth Dale and Jane Blaffer Owen Family.

timed for its bridal-white display in the surrounding fields. Pilot friends from the exiled Royal Norwegian Air Force flew planes overhead, dropping wedding wishes below. Jane described the nuptials as glorious. Witnessing the transformation of Ste. Anne provided the newlyweds with a tangible example of an adaptive approach to restoration.

On the return drive to Houston, Kenneth detoured to New Harmony so his bride could experience the town. He provided a brief history of Owen ancestry and led Jane through the 1859 Gothic Revival David Dale Owen Laboratory, which had been adapted to a residence by the time Kenneth was born in 1903.[11] Though "the Lab" was the only property remaining in the family, K. D. also showed her the adjacent Corbin home (Rapp–Maclure–Owen House) and the Harmonist granary, which had served as a geologic laboratory for William Maclure, followed by the Owen brothers, David Dale and Richard.[12] The expansive surrounding countryside previously owned by the Owens hinted at their early successes. The thirty-seven-year-old groom had a pressing reason to return to the Lab: the first New Harmony Memorial Commission considered condemnation as a potential way to acquire historic

THIS FAIRY-TALE CASTLE WAS BUILT BY ROBERT OWEN'S SON DAVID TO HOUSE EXPERIMENTAL LABORATORY OF NEW HARMONY'S COMMUNAL OWENITE SECT

Life Visits New Harmony

A little Indiana town on the Wabash was setting for two strange utopias more than a century ago

Figure 1.3. Kenneth's first priority was to renovate his childhood home, the Gothic Revival David Dale Owen Laboratory, which was featured in the September 17, 1945, issue of *Life* magazine. Photograph copyright 1945 Kosti Ruohomaa and Black Star.

properties.[13] His immediate priority would be attending to its leaky roof followed by a renovation in order to keep it in the family.[14]

For Jane Owen, New Harmony possessed a historic depth that her native Houston lacked. When she arrived in New Harmony as a twenty-six-year-old bride, the town's significance seemed buried under the layers of coal dust that dulled its buildings and homes.[15] She presumed the townspeople had neglected their inheritance but soon learned that efforts had been and were being made to preserve the town's unique history, despite scarce financial resources. The New Harmony of 1941 needed an infusion of youthful energy and philanthropy committed to preserving its history.

REVENUES FROM THE OIL INDUSTRY

Although K. D. and Jane Owen each possessed financial independence through resources from the oil industry, her family's assets were more substantial than his. The discovery of oil in Texas during the early nineteen hundreds at Spindletop and other oil fields influenced her maternal and paternal family fortunes. Her mother's father, William Thomas "W. T." Campbell (1859–1906), was a founder of the Texas Company (later Texaco).[16] Sarah Jane Turnbull Campbell (1860–1951) was the "first woman ever to attend a meeting of the Texas Company's stockholders . . . in Houston with her husband, W. T. Campbell."[17] W. T. met Robert Lee Blaffer (1876–1942), a younger man who was establishing himself in the burgeoning oil industry, and introduced Lee to Sarah Jane "Sadie" Campbell, his daughter. Following W. T.'s death in 1906, his widow was pressured to liquidate her stock in the Texas Company but did not acquiesce.[18] In 1909 Sarah Jane Turnbull Campbell witnessed the marriage of Sadie and Lee at the Campbell home, Argyll Heights, in Lampasas, Texas.[19]

By 1917 Robert Lee Blaffer and others had chartered the Humble Oil and Refining Company (later Exxon).[20] Earlier, Lee Blaffer passed the time waiting for a well to blow in by reading, among other books, Podmore's *Robert Owen: A Biography*, volumes 1 and 2 (1906) and was impressed by Owen's reforms. The book was so influential that he reread it later with Jane, who said her father had "founded the first stock plan in Houston so that employees would own stock in the company for which they worked."[21] Jane added, "Daddy greatly admired Robert Owen's labor reforms; he implemented some at Humble, [including] stocks for employees. So many people over the years have called me and said, 'We are so grateful to your father because the stock went up.' Some were able to buy a better house, provide an education for their children. All because of my father and, indirectly, of course, Robert Owen."[22]

Kenneth worked his way through college. After graduating from Cornell in 1926, he relocated to Texas and became a successful field geologist initially with the Humble Oil Company and benefited from its stock.[23] His expertise resulted in discovering an oilfield with substantial production that secured his financial success and established him as a consulting geologist.[24] By the early 1940s K. D. had founded Gulfshore Oil Company and Trans-Tex Production Company.[25]

EARLY PRESERVATION PROJECTS

After the newlyweds' summer visit in 1941, they returned often to New Harmony to begin their shared vision: restoring the Owen legacy for their future children. By 1945 interior and exterior images of the renovated Lab appeared in *Life* magazine.[26] The couple also wanted to create a pastoral oasis in New Harmony to balance the pressures of life in Houston. Jane said, "I dreamed of New Harmony all my life,

Figure 1.4. Jane Blaffer Owen (second from left) befriended and mentored New Harmony schoolgirls, including (alphabetically) Betty Louise Hardy, Virginia Lee Hardy, Ruth Seamere/Seavors, and Ora Lee Shaw, circa 1945. Photograph by (Robert) Don Blair. Courtesy of Judith Blair Nix and Special Collections, University of Southern Indiana.

Figure 1.5. Kenneth Dale Owen contributed to New Harmony's heritage by acquiring lands previously held by Robert Owen and establishing Indian Mound Farm, which became world-renowned for its purebred Hereford cattle breeding operation under his leadership. Courtesy of the Kenneth Dale and Jane Blaffer Owen Family.

before I knew it existed."[27] Kenneth's hometown was a leveling ground where they lived seasonally adjacent to and interacted with a variety of townspeople, rather than being confined within the exclusive neighborhoods and society of the Blaffers. The novel experience was dramatic for Jane: "I was saved by the poverty of New Harmony."[28] The town also allowed a measure of anonymity where she could shed haute couture in favor of her crafting the earthy simplicity of southern Indiana.[29] Inescapably, she brought an aesthetic and energy typical of cultured urban life to her projects in the perceived Arcadian landscape that did not always mesh with the even-tempered pace of rural Hoosiers who, like her husband, seemed grounded by the agrarian setting.

Kenneth began to reclaim land that Robert Owen had spent half his fortune purchasing from the Harmonists, most of which had been sold by successive generations.[30] K. D. understood that farmland and pastures must be reinvigorated to create a productive agrarian asset. In 1942 Jane, newly pregnant, followed him to the prehistoric midden on the hill known as "Indian Mound" to observe progress clearing overgrown land below. At its crest, Jane was overwhelmed by a mystical experience in which she intuited that endeavors to revive New Harmony would become fruitful only if she would emulate the biblical Abraham's example of building an altar and dedicating efforts to a higher purpose: thus began her inspiration to find an artist capable of designing one for the present time.[31] Kenneth's perspective was pragmatic: he continued purchasing original Owen acreage south of town, including a larger farmstead with a few Hereford cattle. He established Indian Mound Farm, which expanded to include world-renowned Hereford breeding, Guernsey dairy, and farming operations.[32]

The birth of Jane "Janie" Dale Owen was followed a month later by the death of Blaffer Owen's father in October 1942. Associated Press wires reported his death, and later headlines proclaimed: "R. L. Blaffer Leaves Estate in excess of 150,000: widow and 4 children sole beneficiaries of a trust fund set up for the estate." The testamentary estate was about two million dollars;[33] historic standard of living equivalence for that amount in 2018 dollars is about thirty-three million.[34]

Lee Blaffer had encouraged Jane Owen's desire to preserve New Harmony's heritage. After the birth of her second child, Caroline Campbell Owen, Jane decided the family had outgrown the Lab, since Kenneth's aunt resided there year-round. By 1946 Jane Owen purchased a Harmonist house a few blocks away on Steammill, christening it "No. V," and began a hands-on rehabilitation. She dedicated it to her father in a framed note penned on June 15, 1947:

> I want this house to be like my father—sound, unpretentious, fearing only God. May it see things both as they are and as they might be. May it add in its measure, as he did so greatly in his, to the sum of human happiness, and to our understanding of the divine purpose. This, I believe, is the kind of memorial my father would like best.[35]

Sixteen years after his death, in 1958, Jane formalized what she called "a living memorial" to her father with funds she inherited by establishing the Robert Lee Blaffer Trust.[36] Founding trustees included (Robert) Don Blair, chairman; Ora H. Howton, treasurer/secretary; Helen Duprey Bullock of the National Trust for Historic Preservation; Philip Johnson, architect; and Sr. Élise, Community of the Holy Spirit, New York (aka Zoe Euverard). Owen launched building commissions and preservation projects through the Trust and supplemented its coffers, noting that "our trust is far more modest than other trusts. . . . It's not like the Ford or the Rockefeller Foundation." She admitted, "I received some tax relief. I have to give away thirty or forty percent of my income every year[,] and I chose to give it to New Harmony instead of somewhere else."[37]

More than anything else, Jane felt needed: "But it was the women in those days in New Harmony that were saving the remnants of the Harmonist and the Owen periods. And I said, 'They need help.' And Houston, with its increasing wealth, it would have been a pinhead here. But it is everything there. Do you see the difference? What I inherited made a huge difference in this little village."[38] She named each Harmonist-era house purchased over the next decade: Rawlings House, Kilbinger House (its addition, Mother Superior House), Poet's House, and Barrett–Gate House. After

Figure 1.6. Jane Owen visited Iona, Scotland, in 1955, at the invitation of the Reverend George MacLeod, to learn about his restoration of the medieval monastery into the Abbey Church. He became a mentor and encouraged her efforts in New Harmony. Photograph copyright 2014 Margaret Woodson Nea.

purchasing Kilbinger House, Jane Owen sought advice from Lawrence Thurman, director of Old Economy Village, about its Harmonist origins and preservation expertise from Helen Duprey Bullock of the National Trust for Historic Preservation established in 1949.[39] With Bullock's friendship in 1954 came an awareness of the national preservation movement, later including the National Historic Preservation Act of 1966, and the 1976 bicentennial, which was a very active period of preservation across the nation. Jane also learned about the restoration of a medieval monastery at Iona, Scotland, in 1955, through the Reverend George MacLeod, who aided her efforts in New Harmony.

An Education for Patronage

In the 1940s when Kenneth introduced Jane to the small town of his childhood, she envisioned its possibilities from the perspective of her unique childhood experiences and education, which had prepared her for Houston society and patronage. What specific factors influenced her commitment to commission sculpture, architecture, and gardens? In an interview Jane acknowledged, "I had this heritage and this love of art, beauty from my childhood impressed upon me. And here was a little woebegone town that had fallen asleep[,] but it had this great, great historical and cultural and spiritual beginning."[40]

THE BLAFFER FAMILY AT SHADYSIDE

Lining both sides of Sunset Boulevard today, the massive, full-headed live oak trees, whose intertwined and overhanging branches filter the normally intense Houston sunlight, seem to have provided the inspiration for the neighborhood's name, Shadyside. In Jane's childhood, however, the thin, scraggly saplings were, like her, establishing a foundation. She was the second of four children.[41] The Blaffers built a brick house designed by Birdsall P. Briscoe (1876–1971), a Houston architect, in 1920 on one of the two-acre residential lots they purchased from fellow oilman Joseph S. Cullinan that he had developed as Shadyside, on the south edge of Houston in proximity to the Museum of Fine Arts.[42] Jane Owen would later reflect on her mother's aesthetic, saying, "the rooms she designed were what I call chaste, almost monastic. Beautiful in an understated simplicity, not excessive or showy."[43] Life at 6 Sunset Boulevard during the 1920s and 1930s was serene, and neighboring vacant lots gave the property a rural quality and accommodated the family's cows.[44] Jane described her childhood as "idyllic," "a fairytale," "a magic carpet ride" and admitted to having been "a little spoiled."[45] A benefit of the Blaffer home's proximity to Rice Institute and Shadyside neighbors was a continual influx of visitors from around the country and abroad, in addition to Rice's president Edgar Odell Lovett and faculty. As a trustee from 1935 to 1941, R. Lee Blaffer directed oil revenues to Rice Institute (now Rice University).

With the births of the first Blaffer children, the French governess Mademoiselle Suzanne Henriette Glémet became part of the household. The children spent summers on Mlle. Glémet's family farm in France (near Barbezieux Charente) immersed in the French language while Mrs. Blaffer visited artists, galleries, and museums and exposed each child at an impressionable age to art and artists. Jane Owen vividly remembered the powerful experience of seeing Rodin's bronze sculptures when she was about eleven: "Mother had a profound influence on my love of art and beauty."[46] Jane participated with her family in the sacramental life of the Episcopal Christ Church. She later acknowledged that having been able to travel and view centuries-old works of art and stained glass in museums and churches—with Old Testament biblical scenes of patriarchs and prophets to the life of Christ and the saints—gave her a far different experience than images typically created for children.

THE KINKAID SCHOOL, 1920–30

The Blaffers concurred with Margaret Hunter Kinkaid's philosophy that girls should learn science and math and not be restricted to women's subjects. When Jane began attending the coeducational private school in Houston around 1920, the curriculum also included Latin, French, and Spanish.[47] Kinkaid had reached an enrollment of 125 students in 1920 with eight full-time faculty. Lee Blaffer and other parents spearheaded efforts to construct a brick building for the school instead of having classes in the wood-framed Kinkaid home on Elgin Avenue, which they considered a firetrap. Mrs. Kinkaid wanted the proposed school to let in plenty of light; William Ward Watkin, professor of architecture at Rice Institute, designed the U-shaped Spanish revival building.[48] Jane witnessed her father's interactions with the architect. The school's Richmond Avenue campus opened in 1924. Mrs. Kinkaid kept tuition low so that children from different backgrounds could attend and instituted a "simple dressing pledge" in which girls agreed not to wear silk, satin, or velvet dresses or set their hair with the new bobs and permanent waves.[49] Jane especially enjoyed participating in dramatics. With the onset of the Depression during Jane's final year, Mrs. Kinkaid placed an emphasis on community service so that privileged students would grasp its severity.

THE ETHEL WALKER SCHOOL, 1930–33

Jane Blaffer left home to attend the Ethel Walker School for women in Simsbury, Connecticut, originally the Phelps–Dodge estate. "The school's peaceful setting, along with its proximity to the large cities and cultural wealth of the Northeast, parallels

Walker's dual emphasis on inner development and social commitment."[50] Ethel Walker, alumna of Bryn Mawr College, pioneered its "sound body/sound mind approach to learning."[51] Jane continued studies in Latin, French, and English. Her work in art, which included clay and figural work, was deemed "excellent."[52] She accompanied her friend Jane Watson on visits to schools for disadvantaged children during these Depression years. When she graduated in 1933, Blaffer was active on the boards of the yearbook and the *Timepiece*.[53]

JANE STOTT BLAFFER

6 Sunset Road, Sunnyside   Houston, Tex.

Bryn Mawr

Jane is unusual and intellectual. The one quality that is pre-eminent and recognizable is her earnestness and sincerity. Everything that she does she puts her whole heart and soul into and if the outcome falls short of perfection, she is dissatisfied. Jane would die for ideals, and she has a very high class of them. But do not let this present a picture of some white-robed and grim-faced individual. Say not so. To the layman is shown a Jane of capricious fancy and lilting laughs, accompanying every word with innumerable gestures of her beautifully groomed hands. Truly she is well called the class individualist.

Dial Club; Dial Indian Club Team, '32, '33; Library Committee, '31, '32; Chairman Library Committee, '33; Individual Indian Clubs, '33; Yearbook Board, '33; *Timepiece* Board, '33; French Club, '31, '32, '33; Honorable Mention Dramatic Club, '32; French Play, '32; Prize for Room Neatness, '33.

Figure 1.7. The entry for Jane Blaffer in the Graduating Seniors section of the Ethel Walker School yearbook, *Pepper Pot,* in 1933 provides insights into her classmates' assessment of her accomplishments and personality. Her Houston neighborhood of Shadyside was changed to "Sunnyside" to reflect her disposition. Courtesy of Priscilla Jackson, librarian and archivist, the Ethel Walker School.

BRYN MAWR COLLEGE, 1933–35

After high school, Jane entered Bryn Mawr College, which had a progressive foundation thanks to M. Carey Thomas (1857–1935), its first dean and second president, who was an activist for women's suffrage and education that extended not only to the typical college student but also to women in industrial trades and the "campus maids."[54] The campus design reflected Thomas's priorities, and the Philadelphia-based architects Walter Cope and John Stewardson were able to give form and substance to her unique vision. According to Helen Lefkowitz Horowitz's insights into the design and experience of women's colleges:

> M. Carey Thomas built in stone as effectively as she did in academic policy. She shared her era's belief in the power of the physical environment to shape communal spirit and individual character. She brought to Bryn Mawr a strong, feminist commitment to the needs of young women scholars. However inimical to Quaker traditions, she added a love of pageantry and drama. All of this is visible in the Jacobean quadrangles of Bryn Mawr. . . .
>
> Unlike the men who planned domestic places at Smith or seminary settings at Vassar and Wellesley, Carey Thomas had no desire to adapt feminine spaces to academic uses. Rather, she wanted to appropriate the library and the laboratory of men. . . . Carey Thomas held no belief in a separate women's culture. . . . As the visible sign that truth had no sex, the Bryn Mawr campus gave no clue as to the gender of its student body.[55]

Thomas resided in the Deanery on campus until 1933, outliving her companion Mary Garrett, who had been integrated into campus life; in this sense, an atmosphere of inclusiveness settled over the women's college.[56] Marion Edwards Park, the subsequent president from 1922 to 1942, extended the Thomas legacy of academic excellence and relevant social issues while adjusting to changes brought on by the Depression.[57]

During a conversation in 2009 related to her decision to attend Bryn Mawr College, Jane Owen responded with a reflection: "I had read G. G. King's *The Way of St. James,*" she paused, waiting for an affirmation from her editor. "Didn't she write about the medieval pilgrimage route to . . ." Having said enough to prompt her reentry, Blaffer Owen continued, "Yes, dear, Santiago de Compostela." "I became acquainted with Miss Georgiana Goddard King through her book, several volumes, and wanted to study art history under her and archaeology, classical archaeology, under Rhys Carpenter. They were teaching at Bryn Mawr." She then closed her eyes as if returning to the campus in her mind's eye and spoke in a series of associations:

> We knew her affectionately as "G. G." We were intimidated at first sight, her black robe in the distance, a grand dame of academia. In reality, she was very personable, like her persona in *The Way.* We became acolytes, vestals, once in her presence. The other girls, they were furious note-takers, not me, but G. G. outwitted them. She had devised a way around their habit of doing so from prep school days. She lectured with the lights out. I was used to the semi-darkness from candlelight at home. She spoke from her heart; we looked at slides or listened as her words penetrated, forming images in our minds. G. G. King knew everything, was an exceptional teacher. Both were wonderful teachers, [she added, reintegrating Rhys Carpenter into the reflection,] who encouraged the ability to apply what he taught us beyond the classical Greek epoch; he provided the building blocks and trusted us to construct, to make, connections. We would listen to our "nightingale" for hours. Both used the Socratic method.

Opening her eyes, Jane said that G. G. also possessed a solid knowledge of modern art and was a friend of Gertrude Stein. Eyes closed again as she recited by heart King's commandment: "The only way to know anything is to go and look."[58]

Georgiana Goddard King (1871–1939)

Jane Owen indicated that she was first introduced to King's perspective, analytic approach, and literary style by reading *The Way of Saint James* before college.[59] King had spent years traveling, often in austere conditions, through remote areas of southern France and northern Spain in order to document the architecture along the Way of Saint James. Why did the book appeal so strongly to Jane Blaffer? A concise synthesis of scholarship reveals an answer.

Susanna Terrell Saunders's biographical work of 1981 and Janice Mann's recent scholarship provide the most thorough introduction to and interpretation of King's life and work.[60] In reference to *The Way of Saint James,* Mann explains that King's

Figure 1.8. "G. G." Georgiana Goddard King, from the article "Bryn Mawr College" in the June 1935 issue of *Fortune,* highlighting the college's fiftieth year. King's History of Art course had a profound influence on the sophomore Jane Blaffer. Copyright 1935 George Platt Lynes. Copyright Estate of George Platt Lynes. Courtesy of George P. Lynes, II.

"journey provides more than just a framing device for the history and analysis of the architecture and sculpture encountered along the route. . . . Throughout the book she weaves together the present and the past, the legendary and the historical."[61] Thus King draws the reader into her own visceral experience of witnessing art and architecture firsthand, thereby creating a universal, cosmic pilgrimage that transcends time and retains its sacred relevance across the centuries. King's scope resonated with Jane Blaffer's understanding of the interrelatedness of the temporal and the eternal. Mann also notes, "King does not expunge her deeply felt religious sentiments from her text. For her, . . . the aesthetic and the spiritual were joined. . . . Throughout the book she refers to prayer, saints, and the liturgy without irony or cynicism."[62] Given Jane's religious sensibility and familiarity with art, she felt a strong kinship to the author of *The Way of St. James* and wanted to study with the scholar.

Jane's motivation for attending Bryn Mawr (1933–35) was not only affective but also practical. King, who established the Department of Art History in 1913, was highly regarded internationally.[63] As a testament to King's impressive commitment and capabilities, "by 1934, Bryn Mawr's graduate department of art history had been ranked beside those of Harvard and Princeton by the American Council of Education."[64] She was respected not only for her expertise in the architecture and sculpture of medieval Spain and Sardinia but also her knowledge of Italian, Asian, and modern art.[65]

Jane Blaffer would discover that King's courses were quite popular, as much for the content as for the teacher's personality. According to her transcripts, Jane spent her first year at Bryn Mawr fulfilling requirements.[66] In the fall of 1934, she began "taking G. G.," who was sixty-three years old.[67] History of Art was not similar to any other course in Jane's previous academic experience. Reflecting on her time in the classroom, Jane Owen recalled that G. G. did not use prepared lectures, relying instead on an impressive recall of information across multiple disciplines. The dim illumination in the room came from the lantern-slide projector. By making note-taking for memorization difficult, G. G. sought to retrain the observational skills of her pupils as they focused on visual images and internalized impressions of them. King encouraged students to view art from a personal vantage point: how and in what ways did the artist's composition and arrangement communicate and elicit emotion? Yet the process could be unnerving when she called on a student to "speak" to the image. Jane, somewhat reserved, nevertheless responded to the opportunity to articulate her perspective, gained initially through access to art and artists with her mother. The slides and photographs, however, did not supplant the appreciation of actual works. Students were expected to apply what they learned and to develop their abilities through frequent visits to exhibitions.[68] Jane Owen indicated that small informal groups of students would visit the Philadelphia Museum of Art and the Rodin Museum in Philadelphia and those beyond, even venturing into New York City on King's recommendation.[69] G. G.'s commandment to "go and look" is born out of the pilgrimage ethos, to see and experience the built and natural environment personally rather than being restricted to museums and books, anticipating what Jane herself would begin in New Harmony a decade later.

King assigned readings from literature that served as prompts.[70] She especially admired Gertrude Stein and had published a review of *Three Lives* in the June 1913 issue of *International.* Their friendship began in 1902 and was responsible for exposing G. G. to modern art; the Steins introduced her to Picasso's dealer Daniel-Henry Kahnweiler at their Paris apartment.[71] King taught her students about cubism the year *before* the 1913 Armory Show.[72] (By comparison, Sarah Blaffer, during her 1909 honeymoon, experienced art, especially at the Louvre, as a spiritual quest that would lead to collecting.)[73] Since Jane Blaffer possessed a strong background in European literature and art, she appreciated the depth of her teacher's knowledge. On February 15, 1934, G. G. gave an informative presentation in the college commons about understanding Stein's literary works through art.[74] The works of Georges Braque and Jean Lurçat were on exhibit in the commons at the same time.[75] Later, Stein spoke on poetry and grammar in Goodhart Hall on November 15, 1934, when she visited Bryn Mawr for several days in connection with the promotional book tour for *The Autobiography of Alice B. Toklas,* accompanied by Toklas.[76]

King's pedagogy has been described as eclectic, expansive, and engaging. She demanded excellence from her students to heighten their own expectations. In a memorial tribute to the professor, former student Agnes Mongan (Fogg Museum, Harvard) spoke of "King's capacity to arouse, to electrify, to instruct, and to inspire" her students, whom she "inoculated with ideas which leave marks on all their later lives."[77] Jane chose well and remembered; thirty years later, in 1975, when asked about her education during a deposition, she referenced Georgiana Goddard King and Rhys Carpenter.[78]

Rhys Carpenter (1889–1980)

As a sophomore, Jane Blaffer also began the first-year Archaeology course taught by Carpenter, who had just returned to Bryn Mawr after serving as director of the American School of Classical Studies at Athens.[79] He was forty-five years old, at the midpoint of his career, and by all accounts enormously popular with his students.[80] Jane remembered the nickname students bestowed on him, "our nightingale," because of his melodious voice (he was also a poet), his leading questions, and the exciting discussions that ensued. He encouraged his students to "Look with your own eyes" at classical sculpture and architecture rather than being influenced by the interpretations of others, including experts and scholars. Many students were for the first time eager to express their thoughts, insights, and opinions. Carpenter could assert this bold approach because he gave his students a strong foundation from which to "See!"

To establish a common language in the classroom, he motivated his students to internalize quickly through visualization (and memorization) every component of Greek architecture from the ground-level sterobate to the roof-level entablature (with its variations in orders: Doric, Ionic, Corinthian). In a monograph, Carpenter demonstrates that Greek architecture is "ordered and logical" and "harmonises, part with part, and parts with whole."[81] Jane Owen and her classmates drew and constructed models to familiarize themselves with the terminology and its meaning. "We dreamed of classical temples by night and drilled each other by day during the first weeks until we knew it all by heart. We were liberated because there was no more struggling; we knew what Rhys Carpenter meant instantly."[82] Once past the stage of inculcation regarding classical architecture, he introduced Greek sculpture from the vase and frieze to the figures found within or around the temple.[83] Carpenter states his intention "to examine Greek artistic procedure" via "a method sufficiently general to be applicable not to Greek sculpture only, but in all times, and not to Greek architecture alone, but to architecture the world over."[84] (The Barnes Collection at the Philadelphia Museum of Art would have demonstrated to students in this course the importance of cross-referencing art periods.)

Although Carpenter, like King, used the Socratic method of teaching, some specifics about his perspective can be deduced from the Martin Classical Lectures he delivered at Oberlin College the year before Jane attended his class. A detailed analysis of these lectures, published as *The Humanistic Value of Archaeology* (1933), is beyond the scope of this essay, but key passages are helpful for understanding his influence on Jane Blaffer.[85] To enable his students to "look," he explains what happens when an image is turned around: "Only when the familiar forms with all their habitual associations are destroyed can we see the world as it truly appears rather than as we have decided to envisage it" (95). Carpenter establishes parallels between the evolution of "graphic and plastic arts, painting and sculpture" (75). Jane

Figure 1.9. Rhys Carpenter, pictured right, returned from Athens to resume teaching archaeology at Bryn Mawr. Jane Blaffer Owen credits him with refining her appreciation of architecture. Frederick O. Waage and Rhys Carpenter on Mount Hymettus, 1930. Copyright 1930 Homer A. Thompson. Courtesy of American School of Classical Studies at Athens, Archives, Homer A. Thompson Photographic Collection.

remembered the term Carpenter uses to describe the place where the forward progression toward imitative realism reaches the "dead end":

> In modern times, sculpture reached this Dead End of realism in the nineteenth century, painting in the early twentieth century. The chaos in the arts to-day has been ascribed superficially and erroneously to the soullessness of modern mechanistic civilization, to the Great War, to general restlessness, to decadence, to the present depression. None of these has anything to do with it. The imitative arts had completed their development toward imitative realism. (118)

For Carpenter, artists, regardless of media, who reach this place, responded historically by either retracing their path, staying in place, or moving in a new direction. Carpenter expresses his preference when he relates this to the current situation: "The important masters of to-day are all those who, in their revolt against realistic imitation, do not borrow or revive styles, but seek to create them. Even if their value is their novelty, . . . theirs is the hope and the promise" (123). An impression was made: Jane Owen would search for artists, sculptors, and architects who did not want to imitate or revive what other masters had created but who were on the cusp of making their own contributions to their time.

Many students, like Jane, were simultaneously enrolled in the first-year courses taught by Carpenter and King. Although both professors centered their coursework on its historical subject matter, each also related that content across the spectrum of creativity and into the present. The architectural components of the Greek temple learned with Carpenter could also inform the understanding of Romanesque ecclesiastical architecture with King. And both departments shared excellent resources, from glass lantern slides to documentary photographs, readily available for review during and outside class.[86] Blaffer and the other students had lively discussions after class. King and Carpenter were among those rare and gifted teachers who inspire.

Josephine M. Petts (1891–1989)

When Jane Blaffer attended Body Mechanics, she did not realize that it would have a profound effect on her. Josephine Petts, director of Physical Education and Natural Dancing, taught at Bryn Mawr from 1928 until 1946 and integrated the Isadora and Elizabeth Duncan methodology of dance into her courses.[87] She had returned in the fall of 1933, the year Jane began classes, from her fourth summer in Salzburg at the Duncan School of Dance.[88] Working with Miss Petts introduced Jane to a new form of artistic expression in which she could participate physically. Petts also developed an extracurricular Dance Group, and "Jane Blaffer" is listed as a member and performer.[89] The college also welcomed professional dance performances to the campus, such as the Estelle Dennis Group and Jacques Cartier. Edward M. M. Warburg (who had taught at Bryn Mawr the previous year) arranged

Figure 1.10. Bryn Mawr students in the Body Mechanics class practicing Greek rhythms under the direction of Josephine M. Petts, from the June 1935 issue of *Fortune*. Jane Blaffer participated in the class and performed in the Dance Club. Copyright 1935 George Platt Lynes. Copyright Estate of George Platt Lynes. Courtesy of George P. Lynes, II.

for the nascent American Ballet that he founded with Lincoln Kirstein, featuring George Balanchine, to perform February 7 and 8, 1935.[90]

Insight into Petts's influence comes from her "special thoughts" during dance class: "You cannot become sensitive to beauty and joy and not become at the same time, sensitive to ugliness and sorrow. If you are open to one, you will feel all. You must pay the price."[91] Jane Owen believed so strongly in dance as an expressive art that she included it as an area of educational outreach and support for the Robert Lee Blaffer Trust in New Harmony.[92] The joy of dance remained with Owen throughout her lifetime, and she could be seen dancing in her nineties.

TRANSITIONS

About a month before the end of the 1935 spring semester, Jane's father had a health scare, and she returned home. Rather than resume her studies at Bryn Mawr in the fall, she chose "to continue [her] art education [in Houston] and in Europe informally with artists themselves, with creators themselves."[93] Her ability to do so in Europe only lasted a few years. On a trip to Germany with her parents, she happened to see Adolf Hitler (described as a despicable little man) and his entourage in a hotel lobby.[94] Jane, a self-described advocate for peaceful solutions to national aggression, decided to attend the Washington School of Diplomacy, 1938–39, before settling back at home. Her brother, John, brought his friend Kenneth Owen to dine with the Blaffers and to meet Jane.

Blaffer Owen's Early Influences Converge in New Harmony

Jane Blaffer Owen brought a youthful energy to New Harmony, where her formative and educational influences found expression. What she had absorbed from the teachings of Rhys Carpenter and Georgiana Goddard King during college developed into her unique perspective. Jane Owen was drawn to the modern works of her own time for their ability to reveal a dynamic present. She remembered from Carpenter that the materiality of sculptural and architectural forms has a constancy and durability (even as ruins) that provide insights into ancient communities from which we can see and attempt to understand each epoch. Both courses provided a foundation in the language of architecture. Even the Duncan techniques Petts taught had a lasting influence: Jane Owen credited the corporeal experience of dance with enhancing her appreciation of curvilinear design in sculpture and architecture. (While in New York in the 1960s, Owen occasionally attended classes at the Martha Graham School of Contemporary Dance.) Jane also reflected on an adage she had learned during childhood from her mother about patronage: "We must take care of people who can create. The fundamental can be learnt, but the original must be created." Discovering "the original" would often require time. Jane Owen would search for artists, sculptors, and architects who would help her realize her vision for New Harmony and for whom her patronage would enable them to realize their full potential through the creative process.[95] "To mother, it was always the artist who unlocked the great mysteries, who wove the finest nets with which to catch and hold the inexpressible."[96] Sarah Blaffer had unknowingly prepared Jane for encounters in adulthood with Jacques Lipchitz, Philip Johnson, Paul Tillich, and Frederick Kiesler.

MODERNIST INTERVENTION

While in late pregnancy with her third child, Jane Owen reflected on her mystical experience seven years earlier on Indian Mound and her unfulfilled promise to build an altar.[97] On a regime of partial bed rest in Houston, she perused art magazines to stave off boredom and found an article in *Art News* about the works of Jacques Lipchitz, a cubist sculptor. Sensing she had discovered the artist who could translate her feelings into a physical reality, she wrote to him immediately to request a work on loan.[98] The coincidence of the arrival of Anne Dale Owen and a photograph of *Notre Dame de Liesse* (Our Lady of Joy), while in the maternity ward, confirmed her foresight. With the intensity of her spontaneous reaction to the work, she gave it an alternate name, "Descent of the Holy Spirit," when she wrote to him from her hospital bed in April 1950.[99] Lipchitz replied that Father Marie-Alain Couturier had commissioned the sculpture for a modern church at Assy.[100] Jane Owen was already familiar with the Dominican priest's reputation by way of his contact with Houston philanthropists John and Dominique de Menil, who had met him in France before they came to Houston in 1940.[101] Jane especially admired Couturier's ecumenism. From within the Anglican tradition, Blaffer Owen had begun to explore ways to communicate with others and discuss the beliefs that frequently divide people. She believed New Harmony presented the perfect opportunity to reunite the sacred and the profane.[102] Lipchitz's *Descent of the Holy Spirit* as an altar housed within the open church she commissioned in 1957 from Philip Johnson together became a tangible manifestation of her ecumenical outreach.[103]

Through Lipchitz in the early 1950s, Owen became aware of Protestant theologian Paul Tillich. While in New York City for her daughter Janie's polio treatments and surgeries, Blaffer Owen attended some of Tillich's lectures at Union Theological Seminary. She followed the trajectory of his philosophy, read his books and articles,

Figure 1.11. The sculpture *Descent of the Holy Spirit (Notre Dame de Liesse)* by Jacques Lipchitz, as an altar housed under the baldachin within the Roofless Church designed by Philip Johnson: together they became a tangible manifestation of Jane Blaffer Owen's emphasis on ecumenical inclusion to heal divisions. Photograph by Don Blair, May 1, 1960. Courtesy of Judith Blair Nix. From the Collections of Historic New Harmony / University of Southern Indiana.

and felt a comradeship with his provocative idea that the sacred can become manifest in secular modern art. And she discovered connections with what she had learned from Carpenter. Tillich's article "The Lost Dimension in Religion," in the June 14, 1958, issue of the *Saturday Evening Post,* reinforced her approach to the Roofless Church:

> It is the religious question which is asked when the architect, in creating office buildings or churches, removes the trimmings taken over from past styles because they cannot be considered an honest expression of our own period. He prefers the seeming poverty of a purpose-determined style to the deceptive richness of imitated styles of the past. He knows that he gives no final answer, but he does give an honest answer.

In April 1961 she spoke with Tillich about her idea of creating a park in New Harmony to honor him. Frederick Kiesler originally created the design for Paul Tillich

Park, but later Robert Zion and Harold Breen, in association with Johnson's office, modeled a landscape based on it.[104]

Had Jane Owen confined herself to the traditional preservation she pursued in the late 1940s and 1950s, she might have had few detractors. Her commissions for modern architecture, sculpture, art, gardens, and adaptive preservation placed her at odds with some townspeople. Two publications provide insight into tensions between those who opposed and those who supported interventions by Blaffer Owen. In 1975 John Blades highlights Ralph G. Schwarz, first director of Historic New Harmony, who spearheaded a dynamic transformation of the town. Schwarz acknowledges the effect: "Change is a shattering experience when it disturbs existing conditions."[105] One shop worker complains that the town-wide restoration project has raised housing prices and limited availability, while Helen Elliot, a member of the first Memorial Commission, says, "I've always hoped for better days. And now I think they've come." In 1983 Barbara Grizzuti Harrison gives voice to viewpoints from two women: "And don't forget the business Miss Owen has brought into our town and all the people she employs," Kate says, to counter Kathleen's comment about sculpture in the Roofless Church, "I thought we wasn't supposed to idol things."[106] The frenzied pace of restoration projects and the 1979 completion of an athenaeum designed by the architect Richard Meier had the effect of distancing Kenneth from his hometown. He focused on his standardbred horses and resisted the changes like some other townspeople during this period. Once the novel becomes the norm, however, criticism fades.

RESTORING THE
HISTORIC, INTELLECTUAL, AND SPIRITUAL
SPHERES OF INFLUENCE

Much like Robert Owen and William Maclure, who brought to New Harmony treasure and talent in the form of "The Boatload of Knowledge," the best and brightest men and women of their day, Jane Owen committed to bring those who would best represent the spirit of her "present," the modern age. However, New Harmony always had a balance: even with the scientists and educators and artists of the Owen/Maclure experiment, there were also workers and farmers who formed the community. Martin L. McAuliffe Jr. writes in "The Life of the Spirit: Mrs. Jane Blaffer Owen":

> She conceived the idea of a new life for New Harmony as "an historic living community dedicated to continuing and re-animating in mid-America the attributes of individual religious faith, intellect, imagination and creative industry that, together, have made and will sustain our national character." Mrs. Owen has not tried to rebuild New Harmony as a museum piece, but as a living community.[107]

Jane Owen sought to introduce a new generation of townspeople to a living legacy, the greats of their time. Whoever came to create a work of art or architecture, to preach a radical theology, to dedicate a landscape or lead a retreat, to perform through music or dance, or to recite poetry, became a part of the community. Townspeople could relax in a home with Philip Johnson after a ceremony or listen to Paul Tillich in an informal gathering on the lawn beside Poet's House. Perhaps her mentor Tillich best articulates this aspect of Jane Owen's New Harmony:

> When we [Mrs. Tillich and I] met a few people and had dinner with them, something else, beyond the landscape, took us in, the reality of a community which has one thing in contrast to most small communities—it does not suffer from narrowness. It is wide open in all directions, toward India as well as toward Europe and toward all the other sections of the world. And it is open not only geographically, but it is open also in terms of new ideas. And I cannot avoid saying that this is largely due to Mrs. Owen, who has done many things which are very bold and very adequate to our century.[108]

The Couple's Final Preservation Efforts

Blaffer Owen also funded projects to promote and accommodate the town's growing tourism, including restaurants and commercial buildings as well as commissioning Indiana architect Evans Woollen to design the New Harmony Inn (1974) and its expansion (1986). Her early commissions for the Lipchitz sculpture, Roofless Church, and Tillich Park had initiated a shift from an early focus on preservation projects with Kenneth. From the hindsight of her nineties, Jane muses in her memoir: "Unintentionally, I had diverted his attention from the goals we had pursued so passionately in the first decades of our marriage. . . . In retrospect, I can understand Kenneth's need to distance himself from my missionary zeal and seemingly inexhaustible bank account" (142). K. D. pursued his standardbred breeding and training programs in Kentucky and Pennsylvania and traveled to harness racing events. His expertise earned the Hambletonian in 1967, and he was inducted into the Harness Racing Hall of Fame in 1987.

Preservation took many forms for Kenneth but always related in some way to the Owen family. He accepted an appointment to serve on the New Harmony Memorial Commission II and III from the 1970s through the 1990s.[109] When acquiring properties earlier, Kenneth had purchased from the Corbin family heirs two historic buildings in 1948 relevant to his Owen ancestors. One was the house William Maclure's brother had rebuilt, on the foundation of George Rapp's 1822 mansion, by carpenter John Beal in 1844 (in which David Dale and Richard Owen had lived). The other was the Harmonist granary, which David Dale had used as a geological laboratory for sixteen years before building the Lab that became a family residence. With the purchase, Kenneth had asked Earl H. Reed, after meeting through the

Figure 1.12. Paul Tillich and Jane Blaffer Owen during his Pentecost visit to New Harmony to dedicate the ground of Paul Tillich Park, June 2, 1963. Jane Owen agreed with his insight that secular modern art often enables a heightened awareness of the sacred in its modern guise. Courtesy of the photographer, James K. Mellow. From the Collections of Historic New Harmony / University of Southern Indiana.

Figure 1.13. The Rapp–Maclure–Owen House, as it appeared in March 1906, during Kenneth Dale Owen's childhood. The 1844 house was built on the foundation of George Rapp's mansion, which had been destroyed by fire. In 1989 K. D. began supervising its renovation and established the Owen–Maclure Foundation to maintain the historic building. Photographer unknown. Courtesy of Judith Blair Nix and Special Collections, University of Southern Indiana.

Historic American Buildings Survey (HABS), to research the history of the Rapp–Maclure–Owen House and Granary. Reed, a fellow of the American Institute of Architects serving on the preservation committee at the time, was former Head of the Architecture Department at the Armour Institute of Technology (now IIT) from 1924 until 1936.[110]

Forty years later, K. D. slowed his activity in the pursuits that had captivated him for decades. With the sale of his standardbred farm in Pennsylvania in addition to the 1981 herd dispersion of Indian Mound Farm, Kenneth turned his attention again to New Harmony. In 1989 he began supervising the Rapp–Maclure–Owen House rehabilitation.[111] Jane assisted by commissioning murals for the entryway from the Hoosier artist Loren Dunlap. K. D. also preserved early Owen family papers and artifacts there. He believed the former Owen residence to be of such significance that he ensured its survival through his will, which would transfer the house to the Owen–Maclure Foundation, established as a 501(c)(3) in 1992, to be "permanently maintained and preserved due to its educational and historic value."[112]

K. D. had known that the long-neglected circa 1818 sandstone, brick, and wooden Harmonist granary, which had been in precarious condition when he purchased it, would require community effort and funding to restore the massive building. For that purpose, the Rapp Granary–Owen Foundation was established in 1992, with Kenneth and Jane Owen serving on its board as trustees, together with David L. Rice, president emeritus of the University of Southern Indiana; James "Jim" Sanders; Gary Gerard; and Robert Guenther. Through the stimulus of challenge grants from the National Park Service Preservation and the Neighborhood Assistance Program and from the Lilly Endowment, Inc., more than 360 donors contributed a total of 2.5 million dollars by 1999. In keeping with the dual history of the building's use, it would be christened with the names of the Harmonist community leader and the Owen geologist who had spent the most time there, the Rapp Granary–David Dale Owen Laboratory.[113]

Figure 1.14. Rapp–Owen Granary after restoration, with its front elevation reflecting the five-story Harmonist era and its other elevations reflecting the two-story D. D. Owen laboratory era with enlarged Georgian windows. The rebuilt Granary represents principles of both restoration and renovation. Photograph by Fred Reaves. Copyright 2000 Fred Reaves. Courtesy of Fred Reaves / ImageOne Photography and Hafer Architects, Designers, Engineers.

The trustees selected the architectural firm Edmund L. Hafer and Associates because of their historic preservation experience with the Victory Theatre and Old Post Office in nearby Evansville, Indiana. Hafer's project scope included archaeological documentation, historic restoration of the original intact elements, and reconstruction to re-create the original Harmonist-era building with adaptive reuse as a modern conference center.[114] The decision to maintain the dual historic backdrop—its Harmonist and David Dale Owen period uses—enabled the building's exterior to highlight this distinction. The front elevation, with its small windows, reflects the five-story Harmonist period. The other elevations reflect Owen's modifications to the granary, enlarged Georgian windows set in his two-story laboratory. The interior maintains the dual-period representations, with the first floor highlighting the German granary and the second floor showcasing "the geologic and natural science community gathering center with exhibits."[115] The PBS documentary *Old Stones in New Harmony: The Rebirth of the Rapp Granary* follows its restoration–renovation.[116]

In a congratulatory letter to the Granary Foundation trustees, Bill Goodwin, then vice president for Community Development for the Lilly Endowment, Inc., noted, "I am astounded at the huge success you have had with the Rapp–Owen Granary project. In all of my years at the Endowment, this project has to be recognized as the leading example of a community's dedication, perseverance, and effectiveness in realizing the fulfillment of a dream." The restoration–rehabilitation of the Granary by Hafer received an AIA Indiana Design Honor Award for Preservation in 2000. Kenneth Dale Owen and Dr. David L. Rice were together recipients of the Outstanding Preservation Award of Indiana from the State Department of Natural Resources for their roles in the restoration of the Granary.

Recognition and Legacy

At the Indiana statewide 2010 Preserving Historic Places Conference session "Modernism in New Harmony," a distinguished panel of architects (Bernard Karpf, AIA, Richard Meier & Partners; Evans Woollen, FAIA; Joseph Mashburn, AIA, University of Houston; moderated by Kenneth A. "Kent" Schuette Jr., Purdue University) discussed how modernism came to be in New Harmony and how the newer landmarks relate to themes in New Harmony's past: "New Harmony is more than just the Utopian communities of the nineteenth century. Because of unusual leadership provided by Mrs. Jane Blaffer Owen and Historic New Harmony, twentieth-century Modern buildings like the Atheneum, Roofless Church, and the New Harmony Inn also dot the landscape."[117]

As visitors ascend the white steel ramp inside the light-infused Atheneum designed by Richard Meier to an upper floor, they encounter a wall-sized exhibit commemorating the similarities and distinctions between the two pivotal periods in New Harmony's utopian history compared with the present: the Harmonist, Owen/ Maclure community, and the Bicentennial (2014). Reading across the column of its major leaders (George Rapp of the Harmonie Society as well as Robert Owen and William Maclure of the Owen/Maclure Community), the inclusion of Jane Blaffer Owen's name marking the Bicentennial period demonstrates the significance of her commitment, patronage, and determination to revive New Harmony. Her influence has been called "the third wave" and, together with her husband, the "Kenneth and Jane Owen era of restoration."[118] In September 2016 they were selected as posthumous Torchbearers for the State of Indiana Bicentennial relay when the torch traveled through New Harmony.

Notes

My gratitude goes to Jane Blaffer Owen, who encouraged my research and gave her consent to use several photographs as well as selections from our conversations, various interviews she had given to others, and letters. As her personal editor, I worked with her during the research and revision phase of her memoir, which was published posthumously. Some comments from our conversations beginning in early 2009 through June 2010 are directly quoted throughout the essay, but similar comments discovered in my research are cited in endnotes. Personal and business correspondence for Kenneth Dale Owen and personal correspondence for Jane Blaffer Owen have not been archived and are not open for research or publication. Jane Blaffer Owen correspondence related to New Harmony projects has been collected in the Robert Lee Blaffer Trust Archive and the Tillich Archive through the Robert Lee Blaffer Foundation and her Artists Archive and Helen Duprey Bullock Preservation Archive.

1. She penned fragments of her story beginning in 1979, but not until 2003 did she begin writing in earnest. Longhand pages had been typed and organized in various versions from 2004 to 2008. When we began working together in early 2009, I consulted both her own and archival records, including correspondence, journals, forewords, presentation papers, as well as publications and scholarship to aid her during revision.

2. Jane Blaffer Owen, *New Harmony, Indiana: Like a River, Not at Lake: A Memoir* (Bloomington: Indiana University Press, 2015), 23. During her long lifetime, Jane Blaffer Owen was known as Jane Blaffer, Jane Owen, Mrs. Kenneth Owen, and Mrs. Owen. Kenneth Dale Owen was known as "K. D.," Kenneth Owen, and Mr. Owen; therefore, a variety of familial and personal names are used to follow their progression from childhood and young adulthood to a mature married couple and through their legacies as well as to evoke a more intimate portrayal and immediacy. Although Jane Blaffer Owen did not use the contemporary style of Blaffer Owen, she expressed her approval of women who chose to use maiden and married surnames. She lamented the loss of identity that previous generations of women endured by changing their names with marriage and the genealogical omissions that ensued.

3. Donald E. Pitzer, "William Maclure's Boatload of Knowledge: Science and Education into the Midwest," *Indiana Magazine of History* 94, no. 2 (1998): 110–37; and Pitzer, *New Harmony Then and Now* (Bloomington: Indiana University Press, 2011), 50–64.

4. See the National Trust for Historic Preservation website. Other recipients have included Vincent J. Scully and fellow Texans George and Cynthia Mitchell.

5. "New Harmony Loses Champion—Jane Blaffer Owen," *In Harmony,* Fall 2010, 1; Donna Mosher,

"Re-imagining Utopia," *Science of Mind* 82, no. 4 (2009): 22–30; Roger McBain, "New Harmony Legend, Jane Blaffer Owen, Loved Indiana Town," *Evansville Courier and Press,* June 23, 2010; "New Harmony Preservation Patron Dies," press release, Indiana Landmarks, June 24, 2010, indianalandmarks.org.

6. Press release, Indiana Arts Commission, March 2007, in.gov/arts.

7. Rob Schneider, "New Harmony's Angel," *Indianapolis Star,* March 14, 2007.

8. Stephen Fox, "A Life of Harmony: Jane Blaffer Owen, 1915–2010," *Cite: The Architecture and Design Review of Houston* 83 (2010): 8–9.

9. Blaffer Owen, *New Harmony,* xi.

10. Owen, conversation with author, March 25, 2009. Jane Owen provided information in 1999 and 2000 to Patricia Sullivan for inclusion in *The History of Ste. Anne's Country Inn and Spa* (Belleville, Ont.: Essence Publishing, 2001). Portions appear on the Ste. Anne's website: steannes.com; Blaffer Owen, *New Harmony,* 4.

11. Nora C. Fretageot and W. V. Mangrum, *Historic New Harmony Official Guide—Centennial Edition* (Evansville, Ind.: Kellor Crescent, 1914), 13–14, 21–24; Donald F. Carmony and Josephine M. Elliott, "New Harmony, Indiana: Robert Owen's Seedbed for Utopia," *Indiana Magazine of History* 76, no. 3 (1980): 161–261. For more on David Dale Owen's role in adapting buildings in New Harmony, see John F. Sears, "'How the Devil It Got There': The Politics of Form and Function in the Smithsonian 'Castle,'" in *Public Space and the Ideology of Place in American Culture,* edited by Miles Orvell and Jeffrey L. Meikle (Amsterdam: Editions Rodopi, 2009), 60–66. See Robert Dale Owen, *Hints on Public Architecture* (New York: George P. Putnam, 1849).

12. Leonard Warren, *Maclure of New Harmony: Scientist, Progressive Educator, Radical Philanthropist* (Bloomington: Indiana University Press, 2009); Walter Brookfield Hendrickson, *David Dale Owen: Pioneer Geologist of the Middle West* (Indianapolis: Indiana Historical Bureau, 1943); Blaffer Owen, *New Harmony,* 6–11.

13. Blaffer Owen, *New Harmony,* 57–63; Family Papers—Helen Elliott, Organizations, fs 94–102, box XX, folders 95–97, Helen Elliott—New Harmony Memorial Commission I, Working Men's Institute, New Harmony, Indiana; and Josephine M. Elliott Collection, Series: Institutional, folder New Harmony Memorial Commission—General Correspondence, 1939–1955, Historic New Harmony, Inc. Archives, New Harmony, Indiana. For more about the Memorial Commissions, see chapter 3 of this book, by Christine Gorby, "New Harmony as an Evolving Commemorative Environment."

14. State of Indiana, County of Vanderburgh, in the Vanderburgh Superior Court, 1975 Term, No. 71-CIV-2933; "Deposition under Oath of Jane Blaffer Owen, Taken by Defendants, Johnson," 9–11 (hereafter cited as "Deposition"); and Blaffer Owen, *New Harmony,* 8, 11.

15. Blaffer Owen, *New Harmony,* 10.

16. The Hogg-Swayne Syndicate (James Hogg, James M. Swayne, W. T. Campbell, Judge R. E. Brooks, Col. A. S. Fisher) and Joseph S. Cullinan's Texas Fuel Co. and investors founded the Texas Company in 1902. See "From the Great Beaumont Field: What Hogg-Swayne Syndicate Really Is," *Lima Times Democrat,* December 7, 1901, 7; Jane McMillin, "The Spindletop Connection: One Hundred Years Later, a Look at the Lucas Gusher, the Founding of Texaco and a Key Player—Lampasas' Early-Day Entrepreneur W. T. Campbell," *Lampasas Dispatch Record,* January 19, 2001; Diana Davids and Roger M. Olien, *Oil in Texas: The Gusher Age, 1895–1945* (Austin: University of Texas Press, 2002); Blaffer Owen, *New Harmony,* 16–18. For Texaco history, see www.texaco.com.

17. "'First Lady' of Texaco Stockholders," *Texaco Star* 28, no. 4 (1942): 22.

18. A reviewer requested the inclusion of relevant details from probated wills tracing assets ultimately received by Jane Blaffer Owen. Great-granddaughter Amy "Mimi" Campbell-Cole provided copies of wills for W. T. Campbell and Sarah Jane Campbell-Scott. Probate research completed at the

Lampasas County Clerk's office. See March 29, 1906, W. T. Campbell, No. 407, filed in Probate Minutes of Lampasas County 1905–1911, vol. 6, pp. 95ff., estimated preliminary value $300,000. Subsequent filings indicate that "the business of said W. T. Campbell at the time of his death was quite complicated" (98). Claims were reported in the *Galveston Daily News,* April 18, 1909, 19, in Snow et al. vs. R. R. Hazelwood for accrued profits of the Hogg-Swayne Syndicate. Campbell's estate would not be settled for years. See Community Estate of W. T. Campbell, dec'd, Sarah J. Campbell surviving wife, filed No. 411, p. 134. Inventory, p. 142, records assets of $350,000 with total claims due of $104,124. W. T. bequeathed to his wife their homestead and a combination of assets totaling $100,000 and to each of his *four children, one of whom was Sarah Jane "Sadie" Campbell, assets totaling $25,000 in addition to half of the rest and residue equally divided between the four children.*

Sarah Jane Campbell-Scott died April 26, 1951; will dated March 21, 1949, filed in Probate Minutes of Lampasas County No. 1641 (probate documents from various record books have been copied and collected in a blue folder "Cause # 1641 Estate of Sarah J. Campbell-Scott, Deceased"). Her estate bequeathed equally to her four children except that *Sarah Campbell Blaffer had arranged previously for her one-fourth to skip a generation for tax purposes and be divided equally between the four Blaffer children, one of whom was Jane Blaffer Owen.* Although the portion was estimated to be $65,000 gross in August 1952, the probate process endured for years, with a second generation serving as successor executor. Final documentation occurs on April 5, 1996.

19. "Blaffer-Campbell," *Lampasas Daily Leader,* April 23, 1909.

20. These oilmen included William S. Farish (Blaffer and Farish, 1904) as well as Harry C. Wiess and J. Cooke Wilson. See Henrietta M. Larson and Kenneth Wiggins Porter, *History of Humble Oil and Refining Company* (New York: Harper Brothers, 1959), 29–30, 36–37, 50–55; and "Robert Lee Blaffer" entry, *National Cyclopedia of American Biography,* vol. 31 (New York: J. T. White, 1944), 85, with thanks to Stephen Fox.

21. "Recalling Houston's Early Days and Its Oilmen: A Conversation with Jane Blaffer Owen and Elizabeth Gregory, Joe Pratt, and Melissa Keane," *Houston History* 8, no. 2 (2011): 22.

22. Owen, conversation with author, April 30, 2009; and Jane Blaffer Owen, interview by Drs. Joseph Pratt and Elizabeth Gregory, University of Houston Oral History of Houston Project, May 3, 2006, transcribed by Suzanne Mascola, unpublished interview, 10 (hereafter cited as Pratt-Gregory, interview); printed by courtesy of Drs. Elizabeth Gregory and Joseph Pratt and the Kenneth Dale and Jane Blaffer Owen Family.

23. "K. D. Owen Receives Honorary Degree," *New Harmony Times,* May 12, 1987; Patricia Swanson, "Historical Preservationist, Philanthropist Owen Dies," *Evansville Courier & Press,* May 1, 2002.

24. "Kenneth Dale Owen's Contribution to Geology and Historic Preservation to Be Recognized," in *University of Southern Indiana 1987 Commencement Exercises, May 9, 1987,* in association with his honorary Doctor of Science degree. See "Kenneth Dale Owen," *University of Southern Indiana University Notes* 11, no. 35 (1987): 2.

25. Gulfshore Oil Company was incorporated in Texas in 1940 with filing dates in other states, April 13, 1945, and April 16, 1945. See Trans-Tex Production Company filing dates from December 2, 1940, to August 1945.

26. "Life Visits New Harmony," *Life,* September 17, 1945, 133–39; and Blaffer Owen, *New Harmony,* 57. K. D. Owen supervised the (circa 1941–44) renovation by Fred E. Cook with historical assessment from Earl H. Reed, FAIA.

27. Barbara Grizzuti Harrison, "Life's Simple Treasures: Jane Blaffer Owen Seeks and Funds Paradise on Earth," *Vanity Fair,* August 1983, 46.

28. Ibid., 42.

29. George Fuermann, *Houston: Land of the Big Rich* (Garden City, N.Y.: Doubleday, 1951), 47; Harrison, "Life's Simple Treasures," 42; and Blaffer Owen, *New Harmony,* 3–4.

30. Pitzer cites that the Harmonists sold twenty thousand acres (35) and cites $135,000 as the price Owen paid to purchase the town, with $200,000 as the total loss on the New Harmony experiment of his $250,000 fortune (*New Harmony Then and Now,* 48). See Blaffer Owen, *New Harmony,* 21, 47, 57.

31. Harrison, "Life's Simple Treasures," 42; and Blaffer Owen, *New Harmony,* 21–24. On April 21, 2009, Nancy Mangum McCaslin clarified with Blaffer Owen that the experience was neither a vision nor an interior locution.

32. Mrs. O. P. Wolfe, "Acquires Ancestral Acres," *New Harmony Times,* July 23, 1943; history of Indian Mound Farm in "Sale of the Century: Mature Cow Herd & Herd Bull Dispersion" (booklet), August 31, 1981.

33. Blaffer Owen, *New Harmony,* 27. Robert Lee Blaffer used financial mechanisms, such as *inter vivos* trusts, companies, and corporations, for avoiding negative tax consequences and privacy, since probate documents are public. See Robert Lee Blaffer *Decd*, case 32,566, filed Nov. 4, 1942, legacy, Probate Court No. 1, Harris County, Texas. The complex remainder will bequeathed his half of community property and household as well as remainder/residue to his wife and established dividends/interest income in stocks/business during her lifetime; remainder/residue shares would be distributed to separate trusts (references to No. 1, No. 2, and remainder) for each of his four children, with restrictions for the females based on marital status and age. Total value of testamentary estate Robert Lee Blaffer is $2,136,193.68, Inventory page 531. Harris County Clerk's Office probate archive microfilm. At leagle.com, court documents Blaffer v. Commissioner of the Internal Revenue Service Docket Nos. 110835, 110836. 2 T.C.M. 1117 (1943) Sarah Campbell Blaffer v. Commissioner. Estate of R. L. Blaffer, Deceased, Sarah Campbell Blaffer, John Hepburn Blaffer, Jane Blaffer Owen and Cecil Amelia Blaffer, Executors v. Commissioner. United States Tax Court. Entered December 15, 1943, consolidates into one the tax years 1934–37 concerning gift taxes, which provides information about previous contributions to trust funds and the Robert Lee Blaffer Company trusts to benefit the four Blaffer children, *including Jane Blaffer Owen with a gift value of $54,826.22.*

34. Samuel H. Williamson, "Seven Ways to Compute the Relative Value of a U.S. Dollar Amount, 1790 to present," 2016, accessed June 19, 2018, MeasuringWorth.com.

35. Printed by courtesy of the Kenneth Dale and Jane Blaffer Owen Family.

36. The charitable trust was reorganized as the Robert Lee Blaffer Foundation in 2001. See also the second part of this book, "Three Voices in New Harmony," for Ralph Grayson Schwarz, "Reflections on New Harmony," during the 1970s.

37. "Deposition," 54–56, 29, printed by courtesy of the Kenneth Dale and Jane Blaffer Owen Family. Jane Blaffer Owen's will, No. 370201, filed in Harris County, Texas in 2010, has no sections relevant to New Harmony because she funded the Robert Lee Blaffer Trust/Foundation throughout her lifetime.

38. Pratt-Gregory, interview, 16, printed by courtesy of Drs. Elizabeth Gregory and Joseph Pratt and the Kenneth Dale and Jane Blaffer Owen Family; Blaffer Owen, *New Harmony,* 48–50.

39. "Helen D. Bullock," *Newsletter of the Society of Architectural Historians* 11, no. 5 (1967); Jane Blaffer Owen to Herman B Wells, May 17, 1955, Helen Elliot, Organizations, file 37, WMI; Blaffer Owen, *New Harmony,* 33–44, 123–32, 135–39, 171–77.

40. Pratt-Gregory, interview, 7, printed by courtesy of Drs. Elizabeth Gregory and Joseph Pratt and the Kenneth Dale and Jane Blaffer Owen Family.

41. The Blaffer children: John Hepburn (b. 1913), Sarah Jane (b. 1915; Texas State Board of Health, Bureau of Vital Statistics, Standard Certificate of Birth), Cecil Amelia "Titi" (b. 1919), and Joyce Campbell (b. 1926).

42. On Shadyside, see Stephen Fox, "Public Art and Private Places: Shadyside," *Houston Review* 2 (Winter 1980): 37–60; and Christopher Gray, "All the Best Places: Shadyside: An Oasis Carved out of Houston's Bald Prairie," *House and Garden,* August 1983, 46–47. During Jane's first years, the Blaffers rented Walter B. Sharp's The Country Place (circa 1895) at 4301 Main Street. See Dorothy Knox Howe Houghton et al., *Houston's Forgotten Heritage: Landscape, Houses, Interiors, 1824–1914* (Houston: Rice University Press, 1991), 54–56, 188–89, 217–18, 224.

43. Owen, conversation with author, March 31, 2009, printed by courtesy of the Kenneth Dale and Jane Blaffer Owen Family and Nancy Mangum McCaslin.

44. Jane Blaffer Owen describes life in early Houston and Shadyside in a video interview with Melissa Keane and Bill White, City of Houston Oral History Project, March 27, 2008, http://digital .houstonlibrary.org/oral-history/jane-blaffer-owen.php.

45. Emily Deckard, "Mrs. Jane Owen: Do You Know Her?" *Rappite Rap,* February 2007, 6.

46. Rice University Manuscript Collection, Ann Holmes, Fine Arts Collection, MS 546, box 16, folder 3, Taped Interviews "Jane Blaffer Owen," April 3, 1996, printed by courtesy of Ann Holmes Fine Arts Archive Woodson Research Center, Fondren Library, Rice University and the Kenneth Dale and Jane Blaffer Owen Family; Owen, conversation with author, April 30, 2009.

47. From resources made available by Fiona de Young, archivist and assistant librarian, Moran Upper School Library, the Kinkaid School, Houston: Francita Stuart Koelsch, *The Kinkaid School: First Fifty Years* (Houston: D. H. White, 1957; 2nd ed. 1990), Nora Janssen Seton, *The Kinkaid School: A Legacy of Distinction, the First One Hundred Years* (Houston: Kinkaid School, 2006), 19.

48. Marguerite Johnson, *Houston, the Unknown City, 1836–1946* (College Station: Texas A&M University Press, 1991), 243; Koelsch, *Kinkaid School,* 19; and the Kinkaid Archives.

49. Koelsch, *Kinkaid School,* 34.

50. "Our History" and "By the Decade," 2013, ethelwalker.org.

51. Ibid.

52. Academic reports for Jane Blaffer list the following courses: (1930–31) Algebra, Latin, English, French, American History, Art; (1931–32) Geometry, Latin, English, French, English History, Physiology, Art; (1932–33) three Latin courses (Prose, Poets, and Composition), English, French, Physics, Art.

53. *Pepper Pot,* 1933 yearbook, 60, Ethel Walker School.

54. Claire Richter Sherman, "Widening Horizons (1890–1930)," in *Women as Interpreters of the Visual Arts, 1820–1979,* edited by Claire Richter Sherman (Westport, Conn.: Greenwood, 1981), 55. On M. Carey Thomas, see Helen Lefkowitz Horowitz, *The Power and Passion of M. Carey Thomas* (New York: Knopf, 1994); Roberta Wein, "Women's Colleges and Domesticity, 1875–1918," *History of Education Quarterly* 14, no. 1 (1974): 31–47, http://www.jstor.org/stable/367604; and Roberta Frankfort, "Martha Carey Thomas: The Scholarly Ideal and Bryn Mawr Woman," in *Collegiate Women: Domesticity and Career in Turn-of-the-Century America* (New York: New York University Press, 1977), 26–40, which details Thomas's confrontation with the conservative Harvard president Charles Eliot about his "chauvinistic attitude" toward women and education. For articles during Jane's years about changes in the Bryn Mawr Summer College for Women Workers, see issues of *The College News*; Anne L. Bruder, *Offerings to Athena: 125 Years at Bryn Mawr* (Bryn Mawr, Penn.: Friends of the Bryn Mawr College Library, 2010), 98–99; and Karyn L. Hollis, *Liberating Voices: Writing at the Bryn Mawr Summer School for Women Workers* (Carbondale: Southern Illinois University Press, 2004). *Offerings to Athena* also documents special classes for the maids (103).

55. Helen Lefkowitz Horowitz, "Behold They Are Women! Bryn Mawr," 36, in Bruder, *Offerings to Athena,* originally appeared in *Alma Mater: Design and Experience in the Women's Colleges from Their Nineteenth-Century Beginnings to the 1930s* (New York: Knopf, 1984), 117–33. Cope and Stewardson's

"well-publicized success led to important commissions at the University of Pennsylvania, Princeton, and Washington University in St. Louis" (36).

56. Gertrude Stein fictionalized a painful experience in Thomas's life in "Fernhurst," *The Making of Americans*; see Ulla E. Dydo, *Gertrude Stein: The Language That Rises, 1923–1934* (Evanston, Ill.: Northwestern University Press, 2008), 93, 113, 179; and Lillian Faderman, *Odd Girls and Twilight Lovers: A History of Lesbian Life in Twentieth-Century America* (New York: Columbia University Press, 1991), 29–31.

57. Bryn Mawr's first African American student, Enid Cook, graduated in 1931 (Bruder, *Offerings to Athena*, 106). For a feminist critique of Park's tenure, see Elizabeth M. Schneider, "Our Failures Only Marry: Bryn Mawr College and the Failure of Feminism," in *Woman in Sexist Society: Studies in Power and Powerlessness,* edited by Vivian Gornick and Barbara K. Moran (New York: Basic Books, 1971).

58. Owen, conversations with author at the time of the Fourth International Symposium of the American Planning Association, "Cultural Landscapes, Cultural Towns," New Harmony, Indiana, November 12–14, 2009, printed by courtesy of the Kenneth Dale and Jane Blaffer Owen Family and Nancy Mangum McCaslin.

59. Georgiana Goddard King, *The Way of Saint James* (New York: G. P. Putnam's Sons, 1920).

60. Susanna Terrell Saunders, "Georgiana Goddard King (1871–1939): Educator and Pioneer in Medieval Spanish Art," in *Women as Interpreters of the Visual Arts, 1820–1979,* edited by Claire Richter Sherman with Adele M. Holcomb (Westport, Conn.: Greenwood, 1989); Janice Mann, "Georgiana Goddard King and A. Kingsley Porter Discover the Art of Medieval Spain," in *Spain in America: The Origins of Hispanism in the United States,* edited by Richard L. Kagan (Urbana: University of Illinois Press, 2002), 171–92; Mann, "'Hark the Herald Angels Sing': Here's to Georgiana Goddard King (1871–1939)," in *Women Medievalists and the Academy,* edited by Jane Chance (Madison: University of Wisconsin Press, 2005), 111–25; and Mann, "Frontiers and Pioneers," in *Romanesque Architecture and Its Sculptural Decoration in Christian Spain, 1000–1120: Exploring Frontiers and Defining Identities* (Toronto: University of Toronto Press, 2009), 7–45.

61. Mann, "'Hark the Herald Angels Sing,'" 115.

62. Ibid., 117.

63. For King's academic credentials, see *Bryn Mawr College Undergraduate Calendar* 26 (May 1933), 12.

64. Saunders, "Georgiana Goddard King," 210.

65. Ibid., 209.

66. Transcript, "Jane Stott Blaffer," Major Subject English, Year 1933–1934, with course descriptions from *Bryn Mawr College Undergraduate Calendar* 26 (May 1933), published by Bryn Mawr College:

"Required English Comp"—"A study of the forms of composition based upon reading in the prose and poetry of the Nineteenth Century and the present time," 56.

"I Year French"—"The History of French Literature of the Nineteenth Century with practical exercises in the French language," 59.

"I Year Latin"—"A study of Latin Literature of the Republic and of the Augustan Age, with a consideration of its relation to Greek Literature and its influence on modern literature. The reading includes a play of Plautus, a play of Terence, selections from: Cicero's letters, the shorter poems of Catullus, Livy's first decade, Horace's Odes and Epodes and Vergil's Eclogues and Georgics. In addition to the regular meetings of the class, the students have frequent meetings in conferences. In the second semester selections from mediaeval Latin are read in the conferences and assigned for private reading," 77.

"I Year Philosophy"—"1st Semester. During the first semester there will be lectures and readings on Greek philosophy and its relations to the social and scientific developments of the time. Special attention will be paid to Plato and Aristotle and the students will read and discuss selections from their writings. 2nd Semester. During the second semester, after a brief survey of the intervening periods of the Middle Ages and the Renaissance, the philosophy of the Seventeenth and Eighteenth centuries will be selected for special study. Students will read and discuss selections from such thinkers as Descartes, Spinoza, Locke and Berkeley. In the latter part of the semester some of the more characteristic movements of Nineteenth century thought will be treated more briefly," 82.

"Diction"—[The article "Bryn Mawr" in *Fortune*, June 1935, 30, reads, in reference to this course, "It has been said that no woman who talks through her nose can possibly come from Bryn Mawr"].

"Physical Education, Body Mechanics"—[required the successful completion of the Freshman Swimming Test. Owen's swimming skills were superior, even into her nineties].

"Adv. Stg. Oct 1933, Elective French"—[With her fluency in French, it's not surprising that Jane Blaffer received Advanced Standing credit through examination].

67. Transcript, 1934–35 and from the *Bryn Mawr College Undergraduate Calendar* 27 (May 1934) published by Bryn Mawr College for History of Art: "1 Year History of Art"—"Full Year Course. Italian Painting of the Renaissance from the Middle of the Thirteenth Major to the Middle of the Sixteenth Century: Miss King and Miss Shipley. Reader: Dorothea Caroline Shipley, M.A., 1st Semester. During the first semester the Italian primitives are studied, chiefly in the schools of Florence, Siena and Umbria. 2nd Semester. During the second semester the work is devoted to the painters of the High Renaissance, with special attention to those of Venice and the north of Italy, ending with an introduction to Baroque," 75.

68. *Bryn Mawr College Undergraduate Calendar,* the listing for Modern Art reads "Students are expected to make trips to Philadelphia and the neighbourhood to study pictures as often as may seem necessary," 75.

69. Special Exhibitions Timeline, NHPRC project files, Philadelphia Museum of Art, made available by archivist Susan K. Anderson, lists several exhibitions of interest (some were featured in college publications) during Jane Blaffer's years at Bryn Mawr College, including International Exhibition of Sculpture; Prints by Albrecht Durer; Manet and Renoir; Prints from Lessing J. Rosenwald: Piranesi, Blake, van Leyden; Modern Art & Drawings; French Painting, 19th and 20th Centuries (Lea Collection of French Prints); The Romanticists and the Realists: 1860; Impressionist Figure Painting at 1870; Cezanne; Impressionists and Neo-Impressionists; The Post Impressionists of 1890; The Fauves: 1900. The Rodin Museum, which opened in 1929, has the largest collection of works outside Paris. Jules Mastaum commissioned and acquired such works as *The Kiss, The Thinker, The Burghers of Calais, Head of Balzac,* and the first bronze cast of *The Gates of Hell,* among others.

70. Saunders, "Georgiana Goddard King," 219.

71. Some discrepancy exists about where Gertrude and G. G. met; Stein remembered Baltimore as she writes in *The Autobiography of Alice B. Toklas,* while King remembered New York City. Leo and Gertrude had accompanied G. G. to Spain, but during another trip, Gertrude and Alice accompanied her and Edith H. Lowber, G. G.'s photographer, travel companion, and occasional collaborator. King maintained friendships with both Steins. See Saunders, "Georgiana Goddard King," 223–25, 219nn41–42, King to Stein, n.d., Yale University; and Ulla E. Dydo, *Gertrude Stein: The Language That Rises: 1923–1934* (Evanston, Ill.: Northwestern University Press, 2008), 179–80; and Mann, "'Hark the Herald Angels Sing,'" 116.

72. Saunders, "Georgiana Goddard King," 221.

73. Jane Owen, interview, Sandra Curtis, for the Archives of American Art Texas Project, March 12, 1980. Description: Mrs. Owen speaks of the history of the Blaffer family and its involvement in the

art world; speaks about her mother, Sarah Campbell Blaffer, and her development as an art patron; and about the family's art collection. Research Collections, Oral History Interviews, Archives of American Art, Smithsonian Institution, Washington, D.C. In another interview, Jane Owen discusses her mother's patronage: Marguerite Johnston Barnes Research Materials for *Houston, The Unknown City, from 1830–1991*, MS 455, Series I. Oral Histories, 1985–1991. Transcripts & tapes. Interview Jane Blaffer Owen, August 26, 1987, 29. Woodson Research Center, Fondren Library, Rice University.

74. "Miss King discusses Gertrude Stein's Art: Impressionists, Cezanne, and Cubists Show Parallels to Her Writing," *College News*, February 21, 1934, Bryn Mawr College Library, Special Collections, Digital date 2012, triptych.brynmawr.edu, id 3290.

75. "Calendar," *College News*, February 14, 1934, 7, Bryn Mawr College Library, Special Collections, Digital date 2012, triptych.brynmawr.edu, id 3324.

76. "Gertrude Stein Says Poetry Is Loving Name of Anything," *College News*, November 21, 1934, 1, Bryn Mawr College Library, Special Collections, Digital date 2012, triptych.brynmawr.edu, id 3418.

77. Agnes Mongan, "Georgiana Goddard King: A Tribute," *Bryn Mawr Alumnae Bulletin*, July 1937; Diane DeGrazia Bohlin, "Agnes Mongan (b. 1905): Connoisseur of Old Master Drawings," in *Women as Interpreters of the Visual Arts, 1820–1979*, edited by Claire Richter Sherman with Adele M. Holcomb (Westport, Conn.: Greenwood, 1989), 411–34.

78. "Deposition," 20.

79. Transcript, 1934–35, with course description from *Bryn Mawr College Undergraduate Calendar* 26 (May 1934) published by Bryn Mawr College for Classical Archaeology: "I year Archaeology"—"Greek Sculpture and Ancient Painting: Dr. Carpenter and Dr. Swindler. 1st Semester. Greek Sculpture. During the first semester the work is a critical study of the rise, perfection and ultimate developments of sculpture in Greece. The course is intended as a general introduction to the principles and appreciation of sculpture. 2nd Semester. Ancient Painting. During the second semester the course traces the development of ancient painting. The material studied includes Egyptian and Cretan frescoes, Greek vases, Pompeian wall paintings and the paintings from Etruscan sites," 52. Carpenter taught the first semester and Mary Swindler taught the second. See "Rhys Carpenter, Ph.D., Professor of Classical Archaeology and Greek and Holder of a Julius and Sarah Goldman Grant," 12; and "Mary Hamilton Swindler, Ph.D., Professor of Classical Archaeology. Editor-in-Chief, *American Journal of Archaeology*, 1932," 13.

80. Megan Risse, MA, Curator, "Breaking Ground, Breaking Tradition: Bryn Mawr and the First Generation of Women Archaeologists," an exhibition in the Rare Book Room of the Bryn Mawr College Library, Fall 2007, at brynmawr.edu. Rhys Carpenter and the Early Art and Archaeology Teaching Tools reveal the impressive resources available to Jane Blaffer as a student.

81. Although Carpenter had a prolific career with significant contributions to ancient archaeology, excavation, and sculpture, references herein to his work only include those through Jane Blaffer's last year at Bryn Mawr College in 1935. See Rhys Carpenter, "The Esthetics of Greek Architecture," in *The Esthetic Basis of Greek Art of the Fifth and Fourth Centuries B.C.* (New York: Longmans, Green, 1921), 153ff.

82. Owen, conversations with author, New Harmony, Indiana, November 12–14, 2009, printed by courtesy of the Kenneth Dale and Jane Blaffer Owen Family and Nancy Mangum McCaslin.

83. Carpenter, "The Esthetics of Greek Sculpture," in *Esthetic Basis of Greek Art*, 76ff.

84. Carpenter, foreword to *Esthetic Basis of Greek Art*, vii.

85. Rhys Carpenter, *The Humanistic Value of Archaeology* (Cambridge, Mass.: Harvard University Press, 1933). Hereafter cited in the text.

86. Although an overly simplistic consideration, I was intrigued by the visual parallel between the

images of temple ruins (after viewing nearly a hundred lantern slides from the Bryn Mawr classical antiquity collection, now digitized) and Jane Owen's idea for a roofless church open to earth and sky, as if they had created a subconscious impression.

87. Linda Caruso Haviland, "Turning the Corners," *Bryn Mawr Alumnae Bulletin,* Fall 1992, 13–14; and email to author, May 14, 2012.

88. *College News,* October 18, 1933, 2.

89. Articles and announcements in *College News* describe its activities: "Dance Group Recital Shows Grace, Feeling: Result of One Year's Training Produces Artistic Program of Great Merit, Joy In Dance is Seen," April 10, 1935, 1, 6; "Duncan Dance Group Will Do Improvising: Miss Petts Will Lead Dancers in Development of Winter Class Work," March 20, 1935, 4, triptych.brynmawr.edu, id nos. 3597, 3709.

90. "The American Ballet Coming to Bryn Mawr for the Fiftieth Anniversary Fund," in *Alumnae Bulletin,* February 1935, 16–18. Incidentally, Warburg and Kirstein were close friends of Philip Johnson. In 1934 Warburg gave Johnson his first commission to design an apartment suitable for displaying Warburg's art collection. For more information about the relationships between the three and Agnes Mongan as well as additional details about Warburg and G. G. King, see Nicholas Fox Weber, *Patron Saints: Five Rebels Who Opened America to a New Art, 1928–1943* (New York: Alfred A. Knopf, 1992).

91. Linda Caruso Haviland, "Turning the Corners," 13–14, cites reminiscences of Elizabeth Taylor Goshorn (AB '40).

92. Blaffer Owen, *New Harmony,* 25.

93. "Deposition," 20–21, printed by courtesy of the Kenneth Dale and Jane Blaffer Owen Family.

94. Conversation with author, November 13, 2009.

95. In chapter 2 of this book, Stephen Fox places Jane Owen in the context of patronage and modernism.

96. Jane Blaffer Owen, foreword to *Edvard Munch,* edited by Peter W. Guenther, exhibition catalog, Sarah Campbell Blaffer Gallery, the University of Houston, April 9–May 23, 1976, access courtesy of Leslie Scattone, assistant curator of the Sarah Campbell Blaffer Foundation, Houston.

97. Blaffer Owen, *New Harmony,* 65.

98. Jacques Lipchitz papers and Bruce Bassett papers concerning Jacques Lipchitz, circa 1910–2001, Correspondence, Owen, Jane Blaffer, circa 1950–69, folders 35–37, Archives of American Art, Smithsonian Institution (hereafter cited as Lipchitz, Owen); Rosamund Frost, "Lipchitz Makes a Sculpture," *Art News* 49, no. 2 (1950): 36–64; Blaffer Owen, *New Harmony,* 70–71.

99. Lipchitz, Owen, box 3, folder 37, item 20–22, Hermann Hospital letterhead dated April 29, 1950; Blaffer Owen, *New Harmony,* 74–77.

100. Blaffer Owen, *New Harmony,* 72, 117–120.

101. Pamela G. Smart, "Aesthetics as a Vocation," in *Art and Activism—Projects of John and Dominique de Menil,* edited by Josef Helfenstein and Laureen Shipsi (Houston: Menil Collection; New Haven, Conn.: distributed by Yale University Press, 2010), 20–39; "The Assy Church: Famous Modern Artists Decorate Chapel in Alps," *Life,* June 19, 1950; and M.-A. Couturier, *Sacred Art,* trans. Granger Ryan (Austin: University of Texas Press with the Menil Foundation, 1989).

102. "Deposition," 8.

103. Jane Owen and Philip Johnson collaborated on plans for the Roofless Church. For architect–client relationships, albeit domestic rather than public architecture, see Alice T. Friedman, *Women and the Making of the Modern House* (New York: Harry N. Abrams, 1998). Jane's ecumenical goals to foster reconciliation and mutual understanding unfortunately did not extend to the client–architect partnership, which devolved. She explains her perspective on the litigation that followed a decade later

in Blaffer Owen, *New Harmony*, 27. Cammie McAtee examines the Lipchitz and Johnson commissions in chapter 4 of this book, "'The Rib Cage of the Human Heart': Philip Johnson's Roofless Church."

104. Ben Nicholson documents its progression in chapter 5 of this book, "Frederick Kiesler's Grotto: A Promethean Spirit in New Harmony."

105. John Blades, "Rebuilding Utopia along the Wabash," *Chicago Tribune Magazine,* September 21, 1975, 34.

106. Harrison, "Life's Simple Treasures," 54.

107. Martin L. McAuliffe Jr., "The Life of the Spirit: Mrs. Jane Blaffer Owen, in *Profiles of Excellence* (Evansville, Ind.: University of Evansville Press, [1970]) 167.

108. "Estranged and Reunited: The New Being": Professor Tillich's address in the Roofless Church, New Harmony, 1963, is reprinted in the second part of this book, "Three Voices of New Harmony."

109. Although described and archived as II and III, these distinctions actually refer to two phases of the same Memorial Commission, the third being its reactivation: "Bowen Names 20 Persons to NHC," *Evansville Press,* September 5, 1973, including Kenneth Dale Owen and Ralph G. Schwarz; "Commission Will Be Revived to Help New Harmony," *Mount Vernon Democrat,* June 21, 1984; Deborah Burdick, "Three Reappointed to New Harmony Commission," *Posey County News,* July 25, 1995; Branigan Room, Local Files Archive, New Harmony Memorial Commission II and III, Working Men's Institute, New Harmony, Indiana.

110. Reed and Mr. Owen are mentioned in a letter from Jane Blaffer Owen to Herman B Wells, president of Indiana University and serving on the New Harmony Memorial Commission I, May 17, 1955, "New Harmony Memorial Commission Minutes of Final Meeting Held in Indianapolis, Indiana, May 25, 1955," Helen Elliott—New Harmony Memorial Commission I, Working Men's Institute, New Harmony, Indiana, 95. Reed was considered "Mr. Preservation if anyone was in this country" by Joseph Watterson, FAIA; see "Earl H. Reed, FAIA," in *Pioneers in Preservation: Biographical Sketches of Architects Prominent in the Field before World War II,* research material compiled for the American Institute of Architects Committee on Historic Resources in celebration of the centennial of its founding (Washington, D.C.: American Institute of Architects, 1990), 74–75.

111. Blaffer Owen, *New Harmony*, 59–63, 267–75; and Indian Mound Farm booklet: "Sale of the Century: Mature Cow Herd & Herd Bull Dispersion," August 31, 1981.

112. Will dated April 14, 1993: Kenneth Dale Owen, No. 333,741, filed in Harris County, Texas, p. 701-85-1473, probate archive microfilm, Harris County Clerk's Office.

113. Laurel Rold, "The Restoration of the Sandstone Masonry and Adaptive Renovation of the Rapp Granary–David Dale Owen Laboratory 1997–1999," prepared for the Rapp Granary and David Dale Owen Laboratory Dedication, October 9, 1999 (unpublished document), 14, 17: "David Dale Owen's first laboratory, from 1833 to 1834, was in the large kitchen of Harmonist Dormitory One, where the Owen family resided. In 1834 he remodeled Harmonist Shoemaker's shop and used this as his second laboratory until 1843, at which time he established a laboratory and lecture hall in the old Rappite Granary. . . . In 1859, . . . he also designed and supervised construction of what was to be his fourth laboratory," but died prior to using 'The Lab,' which became a residence." This and other documents related to the Granary restoration project were provided to the author by Hafer Architects, Designers, Engineers, Jill Rawley, email to author, January 5, 2017.

114. Rold, "Rapp Granary–David Dale Owen Laboratory," 4.

115. Ibid., 19.

116. *Old Stones in New Harmony: The Rebirth of the Rapp Granary,* produced by Parri O. Black (Evansville, Ind., WNIN PBS, 1999).

117. 2010 Preserving Historic Places Conference: plenary session 2, "Modernism in New Harmony," program, https://www.in.gov/dnr/historic/files/hp-ConferenceAgenda.pdf.

118. Bicentennial Calendar and Timeline, a cooperative project between the Rapp Granary-Owen Foundation and the Indiana Geological Survey for the New Harmony Bicentennial Celebration, 2014. See Dana Arnold and Joanna Sofaer, eds., *Biographies and Space: Placing the Subject in Art and Architecture* (London: Routledge Taylor and Francis Group, 2008).

Figure 2.1. Dedication of Jacques Lipchitz's Suzanne Glémet Memorial Gate, 1962. Left to right: Philip Johnson, Jacques Lipchitz, Jane Blaffer Owen, and the Reverend George F. MacLeod. Similar to European cathedrals, the Memorial Gates were meant to be opened only on special occasions, their "royal grandeur," according to Owen, to stand in stark contrast to Kiesler's humble cave/grotto then being designed. Courtesy of the photographer James K. Mellow and the Robert Lee Blaffer Foundation.

2

Patronage and Modernism

STEPHEN FOX

PATRONAGE IMPLIES THE SIGNIFICANCE not only of an artist, author, or composer in the constitution of a work of art but of an additional agent, the patron. The patron commissions the work and provides the resources needed to ensure its execution.[1] The modern movement in art, architecture, literature, and music tended to exalt the creative authority of the artist–producer and, given the social democratic inclination of much modernist discourse, to displace the patron as both elitist and anachronistic. Yet patronage did not evaporate as modernism supplanted other forms of expression in U.S. culture during the second quarter of the twentieth century. The artist benefiting from modern patronage typically extolled benefactors by identifying them publicly as patrons rather than mere clients. An examination of New Harmony, Indiana, discloses some of the identifying features, and tensions, of mid-twentieth-century modernist patronage in the United States.

Jane Blaffer Owen was the patron of New Harmony, a community that she first visited in 1941 as the bride of Kenneth Dale Owen, a petroleum geologist and the great-great-grandson of the Welsh industrialist and social reformer Robert Owen.[2] Jane Owen's commissions to Philip Johnson to design the Roofless Church (1957–60) and St. Stephen's Episcopal Church (1962–65) and to Frederick J. Kiesler to design *Cave of the New Being*, also called *Grotto for Meditation* (1964–65), figured as part of a larger complex of activities that involved the rehabilitation of historic buildings in New Harmony, new architectural and landscape initiatives, and the production of programs to conserve the exceptional historical significance of the town and promote new forms of community and spirituality, often using art as an instrument. In relying on Johnson, a New York architect, as her cultural arbiter, Jane Owen became part of the circle of mid-twentieth-century American patrons of architecture who sought out modernist forms of representation to advance their cultural, political, and spiritual agendas.

The Modern Patron

In 1942 the Anglo-German architectural historian Nikolaus Pevsner paid tribute to Frank Pick, the recently deceased managing director of the London Passenger Transport Board, by hailing him as the "greatest patron of the arts whom this century has so far produced in England, and indeed the ideal patron of our age."[3] Pick managed London's public transit system and coordinated the agency's industrial, graphic, urban, and architectural design operations during the 1930s. Pick was an enlightened bureaucrat rather than a prince, a gentleman, or a connoisseur. In acclaiming him as a model modernist patron, Pevsner signaled the advent of a new modernist subject, the public servant as conscientious patron of design in a social-democratic polity, and, by inference, the disappearance of the patron as aristocratic subject, whose field of operation was circumscribed by economic privilege and social exclusion.

The history of modern architecture, however, attests to the resiliency of the older patronage model. At the turn of the twentieth century, Ernst Ludwig, grand duke of Hesse-Darmstadt, founded the Artists Colony in Darmstadt and had many of its buildings designed by Josef Maria Olbrich and Peter Behrens.[4] Helene Kröller-Müller began her career as a collector and patron of modern artists and architects in the Netherlands before the First World War.[5] During the 1920s Hélène de Mandrot-Revilliod, Marie-Laure Bischoffsheim, and Charles de Noailles were conspicuous in their patronage of modern architects, artists, filmmakers, and writers in France, as were the American expatriates Sara Wiborg and Gerald Murphy.[6] José Vasconcelos, while Mexican minister of education in the early 1920s, patronized the foremost modern artists of Mexico, awarding them commissions for heroic public murals.[7] Victoria Ocampo in Buenos Aires pursued patronage in a more personal mode, but her orientation was modernist and international, and she used publication as an instrument to promote her "clients."[8] During the 1940s and 1950s, Juscelino Kubitschek de Oliveira, first as mayor of Belo Horizonte and then as president of Brazil, and André Malraux, the French Republic's minister of culture during the 1960s, pursued state patronage of modern architects and artists in a policy of national renewal.[9]

At a much more modest scale, the French Dominican priest Father Marie-Alain Couturier secured commissions for the artists Pierre Bonnard, Georges Braque, Fernand Léger, Jacques Lipchitz, Henri Matisse, Georges Rouault, and the architect Le Corbusier to outfit or design French churches and convents in the postwar 1940s and 1950s.[10] In contrast to Pick, the "anonymous" patron of good design, these patrons conformed to the premodernist subject position of the patron, in part because their patronage seemed motivated by personal passion, even when they worked within large collectives.

American patrons of modern architecture were more likely to be businessmen than public officials or gentlemen of leisure. Leonard Eaton studied the progressive clients Frank Lloyd Wright attracted, some of whom (Darwin D. Martin of Buffalo, New York; Queenie Ferry and Avery Coonley of Riverside, Illinois; Aline Barnsdall in Hollywood, California; Edgar J. Kaufmann in Fayette County, Pennsylvania; Herbert F. Johnson Jr. in Racine, Wisconsin; and H. C. Price in Bartlesville, Oklahoma, and Paradise Valley, Arizona) stand out as patrons because they supported Wright with multiple commissions, often for his most ambitious projects.[11]

Just after the midcentury, a generation of modern architectural patrons emerged in the United States, men (and some women) born largely between 1900 and 1920. Samuel Bronfman (1889–1971), Walter Paepcke (1896–1960), John de Menil (1904–1973), J. Irwin Miller (1909–2004), and Thomas J. Watson Jr. (1914–1993) were corporation executives; Stanley Marcus (1905–2002) was a retail merchant; and Joseph Eichler (1900–1974) and Herbert Greenwald (1917–1959) were real estate developers and builders.[12] John Entenza (1903–1984) was a magazine publisher, A. Whitney Griswold (1906–1963) a university president, and Nelson A. Rockefeller (1908–1979) a public official. Dominique Schlumberger de Menil (1908–1997), the wife of John de Menil, was a teacher, exhibition curator, and museum founder. Phyllis Lambert (born 1927) was the daughter of Samuel Bronfman; she became an architect, curator, and museum founder.[13]

The cultural historian Donald Albrecht coined the term *popucrat* to distinguish postwar patrons of the architect Eero Saarinen (1910–1961) from aristocratic antecedents of the patron subject type.[14] According to Albrecht, "Popucrats advanced a postwar ideal of a United States that was both egalitarian and democratic, on one hand, and a rich global power on the other."[15] The consensus that these postwar business and cultural leaders sought to construct through their support of modern architecture and art was a liberal vision of community, a process that the political scientist Eric P. Kaufmann has analyzed in detail. The postwar liberal consensus was constructed around such general propositions as individual freedom and mobility, economic prosperity, cultural opportunity, especially with regard to education, and the implicit superiority of the middle class.[16] The historian Jackson Lears, in critically assessing this ideology, noted the fixation of midcentury American commentators and critics on matters of taste rather than issues of power and social justice.[17] Under this liberal dispensation, modern styles of representation were markers of modern forms of thought, action, and community. Stylistic representation functioned socially to identify adherents of actual (or imagined) communities to each other and to distinguish them from competing communities. In this context, modern stylistic representation can be understood as encoding both material artifacts and related social practices with a social identity that affiliated the possessor or enactor with the desired community.[18]

Jane Blaffer Owen's interests, activities, and affiliations identify her with the circle of liberal postwar architectural patrons. Her involvement with modern forms of art was encouraged by her friends Dominique and John de Menil and by the architect of their house in Houston, Philip Johnson.[19] Owen's admiration for and acquaintance with the artist Jacques Lipchitz, whose work she came to know through *L'Art Sacré*, the magazine published by the Menil's mentor Father Couturier, led in turn to her awareness of the liberal theologian Paul Tillich.[20] Like the "popucrats" Albrecht identifies, Owen used modern art and architecture to advance a liberal agenda in New Harmony that aimed to renew the community by reinvigorating its exceptional religious and social utopian legacies. In doing so she engaged a dialectic on the relationship of modernity to history that was a central theme of postwar American modern art and architecture.[21]

Owen did not act in isolation. In Columbus, Indiana, 135 miles northeast of New Harmony, the industrialist and banker J. Irwin Miller used modern forms of corporate management, architecture, and spirituality to construct and disseminate a progressive identity for Columbus based on design excellence. Like Miller, Owen mobilized modern art and architecture as "instruments in the formation of a public" (in the words of the anthropologist Pamela Smart) who might identify with and support the complex of practices—historic preservation, community conservation, religious inquiry, and artistic and architectural exploration—that took form under her sponsorship.[22] Owen's modern patronage was a crucial instrument in recruiting political, philanthropic, and institutional support to ensure the perpetuation of the cultural and spiritual programs she began in New Harmony in the 1950s.

The Architect as Modernist "Client"

What analysis of postwar patronage discloses is how modern "clients"—Johnson, Saarinen, Lipchitz—implicated their patrons in social networks that reinforced and legitimized the patrons' undertakings. Johnson was exemplary in this regard. His ability to rouse his clients' enthusiasm for modern art and design can be attributed to his skill, charm, and persuasiveness as a cultural impresario. Johnson's connection to the Museum of Modern Art in New York, first as director of its department of architecture and then as a trustee after 1957, affiliated him with the institution most closely identified with the propagation of modernism in art and design in the United States and with the elite trustees and collectors who supported the museum's programs.[23] That his clients during the 1950s and 1960s included the modern collectors Blanchette Hooker Rockefeller, Emily Hall Tremaine, Joseph H. Hirshhorn, and Nelson Rockefeller, as well as Thomas Watson Jr. and Whitney Griswold of Yale, indicates how Johnson could facilitate connections between his patrons that might link them to metropolitan institutions and high-status individuals through modern art and design.[24] Frank D. Welch in his book *Philip Johnson and Texas* details the connections Johnson made through John de Menil that led to commissions for a house in Dallas from Patty Davis and Henry C. Beck Jr. (the sister and brother-in-law of Owen's sister-in-law Camilla Davis Blaffer), the Amon Carter Museum and the Fort Worth Water Gardens from Ruth Carter Stevenson in Fort Worth, the John F. Kennedy Memorial in Dallas from Stanley Marcus, and the Art Museum of South Texas in Corpus Christi from Patsy Dunn and Edwin Singer.[25]

Lipchitz's career likewise demonstrates the chain of connections with patrons and collectors stemming from Le Corbusier (architect of Lipchitz's Paris house and studio of 1923) to Charles de Noailles in France and Dr. Albert C. Barnes in the United States in the 1920s, to Hélène de Mandrot at Le Corbusier's summer house for her at Le Pradet in the 1930s, to Kaufmann at Wright's Fallingwater in the 1940s, and to Blanchette Rockefeller at her Johnson-designed guest house, Johnson at his own Glass House, and Father Couturier at the Church of Notre-Dame-de-Toute-Grâce at plateau d'Assy in the 1950s, with which Owen would be linked.[26]

Johnson, working in New York, the media capital of the United States, also offered access to national publicity networks because of his connections.[27] Publication of the Roofless Church in *Time*, the *New York Times*, and various architectural journals put New Harmony on the map of public consciousness in the 1960s.[28] Publicity was a powerful instrument in legitimizing modernist endeavors because it demonstrated to local populations the recognition, approval, and praise that could accrue to communities where significant works of modern architecture and art were constructed, especially if these communities were obscure yet also had historical legacies that might plausibly be linked to the new endeavors.[29]

Publicity reinforced the image of liberal community being constructed in New Harmony (and Columbus) in the 1960s because it suggested that modern art and architecture of the highest caliber connected to the histories of these communities in profound and authentic ways, as new construction that was prosaic and unambitious would not have done. Publicity additionally resulted in the construction of narratives, sometimes by recognized cultural authorities, that could be invoked to justify what were often unprecedented, potentially controversial interventions. And because a compelling narrative would tend to be repeated in subsequent reports on the community—which might take the form of a travel article, for instance, rather than one focused on the modern work—this justification tended to become axiomatic.[30]

Johnson, Saarinen, and Edward Larrabee Barnes (an architect of their generation who practiced in New York) functioned as *form givers*—a term popular in American architectural discourse during the late 1950s and early 1960s—not only in the obvious architectural sense of producing distinctive buildings but also because they were cultural arbiters whose advice, judgment, and instruction were sought by patrons eager to acquire the prestige and polish of metropolitan modernism.[31] In the 1950s Saarinen worked with corporate and large institutional clients, and Johnson and Barnes worked with residential and small institutional clients. What made these architects unusual were the relationships they developed with their patrons, which extended beyond individual architectural commissions.

Johnson served as a trustee of the Robert Lee Blaffer Trust at the time he advised Jane Owen to commission Frederick Kiesler.[32] He was instrumental in getting John de Menil elected to the board of the Museum of Modern Art in 1962, served several terms as a trustee of the Amon Carter Museum, and recommended that his domestic partner, David Whitney, organize the opening exhibition at the Art Museum of South Texas, to which Johnson lent works from his collection.[33] Johnson was an elitist rather than an egalitarian. He was pivotal in shifting the center of U.S. architectural culture back to New York City from Chicago and Los Angeles during the 1950s and in establishing the discourse on modern monumentality—to which the Roofless Church contributed—as the dominant American architectural discourse of the 1960s.[34] These achievements were not tied solely to the designs of his buildings. They attest as well to his deftness in constructing consensus for his authority as a cultural impresario by putting together coalitions of patrons (as well as "clients" of his own) who would support the causes he championed.[35]

Jane Owen and New Harmony

Jane Owen found her life's work in resuscitating New Harmony. She described the town when she first saw it in August 1941 as coated with coal dust and resounding with the noises of a short-lived oil exploration boom then taking place along the Wabash River in Indiana and Illinois.[36] Owen's discovery of art had occurred in Paris, at the Musée Rodin in 1927, when she was twelve.[37] She was especially moved by works of sculpture, which is what attracted her to Lipchitz's *Notre Dame de Liesse* (Our Lady of Joy). Owen had studied modern dance and she was attuned to sculpture that was expressive, gestural, and infused with pathos. In 1950 she donated a terra cotta *Madonna and Child* by the Texan sculptor Charles Umlauf to the Museum of Fine Arts, Houston. She commissioned studies for a relief sculpture by Lipchitz in 1952 to be installed on the exterior of the Robert Lee Blaffer Wing of the Museum of Fine Arts, its construction funded by her brother, John H. Blaffer, but the museum declined her offer. She also commissioned work from the young Houston sculptor Carroll Harris Simms, who began the sculpture program at Texas Southern University, Houston's then-segregated African American public university in 1950.[38] It seems to have been less the "modernity" of these works than the intensity with which their artists evoked emotional states that moved Owen, whose friends described her as "intuitive."[39]

Johnson connected with Owen's intuitiveness. She described how inspired she was when she first encountered him in late 1956 and heard his presentation to the trustees of the University of St. Thomas, Houston's Catholic university, after John de Menil had recommended Johnson for the design of a master plan of expansion for the university and offered to pay Johnson's fees if he was hired.[40] In developing the design of the Roofless Church, Johnson worked closely with Owen, and it is clear from her recollections that he was attentive to her vision of the chapel's components, especially its billowing wood dome.

Instead of deriding and dismissing Owen's devotion to New Harmony, as many of the people closest to her did, Johnson responded sympathetically, producing one of the early built works in his career that moved away from the rectilinear modularity of his buildings of the 1950s.[41] Owen gave Johnson the opportunity to explore the geometry of planar deformation, a theme that captivated him throughout his career.[42] With the dome, he produced a work that, like Lipchitz's *Notre Dame de Liesse,* explores expressive conventions that might be described as "feminine" and "intuitive" in dialectical contrast to the "masculine" economy and precision that marked the three buildings Johnson produced between 1957 and 1959 at the University of St. Thomas.

In the context of modernist patronage of the 1950s and early 1960s, the "feminism" of Owen's approach to conserving New Harmony—her gradual rehabilitation of historic buildings, adapting them to contemporary purposes rather than restoring them as museum structures, and regrouping them in spatially cohesive ensembles to support contemporary cultural and spiritual programs—stands out when contrasted with the emphasis on new construction that marked male patrons. At New

Figure 2.2. Philip Johnson was the architect for the Miesian-inspired architecture of Strake Hall and Jones Hall, University of St. Thomas, Houston, 1957–59. Photograph by Frank Lotz Miller.

Harmony, modern art and architecture were used strategically to reinforce the narrative of the community's historical exceptionality and to attract the attention of cultural elites that historic preservation alone might not have achieved.

Owen, like Dominique de Menil and J. Irwin Miller, combined modern forms of art and architecture with modern forms of spirituality. She did this by bringing theologians and religious leaders to New Harmony to speak, to participate in worship, and to study and write. An Anglican, Owen was drawn to liberal theology and the ecumenical movement in the 1950s. Paul Tillich and Henry Pitney Van Dusen, a Presbyterian minister and the president of Union Seminary in New York, with which Tillich was affiliated, came to New Harmony, as earlier had the Indiana-based Quaker theologian Elton Trueblood and George F. MacLeod, a minister of the Church of Scotland, proponent of ecumenism and social justice, and founder of the ecumenical Iona Community based at Iona Abbey.[43] Although Johnson's design for St. Stephen's Episcopal Church in New Harmony was not built, Owen and the Robert Lee Blaffer Trust did rehabilitate a historic barn in New Harmony as the Barn Abbey (Plate 23), a retreat center inspired by the Iona Community, in 1976.[44]

Acting as a modern patron, Owen conferred an aura of sophistication on New Harmony with her projects. This attracted publicity and visitors. Her construction of the New Harmony Inn (1974, which contains a meditation chapel, the Waddams Chapel) by Evans Woollen Associates ensured that visitors could enjoy levels of amenity not customarily available in a small town.[45]

Such efforts helped construct consensus on the importance of preserving New Harmony. In 1973 the State of Indiana authorized a state-level commission, chaired by the former governor Roger D. Branigin, which led to the establishment of Historic New Harmony, a nonprofit historic preservation organization, in 1974. Under the leadership of the founding president, Ralph Schwarz, Historic New Harmony followed Owen's example by commissioning the New York architects Richard Meier & Associates to design New Harmony's second landmark modern building, the Atheneum (1975–79), a visitors' orientation center on the northwest edge of town overlooking the Wabash River. The Atheneum renewed media attention to and praise of New Harmony as the Roofless Church had done twenty years earlier.[46]

Under Owen's sponsorship and with Johnson's initial guidance, New Harmony emerged from obscurity in the 1960s. The combination of exceptional modern art and architecture and a rehabilitated and reconstituted historic fabric that materialized the layers of New Harmony's history as a center of religious and social experimentation gave the community a distinctive profile that surmounted the barriers imposed by small size and geographic marginality.[47] The spiritual and cultural programs that Owen initiated, and which she linked to these sites, sought to continue the process of constructing consensus on what made New Harmony historically significant—its utopian legacy—by instituting programs that supported and "peopled" her vision of liberal community. That such a vision might not be shared by all residents of New Harmony and Posey County indicated the need for continually legitimizing the narrative of cultural exception as well as the tangible benefits to the community that it delivered.[48]

Midcentury Modern Patronage

Mid-twentieth-century modern patronage grappled with the specter of elitism, which seemed to call into question patrons' dedication to American populist values of egalitarianism and democracy, as Albrecht identified them. What patrons confronted in building "for" the general public (rather than as a personal preoccupation) was the need to legitimize unconventional stylistic forms with persuasive narratives that assimilated unconventionality to accepted social practices. The postwar emphasis on representing modern architecture in terms of newness, progressiveness, and "freedom" (Johnson was the coauthor of a polemic on freedom in architectural design) displays the efforts of critics to code modern architecture with ideological associations that would resonate with otherwise skeptical (or merely disinterested) public perceptions.[49] Although the 1950s was the decade in which modernism emerged as the representational style of U.S. corporate and cultural elites, it did so in a context of conservative resistance. Conservatives constructed consensus around fear of communism, a defense of patriotism and religious orthodoxy, and, in the South, Anglo-American racial superiority and African American racial subordination.[50] Populist aversion to modernism in the cultural arena and to moral relativism in the social arena figured strongly as part of the conservative critique of liberalism.[51]

After the completion of the Roofless Church, the mechanics of constructing consensus on how it related to New Harmony's historical distinctiveness and how that distinctiveness was to be interpreted are apparent, at least in historical perspective. New Harmony had been written about in the popular press before Owen arrived; in 1905 it was the subject of a history, *The New Harmony Movement,* by George B. Lockwood.[52] Yet when *Life* magazine visited New Harmony in September 1945 in the wake of publication of Marguerite Young's novel *Angel in the Forest: A Fairy Tale of Two Utopias,* it headlined the town as the "setting for two strange utopias." A brief report in *Fortune* in July 1954, noting the dissolution of an earlier state commission, organized in 1937 to restore the town's historical distinction, began: "A little withered blossom of nineteenth-century socialism has been dropped by the road."[53] After the dedication of the Roofless Church, *utopia* (minus *strange*) was the term most commonly employed in headlines and media stories to characterize New Harmony's historical identity. Modern architecture supported the construction of a revised identity that linked New Harmony's history to religious and social experimentation and the construction of ideal community.[54]

A similar theme was apparent in media stories about Columbus, where, in 1954, Miller, chairman of the board of directors of two corporations based in Columbus, the Cummins Engine Company and the Irwin Union Bank and Trust Company, committed the Cummins Engine Foundation to pay architects' fees for public buildings (including those built by nonprofit organizations, such as religious institutions), if the architects were chosen from a list that, initially, Miller and Eero Saarinen compiled.[55] Miller's architectural patronage was consistent with his actions as a progressive businessman with strong liberal sympathies. A member of the Disciples of Christ Church, Miller became the first layman to be elected president of the National Council of Churches in 1960. He championed the council's support of religious ecumenism and the civil rights movement, and in 1963 assisted the Reverend Martin Luther King Jr. in organizing the March on Washington.[56]

As a patron, Miller operated on a broader scale than did Owen (Columbus, although a small town, is considerably larger than New Harmony), and he mobilized the Cummins Engine Foundation's resources to reach beyond personal and business-related projects to construct a reputation for Columbus as an enlightened, culturally sophisticated community in which professionals recruited by Cummins Engine and their families would feel at home.[57] Publicity functioned not only to identify Columbus outside south-central Indiana but also to legitimize Miller's patronage within Columbus and Bartholomew County and deflect potential resistance to his liberal-elite subject position.[58] Miller sought to perform modernity consistently as a corporate executive, labor employer, community leader, cultural patron, and religious activist, combining responsiveness to democratic egalitarianism with wealth and power in ways that were represented in media accounts as foresighted and socially responsible.

Dominique and John de Menil also bear comparison with Owen as exemplary midcentury modernist patrons. John de Menil was, like Miller, a progressive businessman. He and his family came to Houston from Paris after the German invasion of France in 1940 and remained there after the war ended. Menil headed the Latin American and Middle Eastern divisions of the Paris-based Schlumberger oil field services corporation, which Dominique Schlumberger de Menil's father and uncle founded. After the subsidiaries were reorganized into a single corporation, Schlumberger Ltd., Menil became chairman of its executive committee.[59] Although Dominique and John de Menil (who operated and were identified as a team) attained recognition as art collectors and patrons, their first dramatic exercise of patronage was to commission Johnson to design their house in 1948, the first of many commissions John de Menil directed to Johnson in the 1950s and 1960s.[60]

Dominique de Menil had become involved with the ecumenical movement in the Roman Catholic Church in France in the 1930s, which is how she made the acquaintance of Father Couturier, who became the couple's first guide to contemporary art

Figure 2.3. Xenia S. and J. Irwin Miller in the living room of the Miller House, Columbus, Indiana, in 1972. The house was designed by Eero Saarinen (with Kevin Roche), architect; Alexander Girard, interior designer; Dan Kiley, landscape architect. Photograph courtesy of the Miller House and Garden Collection, 1953–2009 (M003), IMA Archives, Indianapolis Museum of Art at Newfields, Indianapolis, Indiana.

Figure 2.4. John and Dominique de Menil at the Museum of Fine Arts Houston, 1968. The Menils were significant patrons of art and architecture in Houston, building the Rothko Chapel and, after John de Menil's death, the Menil Collection museum. Photograph by Hickey-Robertson. Courtesy of the Menil Collection.

when he too lived in the United States during the war years.[61] Like Miller, the Menils combined modernist patronage with enlightened corporate management practices and a commitment to religious ecumenism and social causes that in Houston in the 1950s were controversial, especially their repudiation of racism and racial segregation.[62] Yet precisely because the Menils were exceptional, these attitudes brought them recognition in the media.[63] They too sought to perform consistently as modernists in all the endeavors that mattered most to them.

The institution that materialized the breadth of their interests is the Rothko Chapel, which they began to plan in 1964 and which was built in Houston in 1970. The Menils commissioned the painter Mark Rothko to execute fourteen large paintings that envelop the octagonal worship space. They commissioned Johnson to design the chapel building in response to Rothko's directives. After the chapel was dedicated in 1971, the Menils began a series of programs there that continue to support the chapel's identification with modern forms of spirituality, religious exchange, social justice, and human rights.[64]

The Roofless Church stands out as a forerunner of the Rothko Chapel. Both are examples of the art chapel, which was associated with Father Couturier, and both were used as sites to promote modernist forms of spiritual and social practice.[65] Johnson's involvement as architect for the pair closes the auratic circle of modern patron–client association linking them.[66] Because Dominique and John de Menil operated in Houston rather than a small town, their architectural patronage did not have the impact of Owen's in New Harmony or Miller's in Columbus. After John de Menil's death, however, Dominique de Menil concentrated her building activities in the Houston neighborhood in which the Rothko Chapel and Johnson's campus for the University of St. Thomas are located. There she constructed a distinctive sense of community by preserving otherwise unremarkable 1920s bungalows, the original buildings of the neighborhood, and having the Houston architect Howard Barnstone paint them gray with white trim, causing them to cohere visually. When Dominique de Menil built the Menil Collection museum (1981–87) in this neighborhood, her architect, Renzo Piano of Genoa, shaped and colored the museum building so that it engaged the bungalows in an art-inspired dialogue on constructing new forms of community.[67]

In New Harmony, Columbus, and Houston, the theme of a modernist–historical dialectic was pursued. In New Harmony, the Roofless Church and eventually the Atheneum were structures in which New Harmony's historical identity as the site of experiments in community were externalized and celebrated. The Roofless Church carried this historical legacy of critical questioning and testing into the present. In Columbus, the modern community, civic, educational, religious, and industrial buildings constructed during Miller's long lifetime expanded on the history of technical innovation associated with the Cummins Engine Company by emphasizing the connection between liberal progressiveness, commitment to excellence, and the economic prosperity of Columbus, a town that conserved its mythic, Middle Western, small-town identity while enjoying cosmopolitan standards of modern architectural production.[68] In Houston this theme was not tied to advancing the city's reputation but to infusing an ordinary, early twentieth-century suburban neighborhood with a new, subtly surreal identity that materialized connections between daily life and modern movements in twentieth-century art, spirituality, and social justice.[69]

One difference between Owen and Miller and the Menils involves their dwellings. Johnson's Menil House in Houston, in its modernist architectural design and eclectic interior design by Charles James, "spatialized" its patrons' cosmopolitan worldview.[70] Miller's pavilion-like house in Columbus (1957), designed by Eero Saarinen, Kevin Roche, and Alexander Girard, with its landscape setting by Dan Kiley, proclaimed Miller's personal identification with modernism.[71] Owen, both in New Harmony and in Houston, lived in houses she did not build. Her New Harmony house was the Rawlings House, a Harmonist house that sits in the shadows of K. D. Owen's great-great-grandfather Richard Owen's residence, the Rapp–Maclure–Owen House of 1844 on Church Street, and the adjoining research laboratory of Richard's elder brother, the geologist David Dale Owen, of 1859.[72] Jane Owen used modernism to negotiate interpretations of the history of New Harmony. Although her personal inclinations were modern, she did not feel compelled to exclude or subordinate her love for New Harmony's historic fabric in order to advance modernist forms and causes.

A fourth modern patron who bears comparison with Jane Owen was the Chicago businessman Walter Paepcke, chairman of the board and chief executive officer of the Container Corporation of America.[73] Like Miller and John de Menil, Paepcke was a progressive businessman. The cultural historian James Sloan Allen demonstrates how Paepcke sought to perform consistently as an exemplary modernist cultural impresario by founding the Aspen Institute for Humanistic Studies in 1949, the Aspen Music Festival in 1949, and the International Design Conference in Aspen in 1951.[74] Aspen, Colorado, was to Paepcke what New Harmony was for Owen: a small, remote, picturesque town of fewer than a thousand people when Paepcke first visited in 1945, which he determined to transform into a magnet for modern culture, thought, performance, and exchange.[75] Like Owen, Paepcke preserved and restored Aspen's small-town fabric and historical buildings while also patronizing the Bauhaus-trained architect, artist, and graphic designer Herbert Bayer, who produced new, modern buildings there.[76] What differentiated Paepcke from Owen was the velocity and scale of Paepcke's activities. He moved rapidly to implement what amounted to a business plan to develop not only new cultural assets for Aspen but recreational and sports activities and infrastructure as well. Paepcke recruited intellectual and artistic celebrities to attract the constituencies he hoped to lure to Aspen and, drawing on his corporate experience, coordinated advertising and public relations campaigns to promote these activities nationally. At the time of his death in 1960, Paepcke was planning to build a series of modern houses in Aspen, which he hoped to commission from the foremost architects in the world.[77]

Allen also documented the consequences of Aspen's rapid transformation: how change aroused the suspicion and mistrust of Aspen residents, incited conflicts over land use and development that eventually rebounded on the institutions Paepcke founded and, by the 1970s, transformed Aspen demographically into a resort community for the rich. The slower, more tentative dynamic of change in New Harmony during the same period meant that new cultural development, although it did not resolve chronic economic problems endemic to a small farming community, also did not exacerbate those problems by pricing residents out of the community.

In her insightful analysis of Owen's patronage in New Harmony, the architect and historian Christine Gorby deduces the ways in which the landscapes shaped under Owen's direction support such subjective emotional states as contemplation, meditation, remembering, and mystery (along with the correlates of mystery: doubt and unknowing).[78] Gorby does not use the word *intuitive* to describe Owen's methods. But the patterns of action she describes imply that intuition, rather than doctrinaire assertion, conditioned the patron–client relationships between Owen and the artists, architects, and landscape architects with whom she worked. Gorby contrasts this attitude with what she describes as a "curatorial" approach to cultural management, which seeks legitimacy through art-historical categorization and cultural interpretation based on distinction and difference.[79] Gorby advances a feminist interpretation of Owen's patronage style. One sees in Owen's consistent preference for what Gorby calls a "spiritual perspective" a disinterest in forms of authority guaranteed by professional reputation alone.[80]

Johnson's unwillingness to address the weathering problems affecting the brick walls surrounding the Roofless Church, which became so acute by the late 1970s that the walls had to be demolished and reconstructed, undermined Owen's trust in him and modern architecture.[81] This episode did give Owen confidence in her own judgment. The extent to which her subsequent projects, especially the landscapes Gorby analyzes, combined professional design and personal intervention indicates that her agenda as a patron was not to assemble a collection of sites and buildings associated with celebrated artists, architects, and landscape architects but to sponsor the construction of spaces that move those who experience them to become more thoughtful, reflective, and spiritually aware human beings.[82]

As a case study in mid-twentieth-century modernist patronage, New Harmony discloses some of the tensions that patrons and their artistic clients had to negotiate as they sought to construct consensus on the virtues of imagined liberal communities through their building projects. It demonstrates how an architect–client could reward a patron with the modern, democratic-egalitarian version of classical glory—publicity—elevating the patron to singularity nationally, perhaps internationally, but also, just as critically, locally. National acclaim bolstered the patron's aspiration to modify her or his community by constructing consensus locally on the virtue of the patron's vision of imagined community, which in the postwar period was most often a liberal vision. Consensus was required to counter populist resistance, not only because of hostility to modern forms of art, architecture, religion, and politics, but, and perhaps more powerfully, because of resentment of the patron's wealth, class superiority, and elite authority.

This case study also illustrates the way that the postwar modernist problematic of the relationship of modernity and history was negotiated in the 1950s and 1960s by constructing narratives, again often through the medium of publicity, that linked modernist works to historical settings or legacies and identified the modernist work as truer in form to the legacy than forms of representation based on historical models. The case of New Harmony suggests the differences that may have pertained because a woman, rather than a man, was the patron. Owen's relationship with Johnson foundered over issues of professional responsibility and accountability. In the case of Frederick Kiesler and the *Cave of the New Being / Grotto for Meditation*, Johnson, in his client role as cultural impresario and arbiter, proposed, and then disposed of, a design that, in retrospect, would seem to have been especially attuned to Owen's sensibility.

Owen used the wealth she inherited to restore the luster of her husband's family name and renew the town with which the Owens were identified. In making this Texas–Indiana connection, she reversed the historical direction of intellectual-capital transfer. The historian José María Herrera has documented the efforts of Robert Owen to redeem his failed experiment at New Harmony by traveling to Mexico City in 1828–29 to persuade the president of Mexico, don Guadalupe Victoria, to sell Texas to him as the site for a new utopian venture.[83] The contemporaries of Robert Owen's children, the inventors and entrepreneurs Gail Borden Jr. and George W. Fulton, came to Texas from Indiana in the 1820s and 1830s: Gail Borden and his brother Thomas surveyed the town site of Houston in 1836.[84] The banker and philanthropist George W. Brackenridge came to Texas from Warwick County as a youth in 1853; he was San Antonio's foremost architectural patron of the late nineteenth century.[85] In the mid-twentieth century, it was a Purdue University engineering graduate from Gary, Gerald D. Hines, who, seven years after Jane Owen's initial visit to New Harmony, arrived in Houston to begin his career. After 1970 Hines, by then Houston's leading investment builder, would join Dominique and John de Menil in being acclaimed—in the *New York Times,* of course—as a modernist patron, his "client" none other than Philip Johnson.[86] That New Harmony, a town of fewer than a thousand people, is capable of serving as a case study of the cultural politics of twentieth-century modernist patrons and clients suggests that cultural agents can operate from tenuous bases of local support as long as they generate cultural capital, as was also demonstrated by a midwestern transplant, the artist Donald Judd, who sought the isolation of an obscure town, Marfa, in the Trans-Pecos region of Texas.[87] In the case of New Harmony, as in Marfa, the marginality and ordinariness of the town became the plane of reality on which the myths of modernism are performed.

Notes

For assistance with the preparation of this chapter, the author gratefully thanks coeditors Ben Nicholson and Michelangelo Sabatino; Patricia Belton Oliver, dean of the Gerald D. Hines College of Architecture and Design at the University of Houston; Joseph Mashburn, professor of architecture, University of Houston; Mrs. Kenneth Dale Owen; Howard Barnstone; Carlos Jiménez; William I. Miller; Kenneth A. Schuette Jr., clinical professor of landscape architecture at Purdue University; Pamela Smart, assistant professor of anthropology at Binghamton University; Cynthia Rowan Taylor; and contributors Christine Gorby, Cammie McAtee, Nancy Mangum McCaslin, and William R. Crout.

1. James Muirhead and Agnes Muriel Clay, "Patron and Client," *Encyclopaedia Britannica,* 11th ed., 20:935–36.

2. The most perceptive published account of Jane Owen is by Barbara Grizzuti Harrison, "Life's Simple Treasures: Jane Blaffer Owen Seeks and Funds Paradise on Earth," *Vanity Fair,* August 1983, 40–55. On Kenneth Dale Owen, see "Deaths: Owen, Kenneth Dale," *New York Times,* May 2, 2002. On the Owen family and New Harmony, see William E. Wilson, *The Angel and the Serpent: The Story of New Harmony* (Bloomington: Indiana University Press, 1964); Donald E. Pitzer, ed., *Robert Owen's American Legacy: Proceedings* (Indianapolis: Indiana Historical Society, 1972); and Donald F. Carmony

and Josephine M. Elliott, "New Harmony, Indiana: Robert Owen's Seedbed for Utopia," *Indiana Magazine of History* 76 (September 1980): 160–261.

3. Nikolaus Pevsner, "Frank Pick," in *Victorians and After*, vol. 2 of *Studies in Art, Architecture, and Design* (New York: Walker and Company, 1968), 191–209.

4. Stanford Anderson, *Peter Behrens and the New Architecture for the Twentieth Century* (Cambridge, Mass.: MIT Press, 2000), 28–29, 49–53.

5. Ellen Joosten, *The Kröller-Müller Museum, Otterlo, Holland* (New York: Shorewood, 1965).

6. Deborah Gans, *The Le Corbusier Guide*, rev. ed. (New York: Princeton Architectural Press, 2000), 122–24; Jacqueline Salmon and Hubert Damisch, *Villa Noailles (Hyères)* (Paris: Marval, 1997); Catherine Laulhère-Vigneau, *La Villa Noailles: Un Aventure Moderne* (Paris: Flammarion, 2001); and Deborah Rothschild, ed., *Making It New: The Art and Style of Sara and Gerald Murphy* (Berkeley and Williamstown, Mass.: University of California Press and Williams College Museum of Art, 2007).

7. Antonio E. Méndez Vigatá, "Politics and Architectural Language: Post-Revolutionary Regimes in Mexico and Their Influence on Mexican Public Architecture," in *Modernity and the Architecture of Mexico*, edited by Edward R. Burian (Austin: University of Texas Press, 1997), 66–71; and Luis E. Carranza, *Architecture as Revolution: Episodes in the History of Modern Mexico* (Austin: University of Texas Press, 2010).

8. Victoria Ocampo, *Victoria Ocampo: Writer, Feminist, Woman of the World,* translated and edited by Patricia Owen Steiner (Albuquerque: University of New Mexico Press, 1999).

9. David Underwood, *Oscar Niemeyer and the Architecture of Brazil* (New York: Rizzoli International, 1994), 51–54, 60–69, 98–101; Nicholas Fox Weber, *Le Corbusier: A Life* (New York: Alfred A. Knopf, 2008), 12–14, 748.

10. Marie-Alain Couturier, *Sacred Art,* edited by Dominique de Menil and Pie Duployé, translated by Granger Ryan (Austin: University of Texas Press, 1989); Weber, *Le Corbusier,* 663–67.

11. Leonard K. Eaton, *Two Chicago Architects and Their Clients: Frank Lloyd Wright and Howard Van Doren Shaw* (Cambridge, Mass.: MIT Press, 1969); Kathryn Smith, *Frank Lloyd Wright, Hollyhock House, and Olive Hill: Buildings and Projects for Aline Barnsdall* (New York: Rizzoli International, 1992).

12. James Sloan Allen, *The Romance of Commerce and Culture: Capitalism, Modernism, and the Chicago-Aspen Crusade for Cultural Reform* (Chicago: University of Chicago Press, 1983). On John de Menil, see *Who's Who in America, 1964–1965,* vol. 33 (Chicago: Marquis Who's Who, 1964), 504; and *Who's Who in America, 1974–1975,* vol. 38 (Chicago: Marquis Who's Who, 1974), number 1: 773, under "de Menil, John." See also William Middleton, *Double Vision: The Unerring Eye of Art World Avatars Dominique and John de Menil* (New York: Alfred A. Knopf, 2018). On J. Irwin Miller, see Will Miller, "Eero and Irwin: Praiseworthy Competition with One's Ancestors," in *Eero Saarinen: Shaping the Future,* edited by Eeva-Liisa Pelkonen and Donald Albrecht (New Haven, Conn.: Yale University Press in association with the Finnish Cultural Institute in New York, the Museum of Finnish Architecture, the National Building Museum, and Yale University School of Architecture, 2006), 56–67. On Thomas J. Watson Jr., see Bruce Gordon, *Eliot Noyes: Pioneer of Design and Architecture in the Age of American Modernism* (London: Phaidon, 2006), 136–85. On Stanley Marcus, see Barbara Koerble, "Buy Design: Stanley Marcus on the Architecture of Merchandising," in *Cite: The Architecture and Design Review of Houston* 35 (Fall 1996): 28–30. On Joseph Eichler, see Ned Eichler, "A Cherished Legacy," in Jerry Ditto and Lanning Stern, *Design for Living: Eichler Homes,* photography by Marvin Wax, introduction by Sally B. Woodbridge (San Francisco: Chronicle Books, 1995), 35–117. On Herbert Greenwald, see Franz Schulze, *Mies van der Rohe: A Critical Biography* (Chicago: University of Chicago Press in association with the Mies van der Rohe Archive of the Museum of Modern Art, 1985), 239–45.

13. On John Entenza, see Esther McCoy, "Arts and Architecture: Case Study Houses," in *Blueprints for Modern Living: History and Legacy of the Case Study Houses,* edited by Elizabeth A. T. Smith

(Cambridge, Mass., and Los Angeles: MIT Press and the Museum of Contemporary Art, 1989), 15. On Nelson Rockefeller, see William S. Lieberman, *The Nelson A. Rockefeller Collection: Masterpieces of Modern Art* (New York: Hudson Hills, 1981). On Dominique de Menil, see Calvin Tomkins, "The Benefactor," *New Yorker,* June 8, 1998, 52–67; *A Modern Patronage: De Menil Gifts to American and European Museums,* introduction by Josef Helfenstein (Houston: Menil Foundation, 2007); and Middleton, *Double Vision.* On Samuel Bronfman and Phyllis Lambert, see Phyllis Lambert, *Building Seagram* (New Haven, Conn.: Yale University Press, 2013).

Although the publisher Henry Luce (1898–1967) did not commission that many distinctive modern buildings, he did use his magazines—*Time, Fortune, Life,* and *House and Home*—to promote modern architects and their buildings. Time Inc. also owned *Architectural Forum* magazine for several decades.

In the introduction to the present book, Michelangelo Sabatino calls attention to the modern design patronage and progressive social and labor practices associated with Adriano Olivetti (1901–1960), chairman of the Italian business machine corporation Olivetti from 1938 to 1960.

14. Donald Albrecht, "The Clients and Their Architect," in *Eero Saarinen: Shaping the Future,* 44–55; Allen, *Romance of Commerce and Culture,* 234, 277–78. Allen profiles the shared characteristics of this generation of cultural leaders on p. 291.

15. Albrecht, "Clients and Their Architect," 46.

16. Eric P. Kaufmann, *The Rise and Fall of Anglo-America* (Cambridge, Mass.: Harvard University Press, 2004), 66–67.

17. Jackson Lears, "A Matter of Taste: Corporate Cultural Hegemony in a Mass-Consumption Society," in *Recasting America: Culture and Politics in the Age of Cold War,* edited by Lary May (Chicago: University of Chicago Press, 1989), 38–57.

18. The social construction of "imagined communities" was proposed by Benedict Anderson in *Imagined Communities: Reflections on the Origin and Spread of Nationalism* (London: Verso Editions / NLB, 1983).

19. The range of Owen's liberal interests—religion, art, social justice, architecture—paralleled those of the Menils. Though they were mutually supportive, an element of rivalry also seems to have affected the relationship between Owen and Dominique de Menil, especially with regard to standards of connoisseurship. See Dominique Browning, "What I Admire, I Must Possess," *Texas Monthly,* April 1983, 200; and Harrison, "Life's Simple Treasures," 45.

20. See Jane Blaffer Owen, interview with Michelangelo Sabatino and Laura M. McGuire, transcript, Houston, 2009; and Jane Blaffer Owen, "Foreword: Memories of Tillich and New Harmony," in *Paul Tillich's Theological Legacy: Spirit and Community,* International Paul Tillich Conference, New Harmony, June 17–20, 1993, edited by Frederick J. Parrella (Berlin: Walter de Gruyter, 1995), vii–ix. Cammie McAtee has identified two published references to *Notre-Dame-des-Liesse* from 1950, one in the last paragraph of Rosamund Frost's article "Lipchitz Makes a Sculpture," in *Art News* 49, no. 2 (1950): 64—an issue containing several articles about art and religion—and the other in the first issue of *L'Art Sacré 1–2,* September–October 1950, on the dedication of Notre-Dame-de-Toute-Grâce du plateau d'Assy with a photograph of Lipchitz's maquette (p. 13) and an introductory article by Father Couturier: M.-A. Couturier, "Historique de l'église," 6. With respect to the Menils, Father Couturier, Lipchitz, and Tillich, see Kaufmann's observations on the essential contributions of refugee European artists and intellectuals (p. 164) and of what he calls the American liberal "Protestant intelligentsia" ("denominational executives, ecumenical Protestant bureaucrats, seminary professors, religious journalists, and Protestant social workers," p. 143) made to "[drawing] cosmopolitan ideas toward the center of American life" (p. 143) in the postwar period (*Rise and Fall of Anglo-America*).

21. The modern dialectic between history and modernity that prevailed prior to the advent of modernism was Darwinian: in architecture and the arts, this position entailed the adaptation of historical forms to contemporary programs. The modernist version of this dialectic was Marxist: modern forms succeeded to positions of authority previously occupied by period-specific forms. Managing the tense, conflicted relationship of modernity and history was a central theme in Johnson's architectural career. Kaufmann notes the process of social bonding promoted by vanguard cultural advocacy in the second triad of the twentieth century (*Rise and Fall of Anglo-America,* 149).

22. Pamela G. Smart's anthropology dissertation provides the most incisive analysis of Dominique and John de Menil's career as collectors and patrons; Smart, "Sacred Modern: An Ethnography of an Art Museum" (Ph.D. diss., Rice University, 1997), ii. Smart expands on this analysis in her book *Sacred Modern: Faith, Activism, and Aesthetics in the Menil Collection* (Austin: University of Texas Press, 2010).

23. *Philip Johnson and the Museum of Modern Art,* edited by John Elderfield, Studies in Museum Art Six (New York: Museum of Modern Art, 1998). Kazys Varnelis dissects Johnson's patron–client web, demonstrating how it changed over time to serve Johnson's changing agenda. See Varnelis, "Philip Johnson's Empire: Network Power and the AT&T Building," in *Philip Johnson: The Constancy of Change,* edited by Emmanuel Petit, foreword by Robert A. M. Stern (New Haven, Conn.: Yale University Press and the Yale University School of Architecture, 2009), 121, 123–26.

24. Stover Jenkins and David Mohoney, *The Houses of Philip Johnson,* afterword by Neil Levine, photographs by Steven Brooke (New York: Abbeville, 2001), 100–103, 116–20, 136–37, 160–62; Kathleen L. Housley, *Emily Hall Tremaine: Collector on the Cusp* (Meriden: Emily Hall Tremaine Foundation, 2001); Martha Mitchell, "Computing Lab," in *Encyclopaedia Brunoniana* (Providence, R.I.: Brown University Library, 1993); and Reuben A. Holden, *Yale: A Pictorial History* (New Haven, Conn.: Yale University Press, 1967), 285, 293, 295.

25. Frank D. Welch, *Philip Johnson and Texas* (Austin: University of Texas Press, 2000), 109–18, 93–101, 152–60, 122–31, 132–49.

26. Jacques Lipchitz with H. H. Arnason, *My Life in Sculpture* (New York: Viking, 1972), 70–78, 96, 123–24, 148, 168, 171–75, 193, 198. An earlier biography of Lipchitz, Irene Patai's *Encounters: The Life of Jacques Lipchitz,* foreword by Andrew C. Ritchie (New York: Funk & Wagnalls, 1961), contains a more detailed account of Lipchitz's association with Jane Owen and New Harmony (vii–viii, 373–79, 388–91, 436). Owen gives her account of her association with Lipchitz in her memoir *New Harmony, Indiana: Like a River, Not a Lake: A Memoir* (Bloomington: Indiana University Press, 2015), 69–84.

27. The autobiography of Peter Blake (1920–2006), an architect and an architectural journalist and editor, illuminates the social networks linking Manhattan media to high culture from the 1940s to the 1970s. See Blake, *No Place Like Utopia: Modern Architecture and the Company We Kept* (New York: Alfred A. Knopf, 1983).

28. On the Roofless Church, see "Buildings in the News," *Architectural Record* 125 (September 1959): 13; William H. Jordy, "The Mies-less Johnson," *Architectural Forum* 111, no. 3 (1959): 122; Robin H. Moore, "A Shrine by Philip Johnson," *Art in America* 47, no. 4 (1959): 70–71; "Return to the Past," *Time,* September 5, 1960, 52–55; "Shingle Shrine," *Architectural Forum* 113, no. 3 (1960): 128; "Culture, Religion, and Architecture in Indiana," *Architectural Record* 128, no. 4 (1960): 15; Henry-Russell Hitchcock, "The Current Work of Philip Johnson," *Zodiac 8* (1961): 64–81; John M. Jacobus Jr., *Philip Johnson* (New York: George Braziller, 1962), 41–42; *Philip Johnson Architecture 1949–1965,* introduction by Henry-Russell Hitchcock (New York: Holt, Rinehart and Winston, 1966), 72–75; Franz Schulze, *Philip Johnson: Life and Work* (New York: Alfred A. Knopf, 1994), 281–82; Welch, *Philip Johnson and Texas,* 69–75; *The Philip Johnson Tapes: Interviews by Robert A. M. Stern,* edited by Kazys Varnelis, Buell Center / Columbia Book of Architecture (New York: Monacelli, 2008), 168–70.

A critical interpretation of the Roofless Church, part of the emerging postmodern critique of modern architecture, is contained in Charles Jencks, "The Candid King Midas of New York Camp," *AAQ Architectural Association Quarterly* 5, no. 4 (1973): 26–42.

29. Allen comments on the role of publicity as a solvent in fusing business with modern art, graphics, and good taste to construct the image of liberality in *The Romance of Commerce and Culture,* 213, 230. Michelangelo Sabatino, in his book *Pride in Modesty: Modernist Architecture and the Vernacular Tradition in Italy* (Toronto: University of Toronto Press, 2010), analyzes the construction of a cultural discourse in twentieth-century Italy on the superiority of modern architecture because of its affiliation with the vernacular's putatively purer, more essential, more authentic relationship to the historical legacy of architecture than historical eclecticism produced.

30. In a phenomenon that is not confined to reporting on New Harmony, journalistic accounts often tell the same story over and over, as can be seen by comparing the following: William E. Wilson, "Pioneers in Paradise," *Holiday,* June 1959, 42–47; William E. Beauchamp, "Hoosier Utopia of Old a Tourist Utopia Now," *New York Times,* September, 8, 1963; Grover Brinkman, "An Indiana Town Settled by Two Early Communes," *New York Times,* June 6, 1971; Howard A. Wilson, "Letters and Comments: Growing Up with a Past," *Yale Review* 66 (June 1977): 628–40; and Nancy Kriplen, "Recalling Past Utopias in an Indiana Town," *New York Times,* April 17, 1994. Kaufmann, *Rise and Fall of Anglo-America,* 146–47.

31. Allen references the traveling architectural exhibition circulated nationally by Time Inc. and the American Federation of Arts, *Form Givers at Mid-Century* of 1959. Allen, *Romance of Capitalism and Culture,* 279–80. Edward Barnes's Indiana connections were through Miller. See *Edward Larrabee Barnes, Architect,* introduction by Peter Blake (New York: Rizzoli International, 1994), 241, 134–41, 190–97.

32. Jane Owen established the Robert Lee Blaffer Trust in 1958 as a charitable trust, chartered in Texas. In 2001 it was superseded by the Robert Lee Blaffer Foundation, an operating foundation chartered in Indiana. See *Guide to U.S. Foundations, Their Trustees, Officers, and Donors* (New York: Foundation Center, 2007), 3:192. Thanks to Nancy Mangum McCaslin for information on the Blaffer Trust.

33. Johnson's relationship with the Art Museum of South Texas in Corpus Christi is the best documented. See Alan Lessoff, "An Art Museum for South Texas, 1944–1980," in *Legacy: A History of the Art Museum of South Texas* (Corpus Christi: Art Museum of South Texas, 1997), 35–44.

34. In the 1950s, cultural authority in American modern architecture was shared between New York, Chicago, and Los Angeles. The identification of Frank Lloyd Wright and Mies van der Rohe with Chicago and the influence of *Arts & Architecture* magazine, which was published in Los Angeles and featured West Coast architects (as well as architects from other parts of the United States and abroad), meant that the discourses of modern American postwar architecture were not dominated by any one metropolitan center. Johnson's advocacy for historical awareness and a broader interest in urbanism and monumentality helped return New York cultural media to a position of unchallenged primacy in the 1960s with respect to architecture. Kaufmann comments on the relative importance of Chicago and New York as centers of modern culture at the beginning of the twentieth century, with Chicago being the more rigorous and progressive, which was especially true with respect to architecture. Kaufmann, *Rise and Fall of Anglo-America,* 145–48.

On modern monumentality, see Stanislaus von Moos, "Playboy Architecture, Then and Now," in *Philip Johnson: The Constancy of Change,* 180; and George R. Collins and Christianne C. Collins, "Monumentality: A Critical Matter in Modern Architecture," in *The Harvard Architecture Review No. IV: Monumentality and the City,* edited by Paul Louis Bentel and Howard Lynn Hopffgarten (Cambridge, Mass.: MIT Press, Spring 1984), 14–35. This *Review* number also contains two important historical documents: Sigfried Gideon, "The Need for a New Monumentality" (52–61); and Sigfried Gideon, Fernand Léger, and José Luis Sert, "Nine Points on Monumentality" (62–63).

35. Johnson deftly interchanged his roles as client and patron to facilitate connections between his patrons and his "clients," as Ben Nicholson demonstrates in his chapter on Frederick Kiesler and the *Cave of the New Being* in this book. See also Varnelis, "Philip Johnson's Empire." Ralph Schwarz is also fascinating in this regard, as his changing relationships with the architects Kevin Roche and Richard Meier (sometimes as Schwarz's patron, other times as his "client") illustrate; see also Ralph Grayson Schwarz in the second part of this book as one of the "Three Voices in New Harmony."

In considering the pivotal roles Johnson played as cultural impresario, Kaufmann's citation of the Italian sociologist Mario Diani is pertinent: "Diani contends that social movements tend to succeed to the extent that leaders of a movement possess 'social capital' in the form of social ties to the mass media, corporate cultural intermediaries, and the state intelligentsia—where dominant interpretations of reality are generated" (*Rise and Fall of Anglo-America*, 180).

36. The White County, Illinois, website notes the oil exploration boom that began in 1939: www. whitecounty-il.gov/history. The American Guide Series' guidebook to Illinois notes the oilfield discoveries that occurred in the region beginning in 1936: Federal Writers' Project for the State of Illinois, *Illinois: A Descriptive and Historical Guide,* 2nd ed., edited by Harold L. Hitchens (Chicago: A. C. McClurg, 1947), 427, 614–16.

Owen's vocation to recover New Harmony was acknowledged as early as 1951 in George Fuermann's book *Houston: Land of the Big Rich* (Garden City, N.Y.: Doubleday, 1951), 47: "Jane Owen's basic passion is the re-creation of Robert Owen's nineteenth-century utopiate, the New Harmony, Indiana, socialist community. She considers New Harmony her 'home,' and she buys up one house after another just as the owners are about to let them become filling stations or other unblessings of civilization. Every home is then restored, but to call it a one-woman Williamsburg effort at a small scale is inaccurate and unfair to Jane Owen. Hers is a magnificent and penny-pinching effort without anything like the great Rockefeller capital that restored Williamsburg. She does much of the restoration work herself, and some of the New Harmony villagers do not even know who she is. Her aim is to save New Harmony as an unmarred example of America's disappearing village life."

37. Owen, conversation with author, February 26, 2009.

38. "Gifts," *Bulletin of the Museum of Fine Arts* 12 (Summer–Fall 1950), unpaginated. On the Robert Lee Blaffer Memorial Wing of the museum, which John H. Blaffer and his wife, Camilla, built in 1952–53, see *The Museum of Fine Arts, Houston: An Architectural History, 1924–1953,* edited by Celeste Marie Adams, *Bulletin of the Museum of Fine Arts, Houston* 15, no. 1–2 (1991): 61–62. On Owen's patronage of Carroll Harris Simms, see John Biggers and Carroll Simms with John Edward Weems, *Black Art in Houston: The Texas Southern University Experience: Presenting the Art of Biggers, Simms, and the Students* (College Station: Texas A&M University Press, 1978), 80. Owen donated a cast of Lipchitz's bronze bust of Gertrude Stein to Rice University in 1953 in memory of her father. Lipchitz and Arnason, *My Life in Sculpture*, 63; Jane Owen, conversation with author, September 29, 2009; and Nancy Mangum McCaslin, conversation with author, September 30, 2009.

39. Cynthia Rowan Taylor, conversation with author, February 26, 2009.

40. Owen, interview with Sabatino and McGuire, 2009. See also Welch, *Philip Johnson and Texas,* 68–69; and Michelangelo Sabatino, "Cracking the Egg: The Transformation of the University of St. Thomas Campus," in *Cite 73: The Architecture and Design Review of Houston* 73 (Winter 2008): 10–17.

41. Publication in the 1980s and 1990s of unbuilt and preliminary designs that Johnson made from the late 1940s on indicates how long he experimented with formally assertive designs before he began to build any of them around 1960.

42. Planar deformation is a compositional theme that Johnson explored over and over from 1960 until he ceased to design around 2000. One of the titles considered for the Museum of Modern Art's

Deconstructivist Architecture exhibition of 1988, for which Johnson was curator, was "Violated Perfection." Although Johnson did not originate the title, and in fact rejected it, the phrase precisely captures the perverse fascination with geometric distortion that propelled him to continually return to the theme of planar deformation. See Franz Schulze, *Philip Johnson: Life and Work* (New York: Alfred A. Knopf, 1994), 393–95; and Peter Eisenman, "Philip Johnson: Romanticism and Disintegration," in *Philip Johnson: The Constancy of Change*, 226–27.

43. Wilhelm and Marion Pauck, *Paul Tillich: His Life and Thought* (New York: Harper & Row, 1978), 276–78; Alexander Leitch, *A Princeton Companion* (1978) at etcweb.princeton.edu. On George MacLeod, see iona.org.uk/OurHistory.

44. See Welch, *Philip Johnson and Texas*, 71, as well as Cammie McAtee's chapter in this book.

45. Gerald M. Allen, "New Harmony Inn: A Triumph of Modesty," *Architectural Record* 159, no. 4 (1976): 101–6.

46. *Richard Meier Architect, 1964/1984,* introduction by Joseph Rykwert (New York: Rizzoli International, 1984), 190–215; Ada Louise Huxtable, "A Radical New Addition for Mid-America," *New York Times,* September 30, 1979; Suzanne Stephens, "Emblematic Edifice: The Atheneum, New Harmony, Indiana," *Progressive Architecture* 61, no. 2 (1980): 67–75; Stanley Abercrombie, "A Vision Continued: Richard Meier's Atheneum, New Harmony, Indiana," *AIA Journal* 69, no. 6 (1980): 126–37; and Kenneth Frampton, "Meier's Atheneum" and Arthur A. Cohen, "Richard Meier, An American Architect," *GA Document 1* (Summer 1980): 30–33, 34–35. In the case of Richard Meier, it was the initial commission for the Atheneum from the New Harmony Commission that led Jane Owen and the Robert Lee Blaffer Trust to then commission Meier to design the Sarah Campbell Blaffer Pottery Shed (1975–78). See *Richard Meier Architect,* 216–19; and Ben Nicholson's chapter on the Atheneum in this book.

47. Such communities as Santa Fe, New Mexico, and Aspen, Colorado, made small size and geographic marginality part of their appeal.

48. Barbara Grizzuti Harrison describes the conflicted reaction of New Harmony's residents to the activities associated with Owen and Historic New Harmony in "Life's Simple Treasures," 54–55. This issue also surfaces in accounts of Columbus.

49. Peter Blake and Philip C. Johnson, "Architectural Freedom and Order: An Answer to Robert W. Kennedy," *Magazine of Art* 41, no. 6 (1948): 228; Kaufmann, *Rise and Fall of Anglo-America,* 173.

50. Although conservative resistance to liberalism in the 1950s was consistently hostile to some modern forms of cultural expression—art, literature, and music, especially during the years that U.S. Senator Joseph McCarthy led an anticommunist crusade, 1950–54—this was much less the case with architecture. Conservative resistance to modern architecture rarely took form as a call to return to the historical eclectic practices dominant before the Second World War. The most notorious attempt to brand modern architecture as subversive (a code word for communist) was Elizabeth T. Gordon's polemic "The Threat to the Next America," *House Beautiful,* April 1953, 126–31, which attacked Mies van der Rohe's Farnsworth House as un-American. Gordon did not advocate a return to tradition, however, but to the competing "American" modernism of Frank Lloyd Wright, as was made clear in a follow-up article by Joseph A. Barry, "Report on the American Battle between Good and Bad Modern Houses," *House Beautiful,* May 1953, 172–73. For an insightful analysis of this episode, see Monica Michelle Penick, "The Pace Setter Houses: Livable Modern in Postwar America" (PhD diss., University of Texas at Austin, 2007). I am grateful to Nancy Mangum McCaslin for calling to my attention the paper by Sarah Wilson on the cultural politics of Father Couturier's commissions in postwar France: "Catholics, Communists, and *Art Sacré*," at www.courtauld.ac.uk/people/wilson-sarah/Catholicscommunists .pdf. Kaufmann observes of the New York modern vanguard that "this tradition was also yoked to a definite sense of intellectual elitism" (*Rise and Fall of Anglo-America,* 158).

51. Populist resentment, rather than supporting some form of return to conservative tradition, is more often invested in a refusal to countenance the authority of cultural arbiters who are judged to be elitist. The historian Daniel Walker Howe examines the origins of American populism as a political force in his book *What Hath God Wrought: The Transformation of America, 1815–1848* (New York: Oxford University Press, 2007). Howe addresses Robert Owen's experiment in New Harmony on pp. 293–95.

52. G. B. Lockwood, "New Harmony Communities," *Nation*, April 2, 1903, 278; and George B. Lockwood, with Charles A. Prosser, *The New Harmony Movement* (New York: Appleton, 1905).

53. "Life Visits New Harmony: A Little Indiana Town on the Wabash Was Setting for Two Strange Utopias More Than a Century Ago," *Life*, September 17, 1945, 133–64. The *Life* article was prompted by publication of Marguerite Young's novel *Angel in the Forest: A Fairy Tale of Two Utopias* (New York: Reynal and Hitchcock, 1945). "Out of Harmony," *Fortune*, July 1954, 167. See also Anne West, "The Place Called New Harmony," *American Mercury* 81, no. 12 (1955): 57–61. West's article is the first to mention K. D. Owen and his family (p. 61).

54. Young's subtitle of 1945, *A Fairy Tale of Two Utopias*; William E. Beauchamp's "Hoosier Utopia of Old a Tourist Utopia Now," *New York Times*, September 8, 1963; John Bayliss's "Utopia Revisited: A Sliver of the New World Retains Its Old World Identity," *Saturday Evening Post*, April 1975, 100–101; and Nancy Kriplen's "Recalling Past Utopias in an Indiana Town," *New York Times*, April 17, 1994, identify New Harmony with the term *utopia*.

55. Will Miller, "Eero and Irwin," 66–67. See also "Columbus Plan," *Newsweek*, February 9, 1953, 74–75; "Businessmen Rebuild an Indiana Town," *Fortune*, July 1954, 92–95; "Columbus, Indiana: A Study in Small-Town Progress," *Architectural Forum* 103, no. 4 (1955): 158–65; John Morris Dixon, "Columbus, Indiana," *Architectural Forum* 123, no. 6 (1965): 40–49; Marilyn Wellemeyer, "Inspired Renaissance in Indiana," *Life*, November 17, 1967, 74–84; "Showpiece on the Prairie," *Time*, December 5, 1977, 68–69; and Robert Campbell, "Modernism Meets Main Street," *Preservation* 50 (September–October 1998): 38–45.

56. Steven V. Roberts, "Is It Too Late for a Man of Honesty, High Purpose, and Intelligence to be Elected President of the United States in 1968?," *Esquire*, October 1967, 89–93.

57. The precursor to Miller's program of architectural intervention in Columbus was an effort championed by Columbus's leading industrialists to ensure that the town was equipped with such infrastructural elements as new school buildings in order to be able to attract white-collar employees. See "Columbus Plan," *Newsweek*, February 9, 1953, 74–75; and "Businessmen Rebuild an Indiana Town," *Fortune*, July 1954, 92–95. The *Newsweek* article does not mention Irwin Miller.

58. Miller's son Will Miller explained the motivation for Dan Kiley's virtuoso off-set planes of arborvitae hedging the street fronts of the Miller property as providing visual privacy without seeming, in a small midwestern town, to have installed a continuous hedge, much less a wall, that would prevent town residents from keeping an eye on the Miller homestead. Anne West's article on New Harmony called attention to the "seven-foot brick wall" K. D. Owen constructed around the Richard Owen House and the Owen Laboratory; see "The Place Called New Harmony," *American Mercury* 81, no. 12 (1955): 61.

59. Anne Gruner-Schlumberger, *The Schlumberger Adventure* (New York: Arco, 1982); and Ken Auletta, *The Art of Corporate Success: The Story of Schlumberger* (New York: G. P. Putnam's Sons, 1984), 30, 46, 50. See also *Art and Activism: Projects of John and Dominique de Menil*, edited by Josef Helfenstein and Laureen Schipsi (Houston: Menil Collection, 2010).

60. On the Menil House, see Welch, *Philip Johnson and Texas*, 36–50; Kathleen Bland, "Glass House Builder Expands on Ideas," *Houston Post*, January 11, 1950; "Art Collection and Home of the John de Menils in Houston's River Oaks," *Interiors* 128, no. 4 (1963): 84–91; James Johnson Sweeney, "Collectors'

Home," *Vogue*, April 1, 1966, 184–93; John Davidson, "Dominique de Menil," *House and Garden*, March 1983, 10–12; Rosamond Bernier, "A Gift of Vision," *House and Garden*, July 1987, 120–29; Schulze, *Philip Johnson*, 202–3; Martin Filler, "The Real Menil," *Magazine Antiques*, September 2008, 78–85.

61. Smart, "Sacred Modern," 89–90; Tomkins, "Benefactor," 56–58.

62. John de Menil's corporate career has not been systematically analyzed; his progressiveness can be inferred from such sources as Stanley H. Brown, "It's 'Slumber-Jay' and It's a Money Gusher," *Fortune*, September 1973, 198–201; Gruner-Schlumberger, *Schlumberger Adventure*, 119–20, 123–24; and Auletta, *Art of Corporate Success*. On the Menils' opposition to segregation, see Jonathan Marshall, "The A.F.A. Convention," *Arts* 31 (May 1957): 10–11.

63. An early example of the media attention John de Menil could command is the report by Saarinen's soon-to-be-wife, Aline B. Louchheim, "Diverse Museums: Institutions of Our Southwest Present a Wide Variety of Aims and Outlooks," *New York Times*, December 27, 1953.

64. Susan J. Barnes, *The Rothko Chapel: An Act of Faith* (Houston: Rothko Chapel, 1989); Sheldon Nodelman, *The Rothko Chapel Paintings: Origins, Structure, Meanings* (Austin: University of Texas Press, 1997), 72–75; Dominique de Menil, "The Rothko Chapel," *Art Journal* 30, issue 3 (1971): 249–51.

65. Germano Celant, *Cattedrale d'Arte: Dan Flavin per Santa Maria in Chiesa Rossa* (Milan: Fondazione Prada, 1998). See also Kim Shkapich and Susan de Menil, eds., *Sanctuary: The Spirit In/Of Architecture* (Houston: Byzantine Fresco Foundation, 2004).

66. Johnson resigned the commission for the Rothko Chapel because he and Rothko could not agree on the design of the building's skylight. The Houston architects Howard Barnstone and Eugene Aubry substantially retained Johnson's design, which they adapted to Rothko's directives. See de Menil, "Rothko Chapel"; and Barnes, *Rothko Chapel*, 81–86.

67. Reyner Banham, "In the Neighborhood of Art," *Art in America* 75, no. 6 (1987): 124–29. As Ben Nicholson observes, people do come to Houston specifically to visit the Rothko Chapel and the Menil Collection.

When interpreted in feminist terms, it is striking how both Owen and Dominique de Menil respected the existing settings in which they undertook new construction, relied on visitors' own sense of discovery rather than seeking to pre-program experiences, displayed a lack of interest in master planning and total design, and relied on landscape as the spatial and experiential binding element in their domains. As Michelangelo Sabatino notes, they even shared an affinity for color: Owen's distinctive shade of gray-green emphasizes the green, while Menil's emphasizes the gray. Both sought to achieve what was most conspicuously missing from much mid-twentieth-century modern planning (as can be seen in Columbus, Ind.): a sense of wholeness that encompasses the new and old, the ordinary and the extraordinary. One thing that differentiated Menil from Owen is that the former did believe in reputations.

68. This theme is reiterated in articles published in the 1970s and 1980s: Beverly Russell, "America Discovers Columbus," *House and Garden*, July 1976, 80–83; J. Bruce Baumann, "A Most Uncommon Town: Columbus," *National Geographic*, September 1978, 382–97; Edna Thayer, "Columbus: The Gem of Architecture," *Horizon: A Magazine of the Arts* 25, no. 3 (1982): 24–31.

69. Lars Lerup, *After the City* (Cambridge, Mass.: MIT Press, 2000), 80; Richard Ingersoll, *Sprawltown: Looking for the City on Its Edges* (New York: Princeton Architectural Press, 2006), 55–56; and Banham, "In the Neighborhood of Art," 124.

70. Pilar Viladas, "They Did It Their Way," *New York Times Magazine*, October 10, 1999, 85–94; Jenkins and Mohney, *Houses of Philip Johnson*, 56–57; Richard Payne, *The Architecture of Philip Johnson*, foreword by Philip Johnson, essay by Hillary Lewis (Boston: Bulfinch, 2002), 46–47; William Middleton, "A House That Rattled Texas Windows," *New York Times*, June 3, 2004; and David Hay, "De Menil Reborn," *Metropolis*, August–September 2004, 98–101.

71. "A Contemporary Palladian Villa," *Architectural Forum* 109, no. 3 (1958): 126–31; "H&G's Hallmark House No. 3: A New Concept of Beauty," *House and Garden,* February 1959, 58–77; and Gary R. Hilderbrand, *The Miller Garden: Icon of Modernism* (Washington, D.C.: Spacemaker, 1999).

72. Wayne Andrews in his book, *American Gothic: Its Origins, Its Trials, Its Triumphs* (New York: Random House, 1975), 74–75, attributes the design of the Owen Laboratory to the New York architect James Renwick Jr. Nancy Mangum McCaslin informs me that research by Historic New Harmony and the architectural historian at the Smithsonian have never been able to substantiate this attribution. Renwick collaborated with David Dale Owen on the design of the Smithsonian Institution's building in Washington, D.C. (1846–55). On the involvement of David Dale Owen and his brother, U.S. Representative Robert Dale Owen, on the formation of the Smithsonian Institution and the design and construction of its building, see Kenneth Hafertepe, *America's Castle: The Evolution of the Smithsonian Building and Its Institution, 1840–1878* (Washington, D.C.: Smithsonian Institution Press, 1984). John F. Sears states that David Dale Owen designed the Owen Laboratory; see Sears, "'How the Devil It Got There': The Politics of Form and Function in the Smithsonian 'Castle,'" in *Public Space and the Ideology of Place in American Culture,* edited by Miles Orvell and Jeffrey L. Meikle (Amsterdam: Editions Rodopi, 2009), 60n39.

73. "Paepcke, Walter," *Who's Who in America* 31 (1960–61): 2214.

74. Allen, *Romance of Commerce and Culture,* 206–12, 261–65, 269–74.

75. Ibid., 132–33, 137.

76. Allen, *Romance of Commerce and Culture,* 128; "Bayer, Herbert," *Who's Who in America* 40 (1978): 1:206; Herbert Bayer, *Herbert Bayer: Painter, Designer, Architect* (New York: Reinhold, 1967), 111–37; and Gwen Finkel Chanzit, *Herbert Bayer and Modernist Design in America* (Ann Arbor: UMI Research Press, 1987), 151–73.

77. Allen, *Romance of Commerce and Culture,* 279–81.

78. Christine Gorby, "Spirit under the Sky," *Landscape Architecture* 94 (June 2004): 36–44.

79. Ibid., 44.

80. Ibid., 36.

81. Ibid., 43. See also Owen, interview with Sabatino and McGuire, 2009.

82. Gorby, "Spirit under the Sky," 41. The Bloedel Reserve on Bainbridge Island, Washington, represents another instance where a patron, Prentice Bloedel of Seattle, worked with such distinguished landscape architects as Thomas D. Church and Richard Haag yet chose to modify their designs to suit his objectives for his 150-acre garden. See William B. Saunders, ed., *Richard Haag: Bloedel Reserve and Gas Works Park* (New York: Princeton Architectural Press and Harvard Graduate School of Design, 1998).

83. José María Herrera, "Vision of a Utopian Texas: Robert Owen's Colonization Scheme," *Southwestern Historical Quarterly* 116, no. 4 (2013): 342–56.

84. Joe B. Frantz, *Gail Borden: Dairyman to a Nation* (Norman: University of Oklahoma Press, 1951); Keith Guthrie, "Fulton, George Ware," *New Handbook of Texas,* vol. 3 (Austin: Texas State Historical Association, 1996), 28–29.

85. Marilyn McAdams Sibley, *George W. Brackenridge: Maverick Philanthropist* (Austin: University of Texas Press, 1973).

86. Mark Seal et al., *Hines: A Legacy of Quality in the Built Environment,* introduction by Paul Goldberger (Bainbridge Island, Wash.: Fenwick, 2007); and Paul Goldberger, "High Design at a Profit," *New York Times Magazine,* November 14, 1976, 76–79.

87. Donald Judd, *Donald Judd: Architecture,* ed. Peter Noever, essays by Rudi Fuchs, Brigitte Huck, and Donald Judd (Ostfildern-Riut: Hatje Canz, 2003); Urs Peter Flückinger, *Donald Judd: Architecture in Marfa, Texas,* translated by U. Spengler (Basel: Birkhäuser Basel, 2007); and Thomas Köhler, *Donald Judd: Architekturen und Projekte, 1968–1994* (Hamburg: Kovacs, 2005).

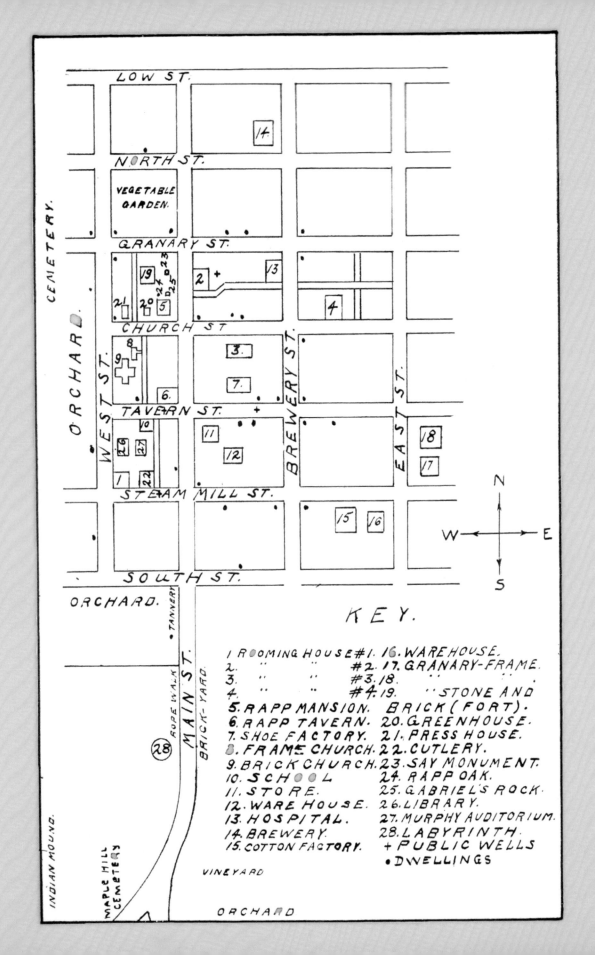

LOW ST.

NORTH ST.

14

VEGETABLE GARDEN.

GRANARY ST.

19 *27* *23* *D25* *2* + *13*

21 *20* *5* *4*

CHURCH ST.

8 *3*
9
6 *7*

TAVERN ST.

10 *11*
16
27 *12*
1 *22* *18*
17

STEAM MILL ST.

15 *16*

SOUTH ST.

ORCHARD.

TANNERY

MAIN ST.

BRICK-YARD.

ROPE WALK

(28)

INDIAN MOUND.

MAPLE HILL CEMETERY

VINEYARD

ORCHARD

CEMETERY.

ORCHARD.

WEST ST.

BREWERY ST.

EAST ST.

N
W — E
S

KEY.

1 ROOMING HOUSE #1. 16. WAREHOUSE.
2.   "   "   #2. 17. GRANARY-FRAME.
3.   "   "   #3. 18.   "   "
4.   "   "   #4. 19.   " STONE AND
5. RAPP MANSION.   BRICK (FORT).
6. RAPP TAVERN. 20. GREENHOUSE.
7. SHOE FACTORY. 21. PRESS HOUSE.
8. FRAME CHURCH. 22. CUTLERY.
9. BRICK CHURCH. 23. SAY MONUMENT.
10. SCHOOL   24. RAPP OAK.
11. STORE.   25. GABRIEL'S ROCK.
12. WARE HOUSE.   26. LIBRARY.
13. HOSPITAL.   27. MURPHY AUDITORIUM.
14. BREWERY.   28. LABYRINTH.
15. COTTON FACTORY. + PUBLIC WELLS
                   • DWELLINGS

3

New Harmony as an Evolving Commemorative Environment

CHRISTINE GORBY

NEW HARMONY is a rich commemorative environment where the evolution of American historic preservation practices during the twentieth century can be analyzed. During this period many individuals and organizations attempted to relate New Harmony's utopian histories to modern conditions. In the early twentieth century, amateur dramatists, social activists, and historians developed, revised, or invented interpretations of the past to activate the community through historical pageants, guidebooks, novels, maps, and other place-based forms of engagement. In the second half of the century, two views of the past were advanced. The first, associated with historic preservation professionals, was a "revised past," informed by residents of New Harmony but ultimately directed to visitors. Grounded in historical research and mapping, it focused on New Harmony's early nineteenth-century history and placed interpretive weight on the Maclurean scientific era that followed the two utopian experiments for which New Harmony is best known. The second view involved an "invented past" associated with Jane Blaffer Owen, who sought to transform New Harmony into a spiritual community for pilgrims. New Harmony represents a distinct case in historical preservation in the United States because it relies on an understanding of both its revised and invented pasts to make itself known.[1]

Lockwood and The New Harmony Movement *(1905)*

George B. Lockwood's book *The New Harmony Movement,* published in 1905, was the first modern history of the Harmonist and Owen utopias.[2] Lockwood not only revived the past; he reframed New Harmony's present and set the stage for celebration of the town's centennial in 1914. The finale to New Harmony's centennial

Figure 3.1. This frontispiece image from a commemorative guidebook marking the 1914 New Harmony centennial authored by Mrs. N. C. Fretageot and William V. Mangrum was the first effort to describe visually the town's historic area. From the Collections of Historic New Harmony / University of Southern Indiana.

observance, the Children's Historical Pageant, marked the first attempt to revise understanding of the town's utopian pasts to nurture place-based, historical consciousness within the community.[3]

Children's Historical Pageant (1914)

The historical pageant was a modern dramatic genre developed by Louis Napoleon Parker in 1905 in the English industrial town of Sherborne, Dorset. When Lotta Alma Clark adopted the "Parker-type" pageant in the United States in 1908, she carried it out as a "series of historical episodes" organized by a community through "cooperation and self-expression," as Parker envisioned it.[4] By 1910 the historical pageant genre had evolved into a distinctly American dramatic form.[5]

Charity Dye, who wrote the New Harmony Children's Historical Pageant, believed that pageantry could become a springboard for community cooperation, civic action, and material progress. Her success in achieving these aims through the New Harmony pageant, though, was limited. Yet pageants continued to be created and performed in New Harmony for almost fifty years after the peak of the U.S. pageantry movement in 1917.

Two other New Harmony residents, Nora Chadwick Fretageot, librarian of the Working Men's Institute, and W. V. Mangrum, superintendent of public schools, wrote the first "official" guidebook to New Harmony for the 1914 centennial.[6] It was subsequently republished in 1923 and 1934.[7] The guidebook described extant and lost historical buildings in New Harmony along with important individuals and material culture from the Harmonist, Owen, post-Owen, and modern periods. The frontispiece map subtly relayed the authors' views on the relative importance of certain buildings and places. This was the first image of New Harmony to suggest a hierarchy of historical buildings and sites through the simple expedient of a graphic numbering system. The map graphically imposed a boundary around the "historic" part of town, a modest, six-block realm, much smaller in area than the original and still-intact Harmonist town plan. The map also highlighted a much richer diversity of historic buildings, both extant and lost, than did the text of the guidebook. These helped give a broader picture of the Harmonist's industrial culture. Examples included the Brewery, Cutlery, Cotton Factory, and Shoe Factory. None of these industrial sites was treated in detail in the guidebook, suggesting they had less value to their interpreters than other buildings, sites, individuals, and artifacts. When the 1914 Centennial guidebook was supplanted by *Indiana: A Guide to the Hoosier State* in 1941, even fewer historic structures were included on the tourist map in the state guide.[8] One value of the 1914 Centennial guidebook map was that for the first time the historic built environment was visualized at a larger scale. It was also the first time a map was oriented to a new tourist constituency. Given this expansive

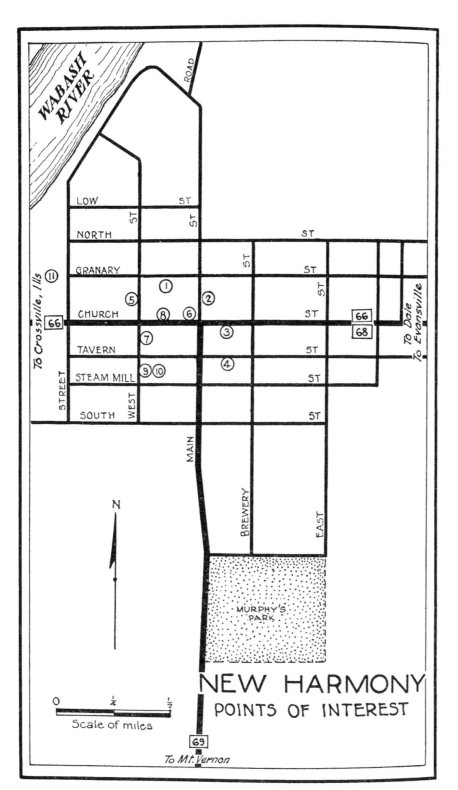

Figure 3.2. New Harmony Points of Interest: map prepared for the Writer's Program–Indiana, 1941. 1 = Rappite Fort; 2 = Community House No. 2; 3 = Tavern; 4 = Schnee House; 5 = Old Fauntleroy Home; 6 = Rapp–Maclure Home; 7 = Rose Door; 8 = David Dale Owen Laboratory; 9 = Workingmen's Institute, Library, and Museum; 10 = Murphy Auditorium; 11 = Rappite Cemetery. Courtesy of Indiana State University, Special Collections, Indiana Collection.

view, the 1914 guidebook map could be seen as a precursor to later, larger, organized efforts to historically preserve New Harmony. Unlike the historical pageant directors, the guidebook map authors did not fully exploit the map's potential to institute modern spatial practices by which to experience the historic town. They were far more cautious. For example, they failed to record automobile historic tour routes, even though three such tours were held during the eight-day Centennial festivities. Although this makes the map appear to be more of a "factual" accounting of the historic built environment during its two best-known utopian periods, certain new spatial orders concerning what was historic and what was not were first imposed through their spatial envisioning of a historic district.

In the Children's Historical Pageant script of 1914, Dye attempted to understand the past in relation to the present and future. She focused on the "active" teaching of New Harmony history through art, music, nature, and place, framing "freedom" as the principle on which both the Harmonist Society and the United States were founded.[9] With respect to the Owen community, Dye linked "freedom" to women's rights, particularly through the Owenite social reformer Frances Wright, to whom Dye accorded an emphasis equal to Robert Owen.[10] Dye's implicit call to redress women's history was taken up by New Harmony's Minerva Society Pageant of 1925, when the Fauntleroy House at 411 West Street was dedicated as a shrine by the Indiana Federation of Clubs to commemorate the founding there of one of the first women's clubs in the United States in 1859.

The place where the historical pageant was performed was critical for embedding this revised historical awareness in the collective consciousness of New Harmony residents. Dye called the pageant setting "an organic part of the performance."[11] More than nine hundred people watched the pageant on a large green space under trees in what residents called the "plaza."[12] The "plaza" was framed to the north and south by two important educational buildings, the Working Men's Institute and the school. The Harmonist Church formerly occupied the school site. Pageant viewers looked to the north where the pageant stage was constructed, with the school facade as a backdrop. Looking west from the plaza was a view of an old Harmonist orchard.

The historical commemoration of New Harmony's past also involved the preservation of buildings. In 1911 Mary Emily Fauntleroy purchased the house of her great-uncle and aunt, Robert Henry Fauntleroy and Jane Dale Owen (daughter of Robert Owen), at 411 West Street, as a filial act of preservation. Fauntleroy continued to live in the house even after she sold it to the Federation of Clubs, serving as "hostess" to tourists until the house museum was temporarily closed during World War II. Fauntleroy also purchased Community House No. 2 at 410 Main Street in 1926 as a deliberate act of preservation.[13] She maintained Community House No. 2 until she sold it to the State of Indiana in November 1940 as part of the New

Harmony Memorial.[14] Easily overlooked but critical to preservation activity were Fauntleroy's efforts to tie the tangible historical material culture of No. 2 with existing civic culture. She did this by offering local organizations second-floor rooms to use as meeting space. Women's clubs engaged in literary, historical, and genealogy activities. The Boy Scouts and a local men's fraternal organization were each given rooms on the same level.

The conceptual value of "preserving" New Harmony was transmitted to a local constituency by opening Community House No. 2 to social and civic functions, especially the "living" women's clubs. Fauntleroy's fostering of historical and civic consciousness, as Helen Elliot later recalled, "was instrumental in stirring up interest in a period when New Harmony was in lethargy about its past and nothing much was being done."[15] It is significant that when Fretageot in the 1934 edition of her *Historic New Harmony Official Guide* gave this building the name "Community House No. 2," she identified both its historical dormitory function and, subliminally, its new civic use.[16] Fauntleroy's acquisitions were the first deliberate acts of historical building preservation in New Harmony.

Fauntleroy's preservation of the Fauntleroy House went against national trends.[17] Unlike most U.S. efforts of this period, where patriotism fueled the preservation of historic buildings, particularly those associated with military heroes, the purchase and protection of the Fauntleroy House recognized women's history and women's organized efforts of self-improvement and education.[18]

Indiana State New Harmony Memorial Commission (1937–55)

The New Harmony Memorial Commission was created by a joint resolution of the Indiana General Assembly (legislature) in 1937 and charged with surveying, purchasing, and restoring historically important properties to create a permanent New Harmony memorial.[19] The commission was also given authority to carry out historical educational programs.

Three factors led to the state government's involvement in the preservation of New Harmony. The first was the expanded role of the State of Indiana Department of Conservation. By 1937 its responsibilities included not only natural site protection but also the preservation of historically significant properties. A second factor, encouraged by a series of Indiana state history conferences held between 1919 and 1921, was the emergence of historic preservation as a research-based enterprise. The third factor was the increased political activity of women's clubs, which led to the appointment of women to state-level commissions focused on historic preservation.

On December 26, 1938, the New Harmony Memorial Commission issued its first report, recommending the purchase of eleven privately owned buildings and the labyrinth ground, with future acquisitions to follow.[20] A group of New Harmony businessmen valued these properties at $57,400. Based on these findings, the commission requested $200,000 from the legislature to complete the memorial.[21] The commission had not yet obtained cost estimates for building restorations and reconstruction of the labyrinth, nor had it established a budget for educational programs. In 1939, when the commission was reauthorized and funded by the state legislature, it was guaranteed $36,000 per annum for four years, or $144,000 in total, to carry out the program.[22]

Three years later, by the time of the commission's last official report, published in May 1942, only three of the twelve properties identified for the memorial—Community Houses No. 2 and No. 3 (called the "Tavern") and the labyrinth site—had been purchased.[23] No restoration work on Community Houses No. 2 or No. 3 had been done, but the labyrinth reconstruction was completed. Options were still outstanding on two additional buildings: the Kilbinger House, an annex to Community House No. 2 at Main Street and Granary Street, and Community House No. 4 at 610 Church Street, popularly known as Thrall's Opera House for its subsequent use as a theater (in 1942 it was a truck garage). Ownership of the Harmonist Cemetery, on West Street between North and Church Streets, reverted to the state after legal ownership could not be determined and the state took the site in 1941 by eminent domain.[24] Three key properties were not yet optioned: the "Rappite Fort" Granary, the Rapp–Maclure Place (Corbin House and Say Tomb), and the Owen Laboratory Home."[25]

Between 1937 and 1939, when building acquisitions were stalled as the commission awaited legislative funding, commission members shifted their attention to other projects, the reconstruction of the Harmonist Labyrinth and the development of educational programs, including a historical pageant and historical reenactments. One member, Bertha Crosley Ball, donated five thousand dollars in 1938 to "restore the maze as the Rapps had it" and to build a replica of the "The Boat Load of Knowledge."[26] The boat reconstruction proved too expensive, but the labyrinth reconstruction was completed in 1941. It was built on property next to the original location because the commission could not reassemble the entire historic site.[27] Soon after, a second adjacent lot was purchased to solve the problems of car access and parking for a growing automobile tourism culture.[28] Hugh A. Sprague served as landscape architect for the project; he collaborated with H. J. Schnitzius of the State Highway Department. Architect Harry E. Boyle designed the inner structure of the labyrinth based on historical and archival research assembled by the commission.

During the late 1930s, when real estate acquisition stalled, educational programs flourished in New Harmony and statewide. The Indiana historian Ross F. Lockridge Sr. of Bloomington, a popular lecturer and writer, was the main organizer of these programs.[29] First elected chair of the commission in 1937 and later director in 1939, Lockridge was the only paid member of the commission.[30]

After becoming director, Lockridge moved to New Harmony to conduct research and work cooperatively with the regional school system and other institutions to develop the state's plans. Lockridge centered educational programming on place-based reenactments derived from pageantry. Embodied experiences were tied to specific historic locations: dancing in the Harmonist labyrinth, stargazing in the Harmonist Cemetery, and shell gathering along the Wabash River as Owenite scientists had done. In the commission's 1942 report, Lockridge described how these programs would "human[ize] historic consciousness" by providing "direct experience and expression."[31] He further envisioned them as annual, ritualized events, instilling ties between citizens, place, and past. Historic sites were treated as primary repositories of historical experience to be continually reinterpreted and acted on, allowing modernity and time, in effect, to evolve together. As performance, historical reenactment "remap[ped] the boundaries between production, reproduction, improvisation and imagination."[32]

The most important educational program promoted by the commission was "The Pageant of New Harmony," first staged in New Harmony in 1937, an epic poem written by Ross Lockridge Jr., son of the commission director.[33] Presented annually from 1937 until 1941 by the commission as a "pilgrimage" event, part of their Golden Raintree Festival, the Golden Raintree Association later restaged Lockridge's pageant in 1946, 1948, 1949, and intermittently, in a modified form, during the 1950s as part of the same festival.[34]

The setting of the first 1937 pageant in the Harmonist cemetery allowed the junior Lockridge to call out the Harmonists who had been buried there, in anonymity in accordance with their religious practice. He ended the pageant with an invocation to the Golden Rain Tree, a symbol of the Owen period (William Maclure reportedly sent the first seeds of this exotic Chinese tree to New Harmony). To Lockridge, the Golden Rain Tree was a symbol of Truth, further reinforcing the righteous evocation of the Owenites' social reforms.[35]

Lockridge Jr. framed Harmonist culture in terms of the vernacular. Regarding spatial environments, the vernacular could be mysterious and "bewitch[ing]" (Lockridge's characterization of the labyrinth), whereas in relation to the Harmonists, Lockridge repeatedly described them as "simple folk" and German "peasant folk."[36] In the pageant script he presented Rapp's idealized religious views as noble yet naive, but he also viewed Robert Owen's social ideals as progressive yet too ambitious and ahead of their time.[37] He incorporated place in the script most effectively through his use of the Fauntleroy House and its links with personalities and events of the post-Owen era, Robert Dale Owen, and the Minerva Society. Although built by the Harmonists, the Fauntleroy House was not portrayed as "vernacular" because of these later post–Owen era associations.[38]

Lockridge Jr. ended the pageant with an "airy fantasy" dance of "woodland creatures" to symbolize the "golden blooms" of the Golden Rain Tree and the "magic" "fantasy" of the Owenite era.[39] Newspaper reports emphasized the spectacle of the pageant with its two hundred volunteer performers and audience of between five and six thousand people. Journalists noted how the yellow-hued pollen of the Golden Rain trees gave New Harmony a glowing allure.[40]

Department of Conservation Preliminary General Plan *for the New Harmony Memorial (1942)*

Several months after the United States entered the Second World War in December 1941, Lockridge Sr. resigned as commission director but continued as a commission member after his administrative duties ended on June 30, 1942.[41] On March 5, 1942, just before Lockridge's departure, Hugh Barnhart, director of the Indiana Department of Conservation, on behalf of the New Harmony Memorial Commission, instructed a team of department staff members to develop the *Preliminary General Plan*.[42] The commission approved the plan one month after its submission on March 25, 1942.[43]

In the 1942 plan, the conservation department team recognized an interpretive incongruity. Because the historical material environment was almost entirely Harmonist in origin, the historical interpretation of the Owen period would be problematic, even though the Owenites' "cultural and scientific" contributions were deemed "more significant historically."[44] The interpretation of the Harmonists in the *General Plan* as nonpolitical, practical, and focused on the production of tangible goods was in sharp contrast to the 1914 historical pageant, which ascribed political and ideological meaning to their legacy.

Although the interpretive aim of the conservation department team was to balance the "true values" of the Harmonists and the Owenites, the department's proposal did not specify how this was to be achieved.[45] Ultimately, emphasis was placed on Harmonist material culture. The team proposed the creation of a twelve-block memorial district near New Harmony's town center. The plan revised the historical hierarchical focal point of the village away from the site of the demolished Harmonist Church to a new axis along Granary Street. A series of proposed new gardens and restored Harmonist houses were to link the blocks along Granary Street. These gardens were emblematic of the "Kingdom of Flowers" for which, the team asserted, the Harmonists were well known.[46] The proposed New Harmony gardens were more reminiscent of the Colonial Revival garden reconstructions at Colonial Williamsburg by the landscape architect Arthur A. Shurcliff than what the historical records indicated for New Harmony.[47]

The Harmonist Cemetery was planned as the western terminus of the Granary Street garden corridor. Wood frame houses around the cemetery were to be razed (except for the Fauntleroy House) and replaced by two rows of fruit trees. These

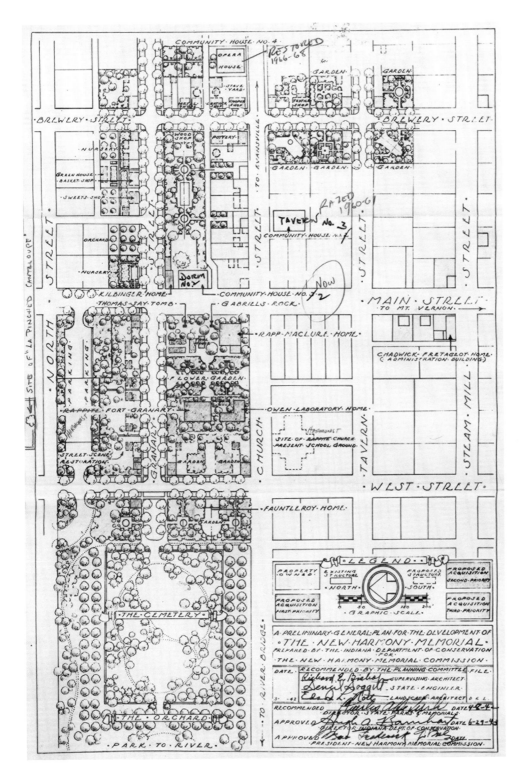

Figure 3.3. *A Preliminary General Plan for the Development of the New Harmony Memorial,* March 1942, not implemented. This plan redirected hierarchical focus away from the Harmonist Church toward Granary Street, where the New Harmony Memorial Commission planned a new tourist path. Open areas were to be dedicated to orchards, gardens, vineyards, barnyards, or craft-based industries. From the collection of the Indiana State Museum and Historic Sites.

plantings were in keeping with the 1824 Pickering and 1832 Weingartner maps, which showed "west orchards" in this location.[48] To the east, the Granary Street gardens ended at Brewery Street, where the Rapp–Maclure house, the centerpiece of the preservation plan, was located. To the south of Brewery Street, more gardens adjacent to restored Harmonist houses were proposed. Although Colonial Williamsburg

Figure 3.4. Inspired by seventeenth-century parterre gardens, Arthur A. Shurcliff planned this physic garden in Colonial Williamsburg in 1937 adjacent to the John Blair House (left). Indiana Department of Conservation personnel proposed similar-type parterres in the 1942 New Harmony restoration proposal. Photograph courtesy of Christine Gorby.

was not cited as a direct reference for the gardens, the "well known gardens of Virginia" were.[49] All the restored Harmonist houses were to contain cottage industries where goods could be made and sold. Weaving, pottery, cooperage, woodworking, metal work, leatherwork, and horticulture were among the uses proposed. These were Harmonist, not Owenite, activities. The Owenites centered their work on educational and other social reforms and scientific work. Their tangible output included a newspaper, numerous scientific publications, illustrations, and specimen collections, but these were not acknowledged. The plan to create a landmark district organized along a linear, pedestrians-only street lined with historic structures used for the sale of handicrafts, demonstrations, and food services was also unmistakably designed with Williamsburg in mind.

Before the Commission could carry out the *General Plan,* a controversial property transaction ensued that defeated the commission's efforts. After accepting the state's contract offer to buy the Rapp-Maclure House, Thomas Say Tomb, and Fort-Granary for thirty thousand dollars, the owners, the Corbin family heirs, rescinded their acceptance.[50] Instead they sold these properties to the Houston-based petroleum geologist Kenneth Dale Owen, a great-great-grandson of Robert Owen, for a higher price.[51] Because commission members considered these properties "the heart" of the memorial, they decided to offer their other state-owned properties for sale to Kenneth Owen in August 1949.[52] Chair Arcada Balz said, "The commission felt that it would take the holdings of both the state and of Mr. Owen to make a memorial worthy of the New Harmony movement."[53] According to newspaper accounts and commission minutes, Owen declined this offer.[54] In a letter summarized in commission meeting minutes, Kenneth Owen and his wife, Jane, stated that they intended to develop an "activities program," in the future, not a building restoration program.[55]

The New Harmony Memorial Commission was the first group to attempt building conservation and educational programming on a large scale in New Harmony. Although commission members lacked direct expertise in historic preservation and real estate acquisition, they engaged consultants who possessed this knowledge. The Department of Conservation was slow to give early support to the commission because it was in transition and lacked adequate understanding to tackle large-scale preservation programs until 1942. Lack of state funding and a strict state legislative budget process inhibited the commission's ability to purchase and restore historic properties quickly. The parceled series of payments they awarded, instead of a lump sum, caused property and restoration costs to escalate. Cultural changes outside the control of the commission, including impending war and labor wage rules, created material shortages and further cost increases.

Nonprofit Preservation Begins: National Trust for Historic Preservation Report (1954) and Dissolution of the New Harmony Memorial Commission (1955)

Beginning in the 1940s and lasting until her death in 2010, Kenneth Owen's wife, Jane Blaffer Owen, emerged as an impassioned preservationist and a patron of modern architecture, gardens, and art in New Harmony. Her projects were clustered along North Street, the northernmost street in the Harmonist community grid, although she accumulated property and historic structures throughout the town. Jane Owen's financial resources gave her the power to carry out significant spatial and interpretive changes to the historical landscape of New Harmony, which were as focused on the present and future as well as the past. Thomas J. Kane, a landscape architect, preservationist, and planner from Pleasantville, New York, who worked extensively in New Harmony, likened Jane Owen's arrival to a critical reawakening for the community, saying that she "gradually re-introduced the community to the world at large."[56]

Following the sale of the Rapp–Maclure House and adjacent properties to Kenneth Owen in 1948, the commission closed the state-owned New Harmony buildings during the Second World War. Subsequent to the war their work slowed significantly. To rejuvenate interest in the New Harmony preservation program, the Golden Raintree Association, a community group first formed to organize New Harmony's annual historical pageant, invited Helen Duprey Bullock, a staff historian and editor at the National Trust for Historic Preservation in Washington, D.C., to visit New Harmony in December 1953.[57] Educated as a social and cultural historian, Bullock was not a trained professional preservationist. Her three-day visit and subsequent six-month study resulted in the June 1954 *Report and Recommendations for New Harmony, Indiana.*[58]

In her report Bullock assessed the state of preservation activities in New Harmony and proposed a new revitalization model. She identified the cause of the memorial commission's ineffectiveness as a lack of preservation professionals among commission members and "unrealistic program[s]" that could not be carried out with the funds allotted, even at "prewar prices."[59] Bullock criticized the commission's purchase and reuse of Community House No. 3 as tourist lodging without first undertaking a "basic program of historical and archaeological study."[60] She also found the memorial commission negligent in their treatment of this building. She did emphasize the need for a hotel in town. Bullock was more positive in her assessment of the Kilbinger House rehabilitation carried out by Jane Owen in 1947. She praised it as an example of the caliber of professional restoration work that should occur in New Harmony.[61]

Bullock was critical of relations between the memorial commission and the public, particularly New Harmony residents. She described how the memorial commission had rebuffed a petition by an unnamed local group that wanted the memorial historic district expanded.[62] At Jane Owen's invitation, Bullock returned to New Harmony in early 1954 to discuss with community members how the preservation program might be restarted. It was during this visit that the public announcement of the dissolution of the state's New Harmony Memorial Commission occurred. Newspaper reports of its impending demise began surfacing as early as June 1953.[63] The commission was formally dissolved on May 6, 1955.[64]

In her report Bullock recommended the formation of a new multi-organization preservation group in New Harmony. Instead, Jane Owen created the private Robert Lee Blaffer Trust in March 1958.[65] Two of the initial five trustees were Bullock and Philip Johnson.[66] Jane Owen's work in New Harmony developed over time as her own spiritual experiences and sensibilities evolved. With her commissioning of the Roofless Church from Johnson in 1957, Jane Owen began to expand her conception of New Harmony as an ecumenical religious community that appealed to people of different faith backgrounds.

Harmonie Associates (1964) and National Historic Landmark (1965)

Following the Bullock report and the dissolution of the New Harmony Memorial Commission, preservation planning in New Harmony lapsed for almost fifteen years. In the early 1960s local groups and state officials began to rethink the past and future due to two impending events: the 150th anniversary of the founding of New Harmony in 1964 and of the State of Indiana in 1966. The loss of Community House No. 3, the Tavern, owned by the State of Indiana, to fire in 1960 did not have the galvanizing effect on the community that the earlier commemorative events had exercised.

New Harmony's approaching sesquicentennial did lead to the revival of the Golden Raintree Association, inactive since the 1950s, in 1964.[67] The association commissioned the Reverend John E. Schroeder to write a "historical drama," "Trumpet, Blow True."[68] Pastor Schroeder strongly emphasized religious themes and focused on Harmonist history, in contrast to previous pageants, which took a more secular view of New Harmony's history.

The historical drama was staged in an auditorium instead of the outdoor setting where previous pageants were performed. The most notable change, in comparison with earlier productions, was that everyday spaces were recast as commemorative locations. The auditorium, church community center, high school gym, 4-H Center, American Legion, baseball diamond, and outdoor "mall" were among the spaces employed.[69] The events staged at these sites had no relation to Harmonist or Owen period histories. Events involved eating, socializing, and entertainment.

Only the opening celebration took place at a historic site, the Harmonist Cemetery. Otherwise, historic places were experienced as part of organized tours led by guides "in authentic costumes."[70] Historic places were no longer inhabited or embodied but observed. Although history, historical traditions, and historical places were not abandoned, they were not the focus of the event. Heritage was at the service of tourism, a marked change from the 1914 centennial and subsequent events sponsored by the Golden Raintree Association and New Harmony Memorial Commission.

As a member of the Golden Raintree Association and as educational director of the Robert Lee Blaffer Trust, the Reverend Nevin Danner, an Evangelical minister and former newspaper editor, was in a unique position to shape Jane Owen's re-visioning of New Harmony as a spiritual pilgrimage destination and, later, to help guide local community group visions of New Harmony as an emerging heritage tourism site. Danner's staff position at the Blaffer Trust was the result of a proposal he submitted to the trustees in 1962 to rejuvenate educational programming in New Harmony.[71]

Danner likened his "enrichment" program idea to the modern "equivalent of 'the boatload of knowledge,'" which he saw as the "path to the future."[72] He proposed organizing conferences for "youth, parents, ministers, and teachers" to provide direct experiences that combined "religion, education, creative arts, and purposeful service."[73] Danner only realized a few such programs. His proposal was more important for reviving historical consciousness among segments of the regional community and devising programs that mainly reconnected to New Harmony's historic religious traditions. He simultaneously added new areas of emphasis including the creative arts and community service, educational traditions Danner believed were more relevant to the needs of modern communities. Although this represented a vision he shared with the Blaffer trustees and Jane Owen, Danner did not deliver the concrete results they expected, and his contract was not renewed.

After the Blaffer Trust discontinued Danner's program, he turned to the Golden Raintree Association to continue it. Danner suggested that the association create a new group from existing membership to maintain the contacts and commitments to programs already made.[74] The association's membership agreed and chartered Harmonie Associates in 1964. This organization supported New Harmony's historic legacy on an even larger scale by expanding programs and by working collaboratively with other organizations at a regional level.[75] One critical difference between Danner's Harmonie Associates and the Blaffer Trust was that he did not attempt to bring his theological interpretation of New Harmony's history to the collective, civic-heritage identity and mission of Harmonie Associates. Danner was cognizant of the need to emphasize different aspects of New Harmony's history that were specific to the identity of each organization.

The three-year plan Harmonie Associates developed was focused on three goals: to secure a state park adjacent to New Harmony for recreational tourism; to purchase and restore Thrall's Opera House (Community House No. 4) and to develop a professional summer theater program in it; and to establish a conference and educational center.[76]

The Harmonie State Recreation Area was opened in 1966 southwest of New Harmony. Governor Roger D. Branigin helped facilitate selection of New Harmony as a site for the state park. Branigin, who was governor from 1965 to 1969, championed preservation in New Harmony. His enthusiasm led to renewed state financial support for and the safeguarding of New Harmony's significant historical material culture.

At the request of Harmonie Associates, Branigin steered funding to New Harmony through the Department of Conservation in preparation for the 1966 State of Indiana sesquicentennial celebration.[77] With Branigin's encouragement, the Indiana Board of Conservation approved funds in November 1964 to purchase Community House No. 4, Thrall's Opera House.[78] In 1965 Branigin approved an additional one hundred thousand dollars to restore the exterior of the opera house.[79] Harry Roll McLaughlin, a preservation architect from Indianapolis, was responsible for the rehabilitation project. Although Harmonie Associates had to struggle to raise funds from private sources to restore the interior, the restored building was dedicated on November 19, 1969.

The third goal of Harmonie Associates, a conference center, a project Danner initiated while at the Blaffer Trust and completed while at Harmonie Associates, was partially realized. Danner initially viewed Community House No. 2 as a location for the conference center, but permission by state officials was given only for its periodic use.[80] This negatively affected his ability to plan a larger program.

In addition to state support, national recognition was bestowed on New Harmony on June 23, 1965, when the National Park Service designated the town a National Historic Landmark District, the highest-ranking historic designation bestowed by the U.S. government.[81] On August 21, 1965, Stewart L. Udall, then secretary of the interior, came to New Harmony to dedicate the commemorative plaque at Church and Main Streets, which attests to New Harmony's "exceptional value in commemorating and illustrating the history of the United States." This was followed in 1966 by listing the New Harmony Historic District in the National Register of Historic Places. New Harmony was recognized once more for its exceptional national significance as a historical site where two "religiously and secularly inspired utopian communities" settled.[82]

New Harmony Master Plan (1969)

In April 1969, following three and a half years of groundwork, the Cincinnati consulting firm of Scott Bagby and Associates and the New Harmony Plan Commission, a committee formed by the New Harmony Town Council, completed *New Harmony: A Master Plan for New Harmony, Indiana, and its Planning Area.*[83] Although the Town Council commissioned the plan to qualify for a federal grant to build a new sewage treatment plant, preservation issues were an important component of the document. These centered on what was needed to support a "tourist industry," which was identified as "the most realistic possibility for [economic] development."[84]

Tourist-related development was proposed in response to the impending construction of Interstate 64 north of New Harmony. The preservation of existing downtown commercial buildings was recommended, as was an increase in landscaped parking areas.[85] The concentration of historic buildings in the northwest quadrant of town was not addressed. Only Community House No. 4 and the Working Men's Institute were acknowledged as tourist assets.[86]

The value of the 1969 master plan was to identify, if not solve, issues related to historic preservation. Unlike the 1942 *General Plan,* this proposal considered regional issues. Yet it perpetuated the 1942 plan's myopic approach to New Harmony. Whereas the 1942 plan addressed only the proposed memorial district, the 1969 plan addressed only the downtown. Neither plan considered the impact of tourism on New Harmony. One critical accomplishment was completion of a sewage treatment plant in May 1972.[87] Without this improvement, such buildings as the New Harmony Inn, commissioned by Jane Owen and opened in 1974, could not have been constructed.[88]

New Harmony Memorial Commission (1973) and Historic New Harmony, Inc. (1974)

In 1973 the Indiana General Assembly authorized a second New Harmony Memorial Commission with the power to recommend legislation.[89] During the first meeting of this group on September 12, 1973, the commission chair, former governor Branigin, recommended legislative approval of a nonprofit foundation to raise funds to support preservation efforts in New Harmony and long-term development.[90] The work of funding, preserving, and interpreting New Harmony would be entrusted to this nonprofit organization, which was to be led by preservation professionals. Following commission and legislative approval of this recommendation, Historic New Harmony, Inc., a not-for-profit organization, was chartered in 1974 to carry out a comprehensive preservation program.[91] From 1974 to 1984, Ralph G. Schwarz, the organization's first president, with cooperation from many preservation consultants and constituencies, was responsible for carrying out the most comprehensive building and landscape preservation program in New Harmony's history.[92]

Entrusting preservation work in New Harmony to professionals was a trend that began with the 1942 general plan and was reinforced by Bullock's National Trust report recommendations of 1954. It was consistent with the rise of preservation professionals and university-based historic preservation programs in the United States during the 1970s. Schwarz had met Jane Owen in Washington, D.C., during the 1950s through Bullock. He first came to New Harmony in 1972 when, on Bullock's recommendation, Jane Owen invited him to become a member of the Blaffer Trust board.[93] Soon after, Jane Owen hired him as a private consultant "to plan and develop" the New Harmony Inn.[94] Schwarz had previously worked in economic development and historic preservation in Bethlehem, Pennsylvania; New York City; and Washington, D.C.

Critical to the success of Historic New Harmony was financial support from the Lilly Endowment, Inc. of Indianapolis, the largest charitable foundation in Indiana, which contributed most of the financial support for the preservation development program. The Lilly Endowment, Inc. initially contributed $1,011,900 in 1974 to Historic New Harmony. From 1975 to 1985, the endowment contributed to this same organization an additional $7,027,000. The endowment also gave $1,525,000 toward the construction of the New Harmony Atheneum, the Visitor's Center designed by Richard Meier. Of this amount, $25,000 was used for planning the building. This made the total contribution by the endowment to Historic New Harmony $9,563,900 between 1974 and 1985, including contributions to both the preservation program and the Atheneum.[95]

Comprehensive Plan (1974), Zoning Ordinance (1973), and Central Historic District Plan (1974)

During the 1970s, the interplay between two views of the past arose. One, associated with preservation professionals led by Schwarz and Historic New Harmony, was a "revised past" informed by local concerns but directed primarily to the development and maintenance of a tourist economy. Interpretation was grounded in rational planning, historical research, and mapping. The second interpretative paradigm was associated with Jane Owen, who attempted to transform New Harmony into an imagined spiritual community for pilgrims.

Landscape architect Thomas Kane led the planning process, which began with a regional planning session in 1972 in which townspeople, members of the New Harmony Town Council, and officials of various state agencies participated. Kane also carried out historical research and mapping and worked with various constituencies, demonstrating his practical, problem-solving approach. His historical research revealed his critical, reflective insight. New Harmony Town Council's president, Foster Tolliver, with whom Kane worked closely, also possessed a commonsense, action-oriented approach. Kane's detailed re-created and modern landscape designs imbued his historical interpretations with authority.

Typical of Kane's problem-solving methodology was his approach to zoning. Most of the historic structures owned by the state were in the northwest quadrant of New Harmony, where they were dispersed among properties still in private owner-ship, many of which were also historic. One zoning provision created a "One Family Historic Residential District" in this area to permit the relocation of historic struc-tures to original Harmonist foundations. New non-single-family residential uses for historic structures were also permitted within the district, including education, interpretation, "craftwork, sales, food service, accommodations and conference space" to support the tourist economy.[96] The Comprehensive Plan of New Harmony (1974) attempted to regulate and plan for change but at a regional scale and for con-stituencies that included heritage tourists and recreational tourists, as well as new permanent residents. Efforts were made to balance the anticipated effects of new development while maintaining the region's historic character and natural beauty. To address anticipated future population growth, a large suburban housing area was projected south of New Harmony, bounded to the east by the State Route 69 bypass, a road project approved in 1968 but not completed until 1999.[97] The 1,500-acre Har-monie State Recreation Area (now Harmonie State Park), established in 1966 south-west of New Harmony, acted as a scenic buffer along the Wabash River.

Not directly related to zoning but key to both regional and local planning were infrastructure improvements to support new construction related to tourism and local needs, almost all of which were completed. Between 1974 and 1977, the New Harmony Town Council invested more than one million dollars in tax revenue to improve electrical supply and road paving, which contributed to preservation goals.[98]

Community sentiment and historical interpretation converged on the preserva-tion of farmland surrounding the town. Zoning measures were enacted to protect the historical agricultural character of New Harmony and increase the tax base.[99]

With the Comprehensive Plan approved, Schwarz and Kane returned to the town scale to develop the Central Historic District Plan. The plan addressed thirty blocks of the town, close to the approximate twenty-two blocks visible in the 1824 Picker-ing map of New Harmony.[100] The Central Historic District Plan was larger than the 1824 Pickering map area because the Harmonist Cemetery and residential blocks south of the cemetery were also included. Increasing the size of the district were five town blocks along North Street owned by Jane Owen, which, in the Harmonist period, were lined with small houses.

Another element designed by Kane was new fencing. It was located throughout the historic residential and business districts. The board, paling, picket, and other

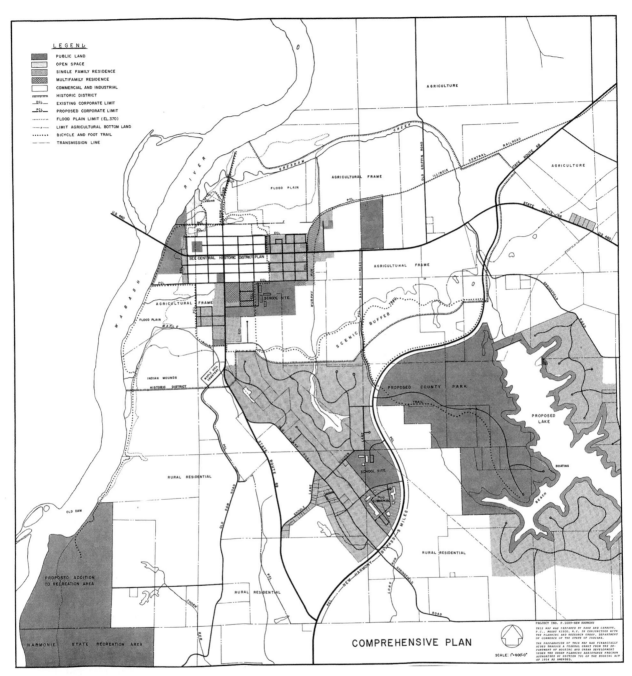

Figure 3.5. Comprehensive Plan of New Harmony, 1974, by Kane and Carruth, P.C., with the Department of Commerce and Planning Research Group for the New Harmony Plan Commission, resulted from a complex planning effort to project future growth while preserving surrounding farmlands from the Harmonist era. Courtesy of Special Collections Department / Iowa State University Library.

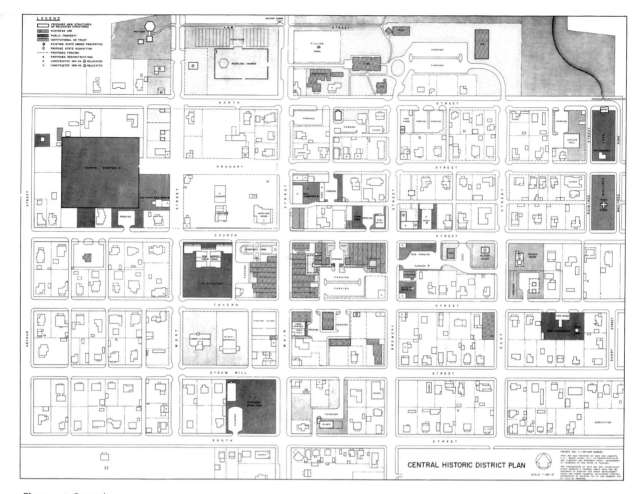

CENTRAL HISTORIC DISTRICT PLAN

SCALE 1" = 40'-0"

Figure 3.6. Central Historic District Plan, circa 1974, by Kane and Carruth, P.C., in conjunction with the Planning and Research Group and Department of Commerce of the State of Indiana. With input from multiple constituencies, key buildings, parks, and lots were identified for their intrinsic value within the town center. Courtesy of Special Collections Department / Iowa State University Library.

Figure 3.7. Kane and Carruth, P.C., designed nine historic and modern fence-types for Historic New Harmony. This paling fence made of bark-stripped cedar or locust was driven into the ground in accord with historic practice; it enclosed a group of log cabins to recall a frontier settlement. Photograph courtesy of Christine Gorby.

types of fencing delineated historical, institutional, and civic environments, and spatially integrated a diverse range of building types and styles. The fencing provides a subtle texture running through the town, knitting disparate elements together.

Interpreting Local History and International Preservation Standards in New Harmony

Schwarz relocated Harmonist structures from other parts of New Harmony to the Historic Residential District to strengthen its legibility. By October 1977, four of the twenty-one structures on the Historic New Harmony tour route had been relocated within New Harmony.[101] Some of these historic buildings were discovered through research and others remained on original foundations or were relocated to new locations once occupied by similar Harmonist buildings. When possible, comparable structures were placed in the same positions on lots as seen on historic maps. The process was simplified because Harmonist construction practices were standardized and the building forms were repetitive and regular. In addition to moving structures within the town, Historic New Harmony purchased, dismantled, relocated, and rebuilt three historic log structures from the region. Although the precedent for moving structures in the United States goes back to the early eighteenth century, the Second International Congress of Architects and Technicians of Historic Monuments, formally organized in 1965 as the International Council on Monuments and Sites (ICOMOS), challenged this practice in its 1964 Venice Charter.[102]

In the Venice Charter agreement, "setting" was declared to be an integral part of an "architectural work."[103] Moving a building from its historic setting was therefore unacceptable unless the structure would otherwise be lost, or where national or international opinion could defend such a position.[104] Many positions defined in the Venice Charter were assimilated to "American preservation thinking," according to the Reverend W. Brown Morton III, an architect, Anglican priest, and preservation and conservation specialist. One example is the first set of rehabilitation standards for historic preservation projects, co-written by Morton and Gary L. Hume for the U.S. Department of Interior and published in 1977.[105] Specific standards in the second edition (1979) in alignment with the Venice Charter affirmed the integrity of a historic building's site and proscribed the practice of moving historic structures unless they would otherwise face demolition.[106]

Jane Owen, both privately and through the Blaffer Trust, moved structures within New Harmony and the region. An early structure moved within New Harmony was the 1814 Harmonist Sadler Shop. The log portion of this double frame-log structure is the only extant Harmonist log house. The Blaffer Trust restored it and used it to first serve refreshments to tourists and later as a guesthouse. It was moved to a strategic corner at Main and North Streets as a distinctive end point terminating the

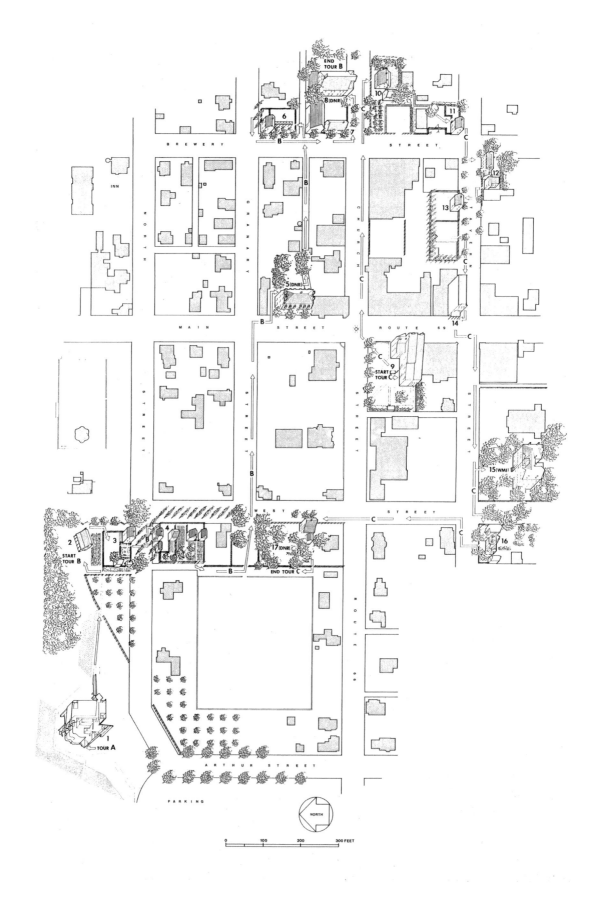

view north on Main Street. Opposite this corner is the Roofless Church, completed in 1960. Pairing the Barrett–Gate House (renamed by Jane Owen for the owners who donated this building to the trust), a structure that represented the beginning of the Harmonist settlement, and the Roofless Church, a structure "symbolic of the new New Harmony," constructed a sense of place that enables visitors to perceive the passage of time in New Harmony.[107]

Two new buildings were constructed by Historic New Harmony to support the tour experience. Amish craftsmen built the Theatre Barn of 1975. Located next to Thrall's Opera House, it houses preproduction uses related to theatrical performances, including scenery painting and prop storage. The Atheneum was completed in 1979, replacing the information center in the center of the downtown. Historic New Harmony also purchased a gas station that it demolished, and it relocated a three-story boiler factory. Another gas station was purchased and reused as an archaeology field laboratory. Historic New Harmony, in cooperation with business owners, restored and rehabilitated many of the commercial facades in the Historic Business District, most built in the nineteenth century.[108]

In 1975, when Historic New Harmony was assessing existing and new proposed building projects, a marketing survey was carried out to evaluate tourism numbers. Minimum estimates were that tourism had the capacity to increase from the existing 50,000 visitors (or 500 people per day) in 1975 to 121,000 (or 1,210 visitors per day) by 1977, to 259,374 annual visitors (or 2,594 people per day) in 1985. To put these figures in context, Old Sturbridge Village, the museum village example deemed closest to New Harmony in concept and facilities, experienced 675,000 visitors in 1973.[109] By 1978, when a majority of changes to the town had been completed, the actual number of visitors reported, just below 200,000, well exceeded the projected tourism numbers of 121,000 for 1977.

Endangered historic structures were preserved using exchange arrangements. Through research, Historic New Harmony discovered that the building on a site where the Town Council planned to construct a medical clinic was a brick Harmonist structure, the Salomon–Wolf House.[110] Historic New Harmony moved the Wolf House five blocks away to a lot that had once contained a comparable structure and was also in a concentrated group of historic buildings.[111] The town then built the Tree of Life Medical Clinic and John's Acre garden, completed in 1976, on the Wolf House site.

Figure 3.8. Historic New Harmony proposed three pedestrian tours (A, B, and C) circa 1970, with building exhibits and planned gardens. Some projects were not completed, but the tour paths are correctly represented and largely followed to this day. Drawing by David Parker. Courtesy of Ralph G. Schwarz.

One New Harmony Town Council goal not met was new affordable housing for people displaced by the restoration program. Planning for new townhouses was done with assistance from Historic New Harmony, and three units were built. None sold because they were too expensive. Further assistance from Historic New Harmony never materialized.[112] Many locals who sold their houses, parcels of land, or businesses to Historic New Harmony, reportedly for high prices, left the community, decreasing its population.

Museum Village Precedent

In terms of types of historical environments, New Harmony most closely resembles a "museum village," an interpretive type developed in the United States in 1923 and derived from Nordic open-air museums. A museum village is a group of historical buildings located on their original site or in a purpose-made setting. They are open to the public for educational purposes. Museum villages typically include such tourist services as restaurants and overnight accommodations. The five most common preservation issues that museum villages must address are spatial organization, temporal limits, restoration practices, interpretive methods, and the historical ideas to be communicated. Although Schwarz never identified New Harmony as a museum village, Harry D. Williams, director of the American Association of Museums, identified it as such in an independent marketing survey he conducted for Historic New Harmony in 1975. Williams compared New Harmony with five museum villages, of which Colonial Williamsburg (1933) and Old Sturbridge Village (1946) are the best known.

The preservation approach that makes New Harmony distinctive is what Schwarz termed a "living community." Historical buildings owned by Historic New Harmony, dating from 1820 to 1845, are set among privately owned historical buildings as well as noncontributing houses, institutional buildings, and gardens. The Harmonist town plan was used as the primary spatial organizing device for buildings and landscapes. New Harmony is surrounded to the south and east by a historically authentic agricultural landscape. The Wabash River is the town's western boundary, and Jane Owen owned most of the property along its northern boundary. Historic New Harmony's preservation efforts were concentrated in a seven-block area in the town's northwest quadrant, part of the seventeen-block Historic Residential District, and in the six blocks leading into and around downtown, part of the Historic Business District.

Tourists experience the structures owned by Historic New Harmony and the state if they follow a linear tourist path marked by Historic New Harmony. The path begins at the Atheneum, the only building in town not aligned with the street grid. It continues through the Historic Residential District and ends in the Downtown Historic District.[113]

Figure 3.9. This path leading from the stepped ramp of the Atheneum directs tourists to the historic area in the town of New Harmony. Photograph courtesy of Ben Nicholson, 2017.

From the Atheneum, visitors progressed down an exterior stepped ramp before being led along a concrete walk and through a five-stile wood fence, designed by Kane and marking the limits of the original Harmonist orchard, to a double log cabin (1852) representing the Anglo-American "pioneer period."[114] This path then leads to the Lenz House, a Harmonist frame building (1820) owned by the National Society of the Colonial Dames of America in the State of Indiana but leased to Historic New Harmony. Across North Street stands a representative group of historic log structures (1814–19) reminiscent of Harmonist houses and barns.

Buildings are organized in small groups along the path to represent three distinct periods: the Anglo-American frontier, the Harmonist Society (1814–24), and the

Maclurean era (1827–60). Schwarz organized the path according to this time line to provide clarity for visitors and enable them to keep track of the personalities and artifacts associated with the multilayered historical legacies of New Harmony.

Historic New Harmony's existing or relocated historic structures were part of an evolving "living" community that altered the concept of time presented to visitors. Unlike Colonial Williamsburg and Old Sturbridge Village, which set historic areas apart from adjoining communities, and instead of demolishing nonconforming structures, as had been the practice at Colonial Williamsburg, Schwarz accepted New Harmony as given.

Several building conservation methods were used by Historic New Harmony, including preservation, rehabilitation, restoration, and reconstruction, depending on the structure and the intended new use. It was not until 1976 that the National Conservation Advisory Council (founded 1973, now Heritage Preservation) came to an understanding of the definition of conservation treatment methods for architecture. Schwarz adopted a contextual, artifact-based approach to interpretation similar to other museum villages, using extant buildings, original historical and scientific texts, maps, and archaeological artifacts found in New Harmony as sources of historical information.

Schwarz did not seek to ascribe political or ideological meanings to the past as Charity Dye had done in the 1914 Children's Historical Pageant. Nor was he influenced by the place-based reconstructive pasts that the New Harmony Memorial Commission enacted during the early 1940s. Schwarz was influenced by cultural ideas embedded in the 1942 general plan, a thematically consistent past heavily influenced by Colonial Williamsburg. Unlike the 1942 plan, which was axial and hierarchical and used the Harmonist Cemetery as a terminus, Schwarz's tourist path was more sinuous, shifting emphasis to a demonstrably new building, the Atheneum. An interpretive claim was made to link the Atheneum to Robert Owen's plan to build his first utopian "Village of Unity," never constructed, to the south of New Harmony.[115]

Absent from Historic New Harmony's interpretation of the past was the ancient, Native American history of the lower Wabash, most evident materially in the burial mounds in and around the Harmonist Cemetery. A second exclusion from the tourist map was any material representation of Owen's utopian society, which sidestepped the failure of the experiment by interpreting it as an enterprise dedicated to discovery and progress, the core tenets of modernity. Schwarz shifted interpretive weight onto what he called the "Maclurean era," the time period after the dissolution of Owen's community. In so doing, Historic New Harmony's interpretative narrative minimized or excluded other important social reformers and educators from this period, especially women.[116]

Schwarz emphasized five of the well-known scientists who stayed in New Harmony after the demise of the Owen community and whose publications and explorations proved quite consequential in the nineteenth century. By linking the relationship between artifacts and their creators (e.g., David Dale Owen's geological surveys, which led to the discovery of iron, supporting U.S. industrialization, expansion, and material progress) to larger concepts of modernity, Schwarz addressed the challenge of limited material evidence for the Owen utopian period. The gallery exhibitions were in three adjacent museums, two in Harmonist houses and one, devoted to the Maximilian–Bodmer Collection, in an adaptively reused nineteenth-century commercial building. Some of the most innovative projects planned by Schwarz addressed the distinctive living and working environments of the Harmonists and Maclure period scientists. One plan was to build a Harmonist hop house and hop garden to enrich the understanding of the Harmonists as consumers, plantsmen, and industrial producers. Schwarz also planned to reconstruct the botanical garden of Thomas Say, who grew unusual specimens in his garden tied directly to his work. Kane completed extensive historical research and drawings for this project, but Historic New Harmony was not successful in funding it.[117]

Figure 3.10. The Harmonists built this hop house outbuilding between 1814 and 1824 as part of their successful distillery operation. Historic New Harmony relocated this structure from another site back to the original location on a new garden designed by Kane and Carruth, P.C. From the Collections of Historic New Harmony / University of Southern Indiana.

Invented and Reimagined Pasts

Alongside Historic New Harmony's construction of a "revised past," Jane Owen crafted another spatial interpretation of New Harmony. Hers was an "invented past," which re-imagined New Harmony as a spiritual destination for pilgrims. Jane Owen's vision developed over time as her own spiritual experiences and sensibilities evolved. An important structure that she purchased in 1947 and transferred to the Blaffer Trust in 1958 was the Poet's House, a Harmonist house on its original foundation. She restored the exterior and rehabilitated the interior "in a manner faithful to the original builders."[118] The most important historic building Jane Owen purchased in this early time period was a brick Harmonist residence, which had been subsequently annexed to Community House No. 2 as its kitchen, later known as the Kilbinger House and leased for a time to Historic New Harmony. Kilbinger House, with its attached Harmonist log cabin, was refurbished by the Blaffer Trust and a guesthouse was added in the 1960s, renamed the Mother Superior House by Jane Owen. She renamed the structures she bought as a reflection of her spiritual narrative and to honor other individuals who helped reenvision New Harmony.

During the 1950s Jane Owen approached historic preservation by purchasing and restoring or rehabilitating Harmonist buildings, a process that the Blaffer Trust continued after its creation. By the mid-1960s the trust began to focus on the present in relation to the past and future. This change in consciousness was evident through the commissioning of modern garden and architecture projects. The three most important architectural projects were the Roofless Church (dedicated 1960), commissioned by the Blaffer Trust, the New Harmony Inn (dedicated 1974), commissioned by Jane Owen through her for-profit Red Geranium Enterprises, and the MacLeod Barn Abbey (dedicated 1976), also commissioned by the Blaffer Trust.

These modern projects expanded on Jane Owen's growing conception of New Harmony as an ecumenical religious community that appealed to people of different faiths through spiritual and educational place-based experiences related to art, social service, and religion. This stemmed from her belief by the mid-1960s that "the needs of our current century are spiritual and psychic [well-being], rather than material or scientific."[119] Her skepticism about the redemptive potential of capitalism and scientism, not coincidentally, was also a critical ideological component of the Harmonist and Owen groups.

The activities of the Blaffer Trust translated Jane Owen's personal worldview into a praxis for preserving. It was guided by her conviction that the present should be understood in relation to the past and future rather than seeking to *reconstruct* a past. The Blaffer trustees cited the Roofless Church as an example of this viewpoint. Even though the trust had the resources to rebuild the Harmonist Church, the trustees chose instead to make a "contemporary" statement.[120] Their "approach to historic preservation" is represented by a passage from Paul Tillich's book *The Religious Situation*:[121]

> To understand the present means to see it in its inner tension toward the future. In this field also, there is such a thing as spiritual perspective and the possibility of finding amid all the infinite aspirations and tensions which every present contains not only those which conserve the past but also those which are creatively new and pregnant with the future.[122]

Preserving was a central design consideration for the New Harmony Inn, a second, important project that Jane Owen commissioned, which was completed in 1974. Located on North Street near the corner of Brewery Street in a large open meadow, the inn was designed by the Indianapolis architect Evans Woollen, of Woollen, Molzan and Associates. Prior to this commission Woollen had designed a small addition to the Red Geranium Restaurant, a for-profit enterprise of Jane Owen that opened in July 1963.[123] Called the Refectory, the simple, modern, rectangular room is dominated by a north-facing glass wall that reveals a dramatic view of nature.

Jane Owen built the forty-five-room inn at a cost of 1.4 million dollars (Plate

22).[124] It was a for-profit venture, unlike the Roofless Church and MacLeod Barn Abbey, which were built by the Blaffer Trust. Because there were few accommodations for overnight visitors in New Harmony, the inn was a much-needed piece of tourist infrastructure.

Gerald Allen, an architectural historian and critic, was the first to explore the relationship of the New Harmony Inn to the "traditions of [the] place where it was built."[125] By the mid-1970s, relating a new building to its immediate surroundings had become a concern of many U.S. architects. This "postmodern" approach involved integrating historical elements into the design of new buildings, addressing the neglect of tradition by earlier modernist architects concerned principally with the expression of function. Woollen abstracted the geometry, composition, and materials characteristic of Harmonist buildings to craft this place-based modern design.

The inn is made up of two structures, the Entry House, where guests check in, suggestive of modestly scaled Harmonist brick houses, and the Dormitory, where guest rooms are located, reminiscent in profile and scale of Community House No. 2. The New Harmony Inn was an exercise of minimalist design within the built environment that makes a distinct impression on those encountering it. This is particularly evident when its simple forms are compared with the complex geometric vocabulary of the Atheneum, the Visitor's Center designed by Richard Meier and completed five years later. Woollen's aim was to integrate the New Harmony Inn into the historic context, while Meier's was to contrast with it. The New Harmony Inn was an exercise in subsuming form within a historic environment. In contrast, the Atheneum was an attempt to expand the existing historic architecture through a distinct, internally consistent, yet empty form. Each building is also a product of its function. When inside the Atheneum, visitors are continually directed back to the landscape and the town yet to be experienced. The New Harmony Inn, as a place where tourists find respite and "home," is a place in which visitors are continually directed inward.

Of this design concept, Woollen said, "We are trying to perpetuate a kind of simple and astringent quality lifestyle the first occupants (of New Harmony) reflected. It is very refreshing for people to be able to go away someplace for a short holiday and see what's almost a monastic existence."[126] Jane Owen agreed. She described the effect they were trying to achieve as emblematic of "early monasteries and shaker communities."[127]

Jane Owen's MacLeod Barn Abbey project, dedicated in 1976, developed by Kane and Robert E. Hatch of Fairfield, Connecticut, was funded by the Blaffer Trust to support Jane Owen's commitment to spiritual ecumenism. A large 129-year-old barn, the Bullard Barn, was dismantled and relocated from the Linus Wolf farm near St. Phillips, Indiana, to New Harmony.[128] It was remodeled to provide modest housing and meeting space for youth retreats and adult conferences focused on education

Figure 3.11. Jane Owen purchased, relocated, and adaptively reused an old barn that is shown here under reconstruction in New Harmony in April 1997. The MacLeod Barn Abbey serves as a retreat location for youth and adult groups to address educational and religious concerns. From the Collections of Historic New Harmony / University of Southern Indiana.

and religious issues. This facility, in part, enabled Danner's earlier vision to offer educational programs to be realized. The site first proposed was where the Atheneum was built. The final site was next to a forest called Our Lord's Wood, also owned by Jane Owen, which features dramatic views of the Wabash River. Jane Owen's name for the building, MacLeod Barn Abbey, imaginatively linked the people who would gather there to a community of monks or nuns. The Reverend George MacLeod, a minister of the Church of Scotland, was the founder and leader of the Iona Community in Scotland. His ecumenical community and social justice agenda inspired Jane Owen. Blaffer Trust documents refer to Iona as New Harmony's "sister community," reinforcing the sense of shared mission Jane Owen hoped to foster.[129]

The interplay between Jane Owen's modern and historic buildings, gardens, and artworks together with the Atheneum and the historic reconstructions of Historic New Harmony made up a significant part of the New Harmony tourist experience, which induces wandering, discovery, and learning. Historic New Harmony's reconstructions constituted a rational counterpoint to Jane Owen's approach, which layered spiritual reconstruction onto the reconstitution of the town by prompting individual contemplation. Jane Owen's notion of contemplation was directed to a community of self-motivated individuals who possess "a certain openness to the world and a genuine participation in its anguish," in the words of the Trappist monk and modern mystic Thomas Merton.[130]

Jane Owen demonstrated how contemporary uses could open up new life in historic environments. As both a contemporary place and a place of the past, New Harmony can be challenging to decipher, given its layers of history. It is in the interplay between the "known," the material and environmental artifacts through which Schwarz and Kane interpreted New Harmony's history to visitors, and the "unknown," the journey through paths and places carried out by Jane Owen with limited, ascribed, and often ambiguous meanings, that individuals are invited to decipher the landscape and reconcile any doubts or confusion they may experience. These interpretive approaches to the past create a richer experience by mixing education and self-reflection.

As a case study, New Harmony is important because it reveals every chapter of the historic preservation movement in the United States. When compared with Colonial Williamsburg, New Harmony stands out because it was not the product of a single vision but of many people and groups contributing their historic consciousness to its preservation over decades. As a place, New Harmony was dependent on community engagement for the development of historic consciousness, whether this was through pageants, reenactments, the living community, or self-reflective spiritual pilgrimages.

The need to sustain familial heritage, express town pride, and serve propaganda interests were behind many of these changing preservation approaches. Cultural changes at the national level, including the rise of the Women's Club and Pageantry Movements and the development of professional preservation standards, also gave rise to shifts in New Harmony preservation strategies.

In addition to a range of interpreters, interpretations, and expressive vehicles, there are at least four "portals" through which New Harmony can be understood: that of the Harmonist sect, the free-thinking Owenites, the frontier scientists, and Jane Owen's imagined pilgrims. Part of its success is how these themes are uniquely addressed in different parts of the material environment. This is unlike themed environments that are dependent on walled enclosures and the exclusion of dissonant messages. For those who come to New Harmony with different needs and expectations, the preserved and contemporary works of New Harmony can be complementary, but they can also be confusing. "Pilgrims" traveling to New Harmony, for example, expecting reflection, rest, or solitude, are confronted with historical fragments whose meanings they are challenged to decipher. Because it is not based on exclusionary preservation or real estate development practices, New Harmony does not offer tourists mass market–driven entertainment attractions. More historic reconstruction and the purging of nonconforming sites and structures would be necessary to carry out such a mass-market scheme. New Harmony is not devoid of consumption, but what is offered here (historical ideas, art in nature, and different ways of thinking) shifts away from consumerist tactics. Unlike other museum villages, a critical part of the learning experience is the attempt to immerse visitors in small-town life. Historic New Harmony employs conventional tourist indoctrination and management tactics to do this. Schwarz, along with Jane Owen, focused more on activating modes of thought than on reenacting ways of life. Their preserving work and that of those who came before them are a testament to the idea that historical culture as an inner pursuit can always be inspired. If there is a cautionary tale applicable to New Harmony, it is that preserving is also dependent on individuals who are willing to become engaged and rethink history.

Notes

The author thanks the following for their assistance with the preparation of this chapter: Ralph Schwarz; Mrs. Owen; Evans Woollen; Jim Sanders and Chris Laughbaum, Robert Lee Blaffer Foundation; Sherry Graves, Margaret Scherzinger, and Ryan Rokicki, Working Men's Institute; Connie Weinzapfel, Historic New Harmony; Amanda Bryden, Indiana State Museum and Historic Sites; Raymond V. Shepherd Jr., Old Economy Village, Pennsylvania; Jennifer Greene, University of Southern Indiana, Evansville; The Lilly Library, Indiana University, Bloomington, for access to the Lockridge text; the contributors to this book, Michelangelo Sabatino, Ben Nicholson, Stephen Fox, Cammie McAtee, and Nancy Mangum McCaslin; and my spouse, Malcolm Woollen.

1. For an overview of the preservation history of New Harmony, Indiana, see Christine Gorby, "Jane Blaffer Owen: Her Modern Spiritual Landscapes of New Harmony, Indiana," *Landscape Architecture: The Magazine of the American Society of Landscape Architects,* June 2004, 36, 38, 40–44; and Gorby, "Jane Blaffer Owen: Her Modern Spiritual Landscapes of New Harmony, Indiana," in *Critique of Built Works of Landscape Architecture,* vol. 8 (Baton Rouge: Louisiana State University, 2003).

2. George B. Lockwood, *The New Harmony Communities* (Marion, Ind.: Chronicle Company, 1902). This edition predates Lockwood's expanded edition, with Charles A. Prosser in the preparation of the educational chapters, *The New Harmony Movement* (New York: D. Appleton, 1905).

3. Charity Dye, *Historical Pageant: Closing the Centennial Celebration, June 6–13, 1914, of the Founding of New Harmony, Indiana, in 1814, Presented by the School Children of the Town Assisted by Their Friends, June 13, 1914, at Early Candle-Light. Book of Words* (Indianapolis: Hollenbeck, 1914), 1–48.

4. Lotta Alma Clark, "The Development of American Pageantry," *Bulletin American Pageant Association* 9 (1914): n.p. For more on the development of pageantry in the United States, see David Glassberg, *American Historical Pageantry: The Uses of Tradition in the Early Twentieth Century* (Chapel Hill: University of North Carolina Press, 1990).

5. Mary Porter Beegle, "The Fundamental Essentials of Successful Pageantry," *Bulletin American Pageant Association* 7 (1914): n.p.

6. Nora C. Fretageot and W. V. Mangrum, *Historic New Harmony Official Guide,* Centennial ed. (Evansville, Ind.: Keller-Crescent, 1914).

7. Nora C. Fretageot, *Historic New Harmony Official Guide,* 2nd ed. (Mt. Vernon, Ind.: Western Star, 1923); Fretageot, *Historic New Harmony: A Guide,* 3rd ed. (Mt. Vernon, Ind.: Western Star, 1934).

8. Writers' Program (Indiana), *Indiana: A Guide to the Hoosier State* (New York: Oxford University Press, 1941).

9. Dye, *Historical Pageant,* 23, 37.

10. Ibid., 34, 42.

11. Charity Dye, *Pageant Suggestions for the Indiana Statehood Centennial Celebration* (Indianapolis: Indianapolis Historical Commission, 1916), 14.

12. Thank you to Margaret Scherzinger, Working Men's Institute Museum and Library, for helpful guidance and personal remembrances about the New Harmony plaza location.

13. Deed of sale from John A. Wilhelm and Annie M. Wilhelm to Mary Emily Fauntleroy, June 22, 1926 (filed June 26, 1926), Posey County, Ind., Deed Book 49, p. 479, County Recorder's Office, Mt. Vernon, Ind.

14. Helen Elliott, "Interview with Rose Broz, Craig Bair, and Todd Mozingo, 16 February 1982," *Mary Fauntleroy and New Harmony In Search of Community,* edited by Robert H. Menke (New Harmony, Ind.: Historic New Harmony, 1996), 133–39. The original source of this interview, "Indiana University Oral History Collection," after an exhaustive number of inquiries, could not be located.

15. Ibid.

16. Fretageot, *Historic New Harmony Official Guide,* 23.

17. For summary accounts of preservation activities in New Harmony, see Donald E. Pitzer and Connie A. Weinzapfel, "Utopia on the Wabash: The History of Preservation in New Harmony," *Cultural Resource Management* 9 (2001): 18–20; and *Posey County Interim Report* (Indianapolis: Historic Landmarks Foundation of Indiana, 2004). For an in-depth article on the restoration of Economy, Pennsylvania, the third and last Harmonist settlement, see Charles Morse Stotz, "Threshold of the Golden Kingdom: The Village of Economy and Its Restoration," *Winterthur Portfolio* 8 (1973): 133–69.

18. Norman Tyler, Ted Ligibel, and Llene R. Tyler, *Historic Preservation: An Introduction to Its History, Principles, and Practice* (New York: W. W. Norton, 2009), 30.

19. *Journal of the Indiana State Senate during the Regular Session of the Eightieth General Assembly Commencing Thursday, January 7, 1937. February 22, 1937* (Fort Wayne, Ind.: Fort Wayne Printing, 1937), 450–89, 517, 677, 751–52, 1101, 1166, 1469.

20. New Harmony Memorial Commission, *Report and Recommendations of the New Harmony Memorial Commission, December 26, 1938* (New Harmony, Ind.: New Harmony Memorial Commission, 1938), 7–8.

21. New Harmony Memorial Commission, "Transcript of Minutes of the New Harmony Memorial Commission," April 23, 1937–July 21, 1939, pp. 1–12, New Harmony State Memorial Collection, box New Harmony Memorial Commission Papers, Indiana State Museum and Historic Sites Archive, Historic New Harmony, New Harmony, Ind. Hereafter cited as Indiana Archive.

22. New Harmony Memorial Commission, "Summary of Expenditure Estimates of The New Harmony Memorial Commission for Fiscal Year 1941–41 and 1942–1943, Including also Expenditures for Real Estate Purchase and Restorations for 1940–1941," transcript, New Harmony State Memorial Collection, box New Harmony Memorial Commission Papers, Indiana Archive.

23. New Harmony Memorial Commission, *The New Harmony Memorial Movement: A Brief Review of Its Origin, Aims, and Progress* (New Harmony, Ind.: New Harmony Memorial Commission, May 1942), 12–13.

24. Ibid., 14.

25. New Harmony Memorial Commission, *New Harmony Memorial Movement,* 11–12.

26. New Harmony Memorial Commission, "Transcript of Minutes of the New Harmony Memorial Commission," December 17, 1938, p. 7, New Harmony State Memorial Collection, box New Harmony Memorial Commission Papers, Indiana Archive.

27. New Harmony Memorial Commission, "Suggested Schedule of Proceedings of New Harmony Memorial Commission," June 15 and 16, 1939, p. 5, transcript, New Harmony State Memorial Collection, box g, folder New Harmony Memorial Movement, Indiana Archive.

28. Helen Elliott, "Letter to the New Harmony Memorial Commission," July 20, 1939, transcript, New Harmony State Memorial Commission, box e, folder E, Indiana Archive.

29. For biographical information related to Ross Lockridge Sr. and his son of the same name, see Larry Lockridge, *Shade of the Raintree: The Life and Death of Ross Lockridge, Jr., Author of Raintree County* (Bloomington: Indiana University Press, 2014).

30. Helen Elliott, "Transcript of Minutes of the New Harmony Memorial Commission [Minutes between April 23, 1937, and June 16, 1939]," April 23, 1937, p. 1, MS, New Harmony State Memorial Commission, box New Harmony Commission Memorial Papers, Indiana Archive.

31. New Harmony Memorial Commission, *New Harmony Memorial Movement,* 19.

32. Mark Franko and Annette Richards, *Acting on the Past: Historical Performance across the Disciplines* (Hanover, N.H.: Wesleyan University Press, published by University Press of New England, 2000), 6.

33. Ross Franklin Lockridge Jr., "A Pageant of New Harmony, to Be Presented at the Festival of the Golden Rain Tree, June 20, 1937," June 20, 1937, pp. 1–60, transcript, Golden Raintree Association New Harmony Pageant Collection, box 2, Golden Raintree Association / New Harmony Pageant Collection, folder 1937, Working Men's Institute, New Harmony, Ind. Hereafter cited as WMI.

34. New Harmony Memorial Commission, *Report and Recommendations,* 4; New Harmony Memorial Commission, *New Harmony Memorial Movement,* 21; Ross Franklin Lockridge Jr., "A Pageant of New Harmony, To Be Presented at the Festival of the Golden Rain Tree, June 20, 1937, June 22, 1946, June 20, 1948, June 10, 1949" (New Harmony, Ind.: s.n.), 1–25.

35. Ross Franklin Lockridge Jr., "A Pageant of New Harmony, To Be Presented at the Festival of the Golden Rain Tree, June 20, 1937," June 20, 1937, pp. 60, and 27–28, 33, 39, 49, transcript, Golden Raintree Association New Harmony Pageant Collection, box 2, folder 1937, Golden Raintree Association / New Harmony Pageant Collection, WMI.

36. Ibid., 21, 22, Prologue, 11, 20, printed by courtesy of the Estate of Ross Lockridge, Jr. and Golden Raintree Association / New Harmony Pageant Collection, WMI.

37. Ibid., 22, 47.

38. Ibid., 55–56, printed by courtesy of the Estate of Ross Lockridge, Jr. and Golden Raintree Association / New Harmony Pageant Collection, WMI.

39. Ibid., 60, printed by courtesy of the Estate of Ross Lockridge, Jr. and Golden Raintree Association / New Harmony Pageant Collection, WMI.

40. "Golden Rain Festival Opens at New Harmony," *Pharos-Tribune* (Logansport, Ind.), June 21, 1937; and "Five Thousand Witness This Pageant," *Hammond Times,* June 22, 1937.

41. New Harmony Memorial Commission, "Minutes New Harmony Memorial Commission," April 8, 1942, transcript, New Harmony State Memorial Collection, box New Harmony Memorial Commission Papers, Indiana Archive.

42. Richard E. Bishop, Denzil Doggett, and Edson L. Nott, "A Preliminary General Plan for the Development of the New Harmony Memorial," Indiana Department of Conservation for the New Harmony Memorial Commission, March 25, 1942.

43. Helen Elliott, "Minutes New Harmony Memorial Commission," April 8, 1942, MS, New

Harmony State Memorial Commission, box New Harmony Commission Memorial Papers, Indiana Archive.

44. Bishop, Doggett, and Nott, "Preliminary General Plan," n.p.

45. Ibid.

46. Ibid.

47. Charles A. Birnbaum and Mary V. Hughes, "Introduction: Landscape Preservation in Context, 1890–1950," in *Design with Culture: Claiming America's Landscape Heritage*, edited by Charles A. Birnbaum and Mary V. Hughes (Charlottesville: University of Virginia Press, 2005), 1–18.

48. William Pickering, *A plan of the town of Harmonie in Posey County, Indiana. The property of Frederic Rapp* (1824); Walrath Weingartner, *Town of New Harmony in 1824, founded by the Harmony society in 1814* (1824).

49. Bishop, Doggett, and Nott, "Preliminary General Plan," n.p.

50. Alvin E. Meyers [deputy attorney general, State of Indiana] to Mrs. Marcia Corbin Ford, Mr. Harry Cuyler Ford, September 16, 1948, p. 2, transcript, Arcada Balz L9, box 1, Manuscripts & Rare Books Division, Indiana State Library, Indianapolis.

51. Deed of Sale from Helen Corbin Heinl, Robert D. Heinl, Robert D. Heinl Jr., Nancy Gordon Heinl, Marcia Corbin Ford, and Harry Cuyler Ford, to Kenneth Dale Owen, September 14, 1949 (filed September 14, 1949), Posey County, Indiana, Deed Book 62, 315, County Recorder's Office, Mt. Vernon, Ind.; and Helen Elliott, *In Retrospect* (New Harmony, Ind.: Elliott, 1976).

52. "Time Running Out for New Harmony Memorial Board," *Pharos-Tribune* (Logansport, Ind.), April 27, 1955.

53. "State New Harmony Holdings Offered to Wealthy Texan," *Pharos-Tribune* (Logansport, Ind.), August 13, 1949.

54. "Commission May Sell New Harmony Holdings to Robert Owen Descendant," *Terre Haute Star,* August 12, 1949; and "State New Harmony Holdings Offered to Wealthy Texan"; Helen Elliott, "[Minutes New Harmony Memorial Commission]," July 6, 1949, p. 1, MS, New Harmony State Memorial Commission, box New Harmony Commission Memorial Papers, Indiana Archive.

55. Elliott, "[Minutes New Harmony Memorial Commission]," n.p.

56. Thomas Kane, "The Preservation and Restoration of Historic Landscape," in *Proceedings of Historic Preservation Conference: New Skills for Architects, Landscape Architects, Planners and Preservationists, December 2–3, 1977,* edited by David Johnson and David R. Hermansen (s.l.: s.n., 1977), 156.

57. Gladys C. Alsop, "Record [minutes]," December 7, 1953, p. 39, MS, Golden Raintree Association, New Harmony Pageant Collection, box 1, Folder Golden Raintree Association 1951–1975 + 1979, WMI.

58. Helen D. Bullock, "National Trust Report & Recommendation for New Harmony, Indiana," unpublished report (Washington, D.C.: National Trust for Historic Preservation, 1954), 1–11.

59. Ibid., 2–3, printed by courtesy of the National Trust for Historic Preservation.

60. Ibid., 3, printed by courtesy of the National Trust for Historic Preservation.

61. Ibid., 9.

62. Ibid., 2.

63. "Commission Fails at New Harmony," *Vidella-Messenger* (Valparaiso, Ind.), June 23, 1953.

64. "Harmony Project May Be Dropped," *Anderson Herald,* June 20, 1953; "Commission Fails at New Harmony," *Vidella-Messenger,* June 23, 1953.

65. "Trust Indenture [Robert Lee Blaffer Trust]," March 3, 1958, pp. 1–12, transcript, box 2, Robert Lee Blaffer Trust, Robert Lee Blaffer Trust Archives, Robert Lee Blaffer Foundation, New Harmony, Ind. Hereafter cited as Blaffer Trust Archives.

66. The first trustees of the Robert Lee Blaffer Trust were Don Blair, Ora V. Howton, Philip Johnson, Helen Bullock, and Zoe Euverard (also known as "The Sister Élise, CHS"). During the first meeting of the Trust on May 13, 1958, Blair, the only New Harmony resident, was elected chairman. Howton was elected secretary. She was also the bookkeeper and manager of the Texas office of Sarah Campbell Blaffer, Jane Owen's mother. Johnson, by this time a well-known East Coast–based modern architect, was named the "Consulting Architect" for the Trust. Bullock was a respected historian who worked for the National Trust for Historic Preservation in Washington, D.C. She mainly advised the Trust on preservation-related matters. Euverard was a member of a monastic religious order for women in the Episcopal Church called the Community of the Holy Spirit, founded in 1952 in New York City. See Ora V. Howton, "Minutes of the Initial Meeting of the Trustees of the Robert Lee Blaffer Trust," May 13, 1958, pp. 1, 7, transcript, box 19, Robert Lee Blaffer Trust, Blaffer Trust Archives.

67. Josephine Elliott, "Record [Meeting Minutes]," February 5, 1964, p. 43, MS, Golden Raintree Association New Harmony Pageant Collection, box 1, folder Golden Raintree Association 1951–1975 & 1979, WMI.

68. John E. Schroeder, "Trumpet, Blow True" (Tell City, Ind.: Key Productions, 1964), pp. 1–82, transcript, Harmonie Associates' Records, box 1, folder Beginnings-Golden Raintree Association, WMI.

69. *Souvenir Program for the 150th Anniversary Celebration* (New Harmony, Ind.: Official Committee, 1964), n.p.

70. Ibid.

71. Nevin E. Danner, "Some Ideas Submitted to Mrs. Kenneth Dale Owen and the Blaffer Trust—Concerning: A Possibility for the Enlargement of the New Harmony Commitment," April 26, 1962, transcript, box 10, folder Reverend Nevil E. Danner, Blaffer Trust Archives, New Harmony, Ind.

72. Ibid.

73. Nevin E. Danner, "Revision of the Proposal Made to Mrs. Kenneth Dale Owen and the Blaffer Trust to Provide a Six Month Demonstration Period for the Testing of a New Harmony Program," 1962 [November], pp. 1–2, transcript, box 10, folder Reverend Nevil E. Danner, Blaffer Trust Archives.

74. Mrs. Clifton E. Couch, meeting minutes, August 17, 1964, transcript, Harmonie Associates' Records, box 1, folder Beginnings-Golden Raintree Association, WMI.

75. Ibid.

76. Nevin E. Danner, "Release from Harmonie Associates," January 16, 1965, transcript, Roger Douglas Branigin Papers 1964–1968, Container 104, Franklin College, Franklin, Indiana.

77. Nevin E. Danner, "Notes on Ten Proposals for Study and Action in the Development of New Harmony, Indiana, as a Center for the Renewing of American Life and Purpose, Prepared for Governor Roger Branigin," February 3, 1965, transcript, Harmonie Associates' Records, box 1, folder Correspondence Governor Roger D. Branigin, WMI.

78. "Approve Plans to Purchase Old Opera House," *Vidette-Messenger* (Valparaiso), May 14, 1964, 11; "Opera House Purchase Set," *Anderson Daily Bulletin,* November 16, 1964, 17; "Branigin Calls Monthly Talks on Budget," *Anderson Herald*, December 10, 1965, 27.

79. Josephine Elliott, meeting minutes, Golden Raintree Association, October 18, 1965, MS, Golden Raintree Association New Harmony Pageant Collection, box 1, folder 8 Golden Raintree Association-President's Personal Papers, WMI.

80. Anton Hulman Jr., "Of New Harmony, Indiana, for Use of Dormitory Number Two," May 5, 1965, p. 1, transcript, Harmonie Associates Records, box 1, folder Correspondence State Department of Conservation, WMI.

81. National Historic Landmarks Program, "New Harmony Historic District, National Registration

Number 66000006, 23 June 23, 1965," *National Park Service,* accessed October 3, 2012, https://npgallery.nps.gov/AssetDetail/NRIS/66000006.

82. National Register of Historic Places, "Harmony Way Bridge, New Harmony, Posey County, Indiana, Item Number 07001030," *National Park Service,* 2007, accessed October 3, 2012, https://www .nps.gov/nr/listings/20071012.HTM.

83. New Harmony Plan Commission and Scott Bagby and Associates, *A Master Plan for New Harmony, Indiana, and Its Planning Area* (New Harmony, Ind.: The Commission, 1969), 1–65.

84. Ibid., 42.

85. New Harmony Plan Commission and Scott Bagby and Associates, *A Master Plan for New Harmony, Indiana,* 40–41.

86. Ibid., 36.

87. Foster Tolliver, interview by Vincent A. Giroux, November 16, 1977, pp. 4, 7, interview 77–038, transcript, Oral History Interviews of the History of New Harmony, Indiana Oral History Project, Indiana University, Bloomington.

88. Ibid., 5.

89. "Local Government Units Get First Choice in Purchase of Used State Police Vehicles," *Pharos-Tribune & Press* (Logansport, Ind.), April 24, 1975; Herb Marynell, "New Harmony Commission Dislikes Its Own Name," *Evansville Press,* September 13, 1973.

90. Marynell, "New Harmony Commission Dislikes Its Own Name."

91. "Minutes New Harmony Memorial Commission," March 9, 1974, p. 3, transcript, Harmonie Associates' Records, box XI, folder New Harmony (Memorial) Commission, WMI.

92. Ralph Schwarz is a well-known and respected preservationist consultant, author, and historian. In addition to his former role as director of Historic New Harmony, in New Harmony, Indiana, Schwarz has acted as adviser to the president for the National Trust for Historic Preservation, Washington, D.C., and performed as a senior advisor for A Living Memorial to the Holocaust Museum of Jewish Heritage, New York City. Schwarz has served as a consultant to the National Museum of Industrial History, Smithsonian Institution, in Bethlehem, Pennsylvania. He was also director of operations at the Ford Foundation in New York City.

93. D. W. Vaughn, Ralph Schwarz, William Sorrels, and Frank Munger, "New Harmony Still Making History," *Evansville Press,* June 19, 1978, 12; and Ralph Schwarz, interview by Christine Gorby, Williamsburg, Va., March 5–6, 2012.

94. Herb Marynell, "Newcomer Goes to Work for Town," *Evansville Press,* September 12, 1973, 39.

95. Thank you to Lilly Endowment, Inc., for providing this financial information.

96. Kane, "Preservation and Restoration of Historic Landscape," 158; Board of Trustees Town of New Harmony, Indiana, "Comprehensive Zoning Ordinance," April 10, 1973.

97. National Register of Historic Places, "Harmony Way Bridge, New Harmony, Posey County, Indiana, Item Number 07001030."

98. Ralph Schwarz, "Historic New Harmony," in *Proceedings of Historic Preservation Conference: New Skills for Architects, Landscape Architects, Planners and Preservationists, December 2–3, 1977,* edited by David Johnson and David R. Hermansen (S.I.: s.n., 1977): 93–116.

99. Kane, "Preservation and Restoration of Historic Landscape," 157; Tolliver, interview by Giroux, 20–21.

100. Pickering, *Plan of the town of Harmonie.*

101. Historic New Harmony, Inc., "Recap of Analysis of Expenditures of Macleod Youth Hostel—Site #1," February 7, 1977, transcript, box 11, Blaffer Trust Archives.

102. John O. Curtis, *Moving Historic Buildings,* Heritage Conservation and Recreation Series 9

(Washington, D.C.: U.S. Department of the Interior, Heritage Conservation and Recreation Service, Technical Preservation Services Division, 1979), 11.

103. Second International Congress of Architects and Technicians of Historic Monuments, "International Charter for the Conservation of Restoration of Monuments and Sites (The Venice Charter, 1964)," ICOMOS, accessed March 31, 2013, https://www.icomos.org/charters/venice_e.pdf.

104. Ibid.

105. W. B. Morton and Gary L. Hume, *The Secretary of the Interior's Standards for Historic Preservation Projects: With Guidelines for Applying the Standards,* Heritage Conservation and Recreation Service Series 7 (Washington, D.C.: U.S. Department of the Interior, Heritage Conservation and Recreation Service, Technical Preservation Services Division, 1979).

106. Ibid., 5, 8.

107. Harry Fisher, Memo to the Blaffer Trust and Jane Owen [Attachment "Copy for Short Brochure"], April 10, 1962, p. 2, transcript, box 7, folder Robert Lee Blaffer, Blaffer Trust Archives.

108. Schwarz, "Historic New Harmony," 103.

109. Harry D. Williams, "The Business Outlook for New Harmony, Indiana or Does Historic Restoration Pay?," March 21, 1975, pp. 6, 16–17, transcript, MS 655 Thomas Joseph Kane Papers, box 17, folder 5, Special Collections Department, Iowa State University Library, Ames.

110. Schwarz, "Historic New Harmony," 102, 107–8.

111. Ibid., 107–8.

112. Tolliver, interview by Giroux, 16–17.

113. Separate tickets were required for state-owned and Historic New Harmony–owned buildings, complicating the tourist experience. The singular path helped remedy this situation, as both state-owned and Historic New Harmony–owned buildings were incorporated along the journey.

114. Darrin Rubino, untitled report, 2C file, Historic New Harmony Archives, New Harmony, Ind.: According to tradition, the cabin was presumed to date from pre–Revolutionary War 1775; however, samples from pieces of wood taken from it by Dr. Darrin Rubino of Hanover College were tested, and "the dendrochronology results date the construction to late April 1852." It was originally located in Posey County and had been relocated South of Route 66 before the Blaffer Trust relocated it to its present location. The University of Evansville used it as a pottery studio for a decade until Historic New Harmony purchased the cabin in 1977.

115. Donald Pitzer, "The Original Boatload of Knowledge down the Ohio River: William Maclure's and Robert Owen's Transfer of Science and Education to the Midwest, 1825–1826," *Ohio Journal of Science* 89, no. 5 (1989): 128–42.

116. Allotting greater significance to the scientific work resulting after the Owenite Society demise was not a new interpretation. Circumventing the importance of the ideological ideas of Robert Owen was, however, a change. In the post-Owenite Society, individual achievement was emphasized over collective success. The difficulty, then, of whose accomplishments to emphasize and interpret was compounded given so many contributing individuals and limited amounts of interpretive space.

117. Schwarz, interview by Gorby.

118. Don Blair, "Report to the Trustees of the Robert Lee Blaffer Trust," December 31, 1958, p. 2, transcript, box 19, folder 1958, Blaffer Trust Archives.

119. Robert Lee Blaffer Trust, "Draft Open Letter to Be Printed," n.d. [circa 1960s], p. 2, transcript, bMS 649 Paul Tillich Papers, Andover-Harvard Theological Library, Harvard Divinity School, Cambridge, Mass.

120. Robert Lee Blaffer Trust, "Draft Open Letter to Be Printed," 2.

121. In an unsigned letter written by Jane Owen to Paul Tillich in 1959, she recollected first hearing

Tillich speak at the Union Theological Seminary in New York in about 1954. In the same letter Owen also stated familiarity with some of his writings, but it was not clear whether this preceded or followed her attendance of Tillich's Seminary lecture. These works, she said, began with Tillich's book *The Religious Situation* and ended with his November 1955 lecture at Connecticut College titled "Religion and the Visual Arts." See Paul Tillich, *The Religious Situation* (New York: Meridian Books, 1932); Jane Owen, letter to Paul Tillich [unsigned], May 19, 1959, transcript, Tillich Archive, folder Tillich Park-Building & Design, Paul Tillich Archive, Robert Lee Blaffer Foundation, New Harmony, Ind.

122. Robert Lee Blaffer Trust, "Draft Open Letter to Be Printed," 2. In *The Religious Situation*, Tillich expressed his view that with capitalism religious tradition had been severed and, with this, came a "rejection of the spiritual." He believed a new "modern religious consciousness" was needed to address this new modern condition for which he stated there was no consciousness. In his book he explored how architecture and other "creative arts" could be used to "express metaphysical meanings," but he was clear that the creative arts could not "produce" meanings. As the most realistic of the creative arts because it was constructed, architecture had been employed mainly to serve the economic needs of the new capitalistic culture. Yet, because of the realism associated with producing architecture, Tillich still also saw great potential in transforming the functional needs for which architecture was being used into what he called "mythical" ones. See Tillich, *Religious Situation*, 89, 91, 93. The creative arts, according to Tillich, included art (painting, sculpture, architecture, dance) and literature, but not gardens or landscape architecture. Jane Owen expanded this conception by including landscape architecture and the garden arts as a key aspect of her reconceptualization of New Harmony.

123. "'Red Geranium' Will Open On Next Tuesday Evening," newspaper clipping, June 11, 1963, Jane B. Owen and Robert Blaffer Trust Papers, folder Robert Lee Blaffer Trust–Jane B. Owen–1959, WMI.

124. Historic New Harmony, Inc., "Tour Guide," circa 1975, transcript, Series III–Bound Records of the New Harmony Community, vol. 88, p. 69, WMI.

125. Gerald Allen, "The New Harmony Inn: A Triumph of Modesty," *Architectural Record* 159, no. 4 (1976): 105.

126. Herb Marynell, "Harmony Inn Reflects Old," *Evansville Press*, May 1, 1974, n.p., accessed June 7, 2012, Browning People Studies, http://local.evpl.org/.

127. Ibid.

128. Herb Marynell, "Log Barn Center Planned," *Evansville Press*, August 8, 1974, n.p., accessed June 7, 2012, Browning People Studies, http://local.evpl.org/.

129. Robert Lee Blaffer Trust, "Dedication of Paul Tillich Park, New Harmony, Indiana," program leaflet, June 2, 1963, transcript, bMS 649 Paul Tillich Papers, Andover-Harvard Theological Library, Harvard Divinity School, Cambridge, Mass.

130. Thomas Merton, *Mystics and Zen Masters* (New York: Farrar, Straus and Giroux, 1999), 204.

4

"The Rib Cage of the Human Heart"

Philip Johnson's Roofless Church

CAMMIE MCATEE

ENCLOSED BY AN ALMOST UNINTERRUPTED PERIMETER WALL but open to the sky, the Roofless Church lies somewhere between architecture and landscape architecture. Intended to be a spiritual retreat open to members of all religions as well as those without defined conviction, since its inauguration on May 1, 1960, the Roofless Church has functioned as a contemplative space occasionally animated by religious services and rituals organized by a wide variety of groups.[1] Standing on the northernmost edge of New Harmony in an area composed of restored nineteenth-century domestic buildings and more recent additions, its brick walls at first glance evoke nothing more than a modest suburban church enclosure.

As one of the important architectural sites of a broadly defined historic New Harmony, today the Roofless Church is usually approached from the Visitor's Center—Richard Meier's New Harmony Atheneum—to the west. From this direction, the soft profile of a dome rising high above the red brick walls first comes into view. This intriguing construction draws visitors along the perimeter walls to enter through an oak door on the south side. Inside, the sixty-foot-high wood structure continues to command all attention. Its rustic form and rugged surface come as a surprise even to the prepared visitor; the undulating curves and the wood-split shingles covering it bring to mind natural and vernacular forms rather than the sleek industrial modernism for which its architect was then closely associated.

If often referred to as a shrine or reliquary in reference to the work of religious art it shelters, the architectural element that dominates and animates the Roofless

Figure 4.1, top. Philip Johnson's Roofless Church (1957–60) viewed from cornfields on the north side of New Harmony. Drawing its strength from an interplay of Miesian principles, historic precedent, and a fascination with curvaceous shapes, the building marked a significant shift in the architect's work in the late 1950s. Photograph courtesy of Ben Nicholson, 2005.

Figure 4.2, bottom. The restraint of the main entrance on North Street is a perfect foil for the dynamic shape of the domed shrine inside the Roofless Church's perimeter walls. Photograph courtesy of Cammie McAtee, 2006.

Figure 4.3. The domed shrine viewed from the "crossing" of the Roofless Church. Photograph courtesy of Cammie McAtee, 2006.

Church is best described as a dome, a canopy, or even a *baldacchino*. At the same time, the structure is also suggestive of Eastern temples and pagodas. Its open, billowing shape appears arrested in time, the deep folds frozen even as they flow over six wooden supports, each anchored by a giant egg-shaped limestone footing. The stones are in turn encircled by granite pavers laid in a fan pattern that echoes the curves of the canopy's lobes. Tucked beneath the dome's exposed arches and ribs and encircled by a low granite wall is Jacques Lipchitz's *Descent of the Holy Spirit* (1946–55), a bronze sculpture of the Virgin Mary. By day, the dome takes center stage, its interior only partially illuminated by an obscured oculus. By night, the sculpture's mystical content is given full expression by concealed lights that also throw the structural elements of the dome into sharp relief (Plate 12).

I have chosen to open this essay with a description of the optic and haptic qualities of the Roofless Church. The materiality of Philip Johnson's work has not typically been taken as the starting point for an analysis of his work. But by any standards, the Roofless Church is hardly a typical project. It was an exceptional commission offered by an equally exceptional client, who not only gave Johnson the chance to explore new directions in his architectural work but also afforded him the opportunity to realize the forms of long-held ideals. Confiding in him her dream to raise a church with "only one roof—the sky," the only space "vast enough to hold all worshipping humanity," Jane Blaffer Owen both demanded and inspired an extraordinary response from her architect.[2]

Although the Roofless Church is an unusual work even for an architect known for his changeability, we would hardly be expected to know this. Fourteen years after his death, Johnson the critic, Johnson the historian, Johnson the provocateur, and Johnson the tastemaker continue to overshadow Johnson the architect. The enigmatic immateriality of Johnson's celebrity has been stressed at the expense of understanding the materiality of his architecture; the power of the designing mind still overwhelms the designer's hand. In light of his fame, surprisingly little scholarly work has focused on Johnson's architectural production—only a few of his works have been closely read—and there has been no in-depth analysis of the Roofless Church since the early 1960s. New Harmony's out-of-the-way location undoubtedly contributed to its obscurity, as did Johnson's long silence about it. Less than ten years after the church's completion, serious structural defects in the brick walls became apparent. A lawsuit resolved the physical problems but brought an end to the close relationship between the architect and his client. If these difficulties caused Johnson to distance himself from the Roofless Church and Owen—from then on he rarely spoke of the project—he nevertheless remembered it as having the greatest of potential, telling Robert Stern in 1985, "It should have been the perfect job."[3]

The Roofless Church offers an opportunity to go past the limited view of Johnson's architectural work. The commission came at a crucial moment in his architectural development. Johnson's work from the mid-1950s shows him to be in the midst of a sea change, leaving behind the Miesian strictures that had defined his earlier work and helping him to realize his own architectural directions. Though history was ever present in Johnson's work, its presence became more palpable than it had been in the past, with the Miesian vocabulary now coexisting—or cohabiting—with an increasingly diverse assemblage of elements drawn from a broad sweep of historical periods. Simply put, the projects of these years reveal an inventive if restless mind. But if it was, as Johnson said, a "wandering," the paths he took through history were much less random than he would have us believe.[4]

The origins of Johnson's design, especially for the domed shrine, aroused much speculation as it neared completion. The critical eye of the late 1950s and early 1960s tended to see the Roofless Church as a manifestation of a larger move toward historicism, even eclecticism, within the architect's work. The more recent lens has read it through regionalism or contextualism. But what few attempted to explain was how the Roofless Church came to be or to consider the possibility that deeper significance may be concealed within the many layers that lie beneath the taut wrap of the dome's shingled surface. This essay offers the first deep reading of the domed shrine set within its enclosed garden.

The Descent of the Holy Spirit *on New Harmony*

New Harmony was at perhaps its lowest point when Jane Owen first visited as a newlywed in 1941. Photographs taken for the Historic American Buildings Survey in 1940 confirm what she later recalled: "It was devastation, a paradise lost."[5] Though her initial contributions to the town focused on rehabilitation, she came to understand that New Harmony's strength lay in its potential to become a laboratory for ideas. She did not want it to be frozen in time, irrelevant to and disengaged from the present. She envisioned New Harmony's resurgence as a destination for spiritual and creative awakening. Rebuilding would become a critical part of her project to revive the community. She instigated and funded a program of renewal that focused on the construction of new architecture. While continuing to support restoration efforts, Owen also commissioned, between the 1950s and 2010, nine major architectural and landscape architecture projects, as well as numerous smaller art installations for sites throughout New Harmony.[6]

Her vision for the town was intimately connected to her religious beliefs. Grounded in the Episcopal Church, her faith grew to encompass the breadth of world religions. Out of this a desire to raise a church without a roof was born. Her idea for the Roofless Church arose from her recollection of a passage by the novelist George Sand that may derive from *Devil's Pool* (1851):

Figure 4.4. By 1940 the Harmonist legacy of New Harmony was in danger of being lost. The Jacob Schnee House (1815) was among the buildings in ruin recorded by the Historic American Buildings Survey photographer Lester Jones in 1940. Photograph courtesy of Library of Congress, Prints and Photographs Division, HABS IND, 65-NEHAR, 6–2.

> Happy the peasant of the fields! . . . I see the seal of the Lord upon their noble brows, for they were born to inherit the earth far more truly than those who have bought and paid for it. . . . But he lacks some of my enjoyments, those pure delights which should be his by right, as a workman in that immense temple which the sky only is vast enough to embrace.[7]

The ideal of embracing all faiths became the cornerstone of her religious conviction, and a dream of building a monument that would embody this ideal and memorialize the two groups of communitarian founders of New Harmony grew alongside her expanding ecumenism.[8]

Owen's project for the town's renaissance as a spiritual center began with a mystical experience. In the spring of 1942, pregnant with her first child, Owen had a revelation while visiting a place known as Indian Mound on the farm of her husband,

Kenneth Owen, south of New Harmony (Figure I.4).[9] Located just outside of the town, the site overlooking the Wabash River had long been revered by the townspeople as a place of solitude and calm. Kenneth Owen strongly shared these feelings. Humbled by the intense sensations that overcame her on that spring day, Jane Owen felt directed to build an altar on the mound and believed that only by making this physical offering could her dream—to bring New Harmony back to spiritual, cultural, and economic well-being—be realized. Much later she wrote: "I chose sculpture as my bridge between civilizations and my ally when pondering how to keep my covenant."[10]

Eight years would pass before she began to identify potential artists for a work to mark this site. As a first step Owen wrote to several of them in early 1950 asking to borrow a sculpture for a May Day celebration she was organizing for her children. She requested works representing the rebirth of spring, expressed in the forms of a pagan goddess or the Blessed Virgin Mary. The artist whose work most interested her was that of the French sculptor Jacques Lipchitz (1891–1973), then living in New York. Upon seeing Lipchitz's work in an art journal for the first time that spring, Owen was moved by the roughness of his maquettes and the way he described his "heavier than air" sculpture as "aerial transparencies."[11] After several exchanges by mail and by telephone, their communication opened by Alfred Frankfurter, editor of *Art News,* and eased by her fluency in French, Owen told Lipchitz that she was interested in a work appropriate for "la Colline Sacré," a holy hill, by which she meant the site of her mystical experience.[12] Lipchitz sent her photographs of a sculpture he was working on in his New York City studio, a Virgin Mary, which the French Dominican priest Father Marie-Alain Couturier had commissioned four years earlier as part of his artistic program for the Church of Notre-Dame-de-Toute-Grâce in plateau d'Assy, Haute-Savoie, France (1937–50).[13] Haunted by the image of the faceless draped Virgin with outstretched arms encircled by a tear-shaped canopy, Owen found her way to Lipchitz's Twenty-third Street studio in September. The artist outlined his conditions: she would support the fabrication of three castings, one for Assy, one for himself, and one for her. Her financial support allowed Lipchitz to work single-mindedly on the sculpture and to produce bronze casts of the maquette over the next ten months.[14] The connection to Father Couturier only increased the work's significance to Owen. Though they never met, she subscribed to his journal *L'Art Sacré* and, through their mutual friends the Houston art collectors Dominique and John de Menil, knew of and greatly admired his project to bring the Roman Catholic Church and modern art closer together.[15] The concept of the modern art chapel Father Couturier pioneered became one of the paradigms for Owen's architectural project. She later memorialized his spiritual and, by his initial commission of Lipchitz, material contributions to it on the reconstructed perimeter walls of the Roofless Church.[16]

Figure 4.5. Jacques Lipchitz in his Twenty-third Street studio, New York, with a full-scale maquette for the first version of *Notre-Dame-de-Liesse* (1946–52). The title given to the sculpture refers to its original commission for the Roman Catholic church of Notre-Dame-de-Toute-Grâce in plateau d'Assy, Haute-Savoie, France. Photograph by Paul Weller, 1949/1950. Source unknown.

When Owen saw the maquette, she immediately felt that the work belonged in New Harmony. While the Virgin's association with the rose, sacred to the Harmonists, presented an appropriate metaphoric connection, Owen also read the gesture of the Virgin's open arms as one of sowing, a fitting nod to the site on Indian Mound Farm.[17] Her facelessness, like that of the Unknown Soldier, Owen later described, "speaks to our minds and hearts. May she be every woman, regardless of color, continent, or creed, and may her strong, outstretched hands, which give and forgive, help lead mankind to peace."[18] For Lipchitz, New Harmony offered the opportunity to rectify what he felt were serious limitations to the presentation of his sculpture in the church at Assy.[19] In a letter to Father Couturier in late September 1950, Lipchitz joyfully announced that the finished bronze would be placed simultaneously on the baptismal font at Assy and at the "top of a hill in the middle of the vast plains of the New World."[20] In early October 1950 he made a two-day visit to decide on the position of the sculpture "en plein air de la Nouvelle Harmonie."[21] Owen also hoped that Lipchitz could help win over Kenneth Owen to the idea of placing it on Indian Mound. Though they were both disappointed by his continuing opposition, soon after returning to New York Lipchitz reported to Father Couturier that the sculpture was "as it were, the Guardian Angel of this region; she protects New Harmony from floods, and as such, is already venerated by the population."[22]

Unfortunately, no similar force protected the unfinished sculpture. A fire on January 5, 1952, destroyed Lipchitz's Twenty-third Street studio and many of the works in it, including the maquette of the Virgin. The tragedy, however, inspired revisions that Lipchitz felt significantly improved the work. In 1955 the first casting of *Notre Dame de Liesse* (Our Lady of Joy) was placed in the church at Assy; in June 1956 the second arrived in New Harmony; and, through Owen's efforts, a third was installed in the cloister of the medieval Benedictine (now Presbyterian) monastery of Iona Abbey on the Isle of Iona, Scotland, in 1959.[23] To make the sculpture relevant to its setting in New Harmony, Owen suggested an alternative name, *Descent of the Holy Spirit,* which was how she had described the work in her April 1950 letter to Lipchitz responding to the photograph of the first maquette.[24] In Iona, "Holy" was removed from the name in deference to anti-Catholic sentiment. The New Harmony casting remained homeless until the Roofless Church was completed in 1960.[25]

Owen's spiritual beliefs underwent a significant refocusing in the 1950s. Through Lipchitz, she met the Protestant theologian Paul Tillich (1886–1965), who became her spiritual mentor.[26] Lipchitz, who had first encountered Tillich at the Jewish Theological Seminary in New York, was extremely excited about his ideas and his empathy with artists, favorably comparing him with Father Couturier. Forced to leave Germany in 1933, Tillich had become one of the most important theologians in the United States in the postwar period. He was a professor and preacher of great renown, and his accessible writings touched a broad public. Tillich's work was exceptional in its depth and scope, not only in philosophy and Christian theology but also in non-Western religious thought. Perhaps no work was more influential than his short, powerful book *The Courage to Be* (1952), in which he examines existential anxiety and the dilemma of meaninglessness—increasingly seen as the greatest challenge facing contemporary society—and introduces the meaning of courage as a remedy.

These issues carried into Tillich's progressive thinking about the role art and architecture played in religious experience. He persuasively argued that only abstract, modern forms could convey significance and redeem meaninglessness, both key concepts in postwar American culture.[27] Tillich was often invited to speak about the relationship of art and religion at various institutions, including the National Gallery of Art and the Museum of Modern Art, and his ideas were well received within architectural circles. The architectural historian and critic Sibyl Moholy-Nagy had studied with Tillich at the University of Frankfurt in the late 1920s and maintained a connection with him when he taught at Union Theological Seminary (1933–55) in New York.[28] Through the Museum of Modern Art, Johnson too had contact with Tillich, who was invited in 1953 to address the opening of the museum's new galleries and sculpture garden designed by Johnson.[29]

Tillich's ideas reached architects through his participation in a roundtable discussion with religious leaders and a group of architects, among them Pietro Belluschi and Albert Christ-Janer, organized by *Architectural Forum* and published in the December 1955 issue. Presented in the journal as one of the "Men behind the Blueprints," Tillich forcefully argued against the use of traditional Christian symbols, advocating instead for the "ideal of holy emptiness."[30] Here Tillich touched on a contentious issue in current architectural discourse. The completion of Ludwig Mies van der Rohe's very spare Robert Carr Memorial Chapel at the Illinois Institute of Technology in Chicago (1949–52) had sparked a debate on the limits of architectural emptiness. Even Johnson, Mies van der Rohe's foremost supporter, was taken aback by its starkness and later cited it as the catalyst for his turn to other sources. Two projects by Eero Saarinen—an interdenominational chapel for Brandeis University designed in collaboration with Matthew Nowicki (unrealized, 1949) and a chapel at Massachusetts Institute of Technology (1950–55)—were often presented as exemplary illustrations of this ideal. Saarinen exploited the expressive potential of his primary material (sun-baked, wood-fired bricks laid to accentuate their irregularity) to its fullest, the dramatic lighting accentuating not only the serpentine wall but also the individual bricks, which seem to almost writhe. Saarinen can be credited, along with such architects as Le Corbusier, particularly the Unité d'Habitation (1945–52), and Louis Kahn, whose Trenton Bathhouse was completed the same year as the MIT Chapel, with the new emphasis in postwar architecture on the expression of

Figure 4.6. Eero Saarinen's vision of sacred space as embodied in his MIT Chapel (1950–55), Massachusetts Institute of Technology, Cambridge, Massachusetts, was a paradigm for architecture in the 1950s. Chapel altar with Harry Bertoia's screen photographed by Balthazar Korab, circa 1955. Photograph courtesy of Library of Congress, Prints and Photographs Division, Balthazar Korab Archive at the Library of Congress, LC-KRB00-230.

raw materiality. The Roofless Church must also be seen within this architectural culture context.

Tillich, whose ideals would have an important impact on the Roofless Church, went further into the question of what might constitute meaningful forms in Protestant churches, advocating publicly in 1962 that architecture would be enriched by "Abstract, nonrepresentational works [which] can have great symbolic power, often far more than realistic forms."[31] He concluded with the assertion that "*only* by the creation of new forms can Protestant churches achieve an honest expression of their faith."[32] Owen's religious vision drew from Tillich, who believed that those rooted in their own faiths would be open to the faiths of others. She was equally moved by his insistence that each epoch create its own art forms and his conviction that religion and contemporary art were integrally related phenomena. Both conclusions became touchstones for her plans for the Roofless Church.

Giving Form to the Roofless Church

In retrospect it is not surprising that it was through Dominique and John de Menil that Jane Owen met Philip Johnson. The Menils' house in Houston, designed by Johnson in 1948, launched what would become a very successful career for the architect in Texas. John de Menil, who believed Johnson to be a significant talent, threw his support behind him and in June 1956 basically procured the architect's largest commission to date: the master plan of the new campus of Houston's Catholic university, the University of St. Thomas (1956–59). Owen knew the Menil house well and followed the progress of the campus commission, attending Johnson's November 1956 lecture at St. Thomas, where she heard him speak passionately about architecture as first and foremost art.[33] Four months later, she found herself turning to him for help in solving the problem of her homeless sculpture, a suggestion made by John de Menil during a chance meeting on a return flight to Houston from New York. As she later recalled, de Menil extolled Johnson's understanding of art as well as architecture: "You would find Philip very sensitive to your most unexpressed wishes. I would go so far as to call him clairvoyant."[34] Although she appreciated Johnson's intellect and what she later characterized as his "restrained approach," it was not Johnson's Miesian architecture that drew her to him. It was an unrealized project for a Catholic parish church in Houston, St. Michael the Archangel (1952–53).[35] Learning that the recently organized parish was planning to build a church and school, Owen apparently suggested to John de Menil that he put forward Johnson as architect.[36] The result was what Johnson later claimed to be his "first Romanesque design."[37] He proposed a dramatic spatial experience for the interior of the church. A sequence of soaring vaults, each supported by thin piers and surmounted by an oculus, leads toward a light-flooded altar. Natural light washes the inner arches that frame a series of side chapels. More than fifty years later, Owen still vividly remembered the project, describing it as "something that belonged in North Africa, with a white dome and white walls; very simple, very stunning."[38] In her eyes it was an almost perfect expression of Tillich's ideal of "holy emptiness."

Despite these close connections, it was not until after finally meeting Johnson in early April 1957 at the American Federation of Arts convention in Houston that Owen became convinced that he was the right architect for her project.[39] Clearly briefed by the de Menils in anticipation of this meeting, Johnson was well prepared to respond to her idea of building an unusual church for the town of New Harmony. That he shared her admiration of Lipchitz's work was reflected in the most personal of projects, his own Glass House (1945–49), where the sculptor's *Figure* (1926–30) occupied a prominent place on the lawn.[40] Johnson's intuitive approach and open attitude dispelled any lingering doubts she possessed; as Owen later remembered, "he was the one [architect] with the kind of poetry in his soul for realizing . . . what was only a dream at the time."[41] With no hesitation she offered him the project. Intrigued by her vision and the potential of the project, Johnson accepted.

Owen was the type of client Johnson worked most enthusiastically with: she was cultured and open-minded, committed to modern art, and unfettered by budgetary constraints. Like many of his clients, she remembered him welcoming her ideas and suggestions, and she put complete trust in him, not only hiring him as architect but appointing him a trustee of the Robert Lee Blaffer Trust, which she endowed in June 1958 to fund her philanthropic projects.[42] Over the next ten years, Johnson would also make studies for a "Cave" (1960), a project intended as a counterpoint to the Roofless Church (a commission that was, with Johnson's encouragement, subsequently given to Frederick Kiesler), and design the new Episcopal Church of St. Stephen in New Harmony (unrealized project; 1964–65). He would also consult with the landscape architects Zion & Breen on the design of Paul Tillich Memorial Park (1965).

Owen's recollections of her first meeting with the architect of her church have only recently come to light. Aside from the general concept of an open-air church—a walled and roofless sanctuary—the only programmatic element Owen initially requested was a structure to shelter the sculpture by Lipchitz, her dream of raising such an altar on Indian Mound reborn in the church project. From the start, the altar—the structure enclosing the sculpture—was to evoke the golden rose sacred to the Harmonists.[43] Early in the process she communicated two broader goals to Johnson that brought past, present, and future together: design a monument paying tribute to the religious founders of New Harmony and produce a spiritual focal point for its townspeople.

Johnson presented his first design to Owen just a week after their initial meeting. If his liberty was occasionally checked by the desires of his client and the sculptor, he had a free hand in laying out the site plan.[44] He was sensitive to the inherent ambiguity of the project; was it a problem of architecture, landscape architecture, or both? In this respect, it shared many of the challenges of his first "roofless room," the Abby Aldrich Rockefeller Sculpture Garden at the Museum of Modern Art (1950–53).[45]

Figure 4.7. The Abby Aldrich Rockefeller Sculpture Garden (1950–53) at the Museum of Modern Art in New York was Philip Johnson's first "roofless room." View by unknown photographer, 1953. Photograph courtesy of the Museum of Modern Art. Digital image copyright the Museum of Modern Art. Licensed by SCALA / Art Resource, NY.

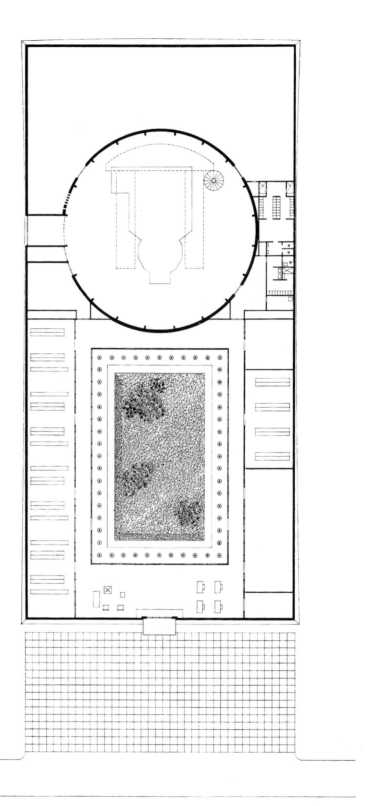

Figure 4.8. The plan of Johnson's Nahal Soreq Nuclear Research Facility (1956–59), Israel, is based on a tense play between the courtyard walls and the reactor core. Drawing copyright J. Paul Getty Trust, Getty Research Institute, Los Angeles (980060). Architectural design copyright the Estate of Philip Johnson; courtesy of the Glass House, a site of The National Trust for Historic Preservation.

0   20   40   60   80

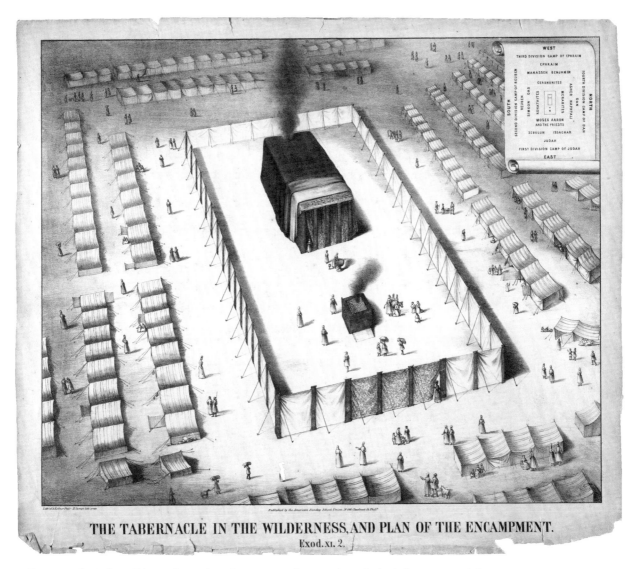

THE TABERNACLE IN THE WILDERNESS, AND PLAN OF THE ENCAMPMENT.
Exod. XI. 2.

Figure 4.9. The Hebrew Tabernacle may have been among the precedents for both the reactor and the Roofless Church. *The Tabernacle in the Wilderness, and Plan of the Encampment, Exod. XI, 2,* printed between 1849 and 1853. Augustus Kollner, lithographer. John Henry Camp, printer. American Sunday-School Union, publisher. Courtesy of Library of Congress, Prints and Photographs Division.

Although no drawings for this initial proposal survive, all evidence suggests that it was conceived as a play between a perimeter wall, broken at only one point, and a freestanding circular structure inside the rectangular enclosure outlined by the wall.

This layout also describes Johnson's contemporaneous design for a nuclear research facility at Nahal Soreq, Israel (1956–59).[46] While Johnson's biographer Franz Schulze and other historians have generally placed the design of the research reactor after that of the Roofless Church, Owen consistently described the first project for New Harmony as being based on that of the reactor. Her recollections, coupled with the speed and sureness with which Johnson laid out his ideas for the church, suggest that its basic outline had previously been worked out.[47] Rather unexpectedly, the two projects had many similarities. The research center comprised a reactor core and research offices organized around an enclosed courtyard, closely modeled on Johnson's favored form of the Greek *temenos*, a bounded open-air space in which a ceremonial structure shelters the sacred object. Another ancient source for a sacred compound was the Hebrew Tabernacle, the first sanctuary built by the Hebrews, predecessor to Solomon's Temple in Jerusalem, and progenitor of the synagogue. Such a symbolic reference undoubtedly resonated in the State of Israel, which in 1968 put an image of Johnson's nuclear reactor on the back of its 5 Lirot note. A portrait of Albert Einstein, since 1940 an American citizen, graces the front.

By this time Johnson had more than passing knowledge of sacred Jewish architecture. He had recently completed his first religious building, the Kneses Tifereth Israel Synagogue in Port Chester, New York (1954–56), and over the course of designing it had become involved in a study of the architectural history of the synagogue by Rachel Wischnitzer, a German émigré architect and art historian.[48] Invited to write the foreword to Wischnitzer's 1955 book, *Synagogue Architecture in the United States: History and Interpretation,* Johnson praised it as a "handbook for architects," especially members of the younger generation who were increasingly finding "history a much more inspiring guide than the bare functionalism of the older generation."[49] To this he added the important proviso: "They are learning to learn without copying and they can tell the difference between imitation and inspiration." Drawing from this "handbook" among other sources, Johnson worked hard to bestow a sacred aura on the nuclear complex, basing his design on one if not two ancient precedents. He said as much in a lecture at Yale in which he also spoke about the design of the Roofless Church, in February 1959:

> In this building we are still designing religion in a way, though it houses a nuclear reactor instead of an altar. . . . The religious overtones were also very conscious in the minds of the clients, when they came not to an engineer but to an architect to do their reactor . . . . It has a monumental presence in the desert that I don't think you can get out of straightforward engineering shapes.[50]

Figure 4.10. The significance of the reactor for the State of Israel is recorded in the 1968 Israeli 5 Lirot note, which features a perspective of the Nahal Soreq Research Facility on one side and a portrait of Albert Einstein on the other. Courtesy of Cammie McAtee.

The projects were clearly closely linked, spiritually as well as formally, in Johnson's mind. He would use the same basic *temenos*/cloister composition—an enclosure with a symbolic focal point—over and over through the late 1950s and beyond.[51]

Johnson first presented Owen with a similarly shaped structure for the focal element of the Roofless Church. Though she accepted the overall scheme, she emphatically objected to the angularity of the dome's design and told him to send the sharp edges of his reactor "back to the Israeli desert where they belong."[52] She remembered admonishing him: "You do not worship God with your elbows, you worship Him with your rounded arms," emphasizing her point physically by gently curving her arms over her head (an Isadora Duncan dance technique)—and an evocation of the profile of *Descent of the Holy Spirit*.[53] She encouraged Johnson to relate the dome's shape to the gentle contours of the Indiana landscape and insisted that he visit New Harmony before going any further with the design.

How engaged Johnson was in the project is reflected in the speed with which he made his first trip to New Harmony. He arrived on April 19, 1957, and for the two days of his visit he stayed in one of the first of the Harmonist houses restored by Owen. She took him on a hayride (a favorite method of sightseeing), and from this vantage point he experienced the rolling landscape of Posey County. Taken aback by the relatively small plot of land Owen had purchased on North Street and concerned that the surrounding buildings would encroach on the church, he encouraged her to purchase the neighboring lots. During the Harmonist years North Street had been a narrow lane, its south side lined with single-family dwellings and its north side— the Roofless Church site—occupied by three houses and an orchard (Plate 7).[54] A planting field stretched farther north beyond the site down to the Wabash River. The land for the project was assembled by bundling together several lots on which stood a barn, some clapboard houses, and a noisome facility for making oil tanks. This end of North Street had also been the focus of Owen's early efforts to restore the Harmonist legacy; several buildings had been relocated to the area. In response to Johnson's concerns, she began to purchase the adjacent lots, eventually more than doubling the size of the site.[55]

Between April and August 1957, Johnson substantially reworked his design.[56] A second review in New York with Owen and Lipchitz, whom his client considered a full collaborator on the project, brought a critical change to the program. During his visit to New Harmony, Johnson had seen Lipchitz's *Descent of the Holy Spirit* and understood that it would occupy a prominent place within the walls of the church. He likely drew from its general shape in his redesign of the dome. It is unknown where the dome was initially placed within the composition, but given the siting of Lipchitz's sculpture at the Glass House, where it played a dynamic role in mediating the relationship between the Glass House and Brick Guest House, Johnson may have envisioned placing it off center. By 1957, however, Johnson's work was increasingly symmetrical. There was no question in the sculptor's mind; for him, the raison d'être of the architecture was to provide a setting for his work. During the meeting he picked up an ink bottle and placed it near the center of the enclosure, indicating that he wanted the sculpture to be located on axis with the single opening—a twelve-foot high door—in the perimeter walls.[57]

The general scheme for a walled enclosure focused on a single freestanding element seems to have inspired more consideration about the function and meaning of the space. Was it a place of communal worship or only of solitary meditation? These questions would stimulate the project's development over the next four months. The duality of the Roofless Church as a place of gathering and a refuge for solitary contemplation was answered by the introduction of a third element, a small chapel where baptisms and marriages could take place. It simultaneously fulfilled Jane Owen's desire for an enclosed space "where one may close the door on his private devotions."[58]

Owen's vision of the Roofless Church as a monument to the past and a religious space for the present and future was formalized in a written document, the June 1958 agreement establishing the Robert Lee Blaffer Trust. Written more than a year after Johnson began design work, the agreement identifies three projects: a "program to embrace and provide cultural and religious phases and activities"; the restoration and preservation of the historic Harmonist buildings owned by the trust; and the design and construction of a "shrine" and, following its completion, a "chapel . . . for the furtherance of their contemplated religious program, both of which will be non-denominational and for the use and benefit of all people regardless of race or creed."[59] To achieve these goals, Owen lent the trust five hundred thousand dollars (the equivalent of almost four-and-a-half million dollars in 2018). The absence of any reference to a "roofless church" in the document suggests that the function of the space as a memorial to the past had taken on more importance.

Lipchitz had a major impact on the direction of its design.[60] For Owen, this was highly desirable, as she wanted artistic collaboration. But it was a relationship of equals in which neither artist nor architect was interested. Johnson's disinclination to enter into such a dialogue had nothing to do with his estimation of the artist. He knew and respected Lipchitz's strong feelings about the relationship between sculpture and architecture and his belief that a building only became architecture through the presence of sculpture.[61] But if sympathetic in principle to the sculptor's position, in practice Johnson had reservations about what he later characterized as Lipchitz's overbearing attitude toward architects. The experience of working with him on Blanchette Rockefeller's Manhattan Guest House, in which Lipchitz's work *Birth of the Muses* (1944–50) had, in Johnson's mind, intentionally overscaled the architecture, left the architect with the belief that the sculptor wanted to, in Johnson's words, "kill the architecture."[62] This battle would be replayed at the Roofless Church, with the dome dominating the sculpture, and the heavy gilded reliefs Lipchitz later created for the ceremonial entrance diminishing the simplicity of the bronze gates and perimeter wall (Plates 9 and 10).[63]

Sometime at the end of July, Owen visited Johnson's office to see the "new" model. She wrote to Lipchitz, who had been away on vacation, to update him. Her description reveals how close the relationship between the sculpture and its domed shelter had become:

> You will be very pleased with the new model. The arches of the roof are higher, which gives the impression of a mighty breath of wind filling a parachute. Our Gentle Lady descends slowly to earth. . . . I would have liked to taste all this with you, particularly the moment of setting into place your statue, for a model, in miniature, has been made of her in order to better understand her desires. We think she will be happy to be completely exposed to those approaching the chapel, so that the triangle seems to hold up the vault of the roof, but the Holy Spirit is covered. Once you have entered her space, you discover the dove.[64]

The letter also indicates that the question of where the sculpture would be positioned was still open, despite Lipchitz's resolute positioning of the ink bottle.[65]

In a letter to Owen of August 13, 1957, Johnson dramatically announced: "We have come to a turning point in our work for you," referring to progress made in the wake of her visit and improvements to the model.[66] Another meeting with Lipchitz was planned for September, but significant developments in the project seem to have been under way before it could take place. On August 27, 1957, Johnson wrote:

> I will hold up on engineering and any more model work until we have a conference. . . .
> I think I had better see you in Houston, since I will not be as harassed there as I would

be here, and we can have more time for talking. I shall come as soon as I get word from the University of St. Thomas and bring all my plans and ideas.[67]

His preference for seeing Owen in Houston was undoubtedly also motivated by a desire to keep Lipchitz at bay. The revised design for the dome called for a wood structure made of laminated ribs and hand-cut shakes. Owen later credited the project's turn in direction to Johnson's time in New Harmony, recalling that it was after his visit that Johnson "finally got the idea," responding with a design that seemed to relate to the natural, built, and spiritual context.[68] To achieve "unity and beauty," Johnson suggested that the walls of the complex be built of Indiana limestone, rationalizing that since it was a "local" material it would cost no more than brick.[69] Not surprisingly, stone proved too expensive, and the walls were built with a warm red brick instead.

An undated drawing (developmentally the earliest among the drawings for the Roofless Church in the Johnson collection in the Avery Architectural and Fine Arts Library at Columbia University) probably made in early 1958, describes the complex defined by the perimeter wall, dome, chapel, and a single portal.[70] The plan also reveals that the site was still relatively modest, with the long dimension of the church oriented north–south, parallel to Main Street, and entered on axis from North Street. The future chapel, which extends out like a hand from the east side of the complex, represented the most significant, if rather awkward, recent development. By May 12, 1958, the plan underwent its last major revision. In expectation that more land would be available, Johnson rotated the main axis ninety degrees and moved the chapel to the south side. The new orientation, aligned lengthwise along North Street, would encourage visitors to walk almost the entire span of the precinct before being granted a view inside through the break, a processional route inspired by those of ancient sacred spaces.

This drawing records another addition to the program. Though it came at the sacrifice of puncturing the *temenos* precinct, at the request of his client Johnson added

Figure 4.11, top. Early undated plan of the Roofless Church with domed shrine, a single entrance, and newly added chapel, which interrupts the regularity of the brick enclosing wall. Courtesy of Philip Johnson architectural drawings, 1943–94, Avery Architectural and Fine Arts Library, Columbia University. Architectural design copyright the Estate of Philip Johnson; courtesy of the Glass House, a site of The National Trust for Historic Preservation.

Figure 4.12, bottom. Plan and north and south interior elevations for the Roofless Church oriented along North Street. Drawing dated May 12, 1958. A balcony on the north wall, an entrance on North Street, and private entrances on the west wall have been added to the composition. Courtesy of Philip Johnson architectural drawings, 1943–94, Avery Architectural and Fine Arts Library, Columbia University. Architectural design copyright the Estate of Philip Johnson; courtesy of the Glass House, a site of The National Trust for Historic Preservation.

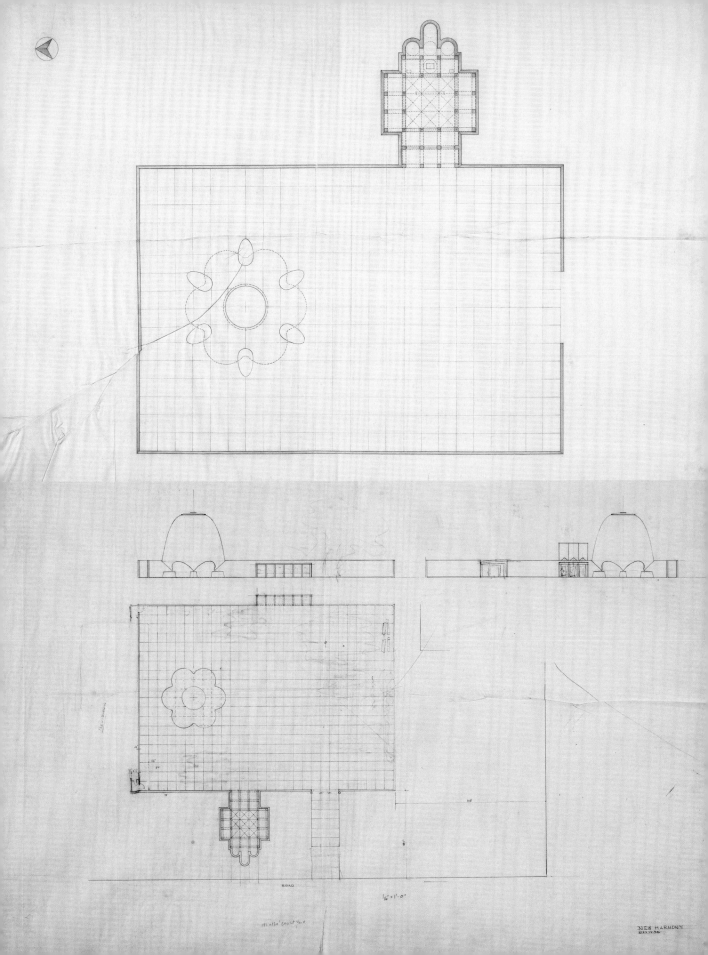

ROAD

1/16" = 1'-0"

NEW HARMONY

a balcony overlooking the low-lying field to the north. Owen had been touched by the request of a friend who saw the plans and asked for a place "where a woman could sit and sew."[71] Though the opening reduced the tension of the uninterrupted walls, it connects the building with the surrounding landscape (Figure 4.1; Plate 6). Its neoclassicism brings to mind the porticos of Karl Friedrich Schinkel's garden architecture at Schloss Charlottenhof, a place Johnson regularly cited as inspiration.[72]

A third new element, a ceremonial entrance, also entered the project. Owen objected to the thin portal as the sole opening and requested an operable gate that was only to be used for special days. Seeing an opportunity to again involve Lipchitz, she asked him if he would make another sculpture for the gate.[73] In the end he created five works, which were installed on the bronze door and gilded in situ in 1962.[74] As the model and final work show, they are arranged around a cross, which splits in two when the gate is opened (Plates 9 and 10). The lowest register holds a pair of thorn-like wreaths, which in their final form frame the Alpha and Omega (the beginning and the end). A smaller pair of rose-like wreaths occupies the space above the cross's arms. Held aloft by a pair of faceless angels, a third wreath of rose boughs encircles a lamb. This triumphant final element surmounts the entire gate structure, remaining in place when the gate swings open on special days. The prominent rose motif enunciated spirit as well as place, addressing both the Virgin and the religious beliefs of the German settlers who established the town.

While these additions answered programmatic needs, they threatened to diminish the tension of the enclosure. Struggling to reconcile the chapel and balcony with the composition, and to answer the problem of the new entrance (which inspired yet more entrances), Johnson sketched into the plan a pair of partially hidden side entrances at the corners of the west end of the enclosure and began working on the expression of the main entrance on the south elevation (see Figure 4.12). The final plan records Johnson's solution: a modest opening on North Street became the everyday entrance; a small, almost hidden door near the northwest corner offered a private entry into the space, likely intended for the celebrant; the monumental gate was on axis with the domed shrine as Lipchitz wished it (the gate also required a small forecourt, which appears in this drawing); an asymmetrically placed balcony opened out on the north side; and, barely perceptibly, the entrance for the future chapel appears on the south wall (see Figure 4.14). The plaza's surface was almost entirely covered by limestone paving stones, with a few openings for flowerbeds (geraniums), trees, and two long hedgerows (Plate 9).

The unrealized chapel merits more discussion here, as it unexpectedly had a trajectory of its own. Although the plans showing the chapel reveal little about Johnson's ideas for the chapel's exterior, we can be fairly certain that Owen's desire for a space where one could withdraw meant that the walls were to be as closed as those of the enclosure. A tripartite entrance to the chapel on the "interior" of the

Figure 4.13. Jane Blaffer Owen, Jacques Lipchitz, and the model for the gates of the Roofless Church. Jacques Lipchitz papers and Bruce Bassett papers concerning Jacques Lipchitz, circa 1910–2001, bulk 1941–2001. Archives of American Art, Smithsonian Institution. Photograph by George Holton. Courtesy of Thomas Holton.

Roofless Church is described on the May 1958 drawing (see Figure 4.12). It seems close in spirit to the entrance as built on North Street (Figure 4.2). The drawing also describes a tall roof rising at least twelve feet above the perimeter walls. That both architect and client believed that they would return to this project and open the Roofless Church's walls a final time was more than just a few notations on a drawing: when the enclosing walls were constructed in 1959, they included a bricked-up knock-out panel, the entrance to the future chapel, an optimistic sign of mutual faith that was erased when the walls were reconstructed in 1976.[75] But well before the decisive break between Johnson and Owen occurred, the plans for the chapel were displaced by a much more ambitious project, St. Stephen's Episcopal Church (1964–65). Though the church would also not go ahead, falling victim to the personal and legal battle over the disintegrating walls of the Roofless Church, the remarkable project gives further insight into Johnson's ideas for the unrealized chapel, fueled as it was by the earlier work.

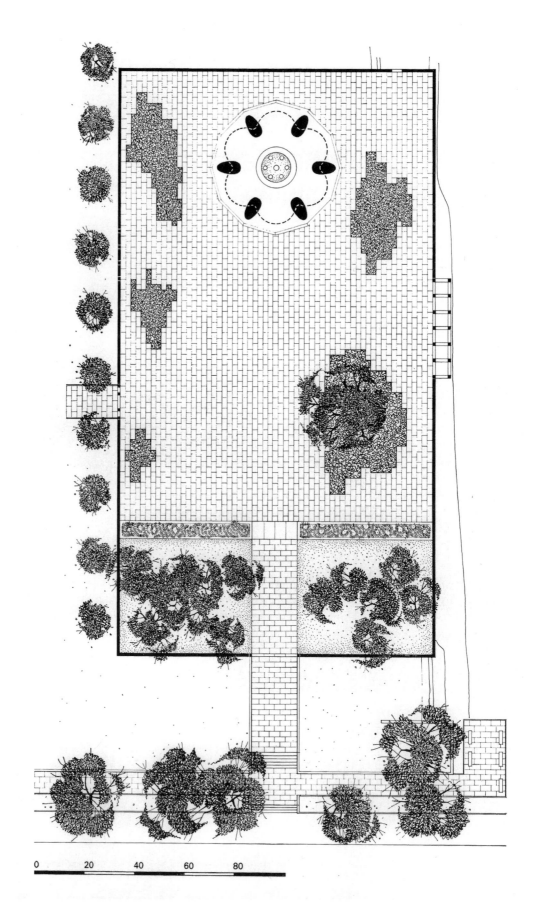

0   20   40   60   80

As a model demonstrates, St. Stephen's was to have maintained the strong theme of light of the Roofless Church, with the undulating blind enclosure walls of its exposed concrete structure surmounted by as many as twenty-seven conical acrylic skylights. It was both a take on the *canon de lumières* of La Tourette (1953–60), for by this time Johnson had been won over to Le Corbusier's work, in 1954 famously making "the play of forms under the light" the fundamental goal of architecture, and a continuation of the nascent ideas for the chapel.[76] Though the plan for the parish church would take on a life of its own, preliminary sketches for St. Stephen's reveal a close connection with the chapel; the two projects share almost identical rounded apses and side aisles (see Figures 4.11, 4.12, and 4.17). The idea of lighting the space entirely from the roof might also have its beginnings in the chapel: it is tempting to

Figure 4.15. The entrance to the future chapel is visible in a photograph taken before the crumbling walls of the Roofless Church were rebuilt in 1976. Unknown photographer, early 1970s. Courtesy of the Robert Lee Blaffer Foundation.

Figure 4.14. Final plan of the Roofless Church showing the main entrance and entrance to future chapel on North Street side, private entrance on west wall, paved courtyard and plantings, domed shrine, balcony, and Memorial Gate and forecourt (the latter unbuilt), 1959. Copyright J. Paul Getty Trust, Getty Research Institute, Los Angeles (980060). Architectural design copyright the Estate of Philip Johnson; courtesy of the Glass House, a site of The National Trust for Historic Preservation.

Figure 4.16. Model of Philip Johnson's unrealized project for St. Stephen's Episcopal Church (1964–65) in New Harmony. Photographed by Louis Checkman in March 1964, this version of the project includes a tower as well as a church with twenty-seven conical skylights. Photograph copyright the Estate of Louis Checkman and J. Paul Getty Trust, Getty Research Institute, Los Angeles (980060). Architectural design copyright the Estate of Philip Johnson. Courtesy of Wayne Checkman and the Glass House, a site of The National Trust for Historic Preservation.

Figure 4.17. The rounded apses and side aisles described in an undated early sketch plan and elevation for St. Stephen's Episcopal Church reveal a close connection with the Roofless Church's chapel. Courtesy of Philip Johnson architectural drawings, 1943–94, Avery Architectural and Fine Arts Library, Columbia University. Architectural design copyright the Estate of Philip Johnson; courtesy of the Glass House, a site of The National Trust for Historic Preservation.

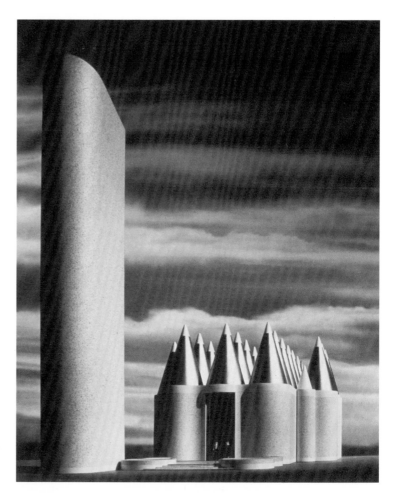

read the triangular shapes above the chapel's entrance as the seed of the dual purpose skylights/steeples of St. Stephen's.

Owen was eager to see her dream materialized and wanted construction to begin in fall 1958, but it was not until January 1959 that working drawings were complete.[77] Site work began in late April. While enough progress had been made on the foundation that a cornerstone could be laid on May Day, 1959 (the rites of spring being especially meaningful to Owen), it was the dome's design that held up construction. The dome encouraged Johnson to continue an investigation of vault forms begun several years earlier and to explore a wide range of "new" forms. It is here that Johnson worked out the approach to architecture he had pursued since the mid-1950s, which he described as "form follows form," a phrase borrowed from the influential Polish architect Matthew Nowicki that Johnson adopted as a rejoinder to the simplistic understanding of the aphorism "form follows function" coined by the Chicago architect Louis Sullivan in 1896.[78]

Johnson made his fullest statement on the design of the Roofless Church in the talk given at Yale in early February 1959, on the occasion of the inauguration of the second solo exhibition of his work at the university. Provocatively extending the title of the exhibition to "Whither Away—Non-Miesian Directions," Johnson not only offered insight into his changing approach to architecture but also disclosed important information about his struggles with the design of the Roofless Church.[79] After positioning his talk as an expression of personal doubt rather than as a manifesto, Johnson stated his allegiance to history as the guiding light of his design process:

> This is not academic revival; there are no classic orders in my work, no Gothic finials. I try to pick up what I like throughout history. We cannot not know history. . . . How could the Roofless Church exist without Bramante . . . ? I have gone back to my own little way of looking at things, which is purely historical, and not revivalist but eclectic.[80]

He concluded this passage by asserting the centrality of form to his work: "In the first place, it's impossible to do architecture without a background of ideas . . . [But] most important to us . . . is the revolution in form—not in ideas, mind you, but in form."

Johnson then went on to describe the Roofless Church, pointing out the model to his audience:

> The Roofless Church is the building I am working on now . . . a shrine out in Indiana for a Texas lady, and the symbol of the town is the rose, so it is the Shrine of the Rose; and that's the Lipchitz statue in the center. This idea comes from many historic sources, primarily the Indian stupa. It is about sixty feet high, fifty feet across, and it is built of shingles, which comes from the stave churches of Norway. The circular shape comes from central planning in any period. A circle has magic meanings, which after

I had designed it I found in Jung, in his description of primitive shapes. It is amusing that I was designing according to Jung; it is a good feeling to be connected with the super-unconscious or whatever it is. . . . [The shrine] is surrounded by a high wall forming a temenos broken only by the portico at the right which looks out over the landscape connected to the fertile Wabash Valley. But I couldn't start on the design of the structure without computers, and the cards are getting stacked high on the floor of the office. In other words, there is nothing simple or direct in the forms of these very strange compound curves.[81]

Typical of Johnson, this description contains an equal measure of frankness and deception about his design sources, more than a little exaggeration, and a dose of self-deprecating humor. These admissions were intended to control interpretations of the Roofless Church by appearing to fully disclose the sources of his inspiration, a strategy Johnson had previously used in presenting his Glass House in 1950.[82]

Of Vaults, Stupas, Shikharas, and Stave Churches

In considering the dome and its sources, the first connection to be made is within the series of vaults Johnson began designing around 1952. The first built example of this direction in his work is the double *baldacchino* inserted within the main bedroom of the Brick House in a renovation of its interior in 1953, but a perspective for a slightly earlier project, recently identified as a nondenominational chapel at Vassar College (1952–53), illustrates the dramatic effects of a similar element within a religious space.[83] Here the meeting space is enclosed beneath a massive canopy that springs up from thin piers, stretching out across the entire span of the sanctuary. As in the bedroom and the project for St. Michael's in Houston, a mysterious light source behind the vaulting simultaneously frames its taut, almost tent-like form and washes the perimeter with light. One "new" element, a single oculus, illuminates the central ritual space. This unrealized interior, especially its oculus, further supports Vincent Scully's claim that the sudden appearance of hung vaults in Johnson's work was a direct result of the architect's visit to Tivoli during the summer of 1952.[84] Scully's reading of the curvilinear shape of the Roofless Church's shrine placed within a sacred *temenos* as another testimony to the powerful lessons Johnson took away from Hadrian's Villa (as well as from ancient Greek architecture) is undoubtedly correct. The Guest House was a test for the Port Chester synagogue begun the following year. The vaults in both contexts function as elaborate scenographic, even trompe l'oeil, devices designed to manipulate the sense of space and heighten the dramatic qualities of light.[85] Compelling similarities also have been discerned between Johnson's vaults and those of John Soane and Basil Spence.[86]

Although fascinated with the scenographic possibilities offered by hung vaults, the effects Johnson designed for New Harmony took him in different directions. Whereas the synagogue's white plaster canopy is held taut like a thin sheet, the undulating shingled surface of the shrine's dome hangs heavily. Its deep folds carry a stronger emotional punch than any of its predecessors. One can only wonder if Johnson was encouraged, even emboldened, by Scully's appreciative reading of the synagogue's tent-like "wind-blown canopy" and his identification of it as an architectural "ur-form" in his influential 1954 article "Archetype and Order in Recent American Architecture."[87] As his statement that it felt good "to be connected with the super-unconscious" shows, Johnson was well aware of the formal as well as symbolic power of archetypal forms.

Considered within Johnson's trajectory as a designer, his experimentation with vaulting and domes seems to, if not climax in the freestanding form of the Roofless Church's dome, take his play of "form follows form" to a new level of complexity. But although the dome neatly falls within the continuum of his research into vault forms,

Figure 4.19. Interior perspective of Philip Johnson's unrealized project for a nondenominational chapel at Vassar College, Poughkeepsie, New York (1952–53). The chapel is one of the earliest of Johnson's "dome" projects of the early 1950s. Courtesy of Philip Johnson architectural drawings, 1943–94, Avery Architectural and Fine Arts Library, Columbia University. Architectural design copyright the Estate of Philip Johnson; courtesy of the Glass House, a site of The National Trust for Historic Preservation.

Johnson's 1959 "confession" of his sources opens up other interpretive directions. The connection between the "stupa"—a Buddhist religious structure that takes its bell shape from early burial mounds—with the "idea" of the "shrine" works well in relation to its memorializing purpose. Johnson may, however, have had a very different Eastern religious structure in mind. It was not the first time he had referred to Indian architecture. In his introductory remarks at the Museum of Modern Art's 1951 symposium "The Relation of Painting and Sculpture to Architecture," he showed a slide of a seventeenth-century Hindu temple, stating, "You can't conceive of it without the sculpture. The sculpture is the building."[88] While this conception all but foretold his later conflict with Lipchitz, it also indicates that a very different type of Indian religious architecture was on his mind. Rather than—or in addition to—the earthbound Buddhist form he cited in his talk at Yale, Johnson was interested in the heavily sculpted surface of the Hindu *shikhara* tower or spire. And indeed, the texture of their stone surfaces could have inspired the rough hand-worked skin of the New Harmony dome. It is impossible to know if Johnson was also referencing the cosmological

meaning of the *shikhara*'s form; at the very least, these sources served to deepen and diversify the cultural and religious origins of his project.

But if by 1959 Johnson was foregrounding non-Western architectural traditions in his explanation of the dome, Owen recalled that their first discussion of the project focused on Norwegian stave churches.[89] Again, it is not difficult to reconcile the finished dome with either the wood-shingled materiality of stave churches or their rounded apses and skeletal structures based on a square or rectangular arrangement of wood "staves" or pillars, which were coupled with transversal beams and arches on which the elaborately carved wooden surfaces were layered. Whether Johnson had firsthand knowledge of these early Norwegian wood structures is unknown, but his interest was very timely, as two English-language publications on the subject came out in the early 1950s.[90] His enthusiasm most likely came from a major exhibition of Viking art that had been shown in Brussels and Paris in 1954. *Art News* (a journal in which Johnson regularly published exhibition and book reviews and which Owen read) featured a long article by Roar Hauglid, the exhibition's curator and stave church expert, that April. The article included an image of a twelfth-century church in Borgund, which Hauglid described as "rising like monsters covered with scales from the mountain hollows."[91] More impetus came from Sibyl Moholy-Nagy's book *Native Genius in Anonymous Architecture* (1957), a groundbreaking study of vernacular architecture addressed specifically to architects. Her discussion includes the stave churches and their close relations, the mountain churches in the Carpathians, the latter illustrated by a line drawing.[92] If these were indeed sources, Johnson saw them much as he had Wischnitzer's study of synagogues, namely, as handbooks for design. This ran counter to Moholy-Nagy's intention; imitation, she warned in the book, "concerns itself only with external form, inspiration with the total concept."[93]

Though Johnson has often been read as an extreme formalist, taken at his "form follows form" word, the fact that the two buildings are both devoted to spiritual purposes cannot be overlooked. The stupa is a reliquary for an artifact of Buddha; its mound-like shape represents a holy mountain sheltering a sacred cave. Hindu temples of this kind also have a cosmological significance, representing the body and the universe. Traditionally, they were set within courts and hypaethral—open to the sky—through the presence of an oculus.[94] Stave churches have been called Gothic churches in wood; their forms arising out of a merger of Anglo-Saxon parish church plans and pre-Christian decorative motifs. They engage both traditions through their structure and decoration. It is tempting to read these two sources in light of Owen's desire for a space that was "non-denominational and for the use and benefit of all people regardless of race or creed." From the client's increasingly syncretic perspective, the merger of a non-Western religious structure with a Norse Christian church was extremely appropriate.[95]

Mounds and Haystacks

But Johnson's citation of two sources does not adequately explain the dome's shape. Here we need to return to Owen's desire that the shape of the shrine reflect its place. It has been previously suggested that another source for the dome was closer at hand: the brick church built by the Harmonist Society in 1822.[96] The second of two churches built in New Harmony, its cruciform-plan appeared to the leader of the Harmonists, Father Rapp, in a dream three times.[97] A relief sculpture of a rose, the construction date, and a reference to Micah 4:8, a text from the Lutheran Bible that was sacred to the group, were inserted in the pediment over the entrance. The full quotation was inscribed on a plaque on the cornerstone of the Roofless Church: "Unto thee shall come the golden rose, the first dominion." According to Rapp's calculation, 1822 marked the beginning of the era of the golden rose, a symbol that held deep meaning as the symbol of the Second Coming and the building of a city of God. The quadripartite plan of the church was oriented according to the cardinal compass points, an organizational principle used by Rapp in his garden designs, in the plan for the town of New Harmony, and again later in the church and town plan of Economy, Pennsylvania.[98]

Described by nineteenth-century visitors as being about 120 feet long in either direction, the four wings of the centrally planned New Harmony church converged on an open gallery surmounted by a low dome. This central space was said to have contained twenty-eight gigantic polished wooden pillars of various woods, often interpreted as a reference to the cedars of Lebanon.[99] The spiritual center of the community during the Harmonist period, the church was converted by the Owenites into their central meeting room, but by the 1870s the structure had fallen into a dangerous state of disrepair. Displeased by the secular repurposing of their former church, descendants of the original Harmonists purchased and then demolished it in 1874, reusing its red bricks to surround the land where the community had buried its dead without grave markers (see Figure 6.4). The remaining bricks were donated for the construction of a school, the former church door with its rose pediment integrated into the new building, where it was known as the "Door of Promise."

The most curious element of the cruciform church was the structure atop the dome. A note made by English visitor William Herbert in February 1823 described it as a "small circular tower of about 10 feet in height . . . surmounted by a silvered globe."[100] This "tower" or lantern is visible in drawings made by the scientific illustrator Charles-Alexandre Lesueur after Robert Owen's purchase of the town in 1825. The most detailed record of what it may have looked like and how it was constructed is found in the set of eight original drawings for the church, attributed to Father Rapp's adopted son Frederick.[101] These drawings indicate that the structure gave access to a musicians' gallery, where the congregation's band was known to have played. Roughly rendered in brown wash in Rapp's drawings, what Herbert called a tower appears to be more of a mound (Plate 3). Its texture starkly contrasts with the even surface of the church's main body, suggesting a wooden, if not shingled, surface in keeping with a series of rough garden structures Rapp built in all three of his towns, which were based on the *Einsiedeley*, a hermitage or shelter of the settler that were popular in Germany in the late eighteenth century.[102] A German garden publication from the end of the century describes the materiality of the *Einsiedeley*:

> It can be a simple, crude little hut, round or square, whose windows are small and whose roof is straw, carried on rough piers, and on whose walls one can trace the ravages of time and weather. It can variously take the form of a wood pile . . . or be assembled out of roots or the bark of trees can be nailed against it. It can depict a cavern or a mound, made up of earth and stone. Whether of stone or wood, it must demonstrate the greatest simplicity and neglect and no trace of artifice.[103]

This description compares equally favorably with the "mound" on the Harmonist Church and the shrine of the Roofless Church.

The conceptual and material similarities between the two structures are striking. A substantial part of Johnson's first visit in April 1957 was undoubtedly spent discussing New Harmony's early history. Moreover, Don Blair (1909–1992), an engineer by profession, a Blaffer Foundation trustee, and Jane Owen's representative throughout the design and construction of the Roofless Church, was as deeply interested as she was in the history of New Harmony and had been in touch with Old Economy Village in Pennsylvania, where Rapp's drawings were located.[104] In his book

The New Harmony Story (1959), Blair reproduced a view of the church as drawn by one of Robert Owen's sons in 1830.[105] How much detail was known in the mid-1950s about the demolished building is an open question, but in a 1959 letter to Tillich asking him to speak at the official dedication of the Roofless Church, Jane Owen intimated that she knew at least as much as Blair, and what is more, "We found the original plans of the destroyed German church, but did not copy them. We have taken, rather, their choice plum, the Rose, which the Germans had carved over each of the four doorways of their church and we are using similar materials—thick wood shingles, pink brick and limestone."[106] Her allusions may have been made to flatter Tillich—the letter also contains references to connections between her father and the Lutheran faith Tillich shared with New Harmony's founders—but they do merit further consideration. By this time, Owen had been in direct contact with Lawrence Thurman, curator of Old Economy Village, who came to New Harmony sometime between 1952 and 1955 to consult on the restoration of one the Harmonist houses.[107] He could certainly have provided her with this detailed historical information about the Harmonist Church. If it is unlikely that Johnson saw the original drawings showing the unusual culmination of the church, Lesueur's sketches of the church showing its rooftop "mound" were easily accessible, and Johnson did call his project the "Shrine of the Rose" while still in the midst of completing its design.[108] The brick walls of the Harmonist cemetery also provided a contextual precedent for the *temenos*. Moholy-Nagy's book on anonymous architecture had raised interest in vernacular buildings, and, although Johnson had mounted a strong opposition to the Bay Region style championed by Lewis Mumford in the late 1940s, the idea of addressing local context was hardly foreign to him, and the obscure references suggested here would certainly have intrigued him.

These references must also be kept in mind when considering Johnson's second New Harmony church, the project for St. Stephen's, for there is just as much evidence that the Harmonist Church as well as his own Roofless Church informed it (see Figures 4.16 and 4.17). Given that the church was to have been located diagonally across the street from the Roofless Church and opposite one of the Harmonist houses Owen had restored, Johnson was clearly seeking to intensify the connections he had begun making in the Roofless Church. While the conical skylights undoubtedly reflect a new enthusiasm for the sixteenth-century Ottoman architect Sinan—in the year he began working on St. Stephen's, Johnson exclaimed to Henry-Russell Hitchcock, "Stanbul and Sinan forever"—the domed kitchens at the Topkapi Palace in Istanbul, the underlying source for the roof plan, the Greek-cross plan of the Harmonist Church also lies beneath those domes (see Figure 4.17).[109] Local newspaper reports suggested that the conical shapes animating the blind enclosing walls were taken from the granaries built by the original settlers, a reading that could be extended to include a formal reference to the origins of modern architecture in the

Figure 4.22. Preliminary elevation for St. Stephen's Episcopal Church (1964–65). The cylindrical shapes were interpreted as grain silos. Courtesy of Philip Johnson architectural drawings, 1943–94, Avery Architectural and Fine Arts Library, Columbia University. Architectural design copyright the Estate of Philip Johnson; courtesy of the Glass House, a site of The National Trust for Historic Preservation.

concrete grain silo, a relationship borne out in an early elevation.[110] Here the symbolic connection the journalists made, encouraged by Johnson, was between church ritual and harvest. It also furthered the liturgical emphasis on the altar, which was envisioned as a communion table accessible on two sides. The "place" reference was materially deepened in this element, which was to be made from New Harmony birch and placed on a dais of Indiana limestone. This was not the only attempt to materially connect the new church with its context; at one point Johnson proposed to cover the concrete surface of the building with cedar shakes, a choice that looks to the Harmonist Church as well as to his own precedent.[111] If the depth of Johnson's allusions to the past might be questioned, what is abundantly clear is that he was very much aware of the historic fabric of New Harmony.

The natural context of New Harmony (more specifically, Indian Mound, the site of the mystical experience that triggered the series of events leading to the materialization of the Roofless Church) may also register in the dome's shape, which

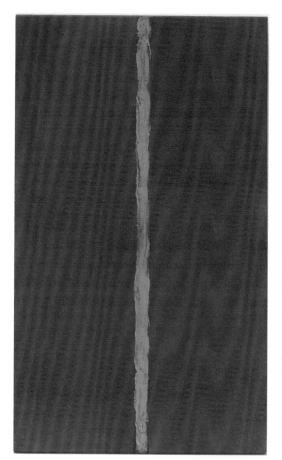

Figure 4.23. Barnett Newman, *Onement I* (1948), oil on canvas and oil on masking tape on canvas, 27.25 × 16.25 inches (69.2 × 41.2 cm). Newman only came to understand this first of his "zip" paintings after his experience with Native American mounds in Ohio in 1949. Gift of Annalee Newman. The Museum of Modern Art, New York. Painting courtesy of and copyright The Barnett Newman Foundation, New York/SOCAN, Montreal (2019). Digital image copyright the Museum of Modern Art. Licensed by SCALA / Art Resource, NY.

Owen specifically requested should respond to the soft rolling landscape of the area. There could be more to this than a simple one-to-one conceptual connection. Johnson may have been aware of the impact Native American mounds had had on the artist Barnett Newman. Like Owen, Newman's experience of Native American mounds in southwestern Ohio during a summer driving trip in 1949 had had a life-altering effect on him. After returning to New York, Newman wrote an important essay about the sensations and realizations that came to him at one of these sites, describing being "confounded by the absoluteness of the sensation, by their self-evident simplicity."[112] As the art historian Richard Shiff has shown, this experience directly related to an important transitional work, *Onement I* (1948), which Newman had painted the year before but only came to understand after facing the Native American mounds.[113] Looking back in 1965, Newman saw the painting as "the beginning of my present life," a characterization with which Owen would undoubtedly have sympathized.[114]

From Sculpture to Mathematical Form to Sacred Geometry

Although the overall shape of the dome was determined within the first few months of the design process, the difficulties in diagramming it for construction worried Johnson for another eighteen months. Its complexities are captured in the so-called theoretical plan, which appears on the cover of the working drawings. The plan shows a central circle surrounded and intersected by six interlocking circles. The outer line describes the edge of the dome canopy; the inner line describes the path of the parabolic curves that generate the arches. A drawing of the hyperbolic paraboloid curves further explicates this relationship (Plate 11). The lines intersecting the central circle include the main axes of the structure and connect the points of the columns, the center points and extreme ends of the piers. These lines join to create a complex web. The drawings show the complicated geometrical construction of the dome. The shape and position of each element is calibrated to support the overarching geometry of the whole structure. For example, the parabolic curve of the arches is echoed in the shape of the stone piers. Change to one element had implications for the entire structure. Thus, what seemed to begin as a sculptural form conceived through an intuitive artistic process—"form follows form"—metamorphosed into a complex geometric composition. From this perspective the dome is simultaneously a work of formal associations and of precise mathematical calculation.

Despite his collaboration with the structural engineer Lev Zetlin on the casing of the nuclear reactor, Johnson seems to have had little idea of how challenging the church's dome would be to describe. The calculations of the curvature of the structure and the patterning for the twenty thousand shingles covering it occupied one

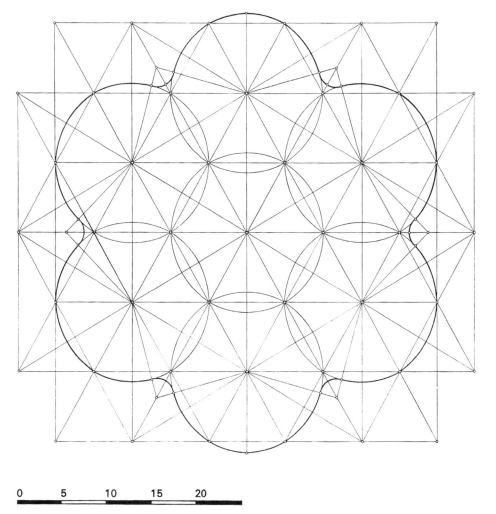

0   5   10   15   20

Figure 4.24. The outer line of the "theoretical plan" of the Roofless Church describes the edge of the dome canopy; the inner line describes the path of the parabolic curves that generate the arches. Drawing copyright J. Paul Getty Trust, Getty Research Institute, Los Angeles (980060). Architectural design copyright the Estate of Philip Johnson; courtesy of the Glass House, a site of The National Trust for Historic Preservation.

Figure 4.25. Don Blair's photographic record of the construction of the dome in the spring of 1960 shows that the elements (Portland footings stones, wooden piers, and arches) were pre-cut and assembled on site. Courtesy of Judith Blair Nix and the Working Men's Institute.

person in his office for an entire year, ultimately proving so complicated that Johnson explored the possibility of using a computer for the calculations.[115] (This was before computers entered architectural practice, and the almost twenty-thousand-dollar estimate for calculations was prohibitive.) Writing to the Blaffer trustees in February 1959, two months before construction was to begin, Johnson apologized for the delay in finalizing the drawings, admitting that "the unexpected engineering complications of the dome have me furious, but at last satisfied."[116]

Johnson was so committed to realizing the design of the dome on his terms that he (briefly) waived his fee to reduce costs.[117] A partial explanation for Johnson's uncharacteristically rigorous pursuit of structural and geometric perfection—nowhere better illustrated than in the almost daily photographs of the construction process taken by Blair—may lie in what Scully called in 1960 the "precisionist strain of American architecture."[118] Opposing this quality to what he called European humanist gestures, Scully saw in American architecture a tendency toward abstract exactitude and idealistic perfection pursued through obsessive attention to structural and material calculation.[119] At the same time, hyperbolic parabaloids had become de rigueur in architecture in the wake of Le Corbusier's Phillips Pavilion at the 1958 Brussels World Exposition.[120] Even so, the fact that Johnson, who consistently privileged effect over structural veracity, would adhere so closely to such strenuous mathematical calculations was more than a little unusual.[121] Something more important was at stake in the geometry of the dome.

Johnson often spoke of his intense interest in sacred geometry, a fascination bordering on an obsession that stayed with him over the course of his career. His client shared his enthusiasm; the first of the Harmonist houses she restored was named No. V in reference to the human body's symbolic and proportional connection to the number.[122] As Johnson said in 1959, "The circle has magic meanings," going even further to make a direct connection with Bramante. Mention of the sixteenth-century architect immediately brings to mind his Tempietto (San Pietro in Montorio, Rome, circa 1502). If Johnson was indeed thinking of this monument, he selected a singularly potent source, the small temple the embodiment of Renaissance humanist ideals and Platonic and Christian symbolism. That Johnson may have been drawn to its sacred geometry is entirely plausible, since the circle is equated with divine perfection. The cosmological associations of the circular building as an image of the world, as Palladio said of the Pantheon, would also have been attractive to both Johnson and Owen. The shape of the limestone piers—the egg associated with geometric perfection as well as with rebirth and the Resurrection—fits well among the constellation of references.[123]

Another source, especially persuasive for explaining the Roofless Church's still-enigmatic "theoretical" plan, was at once close at hand and much farther back in time, connecting the dome to the ancient origins of architecture. In 1955 a reproduction of

PERSECTA 3 *The Yale Architectural Journal*

Figure 4.26. The idea for the "theoretical plan" of the Roofless Church may have come from a medieval mason's mark reproduced on the cover of *Perspecta: The Yale Architectural Journal* in 1955. Courtesy of *Perspecta: The Yale Architectural Journal*.

a medieval mason's mark appeared on the cover of *Perspecta: The Yale Architectural Journal*. This issue had special significance for Johnson, who from the start had been a generous supporter of the student journal, the brainchild of his good friend and ally the late George Howe. Dedicated to Howe's memory and organized around the theme "Architecture and Craftsmanship," the issue contained not only Johnson's infamous 1954 talk at Harvard, "The Seven Crutches of Modern Architecture," which had taken his critique of contemporary architecture to a new level and again presented his belief that the goal of architecture was to produce art for all to see (an especially fitting tribute to Howe), but also an essay revealing the first fruits of Moholy-Nagy's work on anonymous architecture. This article included more than a few photographs that would have caught the eye of the Roofless Church's architect and client.

It is, of course, the mason's mark that is most compelling for the "theoretical" plan. Although the image's source was not given, it was likely reproduced from an analysis of the geometry of medieval stone masons' marks, *Studien über Steinmetz-Zeichen* (1883), by the Austrian architect Franz von Ržiha. This work and other attempts to decode the meaning of Greek and Gothic geometry had been brought back into play by more recent efforts to uncover the secrets of the Golden Section and "Divine Proportion," most notably by the mathematician Matila Ghyka in his 1946 study *The Geometry of Art and Life*. Le Corbusier's theory of the Modulor made the subject even more germane to contemporary architecture, and in 1951 and 1952 architects on both sides of the Atlantic debated whether divine proportion should be adopted as the basis of architectural design. Johnson was directly involved in these discussions: he participated in the Museum of Modern Art's "De Divina Proportione" conference held in March 1952.

While Johnson's library includes Ghyka's earliest book on proportions as well as Miloutine Borissavliévitch's study *The Golden Number and the Scientific Aesthetics of Architecture* (1958), his recent move away from Mies coupled with his dislike of Le Corbusier's theories make it unlikely that he would have been willing to commit himself to even more stringent rules, even if they offered the promise of revealing

144

CAMMIE MCATEE

ancient secrets.[124] The two plans also reveal important differences. Whereas the star-pentagram defines the medieval mark, Johnson's complex geometry obeys only its own geometric logic. The mason's mark must be entered into the list of formal inspirations for the plan of the dome, but it must be understood as representing the idea, not the practice, of sacred geometry.

Johnson's citations in his Yale talk of Bramante and central planning also reflect his awareness of Rudolf Wittkower's *Architectural Principles in the Age of Humanism* (1949), a book that was extremely influential among modern architects in the 1950s.[125] The book is partly based on a close reading of Francesco di Giorgio Martini and Leonardo's centrally planned churches. Drawings for these projects count among the plausible reference points for Johnson's circle-filled shrine. There is also direct evidence linking the design to Wittkower's careful analysis of harmonic proportions. On a sheet of drawings defining the curves of the parabolic ribs, a note explains that they will be calculated on the basis of a system of "harmonic progression," a subject to which Wittkower devoted an entire chapter. What this drawing suggests is that Johnson's "borrowing" from Francesco, Leonardo, and Bramante went beyond composition and proportion, however, to draw on Wittkower's main focus, the symbolic meaning of centralized church plans. Like the medieval mason's mark, the presence of these references within the dense layers of the domed shrine reflect a desire to instill something at once mystical (Harmonist) and rational (Owenite) within the project.

The resonance these ideas found with Jane Owen might be further explained by Tillich's views on modern church design. In his 1955 discussion of contemporary church architecture, the theologian considered how mysticism could be conveyed. Dismissing the idea of replicating shapes and styles of the past, he offered geometric forms as powerful sources for holy expression in a rational time:

> What we can do that was not done before is to use mathematical forms, pieces of color put together, and I think this is adequate to our feeling in which all forms of life have been brought down to geometric forms. We seem not to be able any more to understand the organic-forms in the way in which we did in former centuries but we are much better able to understand the underlying spiritual power of geometrical forms. We should not say that religious life must express itself in organic forms if it is the real possibility of our time to express it in cubic forms.[126]

He concluded his talk on the "principle of honesty": "There is truth in every great work of art, namely the truth to express something; and if this art is dedicated to express our ultimate concern, then it should be not less but more honest than any other art." In light of Owen's interest in religious symbolism and commitment to abstraction as well as faith in Tillich, Johnson's deeply embedded allusions as well as commitment to structural "honesty" would have found a uniquely receptive audience.[127]

Baroque Space

Johnson made a second and more revealing statement about his approach to the design of the church in December 1961. Two months earlier, the German historian and critic Jürgen Joedicke, in an article summarizing the past thirty years of modern architecture, pointed to Francesco Borromini's Sant'Ivo alla Sapienza in Rome (1643–60) as a formal source for the Roofless Church's dome.[128] Though Johnson had not publicly responded to critics' interpretations connecting the design with the work of other architects, Joedicke's comments touched a nerve. In a letter that was subsequently published in the first monograph on his work, Johnson categorically rejected the critic's reductive reading, sharply replying: "Borromini should not be mentioned in connection with my work. The New Harmony shrine is pure form—ugly or beautiful—but pure form."[129]

Joedicke was far from being the first to suggest this source; by the early 1960s, more than one observer had raised the possibility of a formal connection between the Roofless Church and baroque architecture, and parallels were drawn between its dome and that of Borromini's Sant'Ivo.[130] And indeed, in formal terms, Sant'Ivo's dome has rather lobe-like niches that undulate in a manner that are not dissimilar to the canopy of the Roofless Church's dome (see Figure 4.3 and Plate 11). If in built form the disparities between the two structures are more striking than the similarities, on paper it is the similitudes that stand out. Placed side by side, the geometrical diagrams of Sant'Ivo's stepped lantern and the reflected ceiling plan of the Roofless Church are nearly identical. In light of the compelling formal connections, Johnson's protest needs to be carefully considered.

On one level, what likely irritated Johnson was the implicit criticism that he had merely copied the work of another architect. The stakes for contemporary American architecture as well as for Johnson were very high; if he had copied Sant'Ivo, it would have been a clear-cut example of the eclecticism with which Joedicke and other European critics were charging American architects. It was one thing to be a self-styled eclectic but a different thing altogether to be practicing eclecticism, and Johnson was long on record as having denounced the latter. In his Yale lecture he took pains to distinguish between historicism and eclecticism, and more than ten years earlier he had outlined a way to return history to architecture that was not based on copying historical precedents. In a plea for "architectural freedom and order" co-written with Peter Blake in 1948, Johnson stated: "The great successes of form, of scale and of monumental impact are for *us* to emulate—not as copyists, but using the language of our new architectural vision and retaining only the spirit of this past work."[131]

But as is well known and evident in the project for the Roofless Church, illustrations in books occupied a central place in Johnson's design process, and so it is to the drawings in these publications as much as the interpretations they support that we

Figure 4.27. Though Johnson denied the connection, many critics saw Francesco Borromini's Sant'Ivo alla Sapienza, Rome (1643–60), as an important formal source for the dome of the Roofless Church. Courtesy of Nicholas Adams; copyright 2014.

must look. As a member of the upper echelons of architectural history who could count Margot Wittkower and Rudolf Wittkower as well as Henry-Russell Hitchcock, Vincent Scully, and Sibyl Moholy-Nagy as personal friends, Johnson was well aware of trends in architectural scholarship. He was likely cognizant of the recent increase in scholarly interest in Borromini. In 1958, as Johnson was completing the design of the dome, Rudolf Wittkower's Pelican volume on the art and architecture of Italy from 1600 to 1750 came out.[132] In his analysis of the baroque church's geometry, Wittkower drew on the recent work of Leonardo Benevolo, who, in a 1953 article, had included a series of theoretical plans showing a six-pointed star superimposed over Sant'Ivo's dome.[133] One of them, interestingly, was taken from Sigfried Giedion's

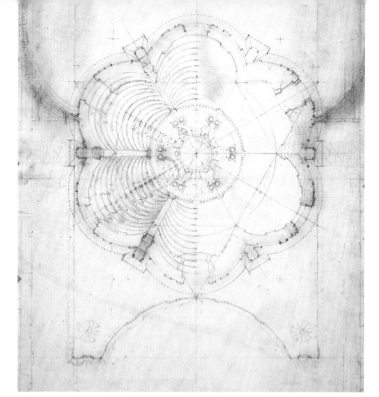

Figure 4.28. Plan of the stepped lantern of Francesco Borromini's Sant'Ivo alla Sapienza, Rome, circa 1645. Drawing courtesy of Albertina, Vienna.

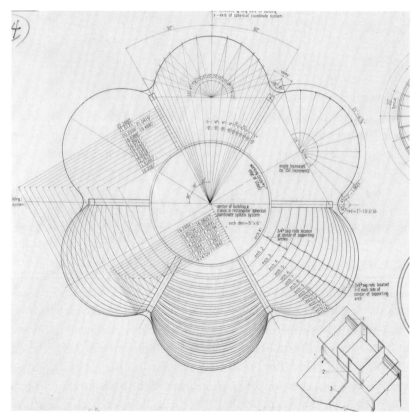

Figure 4.29. A detail from a sheet of drawings for the reflected ceiling plan (1958, revised 1959) of the Roofless Church's dome shows strong similarity between its plan and that of the lantern of Sant'Ivo alla Sapienza. Courtesy of Philip Johnson architectural drawings, 1943–94, Avery Architectural and Fine Arts Library, Columbia University. Architectural design copyright the Estate of Philip Johnson; courtesy of the Glass House, a site of The National Trust for Historic Preservation.

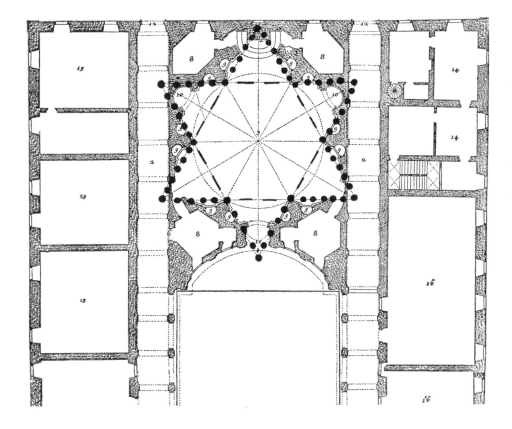

Figure 4.30. Published in Sigfried Giedion's *Space, Time, and Architecture: The Growth of a New Tradition* (1941), this plan of Sant'Ivo with a six-pointed star super-imposed over the dome was readily available to Philip Johnson. Source of image unknown.

section on Borromini in *Space, Time, and Architecture* (1941). In light of Johnson's fascination with sacred geometry, he was surely intrigued by the symbolic associations Giedion and Wittkower made. Another potential connection has been more recently raised by Elisabeth Kieven, who noted that Borromini described the dome as a "six-petaled rose" and called the lantern the "tempietto."[134]

It is difficult to dismiss the visual evidence that makes Johnson's protest against Joedicke more than a little suspect. Even Moholy-Nagy was hard-pressed to discount Sant'Ivo. Responding to a copy of his letter to Joedicke, she scolded Johnson for paying attention to him. At the same time, she could not understand why Johnson so resented the connection, underlining the formal similarities:

> It puzzles me that you object to being likened to Borromini on grounds of "pure form" which you rightly claim for New Harmony. It was my impression that the shrine belongs inseparably to the temenos enclosure—the undulated form to the rectilinear void. There is a relationship there to S. Ivo and its court and quite particularly to the first design of the Collegio di Propaganda Fide.[135]

Given that Moholy-Nagy perhaps best understood Johnson's intellectual meaning of "pure form," his denial must be considered through his design method.

When Johnson differentiated his dome from that of Borromini, he called it "pure form—ugly or beautiful—but pure form." What is patently clear is that Johnson did not merely lift the forms of the stupa or the Tempietto. In his play of "form follows form," he engaged a wide range of sources in ways that went far beyond their shape, proportion, or materiality to embrace historic and even symbolic associations. The unusually rigorous geometrizing of the dome's curves was a step, but only a step, within a painstaking process of formal assimilation, abstraction, and rationalization. All the forms discussed here and several others—those taken from nature, from diverse architects, cultures, countries, periods, styles, high art, and vernacular architecture—live within the shape and meaning of the Roofless Church's dome. Johnson's choices reveal that he was not merely playing fast and loose with a group of wantonly chosen forms as he was so often accused. A close reading instead reveals a meaningful engagement with the rich world of forms and a design process that was open to the symbolic meaning as well as committed to the aesthetics of "pure form." From this perspective, "pure form" must be read as an achievement won through a complex design process that goes beyond mere geometry.

"The Rib Cage of the Human Heart"

As enlightening as it is to parse the layers of the shrine's dome as a way of revealing Johnson's design method, the Roofless Church is much more than an assemblage of references and fragments. Johnson's uncompromising geometric rigor alone suggests that there is another level of meaning. To approach this, it is necessary to return to his purest version of the Roofless Church. As we know, he imagined it as a completely enclosed space, its walls and floor entirely surfaced with white limestone, a single door the only point of access. The focal point was a domed altar, which, though first conceived as also being clad in limestone, was quickly reimagined materially as a more "natural" structure. If on a much greater scale, Johnson's project for the Franklin Delano Roosevelt Memorial competition in 1960 gives an idea of how he may have envisioned this stone structure.[136] The tension between the uninterrupted walls, the open sky, and the altar would have been almost excruciating; the intense focus on the altar as the sole object in the space almost unbearable—or sublime—in emotional terms.

At this juncture I would like to return to Barnett Newman's reaction to the Ohio Native American mounds. In "Prologue for a New Aesthetic," the artist dismissed the spatial experience of the work itself or its relationship to the surrounding landscape as secondary at best, bringing the experience down to "not the *sense* of time but the physical *sensation* of time." [137] In that moment, in that place in Ohio, Newman lost all sense of "space and its manipulations" and discovered that "only time can be felt in private." Like Owen, Newman translated this experience into a religious expression, years later describing how it had motivated him to encode within his work "the idea of making the viewer present: the idea that 'Man is Present.'"[138] The philosopher

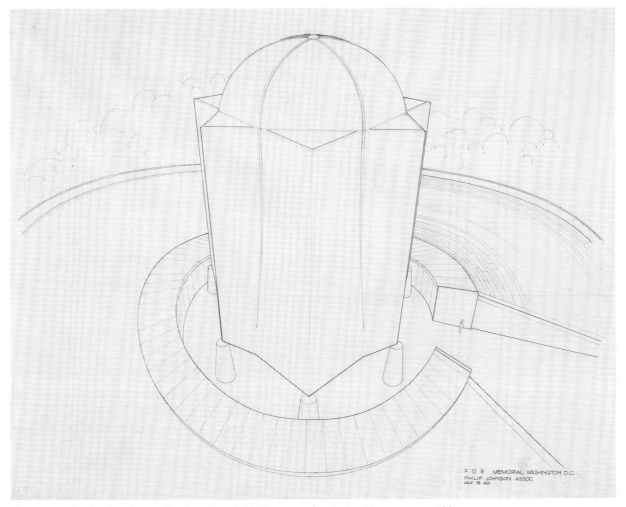

Figure 4.31. Closely related to the Roofless Church, Philip Johnson's entry into the 1960 competition for the Franklin Delano Roosevelt Memorial in Washington, D.C., further illustrates the tension the architect wanted to create between enclosure and memorial. Courtesy of Philip Johnson architectural drawings, 1943–94, Avery Architectural and Fine Arts Library, Columbia University. Architectural design copyright the Estate of Philip Johnson; courtesy of the Glass House, a site of The National Trust for Historic Preservation.

Jean-François Lyotard has interpreted Newman's desire to condense "Indian space and Jewish space" as an attempt to "capture 'presence,'" which Lyotard defines as "the instant which interrupts the chaos of history and which recalls, or simply calls out that 'there is,' even before that which has any signification. It is permissible to call this idea 'mystical,' given that it does concern the mystery of being."[139] This is a potent idea for thinking about Johnson's domed shrine, especially if we imagine it as its architect originally did, with its walls closed.

Having no way to determine if Johnson was familiar with Newman's epiphany, I am not suggesting that they lie behind his concept for the Roofless Church. But the concept of the "presence of time" raises an intriguing alternative to reading John-son's historical, formal, and material choices as being driven by his client's desire for contextual references. When Johnson was forced to give up limestone for the perimeter walls, he turned to a warm red brick, a choice that has typically been related to the walls of the nearby Harmonist Cemetery. I have also suggested that the inspiration for both the dome's shape and materiality came from the lantern of the demolished Harmonist Church. However, with exception of the Indiana limestone, none of the other major materials were "native" to New Harmony: Calvert Rose Red Range brick from Maryland was used for the walls; amethyst-colored granite from Quebec for the paving stones of the dome; southern pine from Wisconsin for the arches and ribs; and the split cedar shakes came from Oregon. The range of materials would seem to reflect a broad interpretation of context, one with a national, if not continental, scope.[140] A contextual reading is ultimately unsatisfying for interpret-ing what has been revealed to be a very complex and multilayered project. I would instead like to posit the idea that these historical, formal, and material layers were quite consciously compressed to express the spiritual and communitarian human "presence of time" and the "mystery of being."

Jane Owen expressed frustration with simple one-to-one formal connections, but she too had a representational association with the dome. She called it the "rib cage of the human heart," a metaphor that conveyed the intensity of her feeling for the spiritual and physical relationship of the shrine and the sculpture it safeguards.[141] She took pleasure in the coexistence of a Christian understanding of the form as a rose and a Buddhist one as a lotus blossom. In a description written soon after the church's inauguration on May Day 1960, she contemplated the wide-ranging readings the dome elicited to arrive at a holy conclusion:

> The dome may be taken for an eastern or a western flower, for a haystack, the spinna-ker of a sailing ship, or any other image familiar and important to the visitor. It is more likely that beyond any historic or personal influence the architect was deeply moved by the unseen power to which the *Descent of the Holy Spirit* bears witness and that, like other church architects before him, reverently and humbly exploited his art to its fullest, that the Creator and not the creature receive the hymn of praise.[142]

Her recognition of the inherent ambiguity of the dome's form brings to mind Umberto Eco's concept of the "open work." His theory helps explain the relationship between the dome as a work of architecture and the seemingly infinite possibilities it seems to offer for interpretation. For Eco, the work of art is simultaneously a "com-plete and *closed* form in its uniqueness as a balanced organic whole . . . [and] an *open* product on account of its susceptibility to countless different interpretations."[143] From this vantage point, "every reception of a work of art is both an *interpretation*

Plate 1. Karl Bodmer (Swiss, 1809–1893), *New Harmony on the Wabash,* 1842, engraving with hand-colored aquatint. In 1832 naturalist Prince Alexander Maximilian and artist Karl Bodmer stopped in New Harmony on their expedition across the American continent. Courtesy of Joslyn Art Museum, Omaha, Nebraska, gift of the Enron Art Foundation, 1986.49.517.2.

Plate 2. Banks of the Wabash River below Indian Mound, New Harmony. The undisturbed landscape at New Harmony has changed little over two hundred years. Photograph courtesy of Ben Nicholson, 2016.

Plate 3. Elevation for the original Harmonist Church attributed to Frederick Rapp in 1822. The church, which stood until 1874, is shown surmounted by a shingled lantern. Drawing courtesy of Pennsylvania Historical and Museum Commission, Old Economy Village.

Plate 4. The Harmonist Cemetery of unmarked graves, seen from the Atheneum. The cemetery is bounded by a wall erected by the last generation of Harmonists, circa 1874, with bricks from the demolished Harmonist Church. Photograph courtesy of Ben Nicholson, 2017.

Plate 5. The secular educators Robert Owen, William Maclure, Thomas Say, Charles-Alexandre Lesueur, and Marie Louise Fretageot are depicted in a watercolor painting by John Chappelsmith, *Man Makes HIS Own Existence: The Founders, Manual Training School, New Harmonie, Indiana*, 1827. From the collection of the Indiana State Museum and Historic Sites.

Plate 6. Jane Owen and the architect Philip Johnson in front of the balcony of the Roofless Church at the May Day Dedication, 1960. Photograph by John Doane. From the Collections of Historic New Harmony / University of Southern Indiana.

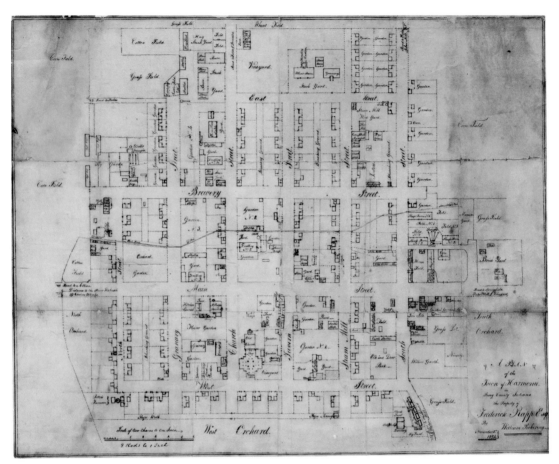

Plate 7. "A plan of the Town of Harmonie in Posey County, Indiana, the Property of Frederick Rapp Esq., by William Pickering, November 5th, 1824." This plan of New Harmony was used by George Rapp for the sale of New Harmony to Robert Owen in 1824. Photograph by John Doane. From the Collections of Historic New Harmony / University of Southern Indiana.

Plate 8. Acknowledging Charles Fourier's Phalanstery community, the architect Stedman Whitwell designed *Community Upon a Principle of United Interests, as Advocated by Robert Owen,* circa 1824. A version of the community was to be situated on a plateau, three miles from New Harmony. Courtesy of the New Lanark Trust.

Plate 9. Postcard of the Roofless Church, circa 1965, showing Jacques Lipchitz's gilded bronze sculptures and the dome over his *Descent of the Holy Spirit.* The original pavement of Indiana limestone was later removed, as it was deemed too hot to walk on during the summer. Courtesy of the photographer James K. Mellow.

Plate 10. The east-facing Lipchitz gates (1959–62) to the Roofless Church are in two parts. The inward-facing pair is a protective barred gate, and the outward-facing pair holds only the sculptures. The gates were restored and regilded by the Robert Lee Blaffer Foundation in 2016. Photograph courtesy of Ben Nicholson, 2017.

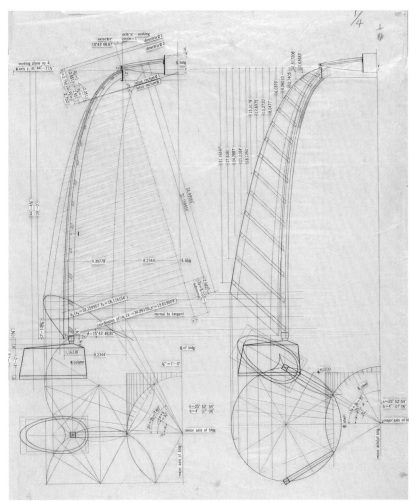

Plate 11, above. Elevation, section, and plans for the hyperbolic parabaloid curves of the dome of the Roofless Church, n.d. (1958–59). This drawing explains how the shape and position of each element is calibrated to support the overarching geometry of the whole structure. Courtesy of Philip Johnson Architectural Drawings, 1943–94, Avery Architectural and Fine Arts Library, Columbia University. Architectural design copyright the Estate of Philip Johnson; courtesy of the Glass House, a site of The National Trust for Historic Preservation.

Plate 12, below. Dome of Philip Johnson's Roofless Church (1957–60) and Jacques Lipchitz's *Descent of the Holy Spirit* (1946–55), photographed before 1966. This dramatic night view captures the formal relationship between the sculpture and the structure designed to shelter it. Photograph by Bert Van Bork. Courtesy of the Estate of Bert Van Bork.

Plate 13. Frederick Kiesler's bronze model of *Grotto for Meditation* for Paul Tillich Park, 1963. Two models were made, for Jane Owen and for Paul Tillich. Copyright 2018 Austrian Frederick and Lillian Kiesler Private Foundation, Vienna. Sculpture courtesy of Albertina, Vienna.

Plate 14. Conceptual sketches of six different schemes for the cave/grotto that includes an elevation of Philip Johnson's Roofless Church, 1962. Drawing copyright 2018 Austrian Frederick and Lillian Kiesler Private Foundation, Vienna.

Plate 15. Frederick Kiesler discusses his *Grotto for Meditation* in Paul Tillich Park with his structural engineer Dr. Paul Rongved and his assistant Len Pitkowsky in October 1964. The wall around the park is complete, and positions for the Grotto and Fish are laid out. Photograph by John Doane. Courtesy of Special Collections, University of Southern Indiana.

Plate 16. Frederick Kiesler and Jim Benton, the New Harmony contractor, inspect prototypes for the concrete shell and mound of *Grotto for Meditation,* 1963. Copyright 2018 Austrian Frederick and Lillian Kiesler Private Foundation, Vienna.

Plate 17. Carol's Garden, south view from entry gate to gravel path, hostas, Bradford pear trees, and fountain. Jane Blaffer Owen designed the overall plan of the garden in memory of her daughter, and artists were commissioned to design the fountain, benches, and other elements. Photograph courtesy of Christine Gorby, 2000.

Plate 18. A footpath winds through the earthen berms and Norwegian spruce trees of Paul Tillich Park (1965). Granite boulders carved with Tillich's words lead to his gravesite. James Rosati's sculpture *Head of Tillich* (1967) is in the background. The landscape architect Robert Zion based his design on Frederick Kiesler's plan for the site. Photograph courtesy of Michelangelo Sabatino, 2015.

Plate 19. A labyrinth for New Harmony, drawing attributed to Frederick Rapp, circa 1815. This nine-circuit design is for a garden of relaxation, with instructions for the type of fruit trees, including wild pear, plums, and cherries, to be planted (espaliered?) between the paths. Courtesy of Pennsylvania Historical and Museum Commission, Old Economy Village.

Plate 20. Cathedral Labyrinth, view of labyrinth with fountain and Harmonist Cemetery in background. Dedicated in 1997, the labyrinth is a reproduction of the medieval Chartres Labyrinth in France. This project was carried out by Kenneth Schuette and Rob W. Sovinski, professors of landscape architecture at Purdue University. Photograph courtesy of Ben Nicholson, 2017.

Plate 21. The Granary (or "Old Fort," as it is colloquially known), showing three phases of its use before its restoration in 1999: the 1814–22 Harmonist Granary, the 1843–59 David Dale Owen Geological Laboratory (at right), and grain mill (1905). Photographer unknown. Courtesy of Special Collections, University of Southern Indiana.

Plate 22. The New Harmony Inn and Entry House. Architect Evans Woollen partly used the vernacular Harmonist buildings to create this modern lodging. Woollen Associates, architect, 1975. Courtesy of Library of Congress, Prints and Photographs Division, Balthazar Korab Archive at the Library of Congress.

Plate 23. The MacLeod Barn Abbey was relocated and modeled on a vernacular Kentucky tobacco barn. It was built as a retreat and place of meditation. Robert Hatch, architect, 1976. Photographer unknown. From the Collections of Historic New Harmony / University of Southern Indiana.

Plate 24. Sarah Campbell Blaffer Potter's House. Richard Meier & Partners, 1978. Photographer unknown. From the Collections of Historic New Harmony / University of Southern Indiana.

Plate 25. Richard Meier included *Che* (1977) in an exhibition held in New Harmony in 1979, *Richard Meier: Collages and Architectural Drawings.* The collage loosely anticipates the limbs, panels, iconoclasm, and rotated grids of the New Harmony Atheneum. Collage courtesy of Richard Meier & Partners Architects.

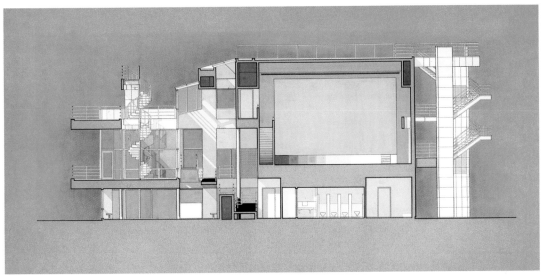

Plate 26. Presentation drawing of an east–west section through the New Harmony Atheneum, 1977. The white building drawn on a colored background reflects Meier's belief that his buildings are not white per se but colored through reflection, showing his indirect participation in postmodern architecture of the mid-1970s. Courtesy of Richard Meier & Partners Architects.

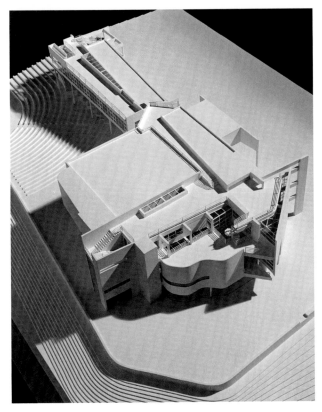

Plate 27. Model of New Harmony Atheneum, 1973. This early version of the scheme shows the amphitheater and study center to the east, subsequently eliminated from the program. Richard Meier & Partners Architects. Courtesy of Richard Meier & Partners Architects and Ezra Stoller. Copyright Esto. All rights reserved.

Plate 28. Nineteenth-century log cabins, relocated adjacent to the Atheneum, are representative buildings from two of New Harmony's Utopian eras. Photograph courtesy of Ben Nicholson, 2008.

and a *performance* of it, because in every reception the work takes on a fresh perspective for itself." The dome is therefore finite in its formal configuration and "open" in the "'readings' it invites."

However, it is Tillich's reaction to the Roofless Church that is perhaps the most enlightening. When he visited in 1963, he paid it the highest compliment Owen could have hoped for, telling her that "if out of this terrible century, we find an open church like this one, there is, indeed, hope, even justification."[144] For him, as for her, the church withstood the tide of contemporary meaninglessness and reaffirmed the significance of spirituality. I would argue that its absolute openness to multiple meanings is what drew his admiration. For Tillich and Owen, it was a place where the "New Being" could be actualized.[145] It is worth considering Tillich's definition of the "New Being":

> The New Being is not something that simply takes the place of the Old Being. But it is a renewal of the Old that has been corrupted, distorted, split and almost destroyed. But not wholly destroyed. Salvation does not destroy creation; but it transforms the Old Creation into a New one. Therefore we can speak of the New in terms of a *re*-newal: The threefold "*re*," namely, *re*-conciliation, *re*-union, *re*-surrection.[146]

This vision is a powerful lens for considering the transformative layers in Johnson's design.

The architect, too, recognized that the project had somehow transcended its physical materialization. Johnson thanked his client for giving him "spiritual spaces and curves," and though he was not religious, when his father died in 1960, he asked Owen to hold a memorial service, which took place beneath the skeletal structure of the dome on a frigid winter night.[147] This request also registers an intriguing absence in the Roofless Church, namely, Johnson's signature "irony," the quality Scully so perspicaciously associated with him. After many years and tribulations had passed, Owen also came to a new realization of what they had built together.[148] The "dream of the perfect church for all sorts and for all faiths" had surpassed her greatest expectations to become a "cathedral of earth and sky."

Notes

This essay is drawn from a chapter of my doctoral dissertation, "The 'Search for Form' in Postwar American Architecture" (Harvard University, 2017). I am grateful to Amanda Bryden, Indiana State Museum and Historic Sites; Sarah Buffington, Old Economy Village; David Fishman, Robert A. M. Stern Architects; Gary Gerard, former secretary of the Robert Lee Blaffer Foundation; Sherry Graves, former director, Working Men's Institute, New Harmony; and Diane Roberts of Houston for generously sharing her research on Jane Blaffer Owen. The late John Manley kindly discussed working with Philip Johnson on both the Roofless Church and St. Stephen's Episcopal Church with me in 2008. Nancy Mangum McCaslin, Ben Nicholson, Michelangelo Sabatino, and Stephen Fox have been models of scholarly collaboration. I am especially grateful to Nancy for her close reading of an earlier draft, which corrected and clarified information based on her work with Jane Owen on her memoir. I would also like to extend my gratitude to Laura Foster Nicholson, Docey and Owen Lewis, the staffs of the New Harmony Inn and Robert Lee Blaffer Foundation, and especially the late Jane Owen for their warm hospitality. I thank Neil Levine for suggesting that I look into Barnett Newman's "mound" experience (which opened unexpected directions in my interpretation) and for close readings of the dissertation chapter. A Wyeth Fellowship from the Center for Advanced Study in the Visual Arts, National Gallery of Art, and a dissertation completion fellowship from Harvard University supported my research and writing. I wish to thank the members of the CASVA community, especially Elizabeth Cropper, Peter Lukehart, Henry Millon, Therese O'Malley, Jill Pederson, and Rebecca Zorach for comments on an early presentation of this material. My work benefited from talks to the Latrobe Chapter of the Society of Architectural Historians and the University Art Association of Canada. I am grateful to Réjean Legault for his perspicacious criticism and companionship through the New Harmony adventure, which made it all the more remarkable. This essay is dedicated to Jane Blaffer Owen and her dreams of the future.

1. The Roofless Church falls under the jurisdiction of the Episcopal Diocese of Indianapolis but is available to other religious and spiritual groups.

2. Jane Blaffer Owen, "Philip Johnson's Roofless Church in New Harmony, Indiana," n.d., circa May 1960; reproduced as appendix C in *Wings of the Morning: Memoirs of Joyce Isabella Mann* (New Harmony, Ind.: Mary Lou Robson, 1967), 182. This description is taken from a pamphlet likely prepared around the inauguration in May 1960 (the text notes that the sculptural additions for the gate are not yet completed—they were installed in 1961) and is the fullest published account by Owen on the Roofless Church at the time of its design and completion.

3. After years of silence, Johnson briefly discussed the project in a 1985 interview with Robert A. M. Stern, later published as *The Philip Johnson Tapes: Interviews by Robert A. M. Stern,* edited by Kazys Varnelis (New York: Monacelli, 2008). Stern was surprised: "I've never heard you talk about that commission for the so-called Roofless Church." Johnson spoke very critically of his client and claimed that the rupture in their relationship was personal rather than professional (168–69). Schulze knew Johnson's version of the events and chose not to reveal them in his 1994 biography of the architect (Schulze, pers. comm. with author, December 2011).

4. As in, "Can't we just wander aimlessly?" Philip Johnson comments in Thomas Creighton, "The Sixties: A P/A Symposium on the State of Architecture: Part I," *Progressive Architecture* 42, no. 3 (1961): 127.

5. Quoted in Frank Welch, *Philip Johnson & Texas* (Austin: University of Texas Press, 2000), 68.

6. See the second part of this book, "Three Voices in New Harmony," for Kenneth A. Schuette Jr., "The Jane Blaffer Owen Sanctuary Plan (2013) within Her Vision for New Harmony."

7. George Sand, *The Devil's Pool,* translated by Jane Minot Sedgwick and Ellery Sedgwick (Boston: Little, Brown, 1901), 24–25. The original French, which Owen would have read, is: "Heureux le boureur! . . . Je vois sur leurs nobles fronts le sceau du Seigneur, car ils sont nés rois de la terre bien mieux que ceux qui la possèdent pour l'avoir payee . . . Mais il manque à cet homme une partie des jouissances que je possède, jouissances immatérielles qui lui seraient bien dues, à lui, l'ouvrier du vaste temple que le ciel est assez vaste pour embrasser." George Sand, *La mare au diable,* rev. ed. (Paris: Michel Lévy Frères, 1869), 22–24. Another possible source is an 1838/1839 letter by Sand in which she described the austere fourteenth-century Carthusian monastery of Valldemossa in Majorca, where she, Chopin, and her two children were staying: "We are planted between heaven and earth. The clouds cross our garden at their own will and pleasure, and the eagles clamor over our heads." Quoted in René

Doumic, *George Sand: Some Aspects of Her Life and Writings,* translated by Alys Hallard (Teddington, U.K.: Echo Library, 2006), 76. Again, the original is: "Nous sommes plantés entre ciel et terre. Les nuages traversent notre jardin sans se gêner, et les aigles nous braillent sur la tête." Doumic, *George Sand: Dix conférences sur sa vie et son oeuvre, avec quatre portraits et un fac-similé d'autographe* (Paris: Perrin et cie, 1909), 208.

8. Jane Blaffer Owen first states this conviction in her "Foreword: Memories of Tillich and New Harmony," in *Paul Tillich's Theological Legacy: Spirit and Community,* edited by Frederick J. Parrella (Berlin: Walter de Gruyter, 1995), ix. I thank the late William R. Crout for bringing this text to my attention.

9. Her mystical experience was first discussed by Barbara Grizzuti Harrison, "Life's Simple Treasures: Texas Angel Jane Owen's Earthly Paradise," *Vanity Fair* 46, no. 6 (1983): 42. In her memoir Owen chose to downplay the mysticism, referring to it as "an assumed command from Indian Mound." Jane Blaffer Owen, *New Harmony, Indiana: Like a River Not a Lake: A Memoir* (Bloomington: Indiana University Press, 2015), 66.

10. Blaffer Owen, *New Harmony,* 66. As I will make many references to Jane Owen's memoir, it is necessary to explain their connection to the research and interpretation presented in this essay. I first visited New Harmony in November 2006. During that two-day visit, I met Mrs. Owen through our mutual friend Ben Nicholson. I learned how closely she and Johnson had worked together on the project and how deeply hurt she had been when he failed to act when the walls began to deteriorate. I left New Harmony convinced I had found not only an appropriate architectural project for my study of the question of form, but also an ideal client for my examination of the meaning of form in postwar American culture. When I returned the following spring, Mrs. Owen not only gave me open access to the Robert Lee Blaffer Trust Archives of the Robert Lee Blaffer Foundation, she graciously hosted me at the New Harmony Inn for a week. She was reluctant, however, to say very much, as she had begun working on her memoir in 2004. She verified a few of my ideas, questioned others, but told me little beyond what had already been published by Frank Welch in his book on Johnson's work in Texas. In 2009 Ben Nicholson invited me to contribute to the present book. Unbeknownst to me, Owen was asked to read an early draft of this essay and through it learned of Johnson's harsh comments about the project and his client that had recently been published by Robert Stern (*The Philip Johnson Tapes*). Owen vehemently denied his interpretation of the events leading to their break. For her, what Johnson told Stern was not "worthy of Philip or the creativity of [their] collaboration" (Jane Owen, letter to author, November 2009; printed by courtesy of the Kenneth Dale and Jane Blaffer Owen family). Both sides of their extensive correspondence during the years of the commission have either been destroyed or lost. Her work on her memoir intensified, memory grounded in history through the work of Nancy Mangum McCaslin. Owen shared an early draft of the chapter of her experience on Indian Mound with me, but I was otherwise unaware of her side of the Roofless Church's story until February 2015. What impact that early draft of my essay—the reconstruction of the project's development and the identification of Johnson's sources—had on her memoir I cannot say. The present essay has benefited from and taken into consideration her memories of the events leading up to the commission, the circumstances through which she met Johnson, his initial ideas about the project, and many historical documents that have come to light through her book. There are, however, discrepancies between my historical reconstruction and characterization of the relationships between individuals and her narrative.

11. The source of these illustrations was an article by Rosamund Frost, "Lipchitz Makes a Sculpture," *Art News* 49, no. 2 (1950): 36–39, 63–64. No images of the Virgin appear in Frost's 1950 article; the last paragraph, however, mentions it as a new commission (64). This version of the story is in Irene Patai's biography, *Encounters: The Life of Jacques Lipchitz* (New York: Funk & Wagnalls, 1961), which she completed with the financial support of the Robert Lee Blaffer Trust. Lipchitz's recollections,

published eleven years later, were slightly different and, according to Jane Owen, incorrect, for he recalled that their first contact came soon after Father Couturier published a sketch of the sculpture in 1950. Jacques Lipchitz with H. Harvard Arnason, *My Life in Sculpture* (New York: Viking, 1972), 172. However, it is not impossible that Owen saw the sculpture before contacting the artist, for a photograph by Paul Weller of Lipchitz in his studio with a full-size maquette of the Virgin was published in the New York professional journal *Interiors* in March 1950 (Figure 4.5). For Owen's more detailed account, see *New Harmony*, 69–70.

12. Lipchitz, *My Life in Sculpture*, 172, and Blaffer Owen, *New Harmony*, 70–71. Lipchitz recalls that Owen requested the Virgin sculpture, but Owen remembered specifically wanting a work for a holy hill, meaning Indian Mound.

13. Approaching the artist first through an emissary in 1946, Father Couturier asked Lipchitz if he would be interested in contributing a sculpture to the church. Lipchitz was very much moved by the invitation and, after confirming that Couturier knew he was Jewish, agreed to take on the project without commission, the church only required to cover the fabrication expenses. He also stipulated that the work bear the inscription "Jacques Lipchitz, juif, fidèle à la fois de ses ancêtres, a fait cette Vierge, pour la bonne entente des homes sur la terre, afin que l'Esprit règne" ["Jacob Lipchitz, Jew, faithful to the faith of his ancestors, has made this Virgin for the good will of all mankind that the spirit might prevail"]; and that he be allowed to make an additional two castings. Jacques Lipchitz to Father Marie-Alain Couturier, letter, May 30, 1948; microfilm MS 251, reel 23, subseries II, vol. 18, Father Marie-Alain Couturier Papers, Special Collections, Divinity School Library, Yale University. Hereafter cited as Couturier Papers, Yale. (Unless otherwise indicated, all translations from French are by the author.) In August 1947 Lipchitz wrote to Father Couturier that he would begin working on maquettes for the sculpture and by May 1948 was sending sketches. Later in the spring he produced six small bronze study maquettes. The sketches and maquettes for the work show Lipchitz struggling to resolve how the base of the sculpture would relate to the baptismal font. In the executed bronze, these supports were more clearly articulated as three archangels with a kneeling lamb looking up to the Virgin and beyond. Progress on the project slowed in 1949, and it was not until the following autumn that Lipchitz announced to Father Couturier that the final plastaline model for *Notre Dame de Liesse* was complete and that he was ready to begin the final realization of the sculpture. On Father Couturier's commission of Lipchitz, see *My Life in Sculpture*, 171–76, 193, 197; and William S. Rubin, *Modern Sacred Art and the Church of Assy* (New York: Columbia University Press, 1960), 126–33. Rubin's account was aided by extensive interviews with Lipchitz. Owen added to the history of the three castings of Lipchitz's sculpture in *New Harmony*, 107–20.

14. In addition to the exchange reproduced in Blaffer Owen, *New Harmony* (74–77), Lipchitz also described the New Harmony commission and the possibilities it offered him to his first wife Berthe Kitrosser. In a letter dated October 2, 1950, Lipchitz wrote: "And then She [Virgin Mary] brings another miracle. A family of some importance in the history of America and perhaps the world, in a place called New Harmony, which is historical as well, has asked that I make, at the same time, the same Virgin for New Harmony as for Assy. The consequences of this fact are incalculable. For day to day life, it gives me the possibility first of all to do the Virgin of Assy because for the first time I will be able to get help, which I couldn't do until now. . . . I am happy to be able to announce this good news to you." "Correspondance de Jacques Lipchitz addressée à Berthe Kitrosser (1948–1972)," in *Jacques Lipchitz: collections du Centre Pompidou, Musée national d'art moderne et du Musée des beaux-arts de Nancy* (Paris: Édition du Centre, Pompidou, 2004), 127–28. Based on this information, the dating of the bronze study maquettes in the catalogue raisonné of Lipchitz's sculpture as 1948 is incorrect.

15. Although Father Couturier visited Houston several times, Owen never met him. Some forty

years later she wrote of his significance, referring to him as a first Colossus. Blaffer Owen, "Foreword: Memories of Tillich and New Harmony," vii–viii.

16. The built-in stone inscription reads: "In Memoriam Marie-Alain Couturier O.P. 1897–1954."

17. Jane Blaffer Owen, interview with Michelangelo Sabatino and Laura McGuire, Houston, January 12, 2009, transcript, 22.

18. Owen also interpreted the Virgin's facelessness as a critique of feminism: "Why is the Virgin faceless? Perhaps because the artist sought to contrast the self-effacement of the mother of our Lord with the often self-centered desire of contemporary woman to see her name, her face, and the incidents of her life restated in the world around her." Blaffer Owen, "Philip Johnson's Roofless Church," in *Wings of the Morning,* appendix C, 185.

19. Father Couturier and the architect Maurice Novarina initially planned to place the Virgin on the baptismal font in the baptistery. It was then moved from the font to be freestanding within the baptistery. Ultimately it was shifted to the choir. Lipchitz felt that the ideal context was an intimate space within the church, possibly a chapel with whitewashed walls. Rubin, *Modern Sacred Art,* 132. Also according to Rubin, Lipchitz was especially pleased with the sculpture's second home, the name of the town striking a chord with how he felt about his own spirit at that moment in time (127n3).

20. "She wants the Dove to bring it, together with the baptismal font of the Church of Assy, at the top of a hill in the middle of the vast plains of the New World." Lipchitz to Father Couturier, September 26, 1950, Couturier Papers, Yale. Printed by courtesy of the Estate of Jacques Lipchitz.

21. Lipchitz to Berthe Kitrosser, October 2, 1950, "Correspondance de Jacques Lipchitz," 128. He also wrote, "in order not to waste time, I will do my best to go to New Harmony as quickly as possible" (128). The dates of Lipchitz's visit were October 11–12, 1950. He stayed in the Poet's House, one of the first Harmonist houses restored by Owen. Patai describes Lipchitz's time in New Harmony as being very important to his further work on the Virgin (*Encounters,* 377). On his visit, see also Blaffer Owen, *New Harmony,* 82–84.

22. Lipchitz to Father Couturier, October 18, 1950, Couturier Papers, Yale. Printed by courtesy of the Estate of Jacques Lipchitz. On the reasons behind Kenneth Owen's opposition to the project, see Blaffer Owen, *New Harmony,* 21–24.

23. The New Harmony casting arrived sometime before June 25, 1956, at which date Lipchitz responded to Owen's phone call about a problem with the condition of the sculpture. Lipchitz to Jane Owen, Jane Blaffer Owen Artist Archive in the Green Gothic, Red Geranium Enterprises, Inc., New Harmony. Hereafter cited as Jane Owen Artist Archive. For the history of the Iona casting, see Blaffer Owen, *New Harmony,* 107–13.

24. Jane Owen to Jacques Lipchitz, April 29, 1950; Jacques Lipchitz Papers, box 3, folder 37, Archives of American Art. Hereafter cited as Lipchitz Papers, AAA. Reproduced in Blaffer Owen, *New Harmony,* 74–75.

25. Despite concerted efforts to convince her husband to support her project, Kenneth Dale Owen maintained his objections to constructing anything that would disrupt the natural sanctity of Indian Mound. Jane Owen uses "The Descent of the Spirit" to describe the work (see appendix C in *Wings of the Morning,* 183), but initially and later uses "Descent of the Holy Spirit."

26. During the early 1950s Owen spent considerable time in New York while her eldest daughter was being treated for polio. Based on the timeline of Lipchitz's work on the sculpture, the fact that she brought a copy of Tillich's 1952 book *The Courage to Be* with her to Tillich's lecture, and that her daughter Janie moved to New York for treatment in 1954, Owen probably learned of Tillich between 1952 and 1955.

27. See, e.g., Paul Tillich, "Existentialist Aspects of Modern Art," in *Christianity and the Existentialists,* edited by Carl Michalson (New York: Scribner's Sons, 1956), 128–46.

28. Sibyl Moholy-Nagy to Theodore A. Gill (executive director, Society for the Arts, Religion and Contemporary Culture), October 12, 1970; reel 945, Sibyl Moholy-Nagy Papers, Archives of American Art, Smithsonian Institution, Washington, D.C. Hereafter cited as Sibyl Moholy-Nagy Papers, AAA. Moholy-Nagy mentions "a number of meetings I had with Tillich's students at the Theological Seminary when I gave a genesis of religious environments and discussed the imprint this matrix left on civilization." Printed by courtesy of Hattula Moholy-Nagy.

29. However, Tillich was ill and unable to attend the event. Wilhelm Pauck instead delivered his address. Tillich, "Address on the Occasion of the Opening of the New Galleries and Sculpture Garden of The Museum of Modern Art [1953]," *Criterion* 3, no. 3 (1964): 39–40. Tillich spoke again at the museum on February 17, 1959. For Tillich's writings on art and architecture, including a list of unpublished talks, see John Dillenberger and Jane Dillenberger, eds., *On Art and Architecture* (New York: Crossroad, 1987). One book by Tillich appears in Johnson's private library: *The Future of Religions* (New York: Harper & Row, 1966). I am grateful to Irene Shum Allen for access to Johnson's private library.

30. Paul Tillich, "Introductory Remarks to a Round-table Report on Theology and Architecture," *Architectural Forum* 103, no. 6 (1955): 131–34, 136. Christ-Janer was the principal organizer of the conference. The other participants were Dean Darby Betts, Cathedral of St. John, Providence, R.I.; Rev. Mr. Marvin Halverson, National Council of Churches; Dr. Paul Weaver, president of Lake Erie College, Painesville, Ohio. Tillich's essay was later published under the title "Theology, Architecture, and Art," in *Church Management* (October 1956); and is included in Dillenberger and Dillenberger, *On Art and Architecture,* 188–98.

31. Paul Tillich, "Contemporary Protestant Architecture," in Albert Christ-Janer and Mary Mix Foley, *Modern Church Architecture: A Guide to the Form and Spirit of Twentieth Century Religious Buildings* (New York: McGraw-Hill, 1962), 124.

32. Ibid., 125.

33. In a letter to Johnson in the early 1980s, Owen recalled that hearing him "speak at St. Thomas" in the mid-1950s was the catalyst. Owen to Johnson, January 19, circa 1980, series IV, box 26, folder 1, Philip Johnson Papers, Getty Research Institute. Hereafter cited as Johnson Papers, Getty.

34. Blaffer Owen, *New Harmony,* 146.

35. At the end of a letter to the Houston architect Howard Barnstone, Johnson writes, "Dominique told me about the possibility on the church and I am already hard at work." Johnson to Barnstone, November 20, 1952, folder "3363 San Felipe," Menil Archives, The Menil Collection, Houston. Hereafter cited as Menil Archives. Welch briefly discusses the patronage context of Johnson's project for the church (*Philip Johnson & Texas,* 57). The project was exhibited in a 1981 exhibition at Rice University organized by Stephen Fox on Johnson's and Johnson/Burgee's work in Houston. See correspondence in Fox, "Philip Johnson, Johnson/Burgee: Houston Projects 1950–1980," n.d., folder "3363 San Felipe 01/01," Menil Archives.

36. In 2009 Owen recounted her involvement in the project thus: "John, Dominique and I worked closely together in the beginning, and they were so disappointed. . . . Philip drew this beautiful design—I don't know where it is now—for a church on a flat terrain. . . . And, of course, the bishop had no idea of art—religion, yes, but not art. He turned it down." Blaffer Owen, interview with Sabatino and McGuire, transcript, 14. Printed by courtesy of Sabatino and McGuire and the Kenneth Dale and Jane Blaffer Owen family. See also Welch, *Philip Johnson & Texas,* 57. She does not discuss this project in her memoir.

37. Johnson cited by Stephen Fox in a letter to Kathy Davidson, January 9, 1981, Rothko Chapel Correspondence File 01/01, Menil Archives.

38. Blaffer Owen, interview with Sabatino and McGuire, transcript, 14. Printed by courtesy of Sabatino and McGuire and the Kenneth Dale and Jane Blaffer Owen family.

39. While their first meeting likely took place in early April 1957, the recollections of client and architect depart there. For his part, Johnson recalled it as taking place in a highly informal setting at John de Menil's club: "One day Jane swam up to me and said, "Will you build me a—?" (*Philip Johnson Tapes*, 168). Owen offers a much more detailed account of the meeting in *New Harmony*, 150–52.

40. Johnson placed *Figure* on the lawn of the Glass House in 1949, and its location is noted on all early site plans. In 1951 Johnson added Frederick Kiesler's *Galaxy* (1947–51), which stood to the side of the Glass House until it was destroyed by lightning in 1959. In 1971 an early site-specific work in concrete by Donald Judd, *Untitled,* was constructed near the base of the slope leading to the Glass House. It may have been at this time that Johnson removed the Lipchitz.

41. Jane Owen in conversation with Frank Welch in August 1994, quoted in *Philip Johnson & Texas,* 69. In my conversations with her in 2006 and 2007, she repeated much of what is in Welch's account. On her impressions of Johnson during this initial meeting, see *New Harmony,* 150–52.

42. Johnson was a trustee from 1958 until 1971. He served in this capacity for other projects, among them the board of the Amon Carter Museum in Fort Worth, Texas. In hindsight it is clear that Johnson's appointment to the Blaffer Trust represented a conflict of interest with his position as architect.

43. Blaffer Owen, "Philip Johnson's Roofless Church," in *Wings of the Morning,* 186.

44. Johnson talked a hard line on handling clients. At the AIA's 1953 Central States regional conference, Johnson answered the question "can an architect justify subordinating art to his client's wishes" with a vehement no: "Too many times an architect takes the attitude that his client can call the tune because he's paying the piper. Often the client gets in the way of an architect's creative ability. . . . An architect's first duty is to his art. The real art of architecture is monumentality—something that will make you gasp. . . . This is what every architect has to think about when he picks up his pencil. . . . You can't get this artistic experience by simply following the client's wants. Your client is not an artist. If he were, he probably wouldn't have come to you for assistance." Johnson, quoted in "News," *Architectural Forum* 99, no. 5 (1953): 58. However, despite Johnson's reputation for being uncompromising at the level of art, Owen remembered him as being exceptionally open to her ideas and suggestions. Jane Owen, conversation with author, May 2007.

45. On the museum's sculpture garden, see Mirka Beneš's comprehensive analysis of its genesis, "A Modern Classic: The Abby Aldrich Rockefeller Sculpture Garden," *Studies in Modern Art 6* (1998): 104–51. The garden was first referred to as a "roofless room" in an interview with the landscape architect James Fanning in the *New Yorker,* April 25, 1953, 25; cited in Beneš, 132.

46. Though the site of the research reactor is usually assigned as Rehovot, Nahal Soreq is the more precise location, now home to a research university. Due to the classified status of the records of the Israeli Atomic Energy Commission, little is known about the events leading to the commission of the Nuclear Research Reactor. The Israeli government took the first steps toward receiving international approval for conducting nuclear research with the signing of the International Agreement for Cooperation in the Civil and Military Use of Atomic Energy in 1955. With this agreement signed, the Americans agreed to construct a light water or "swimming pool" type reactor for research purposes only at Nahal Soreq. On March 20, 1957, the Israelis signed the Atoms for Peace Agreement with the United States, taking them a step closer to building a reactor. With American support on the horizon, it seems highly probable that the Israelis started work on both the site and the design sometime between the signing of these two documents. That the nuclear reactor was designed earlier than usually assumed has been confirmed by Zvi Efrat, who dates the start of the project to 1956 in his Hebrew-language study *The*

Israeli Project: Building and Architecture, 1948–1973 (Tel Aviv: Tel Aviv Museum of Art, 2005). For a good summary of the political events leading up to the Israeli government's construction of the Nahal Soreq research reactor, see Joan Ockman, "The Figurehead: On Monumentality and Nihilism in Philip Johnson's Life and Work," in *Philip Johnson: The Constancy of Change,* edited by Emmanuel Petit (New Haven, Conn.: Yale University Press, 2009), 95–96. In addition to her sources, see Peter Pry, *Israel's Nuclear Arsenal* (Boulder, Colo.: Westview, 1984), 6–9; and Avner Cohen, *Israel and the Bomb* (New York: Columbia University Press, 1998).

47. The dating problem of the nuclear reactor is part of a more general one with Johnson's work, since his office used completion dates to order his projects. For the most part the two projects developed side by side. A full set of linen working drawings for the nuclear complex were complete in the fall of 1958, a few months in advance of those for the Roofless Church. Both projects were completed in 1960. Although not conclusive evidence of an early date, an undeveloped site plan for the nuclear reactor is stamped with Johnson's office address at 219 East Forty-Fourth Street, which he opened in September 1956; the rest are stamped with his address in the Seagram Building (375 Park Avenue), where he moved his office in 1958.

48. In her preface to the book, dated May 10, 1955, Wischnitzer wrote: "Above all, I wish to record my debt to Philip C. Johnson for his active interest in this book." Rachel Wischnitzer, *Synagogue Architecture in the United States: History and Interpretation* (Philadelphia: Jewish Publication Society of America, 1955), xv.

49. Johnson, foreword, in Wischnitzer, *Synagogue Architecture in the United States,* vii. The author could not have been aware of Johnson's sympathy for and involvement with National Socialist politics, a period of his life that was then still under wraps.

50. Philip Johnson, "Whither Away—Non-Miesian Directions," lecture, Yale University, February 5, 1959, transcript of talk as given, series VII, folder 13 1959-B, Writings, Johnson Papers, Getty. It was first published in Johnson, *Writings,* edited by Robert A. M. Stern (New York: Oxford University Press, 1979), 227–40.

51. For example, in early 1958 he described his project for Sarah Lawrence College as a village square with "I hope a symbolic 'something,' sculpture perhaps (analogous to the Athene Promachos on the Athenian acropolis) will be strategically placed on the plaza." He added, "(Symbolism has been much underdone of late.)." Johnson, "A New Design for Sarah Lawrence," *Sarah Lawrence Alumnae Bulletin,* February 1958, 7.

52. Blaffer Owen, interview with Sabatino and McGuire, transcript, 6. Printed by courtesy of Sabatino and McGuire and the Kenneth Dale and Jane Blaffer Owen family.

53. Jane Owen, interview with author, May 2007. Printed by courtesy of Cammie McAtee and the Kenneth Dale and Jane Blaffer Owen family. While in college at Bryn Mawr, Owen studied under a student of Isadora Duncan, and she later taught this form of dance informally (see Figure 1.10).

54. This information is taken from a map of New Harmony made for the sale of the town to Robert Owen reproduced in Don Blair, *The New Harmony Story* (New Harmony, Ind.: New Harmony Publications Committee, 1959), 71. The fact that the Wabash River regularly flooded the field just north of the orchard effectively stopped the town from extending any farther north.

55. Purchased in at least two phases (March 4 and May 5, 1959), by mid-September 1959 the lots adjacent to the original site were owned by either Owen or the Blaffer Trust. Plot plan, September 15, 1959, "Maps of New Harmony," Robert Lee Blaffer Trust Archives, Robert Lee Blaffer Foundation, New Harmony, Indiana. Hereafter cited as Blaffer Trust Archives. As work progressed on the project, new threats to the mood Johnson and his client were trying to convey on the area were made. Just as the plans were being finalized, the owner of the property facing the site on the northeast corner of North

and Main Streets announced his intentions to build a motel. The Blaffer Trust quickly moved to buy the property. In 1960 it became the new site for the Barrett–Gate House, the first Harmonist house to be restored by the Trust, with the back of the site redeveloped for Paul Tillich Park in the 1970s, and later for the first building of the New Harmony Inn.

56. Progress may have been hampered during this time due to Johnson's serious illness in May 1957. Sibyl Moholy-Nagy to Johnson, May 30, 1957, letter, series IV, folder 5, Philip Johnson Papers, the Museum of Modern Art Archives, New York. Hereafter cited as Johnson Papers, MoMA Archives. Johnson was first assisted on the design by James Rush Jarrett, his former student at Yale, who worked for him between spring 1955 and fall 1957. By all accounts an exceedingly talented designer, Jarrett worked very closely with Johnson on the Roofless Church during its conceptual phase.

57. Blaffer Owen, "Philip Johnson's Roofless Church," in *Wings of the Morning,* 186.

58. Ibid., 182. Owen does not discuss this project at any point in her memoir.

59. "[Unsigned agreement]," June 13, 1958, "Duplicates," Blaffer Trust Archives. Owen created the Robert Lee Blaffer Trust (named after her father) on March 3, 1958, which became the Robert Lee Blaffer Foundation in 2011. In keeping with the stipulations in the agreement, the chapel was conceived as a second project. Working drawings thus show the chapel as a "future" project.

60. In his memoir Lipchitz wrote "[Owen] had Philip Johnson design a roofless church for my Virgin, and for this church I also made a monumental gate." Lipchitz, *My Life in Sculpture,* 175.

61. Johnson summarized Lipchitz's statement that "a building was not architecture unless it had sculpture on it; it is merely a building; and that the art of architecture had to have sculpture in order to be the art of architecture," which was made in an unidentified broadcast, in his introductory comments to a symposium at the Museum of Modern Art in 1951. See "A Symposium on How to Combine Architecture, Painting, and Sculpture," *Interiors* 60, no. 10 (1951): 100.

62. *Philip Johnson Tapes,* 170. In 1954 Johnson related his experience working with Lipchitz to Selden Rodman, commenting that he "made the sculpture so overpowering that everything else in the room, and the room itself, was engulfed." Johnson added, "I've been told that when it was installed Lipchitz looked at it and said, 'Now they'll never be able to put any other sculpture in *this* room!' and they can't." Selden Rodman, *Conversations with Artists* (New York: Devin-Adair, 1957), 64.

63. Johnson recalled the project as a battle: "Lipchitz tried to demolish any view of the temenos by putting those gates in and making them bright gold. In the end it just became meaningless. So I always entered the other way, as everyone does. And that worked out very well. But it was just the opposite of my original thought there." *Philip Johnson Tapes,* 170. Despite the power struggle, many saw it as a successful collaboration; for example, the art critic Katherine Kuh wrote: "[Johnson and Lipchitz] obviously worked in close harmony to produce a chapel reflecting both the religious freedom and the Utopian philosophy that have distinguished New Harmony's history." Kuh, "Art in America in 1962: A Balance Sheet," *Saturday Review,* September 8, 1962, special section H.

64. Jane Owen to Jacques Lipchitz, August 14, 1957, box 3, folder 36, Lipchitz Papers, AAA. Translated by Leslie Roberts. Original French as well as translation reproduced in Blaffer Owen, *New Harmony,* 331–32n6. It is unclear if this model was the same one that was exhibited in the 1959 Yale exhibition of Johnson's work, by which time all the major decisions had been made about the composition and orientation of the Roofless Church. This model was widely published. There is no visual documentation of any earlier models.

65. Owen added: "Naturally, we await your opinion on where to place your piece. We merely hope that we are on the right path."

66. Johnson also mentions improving the appearance of "the roses" and methods of presenting Lipchitz's sculpture within the photographs he was having made of the model, now lost. Johnson to

Owen, August 13, 1957, "Duplicates," Blaffer Trust Archives. Printed by permission of the Estate of Philip Johnson; courtesy of the Glass House, a site of The National Trust for Historic Preservation. Furthermore, in at least Johnson's mind, the project was far enough along that *Architectural Record* wanted to publish a long piece on it in November. In an internal memo to the editorial staff of *Architectural Forum* dated August 2, 1957, Douglas Haskell reported that Johnson's "shrine in Indiana is committed to a 16-page piece in November [Architectural] Record. (Apparently they are trying a series on the leading architects.)" Haskell to staff, note, August 2, 1957, Douglas Haskell Papers, box 10, folder 6, Avery Drawings Collections, Columbia University. This article, however, never appeared.

67. Johnson to Owen, August 27, 1957; "Philip Johnson Correspondence," Blaffer Trust Archives. Printed by permission of the Estate of Philip Johnson; courtesy of the Glass House, a site of The National Trust for Historic Preservation. The earlier letter also reveals that Johnson was still somewhat of a novice when it came to estimates. In it he proposes a budget of $150,000 rather than the $300,000 he and Jane Owen initially discussed. Johnson to Owen, August 13, 1957. (The construction bids alone came in at over $300,000.) In August 1958 the estimate returned to the original sum. In notes from a phone call with Johnson, Don Blair wrote: "Philip has worked with Jane and come up with a figure of about $300,000.00 for total cost and is satisfied. / The job should get underway as soon as possible with foundation and masonry this fall." Blair, notes, August 19, 1958, Blaffer Trust Archives. Printed by courtesy of Judith Blair Nix.

68. Jane Owen, interview with author, May 2007. Printed by courtesy of Cammie McAtee and the Kenneth Dale and Jane Blaffer Owen family.

69. "Incidentally, we have found that a limestone wall (which heavens knows is as local as they come in this world) will cost no more than a brick wall, so for unity and elegance I propose this stone." Johnson to Owen, August 13, 1957. Printed by permission of the Estate of Philip Johnson; courtesy of the Glass House, a site of The National Trust for Historic Preservation.

70. Owen's recollections of the project development here break from evidence in the drawings. She recalled that the ceremonial gate was added in the first meeting with Lipchitz in New York. Blaffer Owen, *New Harmony*, 155.

71. Blaffer Owen, "Philip Johnson's Roofless Church," in *Wings of the Morning*, 188; and Blaffer Owen, *New Harmony*, 154–55.

72. For example, Johnson illustrated his famous 1961 lecture on Schinkel and Mies with images of plates of Sanssouci from the *Sammlung architektonischer Entwürf: Eine Auswahl von 40 Bildtafeln und erläuternden Texten aus der Ausgabe Potsdam 1841–43* (Potsdam: Riegel, 1841–43). See Johnson, "Schinkel and Mies," in *Schriftenreihe des Architekten- und Ingenieur-Vereins zu Berlin* 13 (Berlin, 1961), 24; English text in *Program*, Columbia School of Architecture, Spring 1962, 14–34; and reproduced in Johnson's *Writings*, 165–81.

73. The timeline for this addition is unclear. Owen's chronology places it in the earliest weeks of the project's development (*New Harmony*, 155). The drawings, however, do not include plans with two entrances until later in the project development. Some information about Lipchitz's role in the emergence of the gate as a major element in the composition comes from an article by William Jordy in 1959: "The large axial portal, which Johnson added at the request of Sculptor Lipchitz, serves only on ceremonial occasions. For everyday use there remains the small side entrance." William H. Jordy, "The Mies-less Johnson," *Architectural Forum* 111, no. 3 (1959): 122. Lipchitz completed the reliefs for the gate a year after the inauguration, and they in turn were inaugurated in 1962. Owen also asked Lipchitz to design a relief sculpture for the facade of the Robert Lee Blaffer Wing of the Museum of Fine Arts, Houston (1952), and a sundial for New Harmony (1956). Lipchitz to Owen, June 20, 1956, Jane Owen Archives. Neither was executed.

74. In 2016 the gates were restored and repainted, and Lipchitz's sculptures were regilded by the Rhode Island artist Luke Randall.

75. Owen describes "bricked-in portals of the south wall will one day lead to a roofed chapel" in the text she wrote soon after the Roofless Church was completed. Blaffer Owen, "Philip Johnson's Roofless Church," in *Wings of the Morning,* 182. She does not mention the chapel in her memoir, although the photograph showing the walled-up entrance appears (245).

76. On Johnson's conversion to Le Corbusier, see Philip Johnson, "Correct and Magnificent Play," review of *Complete Works,* vol. 1946–1952, by Le Corbusier, *Art News* 52, no. 5 (1953): 16–17, 52–53; and "The Seven Crutches of Modern Architecture," *Perspecta* 3 (1955): 40–44.

77. The project took on speed in the summer of 1958. When site work began in May 1958, Johnson put John Brady in charge of the work in New Harmony. In June 1959 Brady was replaced by Robin Moore, who also wrote a brief descriptive article—a "preview"—about the Roofless Church: "A Shrine by Philip Johnson," *Art in America* 47, no. 4 (1959): 70–71. Over the next several months the major decisions about materials were taken based on the agreed budget of $300,000. An almost complete set of working drawings was sent to the client in January 1959 and bids requested in March. On March 25 the bids came in with the local firm of Traylor Brothers (Evansville, Ind.) submitting the winning bid of $332,000. In June the final buildings on the site were demolished and construction began.

78. Louis Sullivan's actual phrasing "form ever follows function," which he first published in his 1896 essay "The Tall Office Building Artistically Considered," was abbreviated by his former partner Dankmar Adler in the same year. See Dankmar Adler, "The Influence of Steel Construction and Plate Glass Upon Style," in *The Proceedings of the Thirtieth Annual Convention of American Institute of Architects,* 1896, 58–64. Nowicki's phrase first appeared in print in 1951. See Matthew Nowicki, "On Exactitude and Flexibility," *Student Publication of the School of Design* 1, no. 1 (1951): 11–18; and Nowicki, "Origins and Trends in Modern Architecture" *Magazine of Art* 44, no. 7 (1951): 273–79.

79. Lecture, "Whither Away—Non-Miesian Directions," transcript. The exhibition of Johnson's recent work at Yale's Weir Hall, titled "Non-Miesian Directions," opened on February 5, 1959. It included much of his recent work on display (renderings, plans, models, and photographs of built structures) as well as his work on the Theatre of Dance at Lincoln Center and his proposals for the overall center. A review of Johnson's lecture appeared the following morning. Herbert B. Rothschild Jr., "Johnson Uses History as Inspiration, Point of Departure for New Architecture," *Yale Daily News,* February 6, 1959.

80. Johnson, "Whither Away—Non-Miesian Directions," in *Writings,* 227.

81. Ibid., 237–38.

82. On Johnson's narrated presentation of the Glass House in the September 1950 issue of the *Architectural Review,* see Neil Levine, "Afterword: Philip Johnson's Glass House: When Modernism Became History," in Stover Jenkins and David Mahoney, *The Houses of Philip Johnson* (New York: Abbeville, 2001), 268–84.

83. On Vassar's plans to build a new chapel, see Lindsay Cook, "The Little Chapel That Could Have Been: Planning for a Community of Faith at Vassar College 1945–1954," senior thesis (Vassar College, May 4, 2010). While the thesis did not reveal much more about Johnson's project, it offers a wealth of fascinating information about the context of the commission.

84. Scully stated this most recently in "Philip Johnson: Art and Irony," in Petit, *Philip Johnson.* He added biographical information that Johnson went at his [Scully's] suggestion following a chance meeting in Venice in the spring of that year (25). Scully himself had only recently visited the site. See Neil Levine, "Vincent Scully: A Biographical Sketch," in *Modern Architecture and Other Essays* (Princeton, N.J.: Princeton University Press, 2003), 16.

85. Johnson admitted this in his conversation with Rodman (*Conversations with Artists,* 65).

86. Two works by John Soane, the Breakfast Room of his London townhouse (circa 1796) and the Court of Chancery (1822–25), are typically raised in connection with Johnson's work. While Johnson most certainly had firsthand experience of the Breakfast Room, drawings for it and the long-gone courtroom are included in Sir John Summerson's 1952 book on the British architect. Another possible source has recently been raised in connection with the Vassar chapel project. Though not realized in this form, early renderings for Basil Spence's Coventry Cathedral (1951–56) describe the vaulting of the nave as a thin concrete shell that replicates the general form of Gothic fan vaults, the smooth vaults carried up by pilotis-like thin piers. As Cook notes, this project was easily accessible to Johnson through a January 1952 article on Spence's design by J. M. Richards in the *Architectural Review,* a journal Johnson closely followed. Cook, "Little Chapel," 23.

87. Vincent Scully, "Archetype and Order in Recent American Architecture," *Art in America* 42, no. 12 (1954): 256.

88. Johnson, "A Symposium on How to Combine Architecture, Painting, and Sculpture," *Interiors,* 100. Unfortunately the illustration is not large enough to identify the exact temple. Johnson's interest is attested by the presence in his library of several books on Indian art and architecture dating from the 1920s and 1950s.

89. Blaffer Owen, *New Harmony,* 151–53.

90. Anders Ragnar Bugge, *Norwegian Stave Churches,* translated by Ragnar Christophersen (Oslo: Dreyer, 1953); and a UNESCO publication: *Norway: Paintings from the Stave Churches* (Greenwich, Conn.: New York Graphic Society, 1955). Despite its title, this latter book also includes photographs of the stave churches. Neither volume appears in the list of Johnson's art and architecture library or among the photographs of his private library. Although Owen indicated that Johnson had visited a stave church, I have not found any evidence he had been to Norway.

91. *Art norvégien: Mille ans de tradition viking* was presented at the Palais des Beaux-Arts, Brussels, and the Musée des Arts Décoratifs, Paris, between March and May 1954. Roar Hauglid, "The Unknown Viking Masters," *Art News* 53, no. 2 (1954): 64. The fact that this issue also included a report on Mies van der Rohe's Convention Hall makes it all but certain that Johnson looked at it.

92. Sibyl Moholy-Nagy, *Native Genius in Anonymous Architecture* (New York: Horizon, 1957), 192. The line drawing is credited to "Library of Congress Collection." Moholy-Nagy began working on the book in 1952.

93. Ibid., 42.

94. I am basing my reading on a 1947 essay that both Johnson and his client could easily have been familiar with: Ananda K. Coomaraswamy, "An Indian Temple: The Kandarya Mahadeo," *Art in America* 35, no. 4 (1947): 285–92.

95. Owen remembered Johnson's discussion of the dual pagan–Christian nature of the stave churches as key to her decision to offer him the commission. Blaffer Owen, *New Harmony,* 152.

96. Stephen Fox makes this suggestion in his succinct description of the Roofless Church in Hilary Lewis and Stephen Fox, *The Architecture of Philip Johnson* (Boston: Bulfinch, 2002), 88.

97. On Rapp's vision, see Karl J. R. Arndt, *George Rapp's Harmony Society, 1785–1847,* rev. ed. (Philadelphia: University of Pennsylvania Press, 1965), 439.

98. Lu Ann De Cunzo, Therese O'Malley, Michael J. Lewis, George E. Thomas, and Christa Wilmanns-Wells, "Father Rapp's Garden at Economy: Harmony Society in Microcosm," in *Landscape Archaeology: Reading and Interpreting the American Historical Landscape,* edited by Rebecca Yamin and Karen Bescherer Metheny (Knoxville: University of Tennessee Press, 1996), 106. I thank Therese O'Malley for bringing this research to my attention.

CAMMIE MCATEE

99. Here I am extrapolating from the similar presence of trees in the center of Rapp's garden in Economy. Ibid., 106.

100. First published in 1825, part of William Herbert's letter is reproduced in Arndt, *George Rapp's Harmony Society*, 284. The dome does not appear in the only known photograph of the Harmonist Church, which was taken just before it was demolished in 1874. I am grateful to Sarah Buffington for bringing this photograph to my attention.

101. These drawings and the late nineteenth-century photograph are held in the archives of Old Economy Village.

102. As De Cunzo et al. note, the similarity of these structures to primitive or first settler dwellings was expressive of the Harmonists' identification with the Israelites' forty years of wandering in the wilderness. De Cunzo et al., "Father Rapp's Garden at Economy," 110–11.

103. Christian Ludwig Stieglitz, *Encyklopadie der burgerlichen Bakunst*, 5 vols. (Leipzig, 1792), 361; translated by Michael Lewis and cited by De Cunzo et al., "Father Rapp's Garden at Economy," 110.

104. Blair assembled a substantial collection of photographs of New Harmony from the 1870s through the 1940s, including photographs of Lesueur's drawings, all of which was later donated to the University of Southern Indiana. He was also a trustee of the Blaffer Trust and worked closely with Johnson. See his books *Harmonist Construction* (Indianapolis: Indiana Historical Society, 1964) and *The New Harmony Story*. According to Sarah Buffington, the architectural drawings held in the archives at Old Economy Village were cataloged through the Federal Writers' Project of the United States Work Projects Administration in 1939–40 (e-mail correspondence with author, February 2010). They were therefore known and accessible. Though neither Owen's nor Johnson's names appear in the records, Blair had contact with Old Economy Village in the late 1940s.

105. Blair, *New Harmony Story*, 6.

106. Jane Owen to Tillich, carbon copy letter, May 19, 1959, Paul Tillich Archive, Robert Lee Blaffer Foundation. Printed by courtesy of the Kenneth Dale and Jane Blaffer Owen family. See Blair's description in *The New Harmony Story*, 6, 21–22. I thank Nancy McCaslin for confirming that Blair was Owen's source.

107. On Lawrence Thurman's involvement, see a 1955 letter reproduced in *New Harmony*, 330n6.

108. As well as existing in books published in the 1930s in the United States and France, copies of Lesueur's New Harmony drawings exist in collections of materials held by families descending from the passengers of "The Boatload of Knowledge," the Owens being only one such family. Charles Alexandre Lesueur, *Dessins de Ch.A. Lesueur, executes aux États-Unis de 1816 à 1837* (Paris: D. Jacomet & cie, 1933); R. W. G. Vail, *The American Sketchbooks of Charles Alexandre Lesueur* (Worcester, Mass.: American Antiquarian Society, 1938).

109. Johnson to Hitchcock, postcard, 1964, box 11, "1964 Correspondence, J-L," Henry-Russell Hitchcock Papers, Archives of American Art, Smithsonian Institution, Washington, D.C. Hereafter cited as Hitchcock Papers, AAA. Printed by permission of the Estate of Philip Johnson; courtesy of the Glass House, a site of The National Trust for Historic Preservation.

110. Fred Fuller, "New St. Stephen's Episcopal Church of Unique Design Will Emphasize Liturgy," *Mt. Vernon Democrat*, circa 1965, newspaper clipping, series II, folder 16, Johnson Papers, MoMA Archives. The article was based on Johnson's presentation of the project in New Harmony.

111. This idea is recorded on a longitudinal section dated December 1, 1964, as well as in several earlier drawings.

112. Barnett Newman, "Ohio, 1949," in *Selected Writings and Interviews*, edited by John P. O'Neill (Berkeley: University of California Press, 1990), 174–75. This text is usually known as "Prologue for a New Aesthetic," as an early draft was titled. The Native American Indian mounds that Newman

visited were very different from the ones in and around New Harmony. I am not suggesting any formal connection.

113. Richard Shiff, introduction to Newman, *Selected Writings and Interviews,* xxi.

114. Newman, quoted in "Interview with David Sylvester," 1965; in Newman, *Selected Writings and Interviews,* 255.

115. Although Johnson claimed in his 1959 Yale lecture that he had resorted to using computers for these calculations, documents in the Blaffer Trust Archives show that this was not the case. In a letter to Blair about the fee structure, Johnson explains: "However, there is included in this fee the work of a specialized mathematician-engineer on our staff who worked solely on the calculations and computations connected with the difficult shapes of the wooden dome. We had decided here at the office that it would be cheaper for the Trust to have us do this work rather than farm it out to the fabricator's shop drawing department. We feel we saved the Trust approximately $10,000.00 by this method. In our files we have a proposal from Computech Inc. for the sum of $19,040.00 to do the computation work alone." Johnson to Blair, September 25, 1959, "Philip Johnson Correspondence," Blaffer Trust Archives. Printed by permission of the Estate of Philip Johnson; courtesy of the Glass House, a site of The National Trust for Historic Preservation. Johnson recognized a good leading line when he saw one and encouraged the diffusion of this myth; a brief mention of the project in *Time* in 1959 states that the "bell-shaped structure . . . proved so complicated that an IBM machine took two weeks to calculate its compound curves" (April 27, 1959, 68). In his interviews with Stern, Johnson said "a kid in the office who was a dynamo" was responsible for calculating the dome's complex geometry (*Philip Johnson Tapes,* 169). Stern identified this person as James Rush Jarrett, but he had left Johnson's office for Rome by the fall of 1957, long before the design moved into calculations. According to John Manley, who was working for Johnson at the time, "it was an older person, possibly East European." Manley, conversation with author, November 10, 2008.

116. In a letter to the secretary of the Blaffer Trust, Johnson wrote in response to a call from Jane Owen, who was "in some perturbation about some financial problems . . . The bills, I admit, have been horrendous. The unexpected engineering complications of the dome have me furious, but at last satisfied." Johnson to Ora V. Howton, February 16, 1959; "Philip Johnson Correspondence," Blaffer Trust Archives. Printed by permission of the Estate of Philip Johnson; courtesy of the Glass House, a site of The National Trust for Historic Preservation.

117. In the February 16, 1959, letter to Howton, Johnson offered to send ten thousand dollars and to give up his architect's fee and only charge office costs, closing with: "Architects, like doctors, should charge commercial clients more than religious clients, don't you think?" Printed by permission of the Estate of Philip Johnson; courtesy of the Glass House, a site of The National Trust for Historic Preservation. This appears to have been a short-lived offer; an invoice from Johnson's office dating to the end of 1959 includes the note: Architectural Fee previously refunded now due/Payment requested $15,000. . . . ," invoice, December 14, 1959, Blair–Johnson Correspondence, Blaffer Trust Archives.

118. Vincent J. Scully, "The Precisionist Strain," *Art in America* 48, no. 3 (1960): 46–53.

119. Scully wrote: "The historical pattern now seems apparent: when closely derived from European work, American forms have always become tighter, more planar and more linear. This seems to occur for two reasons: first, because that relationship is itself a provincial and, in a sense, academic one, which leads toward a drying of the forms involved; second, because there is apparently something intrinsic to the American experience of life that has often made us want to create perfect, repetitive, closed and weightless forms, like neatly pressed suits to mask us anonymously from the world. Puritanism and a lack of confidence in the place and in human action alike have already been suggested as partial explanations for the latter impulse." Ibid., 52–53.

120. In a lecture in Scully's history of architecture course at Yale University in 1958, Johnson waxed lyrical over the Phillips Pavilion. Johnson, "Post-War Frank Lloyd Wright and Le Corbusier," May 2, 1958, transcript, 24–25, series IV, box 2, folder 42a, Johnson Papers, MoMA Archives.

121. Rodman, *Conversations with Artists*, 65. Johnson had some second thoughts about maintaining an uncompromising mathematical setup, in 1977 stating: "Pure mathematics does not necessarily make good aesthetics." Quoted in Calvin Tomkins, "Profiles: Forms under Light," *New Yorker*, May 23, 1977, 78.

122. Blaffer Owen, *New Harmony*, 43.

123. The shape of the cut stones may also refer to the material itself. Indiana limestone is also known as "oolitic," which comes from the Hellenic word for egg.

124. Johnson's Library in his Study at the Glass House holds a copy of Matila Ghyka's *Esthétique des proportions dans la nature et dans les arts* (Paris: Gallimard, 1927). Johnson may have been introduced to Ghyka's ideas through the mathematician's article "Le Corbusier's Modulor and the Concept of the Golden Means," *Architectural Review* 103, no. 614 (1948): 39–42.

125. Henry A. Millon, "Rudolf Wittkower, *Architectural Principles in the Age of Humanism*: Its Influence on the Development and Interpretation of Modern Architecture," *Journal of the Society of Architectural Historians* 31, no. 2 (1972): 83–91. In an interview with Robert Stern, Johnson recalled Wittkower: "What's that one at Harvard that was the greatest help to me? I mean at Columbia . . . Wittkower. Gee, his books on Palladio. I used to go up there before I went to Italy and talk with them both [Rudolf and Margo]. Their enthusiasm was very much like Scully's. . . . You'd sit down to tea because they didn't drink, alas." "Interview #8," New York, September 4, 1985, transcript, 51; Columbia Center for Oral History, Columbia University. This passage does not appear in the edited version of the interviews, *The Philip Johnson Tapes*. Printed by permission of the Estate of Philip Johnson; courtesy of the Glass House, a site of The National Trust for Historic Preservation.

126. Tillich, "Introductory Remarks to a Round-table Report on Theology and Architecture," 134.

127. As the Lipchitz reliefs for the ceremonial gates show, Owen remained committed to religious symbolism as a way to convey meaning. In an interview in the early 1980s she criticized the Rothko Chapel for the absence of such imagery: "I wouldn't call it a *chapel*—tell me if you see *one* religious symbol in it," Owen, quoted in Grizzuti Harrison, "Life's Simple Treasures," 45.

128. Jürgen Joedicke, "1930–1960," *Bauen und Wohnen* 16, no. 10 (1961): 372. Joedicke credited Jordy in "The Mies-less Johnson" with this identification.

129. Johnson to Jürgen Joedicke, December 6, 1961, series IV, folder 5, Johnson Papers, MoMA Archives. A brief section from the beginning of the letter was omitted when the letter was first reproduced in the appendix of John Jacobus's monograph on Johnson. Jacobus, *Philip Johnson* (New York: George Braziller, 1962), 120–22. This omission was repeated in the 1979 volume of Johnson's *Writings* (125–26).

130. Joedicke, in fact, credited William Jordy with making this connection. Jordy saw a rich panoply of precedents and identified the "complex plans and undulating roofs of Hadrian's Villa at Tivoli . . . , work by such late baroque architects as Borromini and Guarini . . . , the Japanese pavilion house," and "the knobby masses of Norwegian wood churches" all at work within the form of the dome ("The Mies-less Johnson"). Jordy was clearly the source for all of Joedicke's information about the Roofless Church as well as the two images (view of the model of the domed shrine and the theoretical plan) he reproduced (fig. 51, p. 372). Hitchcock also stepped into the fray of sources. In a letter to Jacobus, who was in the midst of preparing his monograph on Johnson, Hitchcock encouraged him to visit the Roofless Church and related his own comments on the project: "It seems to me as also to Philip that it has generally been rather badly presented somewhat as if one showed Bernini's Baldacchin in

St. Peter's and ignored the church of which it is the central feature. I at least don't care too much for the shingled object by itself but judge from plans, models and photographs that I should quite like the 'roofless church' as a whole." Hitchcock to Jacobus, November 28, 1961, box 10, "1961 Correspondence, J-L," Hitchcock Papers, AAA. Printed by permission of the Estate of Henry-Russell Hitchcock.

131. Peter Blake and Philip C. Johnson, "Architectural Freedom and Order: An Answer to Robert W. Kennedy," *Magazine of Art* 41, no. 6 (1948): 229. The article was a response to Kennedy's "The Small House in New England," published in the April issue of the journal. Blake and Johnson interpreted Kennedy's appeal for a return to regional forms as eclecticism and a call to anarchy.

132. Rudolf Wittkower, *Art and Architecture in Italy, 1600–1750* (Harmondsworth, UK: Penguin Books, 1958).

133. The decade leading up to the tercentenary of the architect's death in 1667 saw a flurry of publications in Italian, notably an article on Sant'Ivo's geometry by Leonardo Benevolo in 1953 and several articles by Paolo Portoghesi, who would become Borromini's main Italian interlocutor. Leonardo Benevolo, "Il tema geometrico di S. Ivo alla Sapienza," *Quaderni dell'Istituto di Storia dell'Architettura*, no. 1 (November 1953): 1–10, and illus. Benevolo's drawing of the "origine geometrica del 'perimetro teorico' di S. Ivo" became well known as the cover image of Anthony Blunt's 1979 monograph on Borromini.

134. The text "Segue il Lavori del Tamburo, . . . la muraglia p[er] di fuori è formata con sei semi-circoli a guisa d'una rose di sei foglie" is attributed to Borromini by Elisabeth Kieven (*Von Bernini bis Piranesi* [Stuttgart, 1993], 74); cited in Julia M. Smyth-Pinney, "Borromini's Plans for Sant-Ivo alla Sapienza," *Journal of the Society of Architectural Historians* 59, no. 3 (2000): 322, 335n26.

135. Sibyl Moholy-Nagy to Johnson, December 21, 1961, series IV, folder 5, Johnson Papers, MoMA Archives; and reel 944, Sibyl Moholy-Nagy Papers, AAA. Printed by courtesy of Hattula Moholy-Nagy.

136. The domed structure was to have been 124 feet in height, with the 25-foot statue of Roosevelt on a 5-foot pedestal. Johnson to Sibyl Moholy-Nagy, March 1961, series IV, folder 5, Johnson Papers, MoMA Archives.

137. Newman, "Ohio, 1949," 174–75.

138. The critic Thomas B. Hess reported these recollections in *Barnett Newman* (New York: Museum of Modern Art, 1971), 73.

139. Jean-François Lyotard, "Newman: The Instant," in *The Inhuman: Reflections on Time,* translated by Geoffrey Bennington and Rachel Bowlby (Stanford, Calif.: Stanford University Press, 1991), 87.

140. In her one text on the Roofless Church, Owen did take care to list the materials used and their origins. Her intention seems to have been to connect the architecture to its earthly origins. This also brings to mind ideas from Vincent Scully's doctoral thesis, "The Shingle Style: Architectural Theory and Design from Richardson to the Origins of Wright" (1955), which made a visual case for the appropriateness of shingles for contemporary architecture. The final lines of Scully's study seem exceptionally apropos to Johnson's design: "Most of all, the shingle style itself—in its earnest mixture of motives, its quickly fired vitality, and its impatient search for the roots of experience in a newly industrialized world—seems a most poignantly nineteenth-century and American phenomenon. It can serve as a useful memory for us all." Scully, *The Shingle Style and the Stick Style: Architectural Theory and Design from Downing to the Origins of Wright,* rev. ed. (New Haven, Conn.: Yale University Press, 1971), 164.

141. Owen to Don Blair, n.d., circa early 1970s; "Jane—Philip," Blaffer Trust Archives, printed by courtesy of the Kenneth Dale and Jane Blaffer Owen family. The source of this phrase is likely Frost's description of the genesis of Lipchitz's work *The Harpists* (1928): "The harp's back took on the curve and lift of a wing, became in turn a bird, then a rib cage in which a heart might beat." Frost, "Lipchitz Makes a Sculpture," 38.

142. Blaffer Owen, "Philip Johnson's Roofless Church," in *Wings of the Morning*, 187.

143. Umberto Eco, "The Poetics of the Open Work," in *The Open Work*, translated by Bruce Merry (Cambridge, Mass.: Harvard University Press, 1989), 4.

144. Blaffer Owen, "Foreword: Memories of Tillich and New Harmony," xi.

145. Paul Tillich Park was originally conceived as a counterpoint to the Roofless Church. On the cave that Owen commissioned from Kiesler on the advice of Johnson, see the essay by Ben Nicholson with William R. Crout, "Frederick Kiesler's Grotto: A Promethean Spirit in New Harmony." The work originally had the Tillichean name *The Cave of the New Being*, but Kiesler called it *Grotto for Meditation*.

146. Paul Tillich, *The New Being* (New York: Charles Scribner's Sons, 1955), 19–20.

147. Blaffer Owen, interview with Sabatino and McGuire, transcript, 19. On the memorial for Homer Johnson, see Welch, *Philip Johnson & Texas*, 75. In her memoir, Owen added more to the story of the memorial service (*New Harmony*, 177).

148. Jane Owen to Johnson, January 19, circa 1980, Johnson Papers, Getty; printed by courtesy of the Kenneth Dale and Jane Blaffer Owen family. Her reference in the letter to a "cathedral of sky and earth" recalls Reverend George MacLeod's joyous reaction to the Roofless Church—made to Owen, Johnson, and Lipchitz—when he came to New Harmony in May 1962 to dedicate the ceremonial gate.

Figure 5.1. Elizabeth and Frank Haines created a nativity scene of life-sized painted wood and home-spun fabric for the cave/grotto project in New Harmony, 1961. Jane Owen was equally at ease with both folk art and cosmopolitan design. Courtesy of the Frank and Elizabeth Haines Collection of the Ballard Institute and Museum of Puppetry at the University of Connecticut.

5

Frederick Kiesler's Grotto

A Promethean Spirit in New Harmony

BEN NICHOLSON WITH WILLIAM R. CROUT

THE FIRST PHASE of Jane Blaffer Owen's transformation of New Harmony envisaged three major building projects, which would express different aspects of Christianity.[1] The monumental Roofless Church would attest the majesty of Christ, a new St. Stephen's Episcopal Church would address the ministry of Christ, and a cave to house life-sized woodcarvings of the Holy Family would represent the humility of Christ, who, according to ancient tradition, was born in a cave.[2] Together, the three commissions would support an interconnected triadic vision. As it turned out, only the Roofless Church was completed. St. Stephen's Church advanced as far as a set of working drawings. Construction of the cave was canceled soon after the landscape had been laid out and materials purchased, which still languish in a shed more than fifty years later.

The cave is one of the most curious architectural commissions of the twentieth century, if only because it is known by two names: the client's name *Cave of the New Being* and the architect's name *Grotto for Meditation*, which is still used by architectural historians today.[3] It was the work of architect Frederick Kiesler (1890–1965), who was introduced to Owen by New York architect Philip Johnson (1906–2005). Kiesler and Johnson were an unlikely pair: Johnson famously remarked of Kiesler, "he is the greatest non-building architect of our time," to which Kiesler quipped, "Vell, I would say that Philip Johnson is one of the best building non-architects of our time."[4] The commission acquires an even richer aura with the name of the renowned theologian Paul Tillich (1886–1965), which was bestowed on the park where the cave was to be built. Owen created the Paul Tillich Park to honor her mentor.[5]

As the third element of Owen's intended triad, the cave was conceived as an intimate shelter for sculpted softwood images of Mary, Joseph, and Jesus. She commissioned these from Pennsylvania artists Elizabeth and Frank Haines, known for their realistic painted figurines, dolls, and puppets, which were frequently life-sized. In 1958 Owen organized an exhibition of their work in New Harmony, and they had completed the Holy Family commission for her by 1961.[6] Initially, Johnson was commissioned to design the cave to house the Holy Family, and by July 1960 he was making mockups for it with a set of five architectural drawings, which have since disappeared.[7] In an unlikely combination of sentimental artisanal figures and cosmopolitan high art, the project demonstrated Owen's attraction to both elegist and populist art.

In March 1961 Owen made known her desire to create the New Harmony Park on a site to the east of the Roofless Church to honor Paul Tillich.[8] She had met him in the early 1950s at Union Theological Seminary in New York, and his writings and lectures, especially on art and architecture, became a major influence on her vision for New Harmony. When Tillich lectured at Rice University in April 1961, she invited him to tea in her Houston home and offered him the honor of a park, which he accepted with surprised delight. The park was named Paul Tillich Park and was planned to open in 1963.[9] The park was the designated site of the cave, within which would be set the Holy Family sculpture.[10]

Owen was unsatisfied with Johnson's architectural solution for the cave, and sometime during the summer before August 10, 1962, Johnson introduced her to Frederick Kiesler in New York with the expectation that she would commission Kiesler to take on the design of the cave, the centerpiece of Paul Tillich Park.[11] Johnson was a champion of Kiesler and in 1952 had bought a giant wooden Galaxy sculpture for his Glass House property.[12] In their meeting, Owen invited Kiesler to visit New Harmony, and on August 29 she wrote a lengthy letter confirming his visit for the third weekend of October and assured him that after the trustees of the Robert Lee Blaffer Trust met on September 19, a "formal invitation and budget understanding" would be sent. She wrote, "Philip, as I have told you, feels that you are the most qualified man in the world to undertake this delicate and uncommon project. Have you by chance seen Paul Tillich? He would be most interested."[13]

Sometime in September 1962, Johnson wrote to Owen extolling Kiesler's virtues and suggested engaging him "for $5,000 to cover the cost of all the plans for the cave," but it was unusual in that Johnson was simultaneously excited about the commission and skeptical about its resolution:

> He is such a marvelous artist that even if hitches develop later, you will at least have beautiful drawings and models for yourself. I insisted on the $5,000 because he often sends extra bills afterward for expenses that he should not have incurred. So, I recommend your putting everything in writing. It is a pretty stiff fee, of course, but he is very poor, very deserving, and a great artist. We had a wonderful time.[14]

That he referred to Kiesler as an artist rather than an architect is telling. Johnson seems to have thought of the commission in curatorial terms, acting very much like Alfred Barr, founding director of the Museum of Modern Art, in finding a wealthy patron to support a promising artist while advancing the museum's cause.[15] At this point in time Kiesler's long career was still gathering strength, and his *Endless House* had just been exhibited in the *Visionary Architecture* show that opened at MoMA in September 1960.[16]

There may also have been a friendly rivalry between the two architects. Kiesler, at age sixty-seven, had become a leader in the cosmological aspects of architecture and was working on the most important commission of his career, the Shrine of the Book in Jerusalem, housing the Dead Sea Scrolls.[17] Johnson, at age fifty-one, had become a cosmopolitan leader in advocating America's preeminence on the world stage and had just completed the nuclear research center on the coastal plain south of Tel Aviv. Both projects were begun in 1957.

The First Design Phase (1962)

Although Johnson had recommended in September that a contract between the Blaffer Trust and Kiesler be drawn up to execute plans of the cave project for five thousand dollars, it took until December before a contract for fees and building costs was signed between the two parties. Meanwhile, Kiesler could not refrain from beginning to design the project in New York—in advance of the protection of a contract. On October 18, 1962, he traveled to New Harmony as Jane Owen's guest, and had a memorable time with her.[18] Kiesler bought a cheap school composition book and wrote a delightful account of his experiences in which he commingles the necessities of historical record with ethereal musings about the nature of the place. He was attracted by the allure of New Harmony, in which the spirits of generations consecrate the ground, and he clearly wanted to be all of a piece with it. In the composition book he also began to sketch observations, ideas, and construction details for the project. Owen had sparked his imagination.

Kiesler had begun his design process for the cave a couple of weeks before he had come to New Harmony. In New York he made a sketch, dated September 28, 1962, of a dynamic curved fish surrounded by a narrow pool of water, which was to become a key component of the design. His intuition to work with a fish was uncanny, for Owen had a welcome note waiting for his arrival containing a photograph of the recently restored copper weathervane on top of the David Dale Owen Geological Laboratory on Church Street. This was composed of a large river fish, skewered by a spiral rod rising atop a pentagonal dome with a knobby stem; each part was a symbolic reminder representing the great discoveries of the Owenite naturalists: Charles-Alexandre Lesueur's catfish *Ictalurus nebulosus,* David Dale Owen's spiral fossil bryozoan *Archimedes wortheni,* and Thomas Say's blastoid *Pentremites Say,* a pentagonal fossil with a long-ribbed calyx stem (Figure I.2).[19]

While in New Harmony, Kiesler visited the Owen Laboratory, a Victorian confection in the style of New York architect James Renwick Jr., which was to be the base of operations for David Owen's geological surveys into the hinterland of the

United States.[20] Among the collection of rock specimens and molluscs kept there, Kiesler found an irresistible pink conch shell that he made a quick line drawing of, signing it "21st Oct 1962." In no time at all, he had the two elements of his scheme: a cave in the shape of a conch shell surrounded by a swirling fish.

His visit to the site of the cave, the prospective Paul Tillich Park, a lot that extended 125 feet by 87 feet across Main Street from the Roofless Church and adjacent to the Barrett–Gate House, was sketched as a grove of a dozen trees set within the rectangle. The collection of trees was varied. He marked one as a pear, and the others were marked as black dots that he shunted around with his eraser while trying to approximate their location. As a later drawing indicates, Kiesler marked trees already on the northern edge of the site, including a large elm, black locust, Osage orange (*Maclura pomifera*), pecan, walnut, hackberry, and a couple of golden rain trees. Many of these trees are still living. Another drawing shows the site scraped of all trees save three on the north side, in the classic modernist tabula rasa, on which sculptural forms are set down.

The ten sheets of drawings in the composition book are complemented by another ten sketches made on an assortment of odd sheets of paper. It is not possible to determine if the majority of these first conceptual drawings were made in New York or New Harmony, and only two are dated, September 28, 1962, and October 21, 1962, still two months before Kiesler was to sign the contract for the project on December 5. The drawings are distinctive in that they cover the whole range of architectural expression. The venerable cocktail napkin sketch is present, showing the conch shell and fish embracing each other in plan and section. One can almost feel Kiesler's need to get the concept down on whatever is at hand before the idea drifts away. Kiesler made drawings of the site, descriptive drawings of objects, conceptual drawings of what could occur, measured plan views, several details of how it might be built, and different schemes.

One drawing that stands out is a sheet of sketches showing different configurations of the fish–cave combination, with an acknowledgment of the Roofless Church elevation: the fish gets wiggly; the cave is brought into the belly of the fish; the fish has entrance and exit doors cut into its side; the fish's mouth is wide open with the Nativity within; and the fish's head sticks up into the sky like the dome of the Roofless Church (Figure 5.14 and Plate 14). Already Kiesler's scheme had become the counterpoint of Johnson's Roofless Church: a rectangular walled garden that embraces the sky, within which an organic form is set. In Kiesler's version of Johnson's church, the wall is partial and intermittent, his organic forms challenge architectural cliché, and they descend into the ground rather than reach for the sky. Daylight comes through small lenses cut into the roof, a motif that Johnson was to employ two years later for the sky-cones protruding from his design for St. Stephen's Church (see Figures 4.16–4.17, 4.22). In these drawings Kiesler is studying every option. But even at this point in time,

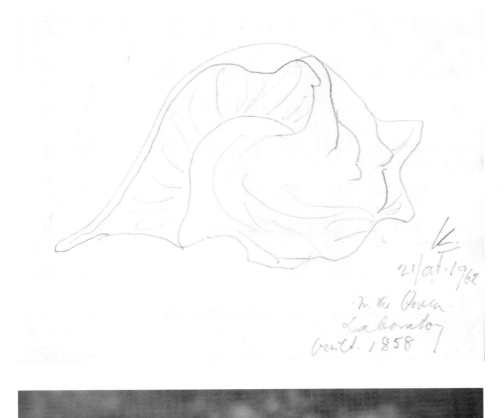

Figure 5.2. A pencil sketch of a conch shell, on which Kiesler modeled his cave/grotto project. "In the Owen Laboratory, built 1858. 21/Oct/1962." The shell form would become the counterpoint to Philip Johnson's billowing Roofless Church dome. Drawing copyright 2018 Austrian Frederick and Lillian Kiesler Private Foundation, Vienna.

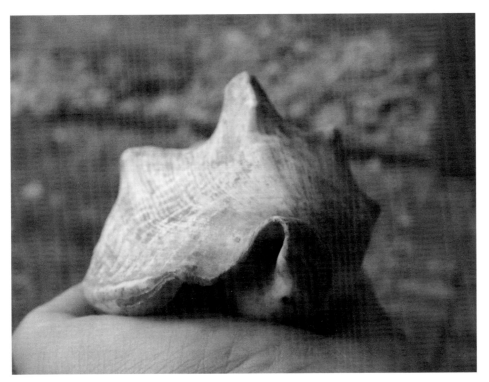

Figure 5.3. The conch shell found in the Owen Laboratory that Kiesler sketched for the cave/grotto design. The naturalist Thomas Say had made New Harmony an important center of conchology study during the 1830s. Courtesy of the Kenneth Dale and Jane Blaffer Owen family. Photograph courtesy of Ben Nicholson, 2006.

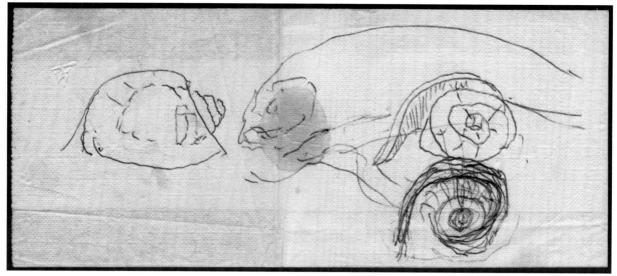

the scale and ambition of his vision were already greater than Owen's intent "for our Holy Family to find shelter at Christmas and for Paul Tillich to be honored."[21]

An especially charming drawing shows the conch shell in the form of a cave with a large opening, through which the sculpture of the Holy Family could be seen (see Figure 5.5). Behind the shell is the big fish with an open mouth, revealing a pool of water. One can imagine boating into the fish's belly, as if this were the Blue Grotto on the island of Capri.[22] On the same sheet Kiesler drew a nursing mother, legs akimbo as she suckles the infant child. The mother and child strike the same pose as the fish and cave, one enveloping the other. In another drawing the composition is a simple plan, in which a stream of water connects the fish with the cave. The pedestal for the sculpture is surrounded by water, which passes beneath the shell's spiral point and then laps around the fish. After considering a number of options, Kiesler arrived at his solution; the design was fixed and the elements were in place. Over the next three years, six versions of this scheme were worked on, with no further modifications of this initial idea.[23]

The drawings of the cave are very grotto-like at this point, as they are shallow and open on one side (see Figure 5.6). The wide opening of the hemispherical form is perfectly symmetrical, and the Holy Family sculpture occupies a pedestal in the center. Light pours in through the wide entrance, supplemented by fifteen or twenty skylights placed on the knobbly points of the shell. There is an overall sense of huge space, as big as the interior of Radio City Music Hall, but then a written dimension of two feet six inches drawn on the sketch reveals its true size. Kiesler seems to have had the scale of his Shrine of the Book in Jerusalem in mind as he struggled with the bite-sized commission in New Harmony. Cramming the life-sized sculptures into a pocket-sized shelter was the challenge, for the magic of a cave is its illusion of infinite scale, a long-standing theme of Kiesler's *Endless House*. As he thought

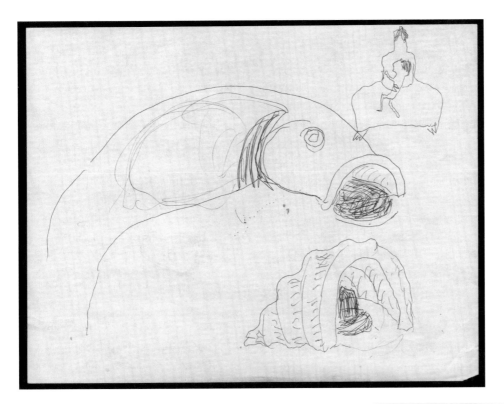

Figure 5.5. Sketch of the fish and grotto, and a mother and child in a sympathetic embrace, indicating the connection that Kiesler sought to make between the two forms of a shell and a fish for *Grotto for Meditation*, 1962. Drawing copyright 2018 Austrian Frederick and Lillian Kiesler Private Foundation, Vienna.

through the design, the drawings have a messy, crumbly aura. There is none of the pink opalescence of the conch shell's interior. Aesthetically, the project is beginning to have the feel of a grotto, both inside and out.

Another series of drawings from this early stage of design are of construction details for the fish, which by this time had changed from being a hollow cavern to a big ninety-seven-foot-long earthen mound covered in limestone flags, mimicking the overlapping scales of a fish. The sketches are inquisitive, showing a mind trying to figure out how to build this unusual fish-mound: they show the hand of an architect wanting to get it right.

Negotiating the Contract

On October 5, 1962, Jane Owen's secretary Dorothy Wood sent a letter to the Houston lawyer Whitfield Huff "Pat" Marshall, who was the chairman of the board of trustees of the Robert Lee Blaffer Trust. She requested that "some sort of contract" be sent to Kiesler for the design of a cave, for which "$12,000 had been appropriated," that would protect the

Figure 5.6. Frederick Kiesler wrote his thoughts on New Harmony in a school exercise notebook. He sketched the elevations and plan of the cave/grotto interior in this book, showing the nativity scene sculpture bathed in skylights. Drawing copyright 2018 Austrian Frederick and Lillian Kiesler Private Foundation, Vienna.

Trust.[24] On November 2, Johnson sent Marshall a draft of the contract, in which he wrote, "Here is a rough draft of something that might cover us with a great man. He is of course a genius and there is no question of 'losing money.' It is a matter of getting something for our money."[25] Marshall sent the agreement to Kiesler on November 5 "for the design of a 'cave' for New Harmony" for which he would receive a fee of $5,000.[26]

Johnson's draft of the contract for Kiesler is at odds with the creative musings of a man at the twilight of his life. Johnson, an established and debonair architect, was getting something down on paper to protect the interests of both Kiesler and the Blaffer Trust. Having already worked with Lipchitz on his sculpture for New Harmony *Descent of the Holy Spirit* (*Notre Dame de Liesse*) and the *Suzanne Glémet Memorial Gate* for the Roofless Church, Johnson knew the importance of having everything laid out transparently.[27] Johnson, founder and former director of the Department of Architecture and Design at the Museum of Modern Art, was trying to get a good deal out of the genius. He recognized that Kiesler was a pioneer of architectural form. Whatever was built in New Harmony should be in the vanguard, if only to enhance Johnson's own brilliant experimentation in the design of the Roofless Church. In a 1994 interview Johnson extolled Kiesler's visionary talent: "Kiesler used forbidden forms . . . [;] Kiesler broke with every tradition . . . [;] Kiesler is still to be discovered."[28]

The one-page agreement, sent to Kiesler by Marshall on his personal stationery on November 6, 1962, was addressed to the architectural partnership of Kiesler and Armand Bartos, with a line for Kiesler's signature.[29] According to the agreement, Kiesler was to provide a set of preliminary sketches, and perhaps a sketch model, for a cave at the cost of $3,500. If the Trust decided to go ahead with the project, a further $1,500 would be paid for supervision of the work. A $5,000 fee, 40 percent of the total $12,000 cost, was a pretty penny for a commission of this size (the equivalent of about $42,000 in 2019).[30]

But Kiesler would have nothing of this arrangement. On November 7, the day after he received the contract from Marshall, Kiesler wrote to Johnson that he wanted a preliminary design fee of five thousand dollars prior to the Trust's decision to build or not build the project. He also stipulated that he would submit drawings "of the proposed shelter cave for the manger group. These would include a smaller and larger version."[31] This was a vital change to the agreement because it would give him legal authority to design a substantially more ambitious scheme than the client's requirement. Kiesler asked for an additional two thousand to three thousand dollars for the "supervision of the sculpture work" and noted that he would provide a model. He also remarked that Owen had verbally agreed to double the budget of the project to between twenty-five thousand and thirty thousand dollars, so Kiesler was aiming for a 25 percent fee, still in the range of what a sculptor might expect for remuneration. He ended the letter by writing, "Let me add that my nominal fee for plans, adjustments and supervising the execution of the sculpture on location is due to my friendship for you and my admiration of Mrs. Owen and her pioneering work in New Harmony."

The next day Johnson wrote a letter to Marshall on his firm's letterhead from 375 Park Avenue, New York, the sleek steel and glass Seagram's Building of Mies van der Rohe, with whom Johnson was partner for that project. Johnson wrote:

Dear Pat:

I enclose Kiesler's letter. I must confess at once that I had discussed $5,000 with him for the plans and, indeed I think I know him well enough to believe that the work that he will do will far exceed the work regularly done by the average architect for such a sum. In other words, the Trust will be the owner of some beautiful drawings, models, water colors and sketches, even if nothing ever gets built, so I would tend to accept his paragraph A.

There is one major point of difference between me and him, and that is that he feels that he is owed the money even if we do not find the plans satisfactory. Since he is more of a sculptor rather than a regular architect, I think we should give into this also.

His paragraph B. and C. are very modest, so that if it should go ahead, they would be easy to accept.

His suggestions of costs of course are entirely imaginary and one of us would have to talk with the builder before any work was started.

What do you think?

Sincerely
Philip Johnson[32]

In everyone's mind, Johnson and Kiesler included, the cave was a sculpture and not a work of architecture, and it was priced accordingly as a work of art. On November 16, 1962, Owen revised the budgetary principles by raising the total cost of the project to fifteen thousand dollars, out of which Kiesler was to receive seven thousand dollars for design and supervision, leaving eight thousand dollars for construction.[33]

Nov 16th 1962

It would defeat the purpose of the Grotto Project if it were to cost more than $15,000.[34] With so many needs facing us all around New Harmony, I could not, in conscience, set aside more than this figure. Furthermore the cave should give an overall impression of modesty and humility—the homely side of the life of our Lord, in contrast to the royal side across the street.

I do not mind giving Mr. Kiesler an additional $2,000 for supervision, which would bring his fee up to $7,000 and would leave a maximum of $8,000 for material and labor.

Since it was my understanding that the latter two commodities could be supplied in New Harmony, I am sure we can keep the costs down. Philip had talked in terms of $12,000 when he was doing the cave.

So, in conclusion, unless Mr. Kiesler can design a cave to come under this outside figure of $15,000, I am afraid we will have to relieve Mr. Kiesler—roll up our sleeves, and make the cave ourselves!

Kiesler replied to Owen on November 23, 1962, and it appeared that the issues were resolved. He wrote: "My enthusiasm remains undiminished, and the ideas for it have by now crystallized clearly in my mind."[35] Owen wrote a note in the margin of the letter to Marshall, "Let's make it $20,000 all told if that's what it takes to please Kiesler. I'd hate to wind up without the cave."[36]

A revised contract went out from Marshall on his law firm's letterhead (Fulbright, Crooker, Freeman, Bates, and Jaworski) on December 5, 1962.

Dear Mr. Kiesler:

With further reference to the proposed shelter at New Harmony for the manger group, I am now pleased to suggest the following arrangement which generally is in line with your letter of November 7 to Philip Johnson and is also, I understand, in accordance with the discussions you have had with Mrs. Owen and Mr. Johnson.

(a) You will submit drawings and perspectives in black and white and in color of the shelter, including a smaller and larger version, and a preliminary site plan on how to locate the cave and how the environment is to be treated. For this work you will receive a fee of $5,000, of which $1,000 will be paid upon your signing this agreement and the remaining $4,000 upon the delivery of the plans called for in this paragraph.

(b) At present the Blaffer Trust intends to proceed with the project if it is determined that the total cost (including your fees) will not exceed $20,000. If the Trust does decide to go forward, you will prepare a small-scale model of the work and you will also supervise the construction of the shelter, for which you will receive an additional fee of $2,000 plus reasonable travel expenses.

As stated above, the Trust has in mind spending only $20,000 on the project, which means that construction could not cost more than $12,000 to $13,000. Mrs. Owen believes (based on her conversations with the local builder) that this can be done, but if you feel otherwise, I wish you would let me know, or talk with Philip about it.

If the agreements set forth in this letter are satisfactory, please sign and return a copy of this letter.

> Yours very truly,
> Whitfield H. Marshall
> For The Blaffer Trust
> ejt
> Accepted: /s/ Frederick J. Kiesler
> cc. Mrs. Kenneth Dale Owen
> Mr. Philip Johnson[37]

In the contract are instructions for smaller and larger versions of the proposed shelter for the "manger group," and also to include a preliminary site plan for the cave, together with a small-scale model of the work. Kiesler, upon signing this contract for a cave, designed to be a shelter for the manger group, immediately sent a copy to Jane Owen, writing, "I am very happy to accept the agreement and to go ahead dreaming, planning and designing your project."[38] She replied with a beautifully written Christmas card, her script set within an oval of embossed holly wreaths, writing "I could not have had more joy or peace at Christmas without knowing that all was settled about our grotto-cave."[39] She looked forward to what would emerge from Kiesler's fertile imagination but, unbeknown to her, the project was turning from being a shelter for a sculpture to something much more substantial, perhaps something that would compete with the Roofless Church.

The Second Design Phase (1963)

Kiesler worked fast, and on January 18, 1963, he wrote Jane Owen enclosing photostats of three plans "for the grotto in New Harmony."[40] Of the three plans of this second scheme, only the drawing of the cave is known to exist. Kiesler was pleased with the solution and hoped that the project would be accepted before he went to Jerusalem in ten days' time so that he could move forward to the working drawings stage.

Owen was very enthusiastic—"predicting your unanimous election to chief mound and cave builder for the Blaffer Trust!" She adds the postscript, "I think the cave should be very still, with only the trickle of water and not have bells. And thank you for the swish in the dolphin's tail!"[41] The dolphin was the third species of swimming creature that Kiesler had drawn.[42]

Kiesler made a ROMA Plastilina model, following the earlier ribbed conch shell drawings but with one essential change: the mouth of the building was plugged by a curvaceous room with entrances to the left and right sides. The project now had a cavernous, unseen, and unknown interior that the visitor must commit to before walking inside. It has become mysterious, lit only by scores of little round skylights peppered over the shell. The skylights are no longer positioned on the tips of the shell's ribs, as was the case for the first scheme, but are set into the valleys of the shell. Inside, the Holy Family has been placed on a rock plinth, and Kiesler inserted a group of visitors in his drawing to give a sense of scale. The sculpture is surrounded with water, and stepping-stones are positioned in the cave's flowing stream so that visitors can walk across to the other side. Narrow benches for rest and meditation run along both walls.[43]

A trickling stream passes out of the cavernous form to the fish under a spiral-shaped window set with colored lights. The spiral was Kiesler's symbol for eternity, which he had used in the *Endless House* a decade earlier. In essence, this second scheme has turned from being a cave to become a dimly lit grotto within a cave, the smaller of the two turned inward, away from the casual gazes of visitors. The

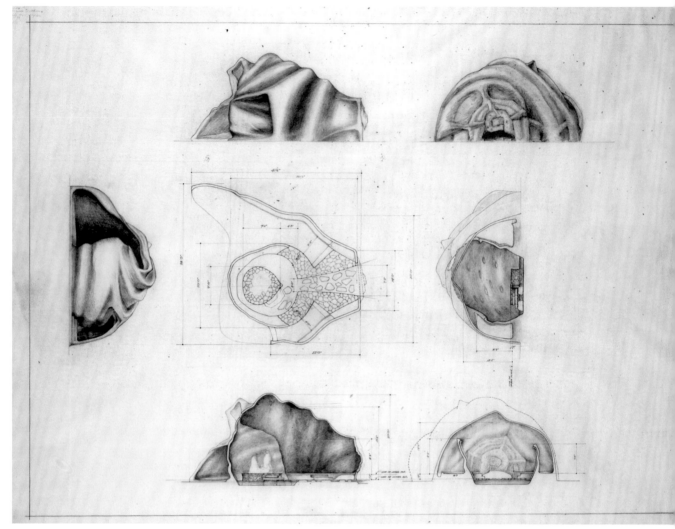

Figure 5.7. The second scheme of *Grotto for Meditation,* designed to conceal the Holy Family from open view and providing interior seating for meditation. Copyright 2018 Austrian Frederick and Lillian Kiesler Private Foundation, Vienna. Drawing courtesy of Albertina, Vienna.

enormous "fish" is recognizable as a dolphin, its head turned to the left rather than the right, as in the first scheme. The dolphin is heavily ribbed, much like the cavernous grotto-esque cave, and sits in a low walled pool of water closely tailored to its shape.

With the first drawings in hand, Owen was eager to share them with Tillich. On January 28, 1963, she wrote Tillich to tell him that the plans for the *"Cave-Grotto of the New Being"* are ready.[44] She described the symbolism of the conch shell as belonging to the lineage of the Owen Laboratory as well as recalling a womb and a hidden heart. Her metaphors were visceral and intense.[45] Tillich would have to wait until early May 1963 before he got the drawings from Kiesler, along with his description: "The fish, in this case the dolphin, a symbol of Christ surrounding the grotto, protecting the Nativity group which is sheltered in a shell of concrete."[46]

BEN NICHOLSON
WITH WILLIAM R. CROUT

Figure 5.8. Frederick Kiesler with the Plastilina model of the second scheme for *Grotto for Meditation,* which creates a cave within a grotto. Kiesler sculpted the clay model with his hands, intensifying its expressionist quality. Photograph copyright 2018 Austrian Frederick and Lillian Kiesler Private Foundation, Vienna.

Naming the Project

Sometime before November 16, 1962, a conversation had taken place between Kiesler and Owen about the project's concept and name. The reasons for this are unclear. The record shows a rich evolution in the project's nomenclature, which was to have far-reaching consequences in how the project was to be understood, both then and now. Owen and Tillich had always understood the project to be a "cave"; Kiesler conceived it as a "grotto." This evolution in terminology can be traced in the many different titles used for the project.[47] It can be fairly assumed that there had been a discussion about the matter, for throughout the correspondence from November 1962 it can be inferred that Owen was struggling to find a title that would express her original intent—for herself, her trustees, and her artist–architect.[48]

In her January 28 letter to Tillich, Owen had described the project as the *Cave-Grotto of the New Being,* and the hyphened title is an indication of the conceptual conflict about to unfold across the project. Owen always wanted a cave for the Holy Family that initially Johnson was to design. With the dedication of the Roofless

Church in 1960, she had begun to think of a contrasting structure across the street representing the humble Lord before she involved either Tillich or Kiesler. She then added the idea that the sheltering cave and Nativity ensemble were a part of a park offered to Tillich on April 3 or 4, 1961, and engaged Kiesler to design the cave for the Nativity.

In her January 28, 1963, letter to her mentor Tillich, when Owen writes, "that the plans for the Cave-Grotto of The New Being are ready," she highlights Tillich's addition, and thereafter the name of the project for them becomes the *Cave of the*

Figure 5.9. Jane Blaffer Owen and Dr. Paul Tillich stand in front of the dedication stone in Paul Tillich Park at Pentecost, June 2, 1963. Kiesler and Tillich advocated different forms of expressionism to redefine religious art. Photograph by Robert E. Eger. Courtesy of the Robert Lee Blaffer Foundation.

New Being.[49] In confirmation of this, on June 2, 1963, Tillich dedicated the Ground of Paul Tillich Park and the Cave of the New Being.[50] In an undated correspondence, thought to be written between January and May 1963 by Owen's secretary, the nomenclature is put this way: "In Paul Tillich Park there will be a grotto to be known as *'The Cave of the New Being.'*"[51] The press release of Dr. Nevin E. Danner, director of program services for the Robert Lee Blaffer Trust, stated, "We welcome Professor Paul Tillich to New Harmony . . . to dedicate Paul Tillich Park and to initiate the construction *The Cave of the New Being,* the design of Doctor Frederick Kiesler."[52] In Owen's letter to Kiesler of May 14, 1963, she writes: "We must consider placing the *Cave of the New Being* further to the east."[53]

A tape-recorded interview between Kiesler and the Reverend Doctor Arthur Hadley, made in October 1964, documents the impasse for the first time. The two parties have separate names for the project, which would become a sectarian dispute between followers of Kiesler and Tillich.

> **MR. KIESLER:** Doctor Hadley, you wanted to make a remark with regard to the water. I know you're interested in it. Because inside the Grotto there will be also places where children can be baptized.
>
> **DR. HADLEY:** Yes. I think that the whole concept of the *Cave of the New Being* as we call it, or the *Grotto of Meditation,* is very dynamic, and your heightened awareness is very true here, that we will be very aware of being washed of sin in the water, and being reborn in baptism. I think this is a very outstanding Christian symbol.
>
> **MR. KIESLER:** Yes it is. And I think it is, in a quite natural way, incorporated inside the Grotto.[54]

The Third Design Phase (1963)

Tillich had not heard from Owen since March 1961 and registered surprise when he learned in February 1963 that the project was going ahead.[55] "I did not think that your kind and very honoring project was still alive, since I did not hear anything about it for such a long time. It slowly took on the character of a dream. . . . I am overwhelmed by the fact that now the dream has become reality again."[56] A week later she replied, "Your letter swept me on to *undreamt* seas of joy. First that you are pleased. Secondly, that you would be in the Midwest through May, for you permit me to hope you can bless the Cave-Grotto at Pentecost, the second of June."[57] Owen sent a copy of this two-page typed letter to Kiesler, with a handwritten note saying, "Let us place 'Cave or Grotto of the *NEW BEING*' on the drawings, because I have always called it that." But Kiesler would not use this name on the drawings, preferring instead "GROTTO for New Harmony, Indiana."

The archival record has no indication of any discussion between Owen, Johnson, Kiesler, and Tillich about the meaning and value of these two quite different names.

It is accepted that Owen settled on the name *Cave of the New Being* and Kiesler settled on the name *Grotto for Meditation.* Because the Kiesler Foundation refers to the project as *Grotto for Meditation,* as do all references to it in the architecture discipline, from this point forward the abbreviated term for the project will change from *cave* to *grotto* in the remainder of this chapter, except for quoted passages.

Kiesler's work schedule on the project was entwined with his work on the Shrine of the Book in Jerusalem. Yet he clearly preferred working on the grotto and wanted to get every aspect of the project right.[58] He knew how important it was to Owen to have the project ready by Pentecost, June 2, 1963, the same day as the 1,400-year anniversary of Iona Abbey in Scotland, which her friend, the Reverend George MacLeod, was organizing. Kiesler wrote to her, explaining that "on the other hand I am sure you will agree that we must be very cautious not to sacrifice the quality of such a beloved work and its execution by rushing it. However I fully appreciate the significance of the date you are aiming at and rest assured that I will try my utmost to align myself to it."[59] Kiesler knew that the ninety-seven-foot-long dolphin would take more time to build, even though Owen suggested that the New Harmony Boy Scouts could help move the earth for site preparation. She now wanted to choose the inscription for a stone plaque at the base of the Nativity group in the grotto and suggested to Tillich that he have Kiesler's drawings and model in his hands to inspire him to find passages from his sermon "The New Being."[60] Kiesler wrote to Tillich that Owen had suggested "Dedicated to the spirit of the new being"; Tillich wrote on the back of the letter: "Estranged and Reunited: The New Being P. T."[61]

Kiesler continued to refine the design, aided by his longtime assistant and later associate Len Pitkowsky.[62] For the first time, the scheme was set on the site in a drawing. The dolphin lay along the north side of a low-walled enclosure, with the grotto right in front of the windows of the Red Geranium Restaurant to the south. Looking at this version of Paul Tillich Park through Lipchitz's reliefs on the bronze gates of the Roofless Church, you would see the snout of the dolphin and the pink hump of the grotto shell. Careful presentation drawings were also made of the dolphin, one version rendered with plant material and the other with a coat of random limestone flags, a design change responding to Johnson's observation that an earthen mound starts to slip at forty-five degrees.[63] The drawings have the appearance of a streamlined Raymond Loewy express train.

The proximity of Kiesler's low-walled *temenos,* with a pair of erotically shaped objects inside, sited adjacent to the Roofless Church was bound to be a provocation to Johnson. Kiesler was not above challenging the authority of the *culturati.* In 1950 Gjon Mili had photographed Kiesler comically perched on a child's stool, struggling to light up a Double Corona. The composition was recalled in Werner Blaser's famous 1965 photograph of Mies van der Rohe, thoughtfully sitting in a MR side-chair smoking a cigar. Kiesler's irreverent humor in selecting suggestive forms

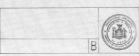

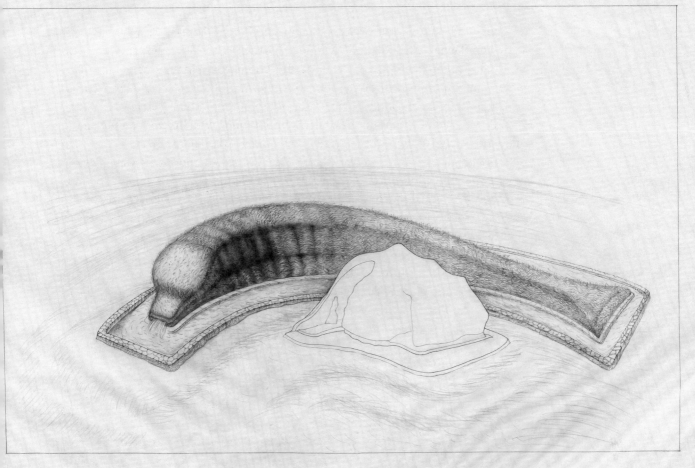

Figure 5.10. Drawing of the dolphin-shaped mound with plant covering surrounding the *Grotto for Meditation.* The grassy covering was seen to be unfeasible because of the sloping design. Drawing copyright 2018 Austrian Frederick and Lillian Kiesler Private Foundation, Vienna.

for the grotto was a scurrilous attack on Owen, Johnson, and Tillich, made at their expense in order to prioritize his own beliefs.

During spring 1963 Kiesler and Pitkowsky spent a month making a pair of clay models of the grotto, the second of which was made in two editions with the dolphin and cast in bronze. Once the models were finished, a fourth set of plans and elevations was prepared and completed on April 9, 1963. Kiesler sent Tillich the new plans with a letter describing the symbolism of the project.[64] A month later the foundry sent Tillich one of the two bronze models following instructions from Owen.[65]

> Dear Dr. Tillich:
> Jane Owen, for whom I have planned, as you know, the grotto for meditation built around the Nativity group, asked me to send you the plans so that we can present to you the idea for the project.

The fish, in this case the dolphin, as a symbol of Christ is surrounding the grotto, protecting the Nativity group, which is sheltered in a shell of concrete.

A source of water is spouting from the base of the group and spreads, flowing quietly through the interior of the grotto out into the open, surrounding the fish.

I do hope you like it. Please accept my reverence and best regards.

> Faithfully yours,
> Frederick J. Kiesler

The fourth scheme, produced in the third design phase, was for the same site but an additional fifteen feet of ground was added to the east so that the grotto could be enlarged in size.[66] The dolphin changed its shape and shadowed the curve of the grotto much more acutely, following the lines of the bronze model. The shell lost all its ribbing and the skylights were gone, leaving only the glow from the two entrances and the light percolating through the colored glass in the spiral window above the outflow of the stream.

In addition to preparing the design drawings, Kiesler was hard at work with the New York engineering firm Strobel and Rongved figuring out how to build the project.[67] Together they designed a thin shell structure made of steel-reinforced concrete. In mid-May 1963, Pitkowsky came to New Harmony to meet the contractor Jim Benton and review the proposed construction. During the visit a new location for the grotto was discussed, as Owen had purchased an additional lot to the east.[68] In her letter, she writes, "We *must* consider placing the Cave of the New Being further to the east, now, because it is *bigger* than I had ever thought it would be, and needs to sit back further from Main Street. Furthermore, it will not thus obliterate the view I have so long enjoyed from the Gate House garden. This is, I am sure you will agree, a subtler solution."[69]

Figure 5.11, top. Portrait of the architect Frederick Kiesler seated in a child's chair, smoking a cigar, photographed by Gjon Mili, circa 1950 (*Life* magazine). Copyright 2018 Austrian Frederick and Lillian Kiesler Private Foundation, Vienna. Courtesy of Gjon Mili / The LIFE Picture Collection, Getty Images.

Figure 5.12, bottom. Portrait of Ludwig Mies van der Rohe in the dining room of his Chicago apartment, 1965. This photograph was taken fifteen years after Mili's photograph of Kiesler, but together the two images of the artist–architects depict the ridiculous and sublime. Photograph by Werner Blaser. Courtesy of Werner Blaser.

Figure 5.13. Kiesler's assistant Len Pitkowsky (1930–2015) reassembles two terracotta models of *Grotto for Meditation* in 2008 that he had assisted with in 1963. The sculptural nature of the models was to prove difficult to scale up to the size of an enclosure. Model copyright 2018 Austrian Frederick and Lillian Kiesler Private Foundation, Vienna. Courtesy of the Collection of the Estate of Frederick Kiesler represented by Jason McCoy Gallery, New York. Photograph courtesy of Ben Nicholson, 2009.

Figure 5.14. Kiesler's bronze model of *Grotto for Meditation* for Paul Tillich Park, 1963. Inside was to be a sculpture of the Holy Family, later exchanged with Kiesler's bronze sculpture *Cup of Prometheus*. Image copyright 2018 Austrian Frederick and Lillian Kiesler Private Foundation, Vienna. Sculpture courtesy of the Robert Lee Blaffer Foundation. Photograph courtesy of Ben Nicholson, 2006.

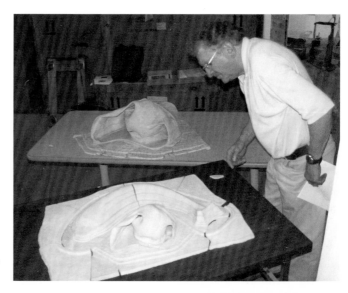

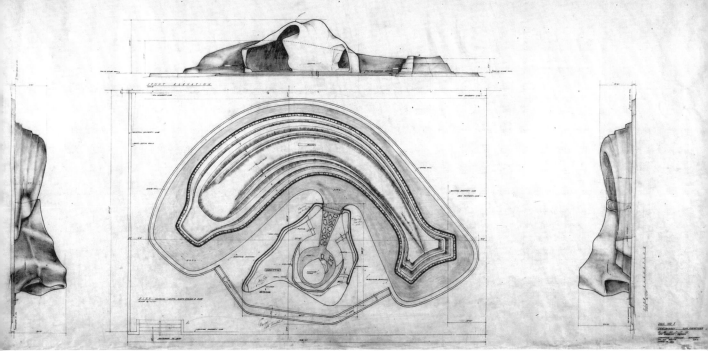

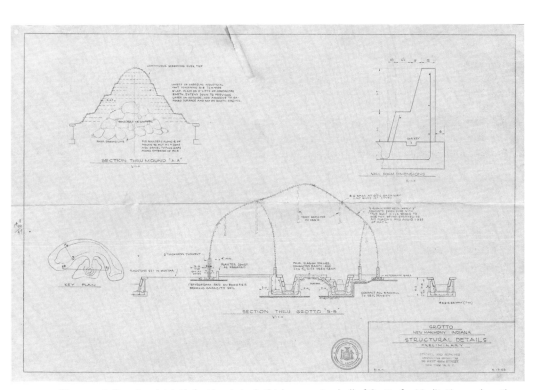

Figure 5.15. Drawing of the fourth scheme for *Grotto for Meditation,* with the dolphin-shaped mound oriented northward, reflecting the terracotta models. Throughout the design process, the site was enlarged to accommodate Kiesler's ever-increasing size of the project. Copyright 2018 Austrian Frederick and Lillian Kiesler Private Foundation, Vienna. Drawing courtesy of Albertina, Vienna.

Figure 5.16. Structural details for the six-inch-thick concrete shell of *Grotto for Meditation* and sections through the boulder and earth fish-shaped mound, and water pools, 1963. Kiesler hired New York engineers to validate the buildability of his organic forms. Drawing copyright 2018 Austrian Frederick and Lillian Kiesler Private Foundation, Vienna.

Dedicating the Ground of Paul Tillich Park and the Cave of the New Being

The original part of the site to the west was laid bare, save for the existing trees and a site for the stone that had been carved for the dedication of Paul Tillich Park on Pentecost, June 2, 1963. In June, the dedication of the ground of Paul Tillich Park and the *Cave of the New Being* by Tillich took place. Owen sought to schedule her major celebratory or dedicatory events on Pentecost or May Day. It was a climactic public event and marked the apogee of the relationship between Kiesler and Owen.[70]

In readiness for the dedication, Kiesler sent Tillich a set of plans and one of the two copies of the bronze model. At the dedication, which Kiesler did not attend, the Reverend Nevin Danner spoke to the press about the symbolism of the dolphin: "Apparently the dolphin is being used because in antiquity it was the symbol of joyfulness, and of mammalian intelligence. Also the skin of the dolphin was used to cover the Hebrew 'Holy of Holies,' and the dolphin may be seen on many European cathedrals."[71]

On July 3, 1963, Kiesler completed the fifth scheme of the grotto. It was the most beautiful scheme yet and masterfully negotiated Owen's wish to include the project while keeping a generous amount of open space with a shade tree in the middle. The grotto and dolphin were moved to the northeast at a forty-five-degree angle, leaving plenty of open space to the west in Paul Tillich Park. A gently scalloped grassy bowl edged by a rise and a line of shrubs and small trees surrounded the grotto and dolphin, making them less visible. Pushing out into the park is a flagstone walkway leading to a large elm tree with a stone at its base, no doubt the one from the dedication, with the words "Estranged and Reunited: The New Being, Paul Tillich, Pentecost June 2 1963" carved on it. Now there was a place for solitary meditation upon the Holy Family in the grotto as well as space for the philosopher–theologian to sit beneath a tree encircled by a ring of students. The project had finally reached a point of calm. Kiesler revealed his deep intuition by designing a place where both the meditative and discursive components of being were given space to thrive. Kiesler visited Tillich and his second wife, Hannah, in their home in East Hampton, New York, around the summer solstice of 1963 and spent an hour in philosophical discourse. Sadly, there is no record of this conversation between the two great men, who approached their work so differently.[72]

In the history of letters, there is a recurring theme of wanting to know what was said between two people in an exchange that was neither heard nor recorded. On the one hand, Tillich and Kiesler could have exchanged pleasantries over a cup of coffee while looking out to the Atlantic Ocean. On the other hand, they could have worked through their respective positions on the relationship of art and spirituality, about which both were passionate and had dedicated their lives to.[73]

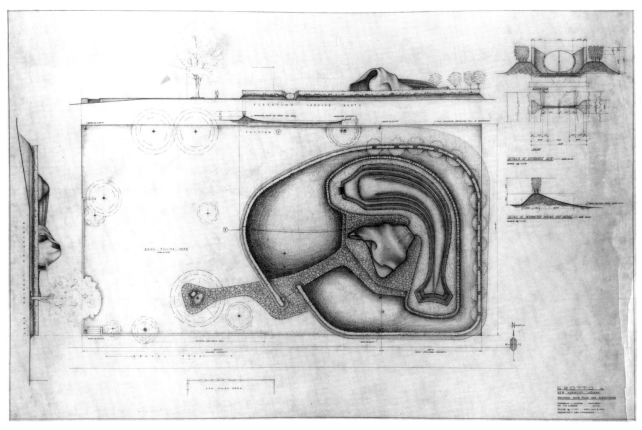

Figure 5.17. Kiesler's fifth scheme on an enlarged site, making room for *Grotto for Meditation* within Paul Tillich Park, at which point the design reaches its maturity. Site plan and elevations, 1963. Copyright 2018 Austrian Frederick and Lillian Kiesler Private Foundation, Vienna.

Everything was apparently progressing according to plan in Kiesler's mind, and he collected estimates from engineering firms for the specialist work needed to design and build the project. In August 1963 Kim Lighting sent him a quotation of $4,283 for the spray, weir, and water flow effects needed for the fountain, and Chemco Engineering supplied samples and instructions for the concrete mix.[74] Adding Kiesler's fee of as much as eight thousand dollars to the lighting estimate of four thousand dollars, the expenses of the scheme were beginning to look problematic: twelve thousand dollars for his labor and the lighting, and nothing had begun to be built. A crisis was in the making. Then his wife Steffi died in early September 1963.

Owen was anxious to have her *Cave of the New Being* completed by mid-November 1963, and she urged Kiesler to make another trip to New Harmony in October to inspect the construction of a test section of the grotto and dolphin.[75] He was not happy with what he encountered (Plate 16). The concrete shell was clearly going to cause a problem, for it was an unlikely surface on which to graft the glass tiles that he had in mind for a covering. But for all this, Owen circulated a letter to her friends on Christmas Day 1963, assuring them that construction of "our cave of wonders" would begin in the early spring of 1964.[76]

The Project Falters and Stumbles

Not much happened between October 1963 and February 1964. Unbeknown to Kiesler, Owen had started an ambitious new project in New Harmony. Johnson was designing a new replacement church for the Episcopal parish, St. Stephen's. The first inkling that the grotto project was no longer on the fast track was a letter to Kiesler from the Blaffer Trust's chairman, Marshall, saying that "it has been determined that we should undertake the construction of the cave and leave the fish for a later date."[77] Pressure was on to finish the project, as Tillich was not in good health, and everyone was concerned that he see through the completed Paul Tillich Park while he still might. Kiesler was dismayed at the news and wrote a letter to Marshall that evokes the idealistic determination of the character Howard Roark in the 1943 book and 1949 film *The Fountainhead*.[78]

> Dear Mr. Marshall:
> Your letter of February 19 reached me in the hospital where I was laid up with a bleeding ulcer.
> I am still in the hospital but expect soon to be released to continue my life at home.
> My answer to your letter and to the Blaffer Trust might be as great a shock to you as your letter was to me.
> In your letter you do not give me any explanation for cutting the project in half but anyone, and certainly Mrs. Jane Owen, knows that the fish and the grotto are insolubly bound together and that means not only spiritually but also structurally.
> Under the circumstances I offer my resignation from the project to leave you free to select any other architect to build a cave of his own design, since mine is copyrighted. I recommend Mr. Howard Barnstone, who lives in Houston and is a friend of Mrs. Owen.
> I regret very much to be forced to this decision, but all my life has been dedicated to consistency of ideas and if I can't follow them to the bitter end I must forsake them.
> I'd like to add that I enjoyed enormously working with Mrs. Owen, but I realized during my last visit to New Harmony that she is restricted in making the final decisions regarding the project. Unfortunately my illness adds another sad detail to the matter and so we'd better drop the whole thing with no ill feeling.
>
> > Sincerely yours
> > Frederick J. Kiesler

Marshall did his best to placate Kiesler and assure him that the fish was still part of the project, but that it was a matter of not having the funds to build the cave and the fish simultaneously.[79] This was probably true, for two weeks later on March 20, 1964, Johnson completed the first set of drawings for St. Stephen's Church.[80] But to presume that it was Johnson who steered the decision to delay building the fish immediately, from his vantage point as a trustee of the Blaffer Trust, is to oversimplify the issue.[81] The situation was further complicated when Kiesler suffered a heart attack a few days later and was confined to bed where "he may have no visitors, make no phone calls or write or even read."[82] But he had recovered enough by March 26, 1964, a week after his trauma, and six months after the death of his wife, Steffi, to marry Lillian Olinsey.

The goal of building the grotto by June 1964, in time for the planned dedication of the completed Paul Tillich Park on Pentecost, began to disintegrate. With Kiesler laid up, and his righthand man Pitkowsky busy installing an exhibition of Kiesler's work at the Guggenheim Museum, no one could travel to New Harmony and oversee construction before Pentecost on May 11, 1964, far too late to have the project ready by June. The dedication was canceled due to the setbacks, yet the project stumbled on.

By June 1964 decisions were again being made regarding the grotto's construction. Two consulting engineering firms, Lev Zetlin and Strobel & Rongved, provided detailed estimates for producing structural drawings, specifications, and oversight of the construction of the project.[83] Owen, in consultation with Johnson, encouraged Kiesler to rest after his illness, writing: "Philip, as you say, believes so in your artistic process that he doesn't want the cave started until you meet with the engineers."[84] Both remained committed to the project. Kiesler wrote to the German–Mexican sculptor and artist Mathias Goeritz, whose friend Juan O'Gorman had tiled a naturally formed grotto with fantastic designs.[85] Kiesler asked him for sources for one-half-inch beige glass tile and for a manufacturer to advise on how to attach the product on wavy surfaces that would be exposed to heavy rain.[86] On July 30, 1964, Kiesler purchased two thousand square feet of Japanese hand-assembled tile. One hundred and nine cartons of the tiles were paid for on October 20, 1964, and delivered to New Harmony, where the unopened cartons could still be found in 2010.[87]

The Promethean New Man

There were dramatic design changes inside the grotto that would change the look and feel of the project. It had become clear that the Holy Family sculpture was far too big for his layout. It was also likely to present adverse environmental problems, as the sculpture was carved in soft basswood, colored with a watercolor paint, and clothed in hand-woven wool and linen. Because the grotto was to have flowing water surrounding the Holy Family, moths and mildew would quickly destroy the figures.

To solve the problem, Kiesler offered Owen his large sculpture *The Cup of Prometheus,* which included a flame mechanism, even though he had to resolve

Figure 5.18. Frederick Kiesler proposed replacing the Christian nativity scene of Frank and Elizabeth Haines in *Grotto for Meditation* with the Greek mythology–inspired wood and bronze sculpture *The Cup of Prometheus* (1956–64). Turning from Christianity to Greek classicism would have radically changed the meaning of the project for Tillich Park. Copyright 2018 Austrian Frederick and Lillian Kiesler Private Foundation, Vienna. Sculpture courtesy of Collection of the Estate of Frederick Kiesler represented by Jason McCoy Gallery, New York.

a financial arrangement with his dealer to do so. As he wrote, he also "denied to sell to Jerusalem which is very much interested because I believe it a perfect fit for the Grotto."[88] Owen agreed and paid him an installment of two thousand dollars, a third of the asking price.[89] To remove the Holy Family from the grotto and replace it with an abstract sculpture of Prometheus was enormously significant, because the whole purpose of the project would completely change. Owen wanted a humble cave for the Infant Jesus, and Kiesler had swapped him out for Prometheus, a Greek demigod with some Christ-like qualities. Kiesler was wrestling the spiritual content of the project out of Owen's hands; having given him part-purchase of his sculpture to substitute for the Holy Family she had become further drawn into his vision.

Prometheus, the Titan who created man from clay and stole fire from the gods, was a popular subject for sculpture during the postwar period.[90] Prometheus represented the New Man, able to confront the gods with technology, an apt metaphor in the Cold War era. On the other hand, Jesus, in Tillich's theological terms, is the bringer of the New Being. Thus while Prometheus represents newness in mankind, Jesus manifests a new reality in nature and history as well as in humankind.[91] It is clear that Kiesler thought *The Cup of Prometheus* was the right expression of newness for the grotto, a place where humankind, fire, and water would commingle.[92]

In October 1964 Kiesler returned to New Harmony for an important set of meetings. His new wife Lillian, his assistant Pitkowsky, and the engineer Paul I. Rongved accompanied him, and Owen arranged for Arthur Hadley to be present. During their visit, on October 4, Lillian Kiesler organized an interview between all members of the party in the Red Geranium Restaurant, which was tape-recorded.[93] Also on the visit's agenda was a photo shoot of the group by John Doane. He photographed Kiesler, Rongved, and Pitkowsky sitting at a table in the Park, with landscape stakes driven into the ground where the foundations of the grotto and fish were to be. The site had been graded, and the retaining walls and steps marked on the plans had been built. Despite the setbacks, the project was finally emerging into a new reality. (Plate 15)

The taped interview is an important record of the project, and

Figure 5.19. Frederick Kiesler discusses the structure of *Grotto for Meditation* with engineer Paul Rongved and assistant Len Pitkowsky in Tillich Park, 1964. The surrounding wall of the park was complete, indicating how close the project came to realization prior to its cancellation. Copyright 2018 Austrian Frederick and Lillian Kiesler Private Foundation, Vienna. Photograph courtesy of John Doane Collection, Special Collections, University of Southern Indiana.

it is far ranging. The interview addresses such diverse topics as the meaning of *Grotto for Meditation* and Kiesler's thoughts on continuous structure, as well as a dialogue with Rongved about the ease of building the project. It contains Kiesler's general observations on the world around him, including the difficulty of sweeping the floor of the Red Geranium with so many chairs around!

Of critical importance to the program of the grotto, Kiesler described his understanding of rebirth, a theme he returned to again and again during his life's work.

> Since the Grotto for Meditation is based on early Christian devotion to the new human being or—at that time—because the New Being is obviously born—and this is again, here, the project for the New Being that will be once more reborn; and we hope you will be. We have today easier means to make the human aware of rebirth, to give birth to himself.

In this excerpt of the taped interview, Kiesler has his own view and interpretation on rebirth, and comes to that question through his practice as an artist.[94] On the other hand, Tillich, the philosopher–theologian, had spent a lifetime articulating the nature of rebirth and the New Being, and although it may seem that the two men were interested in the same issues, what each meant by rebirth was very different.[95]

Father Hadley played an important role in the project, both practically and programmatically, and he fully understood the grotto's role in the complex of buildings that Owen was planning. She wrote a warm letter of thanks to Kiesler and his new wife Lillian, and then articulated the relationship of the three buildings she was working on:

> . . . I wish you could have heard our young Episcopal priest (Fr. Hadley) refer to it as the first *Baptistry* of our era, and one of three different, but integrated parts of a whole—
> 1) Philip's Roofless church, "called by a great clergyman and orator [George MacLeod], 'A *cathedral* of earth and sky.'"
> 2) The small chapel to come and not yet definitive.
> 3) The Kiesler Baptistry in the Grotto-Cave of the New Being, Paul Tillich Park. Let us all pray that this Trilogy gives healing to our times.[96]

In the same letter she agrees with Kiesler that it would be best to lay the foundations in the fall and then erect the structure in early spring of 1965. There was every indication that the grotto was to go forward, with a qualified engineer overseeing the project, and plenty of time for Kiesler to recover from his heart attacks.

Pivotal to the October 1964 trip was the presence of Rongved, who was tasked with working out how to engineer the grotto. During the taped interview, Kiesler pointedly asked Rongved how easy it would be to build the New Harmony project in comparison to the far more challenging Shrine of the Book, for which Rongved was also the engineer; Kiesler got the answer he was looking for:

> **MR. KIESLER:** And in our meetings here with the contractors, we found many suggestions and variations, which they've suggested, which you and I have found very helpful in clarifying the issue. So in a way we are very lucky that we are in a surrounding here, in New Harmony and Evansville, which is, from a contractor point of view, very sympathetic toward this thing we are doing. This is a very encouraging and inspiring aspect, isn't it, for you too?
> **DR. RONGVED:** Yes, yes, absolutely![97]

Kiesler wanted the project well engineered, but he did not want to forfeit expressionist hand sculpting of the grotto. He needed the latitude to manipulate the form on-site and ensure that the concrete be hand-troweled to enable surface decorations to occur as a result of the construction and finishing process.[98] These seemingly contradictory principles of design and construction were reflected in the conundrum of having a highly capable New York engineer working in tandem with a local New Harmony contractor, Jim Benton. Kiesler was still working to get estimates from subcontractors for various aspects of the project, and Pitkowsky drew up a checklist of costs for the grotto still to be determined. A new direction was then taken, to engage Bauer Brothers of Evansville as the general contractor, but the Bauer quotation of

$130,000 for the whole project and $62,000 for the cave alone was not viable, even though Jane Owen had further increased the budget to $60,000. During this period of preparing to build the project, Father Hadley became even more involved, pointedly referring to the project as "the *Cave of the New Being*" in his correspondence.[99] He understood the difficulty of working with a local contractor who has had no experience with such a complex structure and recommended that Kiesler look for a contractor in St. Louis, providing the names of several. Kiesler immediately contacted them and was clearly excited by their expressions of interest, especially when one suggested delivering the project from St. Louis by helicopters.[100]

The Project Spins out of Control

Throughout the commission Kiesler consistently asserted his own agenda, throwing caution to the wind, as if he knew that this was his last architectural project. As an artist, he perhaps wanted to fulfill his vision, of which the *Endless House* was his manifesto, and the project grew conceptually, physically, and financially into something much larger than what Owen originally had in mind. She was willing to encourage his project, to let him release his vision, but the skyrocketing cost of the project, now ten times the original, taxed everyone's patience to the limit. On November 23, 1964, Owen sent Kiesler an airmail letter from Zürich in which she asked him to stop work. As in all her correspondences to Kiesler, her tone is kindly, conciliatory, and respectful.

> Dear Frederick,
> I received lovely pictures of you with Lillian and the expressions of Nature's gold behind you. I was glad that I could have this much of New Harmony and of the author of the New Being's cave here in Zurich.
> The news of the combined cost of the cave and fish caused me great shock, as I am sure it did to you. I simply do not have that much to spend this year, and can only hope my Trustees allow the $60,000 for the cave alone. They are already perturbed over the recent bills, so dear Frederick, please don't do any more work. We must try to gain permission, to at least start the cave now and finish it by May. "'We have promises to keep,' as Robert Frost said so well before me."[101]

What the "promises" she had in mind are hard to know; they may have been her wish to open Paul Tillich Park on time or for Kiesler to remain within the given budget. But whatever her meaning, she hoped that the Blaffer Trust would authorize construction of the grotto, leaving the dolphin until later. Despite this written exhortation, Kiesler continued work on the next version for seven more weeks, oblivious of Owen's polite request to stop work.

Through the long lens of history, it is well that he disobeyed, because his new version, the sixth and final scheme of the grotto, is masterful.[102] He carefully responded

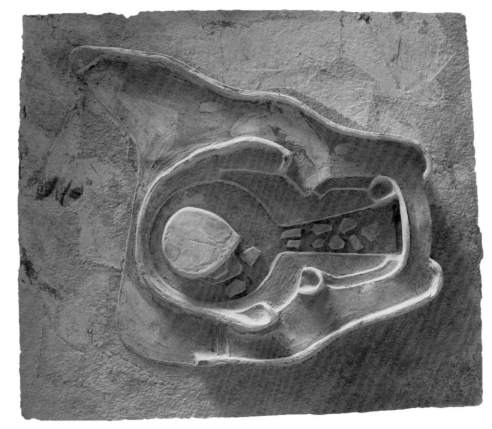

Figure 5.20. Cast plaster model of horizontal floor section for the final scheme of *Grotto for Meditation,* 1965. The design shows a masterful integration of the seating, circulation, and building envelope that expressed Kiesler's concept of Continuity. Model copyright 2018 Austrian Frederick and Lillian Kiesler Private Foundation, Vienna. Courtesy of the Collection of the Estate of Frederick Kiesler represented by Jason McCoy Gallery, New York. Photograph courtesy of Ben Nicholson, 2009.

to the design problems suggested by Father Hadley. The circulation within the grotto was changed to allow for a meditative sitting area composed of four niche seats and a lounging bench placed around the sculpture. This ensemble was separated from the walking path that now included a footbridge over the stream.[103] By January 7, 1965, Kiesler had completed drawings and a finely wrought Plastilina and plaster model for the enlarged version (Figure 5.20).

In the office document "Survey of Work Yet to Be Done at Studio," Kiesler was oblivious of the restraint put on him by his client and was proceeding to draw up the project in its entirety.[104]

GROTTO (NEW HARMONY, INDIANA)

1. Complete revised drawings (plans, sections, details, etc., include "niche" seats)
2. Incorporate mechanical and structural drawings
3. Finish new model. (lower part)
4. Redesign location of grotto in relation to fish
5. Review all questions such as . . .
   a) finishes (type, location, details, etc.)
   b) design of fish in concrete
6. Contact Mr. Benton for estimates

The following week, on January 13, 1965, Kiesler wrote Owen a long, harrowed letter outlining three areas of concern about the project. With this letter she discovered that he had not stopped work; quite to the contrary, the project was getting bigger by the month. He first laid out the reasons why the project had become so expensive, highlighting the different approaches of the prospective contractors, with the St. Louis firm proposing to deliver prefabricated sections by helicopter to the site. To his credit, Kiesler advocated a hand-craftsman-like procedure executed in New Harmony to save on the cost of union labor. The second concern involved the size of the building, for Father Hadley thought the grotto was too small for the expected traffic of thirty to forty visitors each weekend. Kiesler wrote:

> This is the fifth plan we have developed and which takes care of those who want to meditate and those who come as sightseers. There is a low bridge which goes over the interior waterfall so that the visitors can pass from the entrance to the exit without disturbing those who want to meditate on the lower level on one long couch and four built-in niches for individual relaxation. You realize, dear Jane, that this required a great deal of thought and work, but I felt that Dr. Hadley's deliberations were well taken.[105]

In the mind of Kiesler, Father Hadley's observations had demanded action. By preparing this new version of the scheme, Kiesler resolved a potential problem, although he had been directed by Owen to stop work on the project nearly two months earlier.

His third concern must have been the straw that broke the camel's back, as he veered into territory that he had no right to trespass upon. He continued, "If you are interested in building the Grotto you must postpone the work on the Church until the Grotto is finished." That is, she must choose between *Grotto for Meditation* or Johnson's much more expensive new St. Stephen's Church. This letter marked the beginning of the end of the project. Owen had remained loyal to his vision, even though she was warned at the beginning of the project that he was difficult to work with. Now she had been pushed too far.

Alternate Plans for Paul Tillich Park

With Kiesler ignoring Owen's demand that he stop work, the project's continuing sky-rocketing costs, and her anxious doubts that he would be able to finish, Owen realized the project could not be sustained. She sought an appropriate alternative to honor Tillich, and a week later, on January 25, 1965, she summoned Charles W. Kegley to dinner with her daughter Jane Dale Owen and son-in-law Per Arneberg. Kegley was a professor of philosophy at Wagner College and the editor of the Library of Living Theology.[106] At the dinner they discussed a solution to Kiesler's runaway vision of the project that had started out as a humble shelter for the *Holy Family* and had turned into something much larger. At dinner Owen appealed to Kegley in strict confidence, asking him to communicate with Tillich, explain the situation, and ask what would please Tillich.[107] She also asked Kegley for his suggestions for a solution. At the conclusion of this family conclave the warrant for the demise of the project that Kiesler had in his mind had all but been issued.

Although Kiesler's project was stopped due to cost overruns and a change of program, why did Kegley feel that the grotto did not acknowledge that Tillich "deserves a wise honor and perpetuation appropriate to his philosophy"?[108] The paramount issue had become how best to honor Tillich. Were Kiesler's phallic fish and erotic pink conch shell inappropriate metaphors for a memorial to Tillich, irrespective of the program changes and budget overruns that Owen had been stoically absorbing?

The Middle West has precedents for figurative landforms with sacred associations, such as the Great Serpent Mound in southwestern Ohio built in CE 1050, a 1,370-foot long earthen form in the shape of a snake. Were the symbols Kiesler chose seen to be inappropriate?[109] Marguerite Young, a friend of Kiesler's and a historian of New Harmony, had no misgivings about the project's symbolism and saw in it "the entire history of the Utopian search which is an aspect of the search for Eden, the lost innocence of childhood and the entrance into the womb which is the chambered nautilus."[110] An indication of the project's perceived misaligned symbolism was a popular reaction in New Harmony. Although Owen referred to the cave as a womb, others likened the dolphin to a phallus and referred to the whole composition as the procreative combination of the two. Father Hadley took on the thankless task of relaying these sentiments to Owen.

Kiesler may have sought to provoke Tillich with surreptitious irreverence, for he knew the dark power of humor. William R. Crout notes:

> Whatever might be written of Kiesler's motives, Tillich would have graciously accepted in his park a cave with the naturalistic Haines sculptures of the Holy Family. While it is known that Tillich was critical of art in the style of what he called "beautifying naturalism," it is also true that he found symbolic meaning in other styles representing the Nativity, and he himself kept a cherished crèche which he placed under his tree each Christmas. And while it is not known what Tillich may have been told about the Haines sculpture, it is important to know that "The Cave of the New Being" was Tillich's name and that he found symbolically meaningful the tradition that he who was called the Christ, the bringer of New Being, was born in a cave. Tillich makes this expressively clear in his dedicatory address in New Harmony on June 2, 1963.

Between late January and early February, Johnson visited Kiesler's studio in New York to see the "new model" and reported back to Owen that he greatly admired it. But Johnson simultaneously reinforced her doubts with his professional opinion of Kiesler's shortcomings: his advice is tinged with ambiguity, and it began to sound the project's death knell. On February 9, 1965, Owen wrote a heart-wrenching letter to Tillich's wife, Hannah, confiding the depth of her despair and seeking Hannah's confidential help to determine what would please Tillich.[111]

Crout notes that in this letter "the poignance of Jane Owen's tension, and the pathos in her self-consolation, are almost confessionally expressed in what she writes."[112] He goes on to say that she is clearly in a state of despair over what she, her family, and her advisers see as Kiesler's single-mindedness, and it is an agonizing decision for her to terminate the involvement of the important artist, as he is elsewhere considered to be. She could never have imagined that he would have run roughshod over her desire for him to build a simple shelter in the form of a cave for the Humble Lord, even though the Blaffer Trust had signed a legally binding contract with Kiesler for him to propose a larger and smaller version of a cave. And had the free-spirited Kiesler acknowledged that his role in Paul Tillich Park was not going to be the opportunity to release his unfettered vision, it would no doubt have prompted a second letter of resignation from him, but this time final.

One can also feel the tension between the two architects involved. Johnson perhaps felt some degree of responsibility, since he recommended Kiesler to Owen. Reverting to his role of critic and curator, Johnson reinforced Owen's doubt by comparing the opposite working methods of Kiesler and Lipchitz, with whom she was familiar.[113] Johnson remained a supporter of Kiesler's genius but questioned the grotto's viability, but he might have ensured that his ailing friend could get the grotto built by helping him with the practicalities he had trouble with from the start.[114] It should not be forgotten that Kiesler had obtained a quotation for engineering the grotto from Johnson's engineer Zetlin, who was working on St. Stephen's Church, suggesting that Johnson might have helped Kiesler with the engineering and construction.[115] But Johnson had his own structural problems to contend with, as the walls of the Roofless Church were already starting to show signs of efflorescence, which would lead to subsequent collapse.[116] The faulty detailing of the Roofless Church would do nothing to embolden Owen's faith in cutting-edge architecture.[117]

On February 15, 1965, Kegley wrote a letter to Jane Owen expounding on her request that he suggest a project to honor Paul Tillich.[118] He proposed a "Tillich center for the creative interchange of aesthetics or creative art and religion." Kegley did not think that a building for a group of artists to work together for a few weeks would cost too much, claiming "it would be a great challenge to an original architectural mind and would not call for the expenditure of an enormous amount of money, for the simple reason that the more creative it is the more simple it would be." This dream of the philosopher must have sounded eerily familiar after what she had just been through with Kiesler.

Tillich's Cave *and Kiesler's* Grotto *Are Abandoned*

By March 4, 1965, Owen had received the letter from Tillich responding to the appeals of both Kegley and Hannah Tillich for an alternative to Kiesler's design. In his undated letter, Tillich concurred with Hannah and offered the perfect solution for Owen's despairing question of what to do about his park. Tillich suggested that she forget about the "Cave of the New Being" and simply keep the idea of Paul Tillich Park and plant his favorite trees. His letter changed the dynamic of the project and released Owen from her commitment to build her cave and Kiesler's grotto, as well as sparing her the anxiety of humiliation.

> Dear Jane:
>
> Our mutual friend, Charles Kegley, has written me about your difficulties with Mr. Kiesler. I am not surprised, as you can imagine, but I am very sorry that indirectly, I make you so much trouble. I talked at length with Hannah and she made a suggestion with which I wholeheartedly agree. Forget about the whole idea of "the Cave of the New Being" and keep the idea of a Paul Tillich Park. Plant some beautiful trees, among them two cryptomerias in memory of my trip to Japan and two birch trees under which I read Schelling's philosophy of nature. And perhaps a chestnut tree and some lilac bushes and one Xmas fir tree. Unfortunately, there are no linden trees in this country, otherwise, I would add it to the others, because of memories and poems connected with linden trees. You must know that I am a half-pagan adorer of trees. If you want to name the park after me, make a stone with either a relief of me or some words you choose from one of my books or both. This would be for me a real fulfilment of your dream and you would get rid of the problem of having to deal with Mr. Kiesler.[119]

Although Kiesler soldiered on, the words of the letter were prophetic. Kiesler's *Grotto for Meditation* atrophied, and a new park was designed for Tillich planted with the trees of his youthful memories. Relieved that Kiesler was no longer working for her, Owen traveled to Chicago on April 7, 1965, to see Tillich and discuss the trees for Paul Tillich Park before she continued on to New York to visit Johnson and the Reverend Herbert Montague Waddams, Canon of Canterbury Cathedral.[120]

In April 1965 Johnson completed a set of drawings for estimates for St. Stephen's Church. The failing Kiesler suffered another heart attack in June. In a letter to Owen of August 3, 1965, Kiesler again tried to make sense of what had happened.[121] Similar to his letter of January 13, 1965, he outlined the history of his work on the project and his difficulty with the local contractor. He had taken Father Hadley's advice and consulted with the St. Louis engineers, who proposed a practical and affordable plan to build the complex structure. He described how, on his October 1964 trip to New Harmony, Hadley showed him Johnson's plans for St. Stephen's with the accompanying budget of $250,000 and plans to expand the Red Geranium restaurant.

It was clear to Kiesler that his project had been shelved so that the funds intended for his *Grotto for Meditation* could be expended on other projects. Despite the fact that Kiesler knew that the project had been budgeted originally at $12,000, he could not see why he should not continue with the project that now cost $120,000. The following day he wrote to Johnson asking him if he could call for a little chat: "I'm naturally wondering about many things, professionally as well as private."[122]

Upon receipt of Kiesler's letter, Owen and Johnson met in New York, and she quickly composed a letter to the Blaffer Trust's chairman Marshall in which she writes, "Philip thinks K. is entirely mad, and is even claiming to have been chosen to do the sculpture for one of his new buildings when nothing is further from the case."[123] She noted that Kiesler had never returned the bronze maquette of the cave to Tillich or even offered to do so.[124] She allowed Kiesler to keep the two thousand down payment on the *Cup of Prometheus* statue.[125] Her patience with Kiesler had further eroded when she wrote, "Philip also said that Kiesler had said privately to him [Johnson]: 'What does it matter to Jane Owen whether the cave costs 25 or 125 thousand?' 'Unquote!'" She remarked that at Johnson's suggestion, Marshall had to remind Kiesler of the original contract. The project was now over, but it would live on in both Owen's and Kiesler's oeuvre. In terminating the project, Owen would no longer have her cave built according to Kiesler's design, but, through the dedication of the ground in New Harmony for the *Cave of the New Being,* it may have been forgotten but can never be expunged.[126] For Kiesler, *Grotto for Meditation* would be exhibited at the Yale Art Gallery and published repeatedly thereafter.

Robert Zion Designs Paul Tillich Park

While Kiesler was still in correspondence with Owen and Johnson over his involvement with the park, Owen invited the landscape architect Robert L. Zion, of the New York landscape architects Zion & Breen, to New Harmony in early July 1965 to discuss a new design for the park.[127] Zion had been a collaborator with Johnson on the Museum of Modern Art Abby Aldridge Rockefeller Sculpture Garden, as well as the landscape of the Roofless Church, so it was a seamless transition to take on Tillich Park with a minimum of fuss. This is an example of the reinforcement of the New York / New Harmony axis of cultural exchange.

Owen wrote to Tillich: "Plans for a re-born park are on the drawing board of the offices of Robert Zion, and drawings should be ready for your approval by the end of this month. I should also have heard from either or both Lipchitz and James Rosati; both abroad, and both highly recommended for your portrait head or relief. / Mr. Zion and Philip Johnson envisage an imitation German forest with hundreds of conifers (in addition to the trees specifically wished) and small, hidden open spaces—like clearings—where a quotation and a bench can be discovered. But I should allow these two gifted and deeply concerned men to describe Paul Tillich Park in their own words . . . . / You should be hearing from the landscape architects."[128] Robert Zion was the perfect choice of a landscape architect who could design a garden as a German forest, as he was an expert on trees. At this time, he was completing his seminal book *Trees of Architecture and Landscape*.

Tillich enthusiastically approved the design and then sat for Rosati's portrait. The key aspects of his park were now in place. On October 22, 1965, Paul Tillich died. Two months later on December 27, Kiesler followed him to the grave, taking his *Grotto for Meditation* and irascible wit with him.

Johnson moved quickly, and by December his office had drawn up Zion's design and received a quote for 350 spruce trees.[129] The new design mutes the overt symbolism of Kiesler's berms and organic forms and is little more than an abstracted interpretation of what Kiesler had envisioned, but with the addition of Tillich's spruce forest.

In a further development, Hannah Tillich requested that the ashes of Paul Tillich be sent to St. Stephen's Church, New Harmony; on December 23, 1965, Marshall wrote to Cedar Lawn Cemetery in East Hampton, where they were stored.[130] A hastily created gravesite was established in the park, reputed to be the smallest piece of ground owned by the State of Indiana, measuring about six feet by six feet. The gravesite was made ready, and Father Hadley interred the ashes on Pentecost on May 29, 1966, with Dr. Rollo May delivering the homage to Paul Tillich.[131]

Zion's landscape plan had called for rectangular stones to be set among the winding paths, onto which a selection of Tillich's pithy sayings were to be carved. Fortunately, Owen had chosen passages during her meeting with Tillich on April 7, 1965, where their two respective hands had together jotted down thoughts and passages into her loose-leaf notebook, including a list of the trees he wanted. In his hand is "Birch Holunder" and hers "Chestnut extra effort Katalpa May Bugs- and Apple Tree" to which he adds, "-Red."[132] With the trees selected, Owen turns her attention to finding a letterer to carve his words.

She had visited Sir Basil Spence's rebuilding of Coventry Cathedral in England and seen the extensive sculpture and lettering of the German Jewish sculptor Ralph Beyer. Beyer had been interned in England during World War II, where he had met the great architectural critic and historian Nikolaus Pevsner, a friend of Sir Basil Spence. Sometime before June 1966, Owen commissioned Beyer to prepare lettering designs for the passages from Tillich's writings that were initially to be cut into four different-colored rectangular stones, including Charcoal Black, Cold Spring Red, Carnelian, and Lac du Bonnet.[133]

In March 1966 glacial boulders had been shipped to New Harmony that were unearthed by contractors excavating the future route of Interstate 70 in Greenfield, Indiana.[134] A change was then made to the design and the texts were not put on

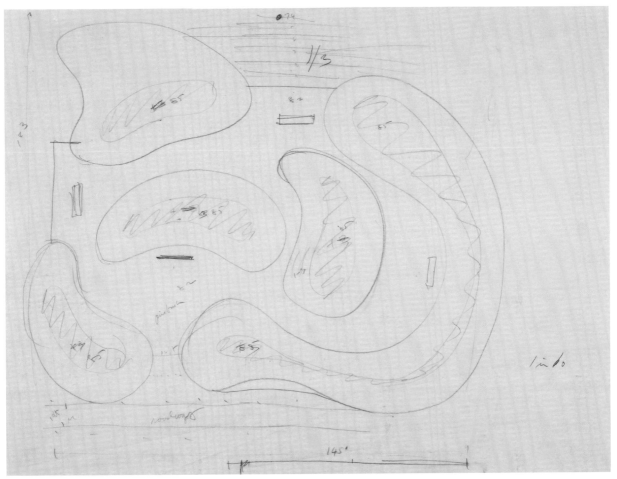

Figure 5.21. Landscape plan for Paul Tillich Memorial Park, prepared by Robert Zion for Philip Johnson Architect, 1965. The design of earthen berms fully acknowledges Kiesler's fish and grotto forms and retains Kiesler's intermittent perimeter wall. Courtesy of Philip Johnson architectural drawings, 1943–94, Avery Architectural and Fine Arts Library, Columbia University. Architectural design copyright the Estate of Philip Johnson; courtesy of the Glass House, a site of The National Trust for Historic Preservation.

the rectangular stones but cut into facets sliced into the free-form granite boulders, which were then arranged along the paths of the newly named Paul Tillich Memorial Park. In addition, the stone that had been carved for the 1963 opening was set at the entrance to the park with Tillich's words:[135]

ESTRANGED

AND REUNITED

THE NEW BEING

PAUL TILLICH

PENTECOST

JUNE 2 1963

Zion's design was, and still is, enchanting (Plate 18). In 1977, a decade after it was built, Grady Clay, editor of *Landscape Architecture* magazine, visited the park with his wife and wrote to Robert Zion: "It is a superb and beautifully simple conception, done with care and to perfection. My wife . . . and I went through very slowly, reading every inscription, and relishing the suspense built up as one goes through the dark quieted tunnels, and came upon the Tillich bust not so much in surprise, for it was obvious that there must be something at the end-of-the-tunnel. Having the bust silhouetted against the lake strengthened its presence and made it hard to leave. . . . The paths are well-trodden, neat and clean. Everything we saw is done with taste and restraint."[136] Clay describes the landscape as evoking dark atmospheric and curvaceous qualities within which are set texts and sculpture; Zion clearly had a feeling for the interior world of Kiesler's visions.

The Legacy of Grotto for Meditation

That Kiesler was marching to a different beat than the other members of the team may come across as if he were the malcontent, but he no doubt thought that they were the ones who were out of step with his inspired visions, long nurtured throughout his lifetime. What were they missing by not giving him free rein to his design sensibilities? While the grotto was being designed, Kiesler was hard at work on *Bucephalus* in the old garage of his summer rental house at Amagansett, Long Island, aided by Pitkowsky. Following a revived interest in Kiesler's oeuvre, in 2009 the *Bucephalus* sculpture was cast in aluminum under Pitkowsky's direction, and it is now possible to speculate what New Harmony lost in not building the grotto.

The interior of *Bucephalus,* named after the horse of Alexander the Great, is nothing short of magical. The ground of the cavernous belly is molded to accommodate a pair of people lying on a padded cowhide.[137] A solitary bulb is set into a dimple in the floor, throwing up light that rakes across the ceiling, sculpted with rune-like poems, a gilded horse head, iconic drawings, and a pair of wings in bas-relief. Reclining in the thick aluminum shell of *Bucephalus,* one feels an intense glow, akin to being in a womb, enveloped by Kiesler's all-encompassing artistry in a space devoid of politics and ego. In *Bucephalus* one sees what was missed in New Harmony: there is no doubt that Kiesler would have let his imagination run out, for he would have had the chance to sculpt his art and scratch his poetry on the inside of the grotto shell. Had he been trusted to make the immersive environment that he had written about, drawn, and modeled so many times throughout his lifetime in a project of this size, New Harmony would have had one more treasure, but the patron flinched at the eleventh hour.

In the years after Kiesler's death, *Grotto for Meditation* was substantiated in print and exhibition. Lillian Kiesler was faithful to her husband's architectural legacy

Figure 5.22. Kiesler carving the interior of *Bucephalus* in 1965, giving a glimpse of how *Grotto for Meditation* may have appeared had it been executed. Copyright 2018 Austrian Frederick and Lillian Kiesler Private Foundation, Vienna. Sculpture courtesy of the Collection of the Estate of Frederick Kiesler represented by Jason McCoy Gallery, New York. Photograph copyright Adelaide de Menil.

and made sure that *Grotto for Meditation* was published as well as exhibited at the Museum of American Crafts in New York and at Yale University.[138] Gone was all mention of the *Cave of the New Being*; the project used the revisionist title *Grotto for Meditation*, the name Kiesler had stuck to and Lillian Kiesler adamantly followed. It is the same name the project retains to this day. After forty years in a dusty cupboard, Owen's cast of the bronze model of *Grotto for Meditation* once more saw the light of day in two exhibitions and is now in the possession of the Blaffer Foundation.[139]

The project lives on in other less explicit ways. Had it been built in the manner and quality that Kiesler had in mind, it would have singled out New Harmony as the place in the United States where the complementary polarities of modernist design and thinking would be witnessed side by side, in much the same way as occurs with Mies van der Rohe's New National Gallery (1968) and Hans Scharoun's fluid Philharmonie (1963) in Berlin's Kulturforum. If Kiesler's project had been built diagonally across Main Street from Johnson's Roofless Church, the pair would demonstrate the formalism of Johnson's geometric Purism and Kiesler's earthy, intuitive expressionist form. The fission between the two adjacent sites would have trumped the struggle over the grotto's concept and name, irrespective of whether it had been named *Grotto for Meditation* or *Cave of the New Being*. The dual name that remains in the shadow of the project is indicative of the tension within modernism over the role that spirituality was to play in architecture. Even the oxymoronic concept of the secular–spiritual confirms the innateness of spirituality in humankind; absent is any inclination toward one specific religion or another.[140]

These conceptual struggles may have proven too big even for Jane Owen's indomitable spirit, despite her respect for cultural and spiritual difference. The correspondence associated with the project demonstrates that she remained loyal to Kiesler's vision long after most people would have given up in frustration. The design process for a cave, which began as a simple shelter to house a Nativity and grew into a project that in Kiesler's mind would be as important as the Shrine of the Book in Jerusalem, overwhelmed everyone involved.

Had the grotto been built, it would have been an immensely bold and lasting contribution to twentieth-century architecture. During the first and second decades of the twenty-first century, Kiesler's free forms became emblematic of what computer-aided design could make possible, both theoretically and in construction. From

Figure 5.23. *The New Harmony Grotto,* 2010, based on Frederick Kiesler's drawings of *Grotto for Meditation.* The sculpture is next to the Gerald Hines College of Architecture, University of Houston, designed by Philip Johnson. The final project of Jane Blaffer Owen, it was digitally fabricated by students under direction of professors Ben Nicholson, Andrew Vrana, and Joe Meppelink. Courtesy of University of Houston and students of Ben Nicholson, Andrew Vrana, and Joe Meppelink. Photograph courtesy of Ben Nicholson, 2011.

2007 on, Owen restored life into her relationship with Kiesler by contributing funds to research an interpretation of Kiesler's New Harmony project. She mulled over the idea of spending one million dollars to re-create it on its original site in New Harmony, while a team of students at the School of the Art Institute of Chicago studied and interpreted the documents and models. In 2010 the project moved to the University of Houston, with Professors Andrew Vrana and Joe Meppelink joining the team. On January 26, 2010, months before her death, she witnessed the raising of a stainless steel interpretation of Kiesler's grotto on the University of Houston campus, adjacent to Johnson's Gerald D. Hines College of Architecture and Design building, an interpretation of Claude Nicolas Ledoux's visionary design for a House of Education (1804).[141] The two structures, one gargantuan and the other diminutive, recall the David and Goliath epic played out in New Harmony. It was to be Owen's last sculpture project; she was finally able to facilitate the rebirth of her patronage and friendship with Kiesler, as well as demonstrate her uncanny ability to commission daring works of art and architecture, whatever they may be.

Kiesler and Johnson were reunited once again, this time in Houston. Owen named the structure *The New Harmony Grotto,* as she wanted to bring a part of the tranquility of New Harmony to Houston for students and visitors. The larger landscape within which the project sits is known as Jane's Garden, reflecting the name given to Carol's Garden in New Harmony, created by Jane Owen in memory of her daughter Carol Owen Coleman.

Johnson predicted at the outset of the commission when he wrote to Owen, "He is such a marvelous artist, that even if hitches develop later, you will at least have beautiful drawings and models for yourself."[142] In this case, the "hitch" was Kiesler's and Tillich's definition of the appropriate space for modern man, articulated by their respective disciplines, which were eerily similar. In this project they knew their times were near and that the building may well become their epitaph and define what they stood for, so the stakes were high. The *Cave of the New Being* and *Grotto for Meditation* were a pole apart regarding what they believed constituted a new symbolism in art. The two giants of twentieth-century art and letters could not agree on a common solution and, as Kurt Vonnegut, the Indiana Hoosier, remarked, "So it goes."[143]

Notes

Text and quotations by and related to Frederick Kiesler are cited from various archives below and reprinted by courtesy of the Austrian Frederick and Lillian Kiesler Private Foundation, copyright 2018.

1. To understand the complexity of Frederick Kiesler's project, it is necessary to understand its theological and spiritual power, and William R. Crout, STB, AM, significantly contributed to this matter. He was former student and editorial assistant to Paul Tillich at Harvard University and founder and curator of the Paul Tillich Lectures at the Memorial Church, Harvard University. Jane Blaffer Owen had recommended to the editors that Crout write a chapter for this book, which he titled "Jane Owen,

Paul Tillich, and New Harmony"; it remained unfinished at the time of his death on February 11, 2015. During the six years of this book's writing, Crout began an extensive correspondence with me for this chapter on Kiesler. We worked extensively in the Tillich Archives at both Andover-Harvard Theological Library and New Harmony and constructed a precise chronology of events. He went on to infuse the chapter with his insights about what took place between Jane Owen, Paul Tillich, Frederick Kiesler, and Philip Johnson. Key passages of his correspondence describing the meaning of the project are published here as notes. He had been present at the Tillichs' East Hampton cottage in August 1963 when the drawing of one of Kiesler's proposed designs arrived. At the time of his death, Crout had completed all his corrections and insights for this text, except for a final review of the notes. In essence, he brought to completion his perspective on Tillich to this chapter on Kiesler and agreed to be named as an author, although he humbly considered himself a reader.

2. Jane Blaffer Owen (JBO) writes to Frederick Kiesler (FJK), undated but after October 23, 1962: "I am so eager to see the beginning of your inspiration, for an Holy Family to find a shelter at Christmas, and for Paul Tillich to be honored," box 12, Robert Lee Blaffer Trust Archives, Robert Lee Blaffer Foundation, New Harmony, Indiana. Hereafter cited as Blaffer Trust Archives. Reprinted by courtesy of the Robert Lee Blaffer Foundation.

3. My thanks to William R. Crout for clarifying the difference between the legally conferred name "cave" as described in the contract signed between the Blaffer Trust and Kiesler (Whitfield Huff Marshall [WHM] to FJK, December 5, 1962, box 12, Blaffer Trust Archives) and the name "Grotto for Meditation" as used by Frederick Kiesler, Lillian Kiesler, the Kiesler Foundation, and architectural historians up until the present day. The fact that the abovementioned persons and institutions universally call Kiesler's unbuilt design *Grotto for Meditation* does not in any sense trump Jane Owen's legal right of naming, according to the contract. The validity and status of her name "cave" is legal, despite all the ambiguities—a name that, as the dedication of the project approached (beginning in late April 1963), she made unambiguously clear. The name "Cave of the New Being" first appears in print in Jane Owen's letter to Tillich of circa April 27, 1963, responding to Eva Shane's letter of April 24, 1963, and that Kiesler's name "grotto for meditation" (lowercase) first appears in print in his letter to Tillich of April 29, 1963. Kiesler persisted with the grotto name despite knowing of Tillich's addition to the name "cave." Kiesler's first use of the title *Grotto, New Harmony, Indiana* on a drawing is dated April 9, 1963, although he had used the term on earlier drawings that are undated. This drawing is #Kiesler AZ 12412, Albertina, Museum, Vienna.

4. "Frederick Kiesler's career spans the entire history of modern architecture. An original member in 1925 of the de Stijl group in Central Europe, he is the greatest non-building architect of our time, but his ideas are profound, his influence enormous. His conception of the 'Endless House,' which I hope will be built, is one of the few original conceptions of our day. . . . Frederick Kiesler's 'Endless House' has existed in his imagination since the early Twenties. Now the possibilities of shell concrete have projected his ideas into the realm of reality." Philip Johnson, quoted in Lloyd Goodrich, "New Talent in USA and Great Reputations," *Art in America* 48, no. 1 (1960): 70–75. Of the several versions of Johnson's remark and Kiesler's riposte that have been quoted in print, this version was reported in a letter by James Healey to the *New York Times* published on October 31, 1993 under the heading "PHILIP JOHNSON, Touché."

5. I sincerely thank William R. Crout for his very close reading of this text and for illuminating me on many aspects concerning Tillich and the Frederick Kiesler project that I had not considered.

6. A photograph dated 1958 shows Elizabeth Haines and Frank Haines in the New Harmony Community House at the opening of their exhibition. University of Southern Indiana, Special Collections, John Doane Collection, MSS 022–0958. It is not known exactly when Jane Owen commissioned

the Haineses to make the sculptures of the Holy Family. The three figures were draped in homespun, woven cloth and embroidered in Jerusalem by Christian Arab refugees. Mary's hair was worn in the style of a married Hebrew woman of the time. That the sculpture recalled Christian, Arab, and Jewish culture would align with Jane Owen's commitment to interfaith issues. "Illinois Shrine Near Highway Attracts Traveler's Attention," *Turtle Mountain Star* (Rolla, N.D.), December 24, 1964. The nativity scene was destroyed by fire in 1970 while in storage in the Rose Bank House, New Harmony. *Mount Vernon Democrat*, February 3, 1970, newspaper cutting in box 12, file "Jane B. Owen," Robert Lee Blaffer Trust Archives.

7. In a letter from Philip C. Johnson (PCJ) to Don Blair of July 12, 1960, he describes having made mockups for a "cave." In a letter from Jane Blaffer Owen (JBO) to her Houston lawyer Whitfield Huff "Pat" Marshall (WHM) of November 16, 1962, she writes: "Philip has talked in terms of $12,000 when he was doing the cave." Both letters are in box 12, Blaffer Trust Archives. Johnson donated five vellum drawings of the cave to the Philip Johnson architectural drawings, 1943–1994, Avery Architectural and Fine Arts Library, Columbia University (hereafter cited as Avery Library), but these drawings, listed in a document titled "Philip Johnson and John Burgee Architects: Work Donated," pg. 2, cannot be located at the Avery Library. Jane Owen had no recollection of Johnson producing a design for the cave and thinks that it might refer to the underground chapel he designed for the south side of the Roofless Church, which had three portals and was to be lined in gold leaf. Jane Blaffer Owen, interview with author, June 2009.

8. "I think the New Harmony Park a wonderful undertaking. I am most sure Dr. Tillich will be happy to hear of it." Niels C. Nielsen, professor of religious studies, Rice University, to Jane Owen, March 9, 1961, file "Tillich Park," Tillich Archive, Robert Lee Blaffer Foundation, New Harmony, Ind. Hereafter cited as Tillich Archive. Printed by courtesy of the Robert Lee Blaffer Foundation.

9. "We cannot break ground for Paul Tillich Park before spring, so there is no immediate hurry." JBO to Paul Tillich (PT), January 28, 1963, box 12, Blaffer Trust Archives. Printed by courtesy of the Robert Lee Blaffer Foundation.

10. JBO to FJK, after October 23, 1962, box 5, file "Corresp. Sept.–Dec. 1962," Lillian and Frederick Kiesler papers, circa 1910s—2003, bulk 1958–2000, Archives of American Art, Smithsonian Institution, Washington, D.C. Hereafter cited as Kiesler Papers, AAA.

11. Frederick J. Kiesler had connections to Houston; he delivered a pair of lectures at the Museum of Fine Arts and Rice University in April and May 1962. James J. Sweeney to Frederick J. Kiesler (FJK), April 13, 1962, and Bill N. Lacy to FJK, in which he writes about the idea of birth and rebirth, May 15, 1962, box 5, file "Corresp. Apr–May 1962," Kiesler Papers, AAA. Owen reports that she first met Kiesler at his studio in New York where Philip Johnson took her later that summer. On August 10, 1962, Kiesler sent Owen Goethe's "Conversations with Eckerman" as a gift. File, "Corresp. Jun–Aug 1962," box 5, Kiesler Papers, AAA. Kiesler relates that when Owen saw Johnson's plans, she said, "'Well, my dear friend, we all love you; but that, after all, is a piece of architecture. What we want is a 'cave.' And in her own words, which amused me very much, was that she said, 'Well, you as an architect of New York, you know very well there's only one cave man who can do that.' She referred, apparently, to my Endless House." *Kiesler Recording, New Harmony, Indiana, Oct 1964*, Lillian Kiesler interviews Frederick Kiesler, [Reverend] Dr. Hadley, Dr. Rongved, and Len Pitkowsky in New Harmony (1964), Austrian Frederick and Lillian Kiesler Private Foundation. Hereafter cited as Kiesler Foundation.

12. Dieter Bogner, *Frederick Kiesler: Inside the Endless House* (Vienna: Böhlau, 1997), 183.

13. JBO to FJK, August 29, 1962, p. 4, box 5, file "Corresp. Jun–Aug 1962," Kiesler Papers, AAA. Printed by courtesy of the Robert Lee Blaffer Foundation.

14. PCJ to JBO, September 1962, box 12, Blaffer Trust Archives. Printed courtesy of the Estate of Philip Johnson; courtesy of the Glass House, a site of The National Trust for Historic Preservation.

15. My thanks to Cammie McAtee for pointing out Johnson's and Kiesler's recent association with the Museum of Modern Art, as well as for revealing to me a cache of Kiesler's letters at the Archives of American Art.

16. Ada Louise Huxtable wrote a glowing review of the *Visionary Architecture* exhibition titled "The Architect as Prophet," for the *New York Times,* October 2, 1960: "With the help of life-size photographs, the spectator can enter Frederick Kiesler's world of 'endless space,' a kind of free-form Fun House, or gelatinous Cabinet of Dr. Calgari." In response to the article, Kiesler then arranged for George N. Cohen, the builder of Wright's Guggenheim Museum, to write a letter to the *Times* describing how practical a structure the *Endless House* was. Box 5, file "Corresp. Aug–Dec 1960," Kiesler Papers, AAA. The MoMA press release for the exhibition is at www.moma.org/docs/press_archives/… /MOMA_1960_0132_108.pdf.

17. At this time of the building of the Shrine of the Book in Jerusalem, Kiesler was in partnership with Armand Bartos.

18. In a letter from FJK to a friend Irma of November 16, 1962, he writes: "I was out of town . . . (in Indiana to look over the site where Mrs. Owen—remember the meta-madness woman in the script?— wants me to build a shrine)." Box 5, file "Corresp. Sep–Dec 1962," Kiesler Papers, AAA.

19. In July 2009 Jane Owen shared a draft of her *New Harmony, Indiana: Like a River, Not a Lake: A Memoir* (Bloomington: Indiana University Press, 2015), in which she described how the design of the weather vane referenced discoveries made by the Owenite geologists and botanists. She also commented how the catfish would have appealed to the earlier Harmonists, because of the long-standing association of fish with Christianity. She asks, "Was the wind that spun the fish telling us that, back to back, science and religion together could accomplish the unrealized hopes of Harmonists and Owenites?" (which were the two divergent communitarian societies of New Harmony's past) (21). Jacqueline Bonnemains, "Dossier 41: Catalogue/Planches in Charles-Alexandre Lesueur en Amérique du Nord (1816–1837)," "Catalogue des Documents du Museum d'Histoire Naturelle du Havre," *Annales du Muséum du Havre* 30, nos. 1–2 (1984).

20. David Dale Owen (1807–1860) was the third son of Robert Owen. He was the state geologist for Indiana (1837–39, 1859–60), Kentucky (1854–57), and Arkansas (1857).

21. JBO to FJK, n.d., early November 1962, box 5, file "Corresp. Sep–Dec 1962," Kiesler Papers, AAA. Printed by courtesy of the Robert Lee Blaffer Foundation.

22. Hotel receipts recently archived by the Kiesler Foundation show that Kiesler visited the Isle of Capri in 1961. Within a morning's drive of New Harmony are several caves, the most notable being Mammoth Cave, in Mammoth, Kentucky; Marengo Cave in Marengo, Indiana; and Cave-in-Rock, at Cave-in-Rock, Illinois. In Jasper, Indiana, is an elaborate Outsider Art grotto, constructed from quartz geodes with lifelike painted figures.

23. In the letter from FJK to JBO, January 13, 1965, Kiesler describes how he had prepared five schemes, although he had actually done six schemes for the large version. Box 5, file "Corresp. Jan–Mar 1965," Kiesler Papers, AAA.

24. Dorothy Wood (DMW) to WHM, October 5, 1962, box 12, Blaffer Trust Archives. Printed by courtesy of the Robert Lee Blaffer Foundation.

25. PCJ to WHM, November 2, 1962, box 12, Blaffer Trust Archives. Printed courtesy of the Estate of Philip Johnson; courtesy of the Glass House, a site of The National Trust for Historic Preservation.

26. PCJ to WHM, November 2, 1962; and WHM to FJK, November 6, 1962, box 5, file "Corresp. Sept.–Dec. 1962," Kiesler Papers, AAA. Printed by courtesy of the Robert Lee Blaffer Foundation.

27. In a letter from Jacques Lipchitz to Jane Owen of May 15, 1960, he writes, "J'irai voir Philip et lui expliquerai comment faire" (I will see Philip and explain to him how to do it). Tillich Archive. Printed by courtesy of the Estate of Jacques Lipchitz.

28. My thanks to Cammie McAtee, who passed on selections of Maria Bottero's interview with Johnson for her book *Kiesler Observed by New York Friends,* typescript, 3 pp. "Alfred Barr and I considered him a great sculptor. The world of emotions, which was then banned from architecture, was so well expressed in his sculpture—which was also very architectural. . . . That was before the Endless House" (1); "Kiesler used forbidden forms. . . . Kiesler broke with every tradition. . . . Kiesler is still to be discovered." "Bottero Interview," 1994, series IV, box 40, folder 5, Philip Johnson Papers, Getty Research Institute, Los Angeles. Printed courtesy of the Estate of Philip Johnson; courtesy of the Glass House, a site of The National Trust for Historic Preservation.

29. WHM to FJK, November 6, 1962, box 12, Blaffer Trust Archives.

30. "A sum of $12,000 has been appropriated sometime back for this edifice." DMW to WHM, October 5, 1962, box 12, Blaffer Trust Archives. Printed by courtesy of the Robert Lee Blaffer Foundation and Inflation Calculator, accessed June 22, 2019, http://www.in2013dollars.com/.

31. FJK to PCJ, November 7, 1962, box 12, Blaffer Trust Archives.

32. PCJ to WHM, November 8, 1962, box 12, Blaffer Trust Archives. Printed courtesy of the Estate of Philip Johnson; courtesy of the Glass House, a site of The National Trust for Historic Preservation.

33. JBO to WHM, November 16, 1962, box 12, Blaffer Trust Archives.

34. This letter of November 16, 1962, from Owen is the first appearance in the correspondence of the term *Grotto Project* in a letter that otherwise uses the term *cave* four times. Printed by courtesy of the Robert Lee Blaffer Foundation. The first textual record of Kiesler using the term *grotto* is in a letter to Owen of January 18, 1963, six weeks after he had signed the contract to design a shelter to house the Haines-designed Holy Family sculpture in the form of a cave. It is highly unlikely that Owen had renamed the cave "Grotto Project." It is more likely Kiesler had introduced the term *grotto* with her, and she was responding to that conversation. This is prime evidence of what Owen called an "evolution" in the project and its naming.

35. FJK to JBO, November 23, 1962, box 12, Blaffer Trust Archives.

36. JBO to WHM, November 16, 1962, box 12, Blaffer Trust Archives. Printed by courtesy of the Robert Lee Blaffer Foundation.

37. WHM to FJK, December 5, 1962, box 12, Blaffer Trust Archives The contract prepared for Kiesler's signature, copy with indicated signature "/s/ Frederick J. Kiesler," is clearly intended to be the legally binding contract for design of a "cave" ("for protection," Dorothy Wood at Jane Owen's behest to Whitfield H. Marshall, chair of the Blaffer Trust and her lawyer, letter dated 10/5/62, Blaffer Trust Archives): the copy is on formal letterhead of Marshall's Houston law firm (Fulbright, Crocker, Freeman, Bates & Jaworski) and is the only letter of Marshall's in the Blaffer Trust Archive in which "For The Blaffer Trust" is typed under his signature (i.e., "William H. Marshall / For The Blaffer Trust") and is the only one containing his signature, boldly signed. Printed by courtesy of the Robert Lee Blaffer Foundation.

38. FJK to JBO, December 7, 1962, box 5, file "Corresp. Sep–Dec 1962," Kiesler Papers, AAA.

39. Christmas card from JBO to FJK, box 5, file "Corresp. Sep–Dec 1962," Kiesler Papers, AAA. This is the second time that Jane Owen uses the hybrid term *grotto-cave*. Printed by courtesy of the Robert Lee Blaffer Foundation.

40. FJK to JBO, January 18, 1963, box 5, file "Corresp. 1963," Kiesler Papers, AAA. This is the first time that Kiesler writes about the project as a "grotto."

41. JBO to FJK, January 22, 1963, box 5, file "Corresp. 1963," Kiesler Papers, AAA. Printed by courtesy of the Robert Lee Blaffer Foundation.

42. Kiesler's decision to substitute a dolphin for Owen's choice of a fish, an important symbol of Christianity, is significant. The dolphin's symbolism for Kiesler is mentioned twice in the correspondence, but why would Kiesler feel so strongly about it? (See notes 60 and 67.) William Crout brought to my attention that "when Kiesler was working on the Shrine of the Book in Jerusalem, also in Jerusalem and the region, was Professor Sheldon Glueck, renowned biblical archaeologist, Reform rabbi, president of the Hebrew Union College, Cincinnati, who during those years (1955–1965) was researching and writing a major and utterly fascinating book titled *Deities and Dolphins: The Story of the Nabateans* (New York: Farrar, Straus and Giroux, 1965] about the prevalence of dolphins as religious symbols in the ancient pagan world, published the year the Shrine was completed (1965). It is quite conceivable that he and Kiesler met in Jerusalem and knew one another." William R. Crout, correspondence to author, November 24, 2013.

43. "If you look at the body of Kiesler's work, meditation is one of the big things. Provide a seat and create an environment to meditate within seclusion." Len Pitkowsky, interview with author, July 13, 2009. Printed by courtesy of Len Pitkowsky.

44. This is the first time the hyphenated name "Cave-Grotto of the New Being" appears from Owen, perhaps attempting a compromise on Kiesler's introduced nomenclature of January 18.

45. JBO to PT, January 28, 1963, box 12, Blaffer Trust Archives.

46. FJK to PT, April 29, 1963, box 5, file "Corresp. 1963," Kiesler Papers, AAA.

47. From September 1962 on Owen referred to the project in her correspondence in eight different ways. She called it a "cave" (9/17/62 to FJK), "Grotto Project" (11/16/62 to WHM), "grotto-cave" (12/??/62 to FJK), "Cave-Grotto of The New Being" (1/28/63 to PT), "Cave-Grotto" (2/8/63 to PT), "the Cave of the New Being" (5/14/63 to Kiesler), "cave of wonders" (12/25/63 to friends), "Grotto-Cave of the New Being" (9/3/64 to FJK), and even referred to the project by two different names in the same letter (9/3/63 to FJK). Printed by courtesy of the Robert Lee Blaffer Foundation.

48. William Crout comments, "My judgment is that Kiesler was reacting strongly to the Jerusalem experience. He was subordinate in recognition to the Shrine's wealthy donor David Samuel Gottesman and his partner Bartos, the donor's consequently very wealthy son-in-law; he was scorned by the Israeli architects, who didn't approve of his partnership in the commission or his ideas; he was overwhelmed by the 'drudgery' of the task; he was deeply disappointed that the São Paulo Biennal of 1960 did not build his *Endless House* as he hoped, which would bestow the international recognition desired; and, importantly, for all these reasons—and probably more—he did not want to be known as 'the cave man,' which is how Johnson introduced him to Jane Owen. I think from the beginning, and certainly with his first visit to New Harmony in October 1962, he began to change the concept and name and to undertake to persuade Jane Owen in his behalf. She tried to be open and accommodating for a time, then realized the conceptual conflict with her whole intent and Tillich's intent of concept and name." William R. Crout, correspondence to author, January 5, 2015.

49. JBO to PT, January 28, 1963, folder "Tillich Park," Tillich Archive.

50. Tillich's full text "For the of Dedication of the Ground of Paul Tillich Park and the Cave of the New Being, Pentecost, June 2, 1963" appears in the second section of this book, "Three Voices in New Harmony."

51. Unsigned and undated fact-checking correspondence to a Mr. Banta (journalist?), possibly from Father Hadley, January 28, 1963–May 17, 1963?, box 12, Blaffer Trust Archives. Printed by courtesy of the Robert Lee Blaffer Foundation.

52. William R. Crout passed away prior to publication, and a reasonable effort followed by the editors to confirm the source of this quotation (press release, Dr. Nevin E. Danner, May 27, 1963), indicated to be among his unprocessed papers (William R. Crout, Personal Papers, accession

no. 2150319) held by the Andover-Harvard Theological Library, Harvard Divinity School, Harvard University.

53. JBO to FJK, May 14, 1963, box 5, file "Corresp. 1963," Kiesler Papers, AAA. Printed by courtesy of the Robert Lee Blaffer Foundation.

54. "Kiesler Recording New Harmony, Indiana," October 1964, tape-recording, the Austrian Frederick and Lillian Kiesler Private Foundation, Vienna, copyright 2018. Transcribed by Ben Nicholson. Printed by courtesy of Ben Nicholson.

55. Owen had discussed a park in New Harmony for Tillich with Niels Nielsen before March 9, 1961. Nielson to JBO, 3/9/61, "Tillich Park," Tillich Archive, New Harmony. Owen then offered Tillich "a garden called Tillich Park" at a tea at her home in Houston when Tillich lectured at Rice University from April 4–6, 1961. Present also were Owen's husband, Kenneth, her daughter Annie, William Houston, president emeritus, and Professor Niels Nielsen of Rice. The formal name for the park is Paul Tillich Park.

56. PT to JBO, February 1, 1963, box 5, file "Corresp. 1963," Kiesler Papers, AAA. Printed by courtesy of Ted Farris as representative of the Estates of Paul Tillich and Hannah Tillich.

57. JBO to PT, February 8, 1963, box 5, file "Corresp. 1963," Kiesler Papers, AAA. Printed by courtesy of the Robert Lee Blaffer Foundation.

58. "The best of all projects that summarizes my life experiences is the Grotto of Meditation. The concept cannot be found in any history of architecture, it supersedes the Shrine with its seven years of drudgery—work with associates, supervisors, government officials and workmen, whose language I could never understand in Jerusalem. But it is done due to the thread of Ariadne that guided me." From the typescript "Continuity: The New Principle of Architecture," in *Frederick J. Kiesler: Endless Space,* edited by Dieter Bogner and Peter Noever (Stuttgart: Hatje Cantz, 2001), 53.

59. FJK to JBO, February 21, 1963, box 5, file "Corresp. 1963," Kiesler Papers, AAA.

60. JBO to PT, February 8, 1963, file "Tillich Park," Tillich Archive. "The New Being" is the title sermon in Tillich's collection of sermons by that name; see Tillich, *The New Being* (New York: Charles Scribner's Sons, 1955), 15–24.

61. FJK to PT, May 13, 1963, file "Tillich Park," Tillich Archive.

62. Up until his death, Len Pitkowsky (1930–2015) oversaw the casting of Kiesler's sculpture and took an active role in archiving Kiesler's papers and drawings.

63. "Johnson's remark eventually led to the plan to construct the dolphin mound as a rubble-filled concrete structure." Len Pitkowsky, conversation with author, July 13, 2009.

64. FJK to PT, April 29, 1963, box 5, file "Corresp. 1963," Kiesler Papers, AAA.

65. Of the two bronze models mentioned in this letter, one is in the collection of the Albertina Museum, Vienna, and has a patinated finish. The second model, with an unpatinated finish, is in the possession of the Robert Lee Blaffer Foundation, New Harmony. FJK to JBO, May 7, 1963, box 5, file "Corresp. 1963," Kiesler Papers, AAA.

66. The site was enlarged twice, first with the addition of fifteen feet on the east, and then again by sixty-nine feet with the purchase of the Alsop lot A3 on May 14, 1963. JBO to FJK, May 14, 1963, box 5, file "Corresp. 1963," Kiesler Papers, AAA.

67. Kiesler was ultimately to work with or get estimates from eight different contractors for the grotto:

1) George N. Cohen, Pres., Euclid Contracting Corp., 101 Park Ave NY, as builder of Guggenheim, supports Kiesler's design of Endless House as logical and had checked its structure with Severud. Box 5, file "Corresp. Aug–Dec 1960," Kiesler Papers, AAA.

2) Strobel and Rongved, consulting engineers, 70 W 40th St., NY [?] for services rendered:

$157.50: estimate for structural design services and overseeing construction with SIKA Chemical Co., NJ, for concrete supervision. Invoice of April 30, 1963, from Strobel and Rongved to FJK, box 5, file "Corresp. 1963," Kiesler Papers, AAA.

3) Jim Farmer, KIM Lighting and Manufacturing Co., 1467 N. Lidcombe Ave, El Monte, CA. Letter July 25, 1963, box 5, file "Corresp. 1963," Kiesler Papers, AAA.

4) Louis Falco, Chemco Engineering, Old Mill Road, Woodbridge, CT, August 15, 1963, advice on concrete. Box 5, file "Corresp. 1963," Kiesler Papers, AAA.

5) Lev Zetlin & Associates, consulting engineers, 145 E 32nd Street, NY, April 22, 1964, estimate for structural design services & overseeing construction. Zetlin worked with Philip Johnson on St. Stephen's Church. Box 5, file "Corresp. Jan–Jun 1964," Kiesler Papers, AAA.

6) Cletus Dressel, Bauer Bros, General Contractors, Evansville IN, October 22, 1964, request for estimate. Box 5, "Corresp. July–Dec 1964," Kiesler Papers, AAA.

7) Richard DeCew, DeCew and DeCew, Lighting and Fountain Equipment, November 4, 1964. Box 5, "Corresp. July–Dec 1964," Kiesler Papers, AAA.

8) "A firm from St Louis" letter from FJK to JBO, January 13, 1965, describing Fr. Hadley's help in securing a contractor for the project. Box 5, "Corresp. Jan–March 1965," Kiesler Papers, AAA.

68. A plat of New Harmony was included with this letter and shows this lot to be A3 (OFLK drawing # pin_6040_0). Kiesler's plan of the third scheme drawn before April 1963 shows the lot to be 125 feet long. The April 9, 1963, scheme shows the lot (A4) measuring 138 feet, which includes a 15-foot addition to the east. The plan of July 3, 1963, shows the lot to measure 207 feet plus the 69 feet of newly acquired Alsop property (A3) to the east.

69. JBO to FJK, May 14, 1963, box 5, file "Corresp. 1963," Kiesler Papers, AAA.

70. This was Tillich's first and only visit to New Harmony, which was made by private plane from Chicago, where Tillich had been appointed to the John Nuveen Chair of Theology at the University of Chicago Divinity School. The plane was provided by Meade Johnson of Johnson & Johnson Co. in Evansville. Tillich's full text may be found in "Estranged and Reunited: The New Being": Professor Tillich's Address in the Roofless Church, New Harmony, 1963, in the second section of this book.

71. "Shell-like Grotto Plans Revealed at New Harmony," unidentified press clipping, May 24, 1963, file "Tillich, Paul. Visit to New Harmony June 1963," Branigin Archive, Working Men's Institute, New Harmony, Ind. Printed by courtesy of the Working Men's Institute.

72. "Paulus had alone a very good philosophical hour with Mr. Kiessler!" Printed by courtesy of Ted Farris as representative of the Estates of Paul Tillich and Hannah Tillich. In the author's opinion this implies a face-to-face visit, but it may have been a phone call. Hannah Tillich to JBO, n.d., July 1963, file "Tillich Park," Tillich Archive.

73. My thanks to Taylor Lowe, an architect and doctoral student at the University of Chicago, who contributed this note on February 13, 2015: "Pragmatically speaking, the relationship between Kiesler and Tillich exists in *almost* its entirety for contemporary historians to analyze and digest. This is because the two *almost* never met. But for a single hour of discourse shared in Tillich's East Hampton home, their entire history together had been apart, mediated only through the emotionally and philosophically charged letters of others. This begs the question: what did they say during that mysterious hour?"

The answer will require historiography that is both speculative and spectral. In the tradition of Marshall Sahlins and Gananath Obeyesekere's epic debate over the rationale of Hawaiian natives for disemboweling, baking, and then gifting the bones of Captain Cook, or Michael Frayn's play *Copenhagen,* imagining the lost meeting between physicists Niels Bohr and Werner Heisenberg, and the onstage repeated "takes" performing possible outcomes of their debates over the atomic bomb, this chapter summons the spirit of that immaterial(ized) hour through the body of digital debate. In *Copenhagen,* the ghosts of the physicists re-created their own hypothetical debates; for New Harmony, the ghosts of Kiesler and Tillich have taken possession of Ben Nicholson and William R. Crout, respectively, in their own epistolary (now e-epistolary) debates over the very issues that would have likely filled that enigmatic hour fifty-two years prior. Though a transcript of that elusive hour eludes us today, the living logos of discourse persists in this contemporary debate between the two scholars of Tillich (Crout) and Kiesler (Nicholson) as their email exchanges play out questions over old discord in New Harmony. This (email) play's the thing wherein they catch the conscience of a missing hour. Printed by courtesy of Taylor Lowe.

74. Chemco to FJK, August 15, 1963, box 5, file "Corresp. 1963," Kiesler Papers, AAA.

75. JBO to FJK, before October 8, 1963, box 5, file "Corresp. 1963," Kiesler Papers, AAA.

76. JBO to Friends, December 25, 1963, file "Tillich Park," Tillich Archive. Printed by courtesy of the Robert Lee Blaffer Foundation.

77. WHM to FJK, February 19, 1964, box 12, Blaffer Trust Archives. Printed by courtesy of the Robert Lee Blaffer Foundation.

78. FJK to WHM, March 9, 1964, box 5, file "Corresp. Jan–Jun 1964," Kiesler Papers, AAA.

79. WHM to FJK, April 8, 1964, box 5, file "Corresp. Jan–Jun 1964," Kiesler Papers, AAA.

80. Blueprints of the four sets of drawings are in the Helen Duprey Bullock Book Room, to the east of the Tillich Archive in Kilbinger House, Robert Lee Blaffer Foundation, New Harmony, Ind.

81. In April 1964 the board members of the Robert Lee Blaffer Trust were Chairman Whitfield Marshall, Vice Chairman Camilla Corbin, Treasurer Ora Howton, Helen Duprey Bullock, and Johnson.

82. Teresa Reese (FJK's secretary) to Camilla Corbin (JBO's secretary), April 3, 1964, box 5, file "Corresp. Jan–Jun 1964," Kiesler Papers, AAA.

83. Lev Zetlin had worked on Johnson's projects, suggesting that Johnson was indeed coming to Kiesler's aid. LZ to FJK, April 22, 1964, box 5, file "Corresp. Jan–Jun 1964," Kiesler Papers, AAA.

84. JBO to FJK, April 5, 1964, box 5, file "Corresp. Jan–Jun 1964," Kiesler Papers, AAA. Printed by courtesy of the Robert Lee Blaffer Foundation.

85. O'Gorman had built his own house that included a natural grotto, as well as the tile-covered UNAM library. See Jacqueline Barnitz, *Twentieth-Century Art of Latin America* (Austin: University of Texas Press, 2001), 175–77.

86. FJK to Mathias Goeritz & Cha-Cha, June 10, 1964, "OFLKS Let 1208/0," Kiesler Foundation.

87. Receipt from Agency Tile Industries to FJK, October 20 1964, box 5, file "Corresp. July–Dec 1964," Kiesler Papers, AAA. In 2010 the tiles were still stored at the north end of the green barn used by Red Geranium Enterprises near the Barn Abbey in New Harmony. By the late 1960s they were being used to decorate bathrooms in the Mother Superior House and elsewhere in New Harmony. They are now lost.

88. FJK to JBO, June 5, 1964, box 5, file "Corresp. Jan–Jun 1964," Kiesler Papers, AAA. See also the section drawing that Kiesler made showing the *Cup of Prometheus* sculpture inside the grotto, "OFLKS #lpf_1078," Vienna.

89. "I gave him $2,000 on a statue that he may *keep.*" JBO to WHM, around August 30, 1965, box 12, Blaffer Trust Archives, New Harmony. Printed by courtesy of the Robert Lee Blaffer Foundation.

90. Owen held that Lipchitz and Kiesler were interested in Prometheus because he symbolized resistance to a rapacious society. Jane Blaffer Owen, conversation with author, summer 2009. Lipchitz designed *Prometheus Strangling the Vulture II,* 1944–45, for the Ministry of Education and Health Building, designed by Neimeyer, Costa, and Le Corbusier in Rio de Janeiro. He was indignant that the maquette he sent to Rio for approval was mounted on the building, indicating that he felt sculpture should be integral with architecture, not attached to it.

91. My thanks to William R. Crout for his brief explication of Tillich's Christological interpretation of Jesus as bringer of the New Being. In a correspondence of November 24, 2013, Crout wrote: "The name 'Jesus' for Tillich refers to the historical Jesus, the man 'Jesus of Nazareth,' about whom almost nothing is factually known but who, by his disciples, beginning with Simon Peter (Matthew 16:16), was called 'the Christ,' Messiah, *Christos* ('the anointed one'), meaning 'He who brings the new reality, the new eon.' Thus Tillich asserts the name should properly be 'Jesus who was called the Christ,' 'Jesus as the Christ,' 'Jesus the Christ,' hence, for Tillich, 'Jesus as bearer, as bringer, of the New Reality, the New Being.' This is the Jesus of the Gospels, who by the writers and their sources in the early confessing community, was believed to be the Messiah, the Christ. Tillich stresses everything written in the Gospels, by Paul, by all writers of the New Testament, is from 'within faith.'"

92. Pitkowsky remarks, "Prometheus celebrates the concept of rebirth, it is a kind of celebration of the beginning, up from the ashes. The original concept for Prometheus was not an object standing in space; it was creating an environment around it. This would have been the perfect project, as it would have provided an entire realm into which Prometheus could be seen." Pitkowsky, conversation with author, July 13, 2009.

93. Jim Benton, the contractor for the grotto, and Jim Brown, Owen's groundskeeper, were both present at this interview. A transcript was made, and excerpts, carefully edited by Kiesler's widow, Lillian Kiesler, who expunged all references to "cave," were published after Kiesler's death in "The Grotto for Meditation, Frederick Kiesler," *Craft Horizons* 26 (July–August 1966): 22–27; and Frederick Kiesler "Grotto for Meditation," *Zodiac* 19 (1966): 19–26. The tape-recording "Kiesler Recording New Harmony, Indiana, October, 1964" is in the archive of the Kiesler Foundation.

94. Pitkowsky pointed out that part of Kiesler's base philosophy is that we should strive to be reborn in our own eyes in our own lifetime. Pitkowsky, conversation with author, July 13, 2009. On the subject of rebirth, Kiesler inscribed the following poem in his 1964 sculpture *Bucephalus*. "Pegasus, never heard before now, to echo forever the tide of poetry, rises to the moon and falls back into the heart of the earth, it cools the fire at the core and gives rebirth to man through the breath of its word, word, word."

95. I am grateful to William R. Crout for his extensive commentary on the contrasting philosophical views of Kiesler and Tillich (quoted here in full): "Kiesler does not grasp (or chooses not to grasp) what Tillich means by New Being, equating it with being 'reborn,' which for Kiesler means 'to give birth to himself.' Tillich's existential realism could never accept this interpretation. While both Kiesler and Tillich write of 'rebirth,' Kiesler's depiction in the quotation is narrowly humanistic, positing a notion of rebirth as the image of the 'self-reborn,' Prometheus: self-rebirth can be accomplished by self-will. Thus for Kiesler humans through their own individual effort and methods can overcome estrangement from self, from others, from the transcendent. This for Tillich—what he calls 'self-salvation'—is existentially illusory. Tillich's whole theology is a critique of the possibility of self-salvation, efforts for which inevitably fail. Humans cannot of themselves heal themselves ('make whole again')—overcome estrangement by their own will, power, and striving, whether by methods legalistic, ascetic, mystical, sacramental, doctrinal, emotional (*Systematic Theology* v. 2, pp. 165–68.) Or, as stated in answering a student's question, for healing people go to friends, lovers, psychiatrists, or 'God,' whatever is meant by that word (for Tillich, symbolically, 'Being-Itself,' the 'ground of being,' the 'power of being')."

"While for Tillich salvation—being made whole—is through 'participation in,' 'acceptance of,' and 'transformation by' the New Being there is one sense in which Tillich's and Kiesler's thought could be said to converge, and that is in respect to Tillich's descriptive (philosophical) analysis of religion as the 'self-transcending dimension' of the human spirit, meaning that the religious question is the question of asking with infinite passion the meaning of one's existence and existence generally. Religion, then, is understood as giving symbols in which this question is answered. With this analysis Tillich would be open to and accepting of the symbol 'Prometheus' as having for Kiesler infinite meaning of newness, assuming that is indeed true for Kiesler: Prometheus, symbol and prototype of 'the New Man,' or 'the reborn man.' The question then becomes the existential validity of experiential participation in and transformation by the reality toward which that symbol points in answering for him the question of ultimate meaning. Thus Tillich would willingly acknowledge the meaning for Kiesler of 'Estranged and Reunited: Prometheus' if 'Prometheus' had that potency as symbol for him (as well as in reality that living power for others for whom he was such a symbol. But Tillich would immediately engage in an incisive critique of a Kieslerian 'Estranged and Reunited: I, Myself')." William R. Crout, original correspondence to author, November 24, 2013; slightly revised by Crout, December 2, 2014.

96. These three buildings were different from those mentioned at the beginning of the chapter. The third building mentioned here was to become the *Chapel of the Little Portion* (aka *Saint Francis Chapel*), designed by Stephen De Staebler and constructed in 1989. JBO to FJK, September 3, 1964, box 5, file "Corresp. July–Dec 1964," Kiesler Papers, AAA. Printed by courtesy of the Robert Lee Blaffer Foundation. William Crout notes that Owen's concern for "healing in our times" was a major concern of hers in all her commissions for New Harmony. It would represent her deep passion for healing and her dedicated intent.

97. "Kiesler Recording New Harmony, Indiana, October, 1964," tape-recording, The Austrian Frederick and Lillian Kiesler Private Foundation, Vienna, copyright 2018. Transcribed by Ben Nicholson. Printed by courtesy of Ben Nicholson.

98. My thanks to Len Pitkowsky for pointing this out.

99. Father Arthur C. Hadley to FJK, November 1, 1964, box 5, file "Corresp. July–Dec 1964," Kiesler Papers, AAA. Printed by courtesy of the Reverend Dr. Arthur C. Hadley.

100. "Both gentlemen [Dr. Hadley and the gardener] begged me not to use him [Jim Benton] but insisted that I call in a large firm from St. Louis which Dr. Hadley knew, to take over the job. I conferred with the representative of the firm the next day but he came with another firm head and insisted that the two firms should do the job prefabricated and deliver it by helicopters to the site in New Harmony." FJK to JBO, August 3, 1965, box 12, Blaffer Trust Archives.

101. JBO to FJK, November 23, 1964, box 5, file "Corresp. July–Dec 1964," Kiesler Papers, AAA. Printed by courtesy of the Robert Lee Blaffer Foundation.

102. Kiesler describes this scheme as the fifth that he had done, but actually it was the sixth scheme. FJK to JBO, January 13, 1965, box 5, file "Corresp. Jan–Mar 1965," Kiesler Papers, AAA.

103. Father Hadley notified Kiesler of three areas of concern: (1) How could the statues be preserved in the wet environment? (2) How would the tiles adhere to the surface in this climatic environment? (3) There were safety issues concerning the slippery unguarded rocks in the stream. Father Arthur Hadley, conversation with author, July 2009. Printed by courtesy of Ben Nicholson and the Reverend Dr. Arthur C. Hadley.

104. Document of circa January 13, 1965, box 5, file "Corresp. Jan–Mar 1965," Kiesler Papers, AAA.

105. FJK to JBO, January 13, 1965, box 5, file "Corresp. Jan–Mar 1965," Kiesler Papers, AAA.

106. Tillich was the subject of volume 1 of this new series, introduced and edited by Charles W. Kegley (CWK) and Robert W. Bretall (New York: Macmillan, 1952), 349 pp., as well as Tillich bibliography and indexes. My thanks to William R. Crout for pointing this out.

107. CWK to PT, January 25, 1965, Kegley's personal papers. Courtesy of Jacquelyn Kegley.

108. CWK to JBO, January 25, 1965, file "Tillich Park," Tillich Archive, New Harmony. Courtesy of Jacquelyn Kegley.

109. Tillich had remarked to Owen, "The symbolism of any valid work of art is inexhaustible." Draft of her memoir, July 2009, p. 104. Printed by courtesy of Ted Farris as representative of the Estates of Paul Tillich and Hannah Tillich. William R. Crout comments, "Tillich believed that in principle 'anything' could become a religious symbol, so naturalistic form as such would not preclude that. What would preclude it would be whether it had ceased to have symbolic meaning, would have 'died' (like the Virgin Mary in Protestantism), for symbols are born and die." William R. Crout, conversation with author, August 27, 2009.

110. Maria Bottero, *Frederick Kiesler: Arte Architettura Ambiente* (Milan: Electa, 1996), 234.

111. JBO to Hannah Tillich (HT), February 9, 1965, file "Tillich Park," Tillich Archive.

112. William R. Crout, correspondence to author, November 24, 2013.

113. "and he [Johnson] cited the entirely different working methods of Jacques Lipchitz. Where Kiesler begins with a delicate, highly-refined model, Lipchitz starts from a rough, crude one which *gains* in power and poetry as it *expands*." JBO to HT, February 9, 1965, Tillich Archive. Printed by courtesy of the Robert Lee Blaffer Foundation. Johnson was an architect who had associated with artists—Lipchitz on the Rockefeller Guest House, Rothko for the Four Seasons murals and the Rothko Chapel—yet these collaborations often ended badly (i.e., both Rothko commissions). On Johnson's working relationship with Lipchitz, see Robert A. M. Stern, *The Philip Johnson Tapes* (New York: Monacelli, 2008), 170.

114. Johnson wrote about Kiesler's *Endless House* to Reid Johnson on March 1, 1965: "In my opinion, Kiesler is one of the seminal artist-architects of our time. There is no one living who has so combined in his thinking the arts of sculpture and architecture. His *Endless House* is his greatest design to date, and for the sake of art and architecture, I can only hope that someday it will be built, and, naturally, during the lifetime of the artist. Its importance lies in the original conception of folding spaces around the viewer, rather than stationary walls and floors, which appear sterile in comparison. It is a work of art the 20th-century would be proud of." Box 5, file "Corresp. Aug–Dec 1960," Kiesler Papers, AAA. Printed courtesy of the Estate of Philip Johnson; courtesy of the Glass House, a site of The National Trust for Historic Preservation.

115. Zetlin was the structural engineer for Johnson's St. Stephen's Church project as well as many other works. New Harmony, "File 302," Avery Library.

116. Owen related that the looming costs of rebuilding the walls of the Roofless Church effectively canceled the St. Stephen's project. The walls of the Roofless Church were finally rebuilt ten years later. Jane Blaffer Owen, conversation with author, June 2009.

117. Kiesler was never in doubt as to the buildability of his projects and went to great ends to maintain his credibility. In a response to Ada Louise Huxtable's comments on Kiesler in her *New York Times* article of October 2, 1960, "The Architect as a Prophet," Kiesler solicited a letter from George N. Cohen, builder of Wright's Guggenheim Museum, attesting to the buildability of the *Endless House*: "I have thoroughly studied it (the Endless House) and made estimates as to cost of execution with engineer Severud (Seagram Building) and found the project to not only be structurally sound but easily applicable to our methods of concrete construction, yet sturdier to weight and pressure than the normal steel, brick or concrete house. The price too compares favorably with customary methods of building, since it restricts the amount of sub-contractors to one main profession, which is reinforced concrete. It might also interest you to know that I executed a construction test in my building yard, to mine and my engineer's full satisfaction." Box 5, file "Corresp. Aug–Dec 1960," Kiesler Papers, AAA.

118. CWK to JBO, February 15, 1965, file "Tillich Park," Tillich Archive, New Harmony. Printed by courtesy of Jacquelyn Kegley.

119. PT to JBO, circa March 1, 1965, file "Tillich Park," Tillich Archive, New Harmony, In. Printed by courtesy of Ted Farris as representative of the Estates of Paul Tillich and Hannah Tillich.

120. "The next day, I have an appointment in New York with Philip Johnson and Canon Herbert Waddams of Canterbury, who have followed the destiny of Paul Tillich Park since its inception and share my sense of urgency about its fulfillment. . . . I feel more like the battered, be-calmed ancient mariner who has just had a heavy albatross fall from his neck, and now glimpses the good water sprites below the surface of the water. They *are* taking hold of our vessel, and shall, I *know* guide us swiftly and surely into a safe harbor." JBO to PT, March 5, 1965, file "Tillich Park," Tillich Archive. Printed by courtesy of the Robert Lee Blaffer Foundation.

121. FJK to JBO, September 3, 1965, box 5, file "Corresp. July–Aug 1965," Kiesler Papers, AAA.

122. FJK to PCJ, August 4, 1965, box 5, file "Corresp. July–Aug 1965," Kiesler Papers, AAA.

123. JBO to WHM, circa August 3, 1965, box 12, Blaffer Trust Archives. Printed by courtesy of the Robert Lee Blaffer Foundation. It is not clear here whether Johnson meant that Kiesler was deranged or "off the wall." Father Hadley remarks that he was taken aback at Kiesler's explosive temper, as when one of Lillian Kiesler's conditions for the 1964 interview—that no tall person could stand in Kiesler's presence—was broken. Father Hadley, interview with author, July 2009. Printed by courtesy of Ben Nicholson and the Reverend Dr. Arthur Hadley. Pitkowsky has no such reservations, remarking that people would often misconstrue Kiesler's energy and enthusiasm and call him mad: "It often happens that when people can't understand something they attribute it to madness. In my experience, Kiesler was never mad. His imagination would take him to places that most other people never got to. They don't understand it. They don't get it. I remember Bartos's project for El Al Airlines, for which Kiesler designed a ticket office in Rockefeller Plaza. Bartos comes to me and says 'Is he crazy?' Even his own partner could not trust what Kiesler was doing, couldn't get it." Len Pitkowsky, interview with author, July 13, 2009. Printed by courtesy of Ben Nicholson. For further recollections on Kiesler's temperament, see Bottero, *Kiesler,* 243. A gentle form of banter about genius and madness permeated the commission. At the beginning of the project in November 1962, in a letter to a friend, Kiesler likened Owen to "the meta-madness woman," so the feelings were mutual (see note 18 above).

124. This is the second copy of the bronze casting. It was a gift to Tillich, but Kiesler never returned it to him. It is now in the Albertina Museum, Vienna.

125. FJK to JBO, June 5, 1964, box 5, file "Corresp. Jan–Jun 1964," Kiesler Papers, AAA.

126. In his resignation letter of March 9, 1964, Kiesler wrote to Owen that she was free "to select any other architect to build a cave of his own design, since mine is copyrighted." It is not known if a legal copyright owned by Kiesler exists for the project. FJK to WHM, March 9, 1964, box 5, file "Corresp. Jan–Jun 1964," Kiesler Papers, AAA.

127. RZ to JBO, July 12, 1965, file "Tillich Park," Tillich Archive.

128. JBO to PT, August 8, 1965, file "Tillich Park," Tillich Archive. Printed by courtesy of the Robert Lee Blaffer Foundation.

129. A contour plan of Paul Tillich Park was made in Johnson's office in December 1965. See "file 305," Avery Library.

130. WHM to James M. Strong, December 23, 1965, box 12, Blaffer Trust Archives.

131. Paul Tillich Park was opened on May 29, 1966, when Tillich's ashes were interred in the park according to an article in the *Evansville Courier & Press,* May 8, 1966.

132. Ten sides of JBO's undated 10" × 6.25" notebook, presumed to be from her April 7, 1965, meeting with Tillich. "Tillich Park," Tillich Archive. Printed by courtesy of the Robert Lee Blaffer Foundation and Ted Farris as representative of the Estates of Paul Tillich and Hannah Tillich.

133. Beyer sent the Blaffer Trust two bills on April 5, 1965, and June 13, 1965, along with three sketches of the blocks he was preparing. "Tillich Park," Tillich Archive.

134. Two bills were submitted to the Blaffer Trust on March 15 and April 5, 1966, by Ralph E. Esarey, geologist, for glacial boulders to be sent to the Paul Tillich Memorial Park. "Tillich Park," Tillich Archive.

135. Printed by courtesy of Ted Farris as representative of the Estates of Paul Tillich and Hannah Tillich.

136. Robert Zion to JBO, September 6, 1977. "Tillich Park," Tillich Archive. Printed by courtesy of the Robert Lee Blaffer Foundation.

137. Kiesler had wanted horsehide, but this could not be found, so cowhide is used today. Len Pitkowsky, conversation with author, July 13, 2009.

138. *Frederick Kiesler,* exhibition at Yale University School of Art and Architecture April 13–May 14, 1967, with catalog. Kiesler took part in the group exhibition *Object in the Open Air,* Museum of Contemporary Crafts, New York, March 25–May 15, 1966.

139. The model was included in the exhibition *Jane Blaffer Owen and the Legacy of New Harmony* at the Gerald D. Hines College of Architecture, University of Houston, April 2–27, 2007, and in the exhibition *Frederick Kiesler: Of the Womb* at the Jason McCoy Gallery, New York, March 11–May 1, 2010.

140. The Rothko Chapel in Houston, designed by Johnson with Howard Barnstone and Eugene Aubry, prompts many of the same issues of secular–spirituality: some see it as a chapel for which Rothko provided the paintings, and others see it as a chapel dedicated to Rothko's genius.

141. In 2010 Ben Nicholson led a design studio with Joe Meppelink and Andrew Vranas at Gerald D. Hines College of Architecture and Design at the University of Houston, with the assignment of studying and interpreting Kiesler's *Grotto for Meditation.* The project evolved into a construction. As of 2017, *The New Harmony Grotto* is still without its interior seating, fountain, and landscape.

142. PCJ to JBO, September 1962, box 5, Corresp. "Sept.–Dec. 1962," Kiesler Papers, AAA.

143. This sentence is taken from the last page of Kurt Vonnegut's book *Slaughterhouse Five* (1969). It is locally understood in New Harmony that Vonnegut's book *God Bless You, Mr. Rosewater* is a veiled description of New Harmony during its halcyon days of the 1950s and 1960s.

Figure 6.1. Philip Johnson located the exterior wall of the Roofless Church in orthogonal relationship with the original New Harmony town plan. He planned a crab apple tree group (beyond right) to flank the brick perimeter wall along North Street of the enclosure. Photograph courtesy of Christine Gorby, 2000.

6

The New Harmony Gardens
of Jane Blaffer Owen

CHRISTINE GORBY

JANE BLAFFER OWEN explored place-based historical consciousness as a way to interpret New Harmony's utopian legacy. Her understanding of the past shaped her aspirations for New Harmony's future. She did not abandon the past, but she did believe that contemporary design best addressed modern conditions. The projects she commissioned externalize tensions between the past, present, and future. Although Owen carried out many projects in New Harmony, including works of architecture and cultural and educational programs, the gardens she commissioned enabled her to explore the construction of affective environments. She trusted in the power of nature to evoke both historical consciousness and unconsciousness as well as relationships between nature, history, and time.[1]

Owen developed four important modern gardens in New Harmony as well as several connecting gardens between 1957 and 1997. Most were commissioned by the Robert Lee Blaffer Trust, which Owen chartered and endowed in 1958 to maintain the historic structures she bought, finance her cultural and educational programs in New Harmony, and commission new works of art, architecture, and landscape architecture.

The four major projects Owen developed were the Roofless Church (dedicated 1960), Paul Tillich Park (dedicated 1963), Carol's Garden (dedicated 1982), and the Cathedral Labyrinth and Sacred Garden (dedicated 1997).[2] Important architects, landscape architects, and artists were commissioned to design the gardens or to create special elements for them. Among them were architects Philip Johnson and Frederick J. Kiesler; landscape architects Thomas Kane, Robert Zion, and Kenneth A. Schuette Jr.; and artists Jacques Lipchitz, Ralph Beyer, Carroll Harris Simms, and Edward Gilbert. Owen also came into direct contact with theologians and writers whose ideas inspired her heterogeneous thinking. Foremost among them were the Reverend Dr. Paulus Johannes "Paul" Tillich, theologian and philosopher; the Reverend George MacLeod, founder of the Iona Community in Scotland; and the Reverend Herbert Waddams, Canon of Canterbury Cathedral in England.

Contemporary Design and Modern Conditions

Jane Owen believed modern design addressed conditions specific to her time. In embracing modernism, she did not reject the past. Working with artists, architects, and landscape architects, she explored the ways modern design expresses the "tensions" between past, present, and future, an idea inspired by Tillich, whose theological and philosophical insights deeply influenced her.[3]

Owen's work as a patron of art, architecture, and landscape architecture occurred during the post–Second World War period, coinciding with the onset of the Cold War (1945–89) and the resurgence of the ecumenical movement. By the late 1950s Owen had shifted her efforts away from the preservation of Harmonist buildings to begin to express a historical consciousness through modern interventions.[4] Her projects were concentrated in the northwest quadrant of New Harmony, where she accumulated significant real estate. The gardens, together with her architectural projects, artworks, and cultural and educational programs, materialized Owen's emerging understanding of New Harmony as a spiritual retreat for "ecumenical religious activity."[5] This spiritual narrative added a new layer to the history of New Harmony.

Interpretations of the Garden

The grove, grotto, mound, labyrinth, pavilion, and wall are elements in the design of gardens. Repeated use has transformed them into formal archetypes capable of affecting historical consciousness and unconsciousness.[6] Jane Owen's landscape architects used centrality, line, square, and circle to form geometries that, in each of the gardens, overlap. These primordial types have been embraced by different faiths since ancient times, leaving them open to a broad range of potential meanings. This breadth corresponded with Owen's desire not to ascribe meaning to the gardens so that visitors might interpret and find meaning on their own terms.

Owen created locations for prayer and meditation, activities central to the monastic way of life and the spiritual journey of the mystic. On one level her gardens are places for individuals to restore mind and soul. Following the monastic example of Christian communal living, her gardens also encouraged people to come together. Her overarching concern was to foster better understanding between people of different religious faiths. "My greatest hope for New Harmony from the beginning," she said, "was that it be a place of healing and reconciliation."[7]

To Owen, the mystical garden was useful as a precept because it was "based on experience, rather than on authority, because it is available to all, not just an elite group."[8] This differed from the ideologies of the Harmonists and the Owenites, which had shaped New Harmony's utopian past. Although Owen's gardens arose from ideological precepts, these precepts are not made explicit to the people who experience the gardens. Not only are they free and open at any time to anyone who wants to experience them, they were also consciously not interpreted by Owen. Encouraging diverse interpretations of place was something Owen accepted and welcomed. "I am ever so pleased," she stated, "when people of different faiths find features relating to their symbols."[9]

The Potential of Nature to Evoke Historical Consciousness and Unconsciousness

Jane Owen's consciousness in the postwar and Cold War period was shaped by her pacifism and desire to prevent conflict. Owen's affinity with modern art and design resonated with her desire to facilitate reconciliation.[10] Education was one instrument with which she pursued this aim:

> This is not to say that there won't be conflict, because there will always be conflict and differences of opinion, but we must use tools to resolve conflict so that there will not be violence. New Harmony was founded in peace and harmony with the hope that education would reconcile all opinion.[11]

Owen's commitment to resolving conflict led her away from an exclusive focus on historic preservation. In addition, she sought to renew New Harmony's utopian heritage by identifying it as a place of pilgrimage and retreat. Gardens, art, and architecture became the instruments with which Owen advanced her ideological agenda. They conveyed spatially her commitment to peace through prayer, meditation, and the healing powers of nature. This was in contrast to the religious beliefs of the Harmonists and the secular practices of the Owenites, who adhered to explicit doctrines. Owen wrote or spoke very little about the interpretation of her gardens. Instead she relied on the Christian symbolism of some of the artworks and poetry plaques that she installed in the gardens to convey messages implicitly.

Owen was skeptical of utopian claims and the ideology of scientific progress. To her, the problems of the world were spiritually based. She grappled with the pious religious beliefs of the Harmonists and the scientific, progressive social ideals of the Owenites. She made reference in her projects to earlier forms associated with New Harmony but resisted the literal replication of historic places. Some of her referents came from outside the history of New Harmony; this was a controversial tactic because New Harmony's own rich histories were obscured.

Owen believed in the potential of modern art, architecture, and gardens to enrich individual lives and foster reconciliation among different religious groups. She, with the designers she commissioned, explored the cultivation of nature to evoke historical *unconsciousness*, especially through prompting meditation and prayer within gardens. Unlike historical *consciousness* in which the past was interpreted to explore its relevance to the present and future, historical *unconsciousness* is a state of mind in which one exists outside "historical time."[12]

History, Time, and Nature

Jane Owen and her designers drew on the relationship between history, time, and nature. Within this relationship the varying, unfinished aspects of nature were recognized and expressed through the effects of weather, growth, and decay, which are found throughout the gardens. This gesture spoke as much to the "beauty" as it did to the "tragedy" of nature.[13] Time in relation to nature was also consciously accelerated: untamed nature was evoked in some gardens to bring the realities of nature and life to bear even more acutely on the awareness of visitors.

She drew inspiration from the theology of Tillich, especially his view of religion in relation to art and science and his call for people to become "reconciled with nature."[14] The dominance of science and technology, according to Tillich, had caused "the estrangement of people from nature, from their own natural forces and from nature around them."[15] The implications for reconciliation went beyond bringing people of different faiths together for spiritual dialogue: it extended to nature itself.

There was a commemorative function in all the gardens she developed. Each garden originated as a place of mourning or remembrance for someone with whom she had personal contact, and each spoke as much to human relationships as historical and cultural events. It could be said that Owen was leading the local community and outside visitors in a public display of personal memorializing, building community by different means than those earlier settlers used.

Artworks, particularly modern abstract figural sculptures, are integral to the commemorative experience of the gardens. The art she commissioned displays her emerging historical consciousness. Her mother, Sarah Campbell Blaffer, influenced her passion for collecting art. Owen said that art was an important part of her mother's personal "spiritual search."[16] The same was true of Owen. Early in the 1930s Sarah Blaffer collected American and European portraits.[17] In the 1960s she chartered and endowed a foundation to collect master works to travel for educational purposes.[18] Although each woman considered art an important teaching tool, Owen's mother believed that she possessed the authority to determine for a public what constituted art of quality. Owen's collecting served a different purpose. She grasped the potential of art to effect emotional change in those who beheld it and thereby change people's attitudes about social problems.

It was through the sculpture Owen placed in her gardens and landscapes that she expressed her Christian beliefs *explicitly.* This ran counter to her inclination not to interpret the gardens. In contrast, the plant textures and forms of the gardens *implicitly* expressed her evolving spiritual interest in Christian monasticism, mysticism, and Eastern religions, which she explored to enrich her understanding of her own Anglican Christianity.[19] The influence of Eastern religious thought on Owen was most evident in the domed canopy of the Roofless Church and the form of Carol's Garden. Owen saw herself as "a struggling would-be Christian"; her interest in other religions was a way to enrich her own Christian faith.[20] She had the sense that she was following a path Tillich, Carl Jung, and Thomas Merton had explored.[21] With these influences came greater emphasis on the experiential through the "individual journey," a path that Owen herself also walked. This was one in which "the individual journey provides more religious and authentic meaning" than statements of doctrine.[22]

The Roofless Church (Dedicated 1960)

The Roofless Church is a walled or "cloistered" courtyard garden containing a tall domed structure that shields the bronze sculpture *Descent of the Holy Spirit,* inscribed in French that translates as "Jacob Lipchitz, Jew, faithful to the faith of his ancestors, has made this Virgin for the good will of all mankind that the spirit might prevail." Philip Johnson, architect of the Roofless Church, ascribed the name "Roofless Church" to Jane Owen, calling it a "fascinating thought."[23] As the project neared completion, Owen wrote that the shrine was constructed "in memory of my very wonderful father, of German descent, and of the German and English idealists who settled New Harmony the first quarter of the last century."[24]

GARDEN ARCHETYPES: THE WALLED GARDEN, CEMETERY

As a spatial form and a historical and cultural concept, the walled garden was used throughout history, translated from the ancient period to the modern era. Johnson used the term *walled courtyard* to describe the Roofless Church. He said the project was derived from an ancient Greek *temenos,* defining it as "a sacred place, a walled place" where "you step into another world."[25]

The medieval monastic walled garden is a useful model for understanding the Roofless Church. This model closely adhered to the formal spatial expression and larger historical and cultural agenda of Owen. Crossing the threshold of a door into a monastic walled garden delivers a spatially powerful experience of the boundary condition.[26] In the medieval monastery the threshold was what stood between ordinary and monastic life, between profane and sacred space. Herrad of Landsberg metaphorically understood the walled monastery garden as an "earthly paradise."[27] Evolving from a space of utility to a place for prayer and meditation, the cloistered medieval garden was imbued with spiritual meaning. For those who lived a monastic life, "earthly paradise" was not understood only as "the church"; it could also be understood as "the Christian soul, a pure conscience, virginity, monastic life, the cloister, the four rivers of Paradise, and heavenly Jerusalem."[28]

These meanings had important consequences for the spatial makeup and imagery of cloistered gardens. Elements were often added to these places to symbolize the meanings associated with earthly paradise: water wells, symbols of virginity, and the four rivers of Paradise were common features. Symbolic artworks and memorials originated with, and were later also added to, the Roofless Church.

From surrounding streets, the Roofless Church appears like a rectangular masonry box sitting back on a corner lot. The spatial progression from the street into the interior garden was designed as a series of layered visual and spatial experiences with potentially diverse historical meanings. Suggestive of the brick-walled enclosure of New Harmony's Harmonist Cemetery, the scale of the Roofless Church's twelve-foot-high perimeter wall was enhanced by a narrow entry walkway from North Street. Although the east wall gate was originally intended as the arrival point, after the addition of the Lipchitz gate that could be closed except for ceremonial use, North Street became the preferred entrance.

Thirty dwarf crab apple trees, planted in a grid along North Street, replicate the line of the long brick wall of the Harmonist "church" exterior on a nearby site. They also recall a small orchard once planted just to the north of this site by the Harmonists.[29] A fragment of this orchard was reconstructed in the 1970s by Thomas Kane to the northwest, next to the Atheneum, which serves as the Visitor's Center for Historic New Harmony. It was in part of this orchard, just to the south of the reconstructed fragment, that the Harmonists buried their dead without headstones, surrounding walls, or markings of any kind. The cemetery was a sacred place to the Harmonists, central to their daily lives, where they prayed collectively three times a day. Only after their relocation to Economy, Pennsylvania, was a Harmonist member directed to return to New Harmony, demolish the Harmonists' brick church, and use the salvaged brick to build a wall around the cemetery.[30] There was an associative meaning, then, between the wall of the Harmonist Cemetery and that of the Roofless Church, one built by a particular religious group to close a chapter in its history, the other opened to people of all faiths.

Johnson said the moment of entry into the Roofless Church conveyed a "concentration of the spirit of religion. When you enter its great doors, peace should come over you."[31] Within the church's enclosure three visual experiences draw the attention of visitors away from the high walls. Directly to the north is a small grove of hackberry trees. A low yew hedge just to the east reinforces this linear view. To the west is the large domed canopy protecting Lipchitz's *Descent of the Holy Spirit,* and to the north is an opening with a shallow balcony projecting out, onto a view of the native Wabash River bottom grasses.[32]

The Roofless Church was conceived as an interdenominational spiritual place.

Figure 6.2. Originally conceived by Philip Johnson as a secondary entrance, visitors soon began using this modest south wooden door of the Roofless Church as the primary arrival point. Photograph courtesy of Christine Gorby, 2000.

Figure 6.5. On first entry to this walled courtyard of the Roofless Church from the North Street entrance, a group of native Indiana hackberry trees are visible on axis, one of a series of directional lines and framed views in this garden. Photograph courtesy of Christine Gorby, 2000.

Figure 6.3, top. This long line of gridded crab apple trees, originally planned by Philip Johnson for the Roofless Church, brings historical recollections to mind, including Harmonist era orchards that once stood on the site and a nearby Harmonist cemetery wall. Photograph courtesy of Christine Gorby, 2000.

Figure 6.4, bottom. A brick cemetery wall is the only tangible reminder of the Harmonists' final resting place, where they buried their dead without markers. The brick wall of the Roofless Church is a reference to this hallowed enclosure. Photograph courtesy of Christine Gorby, 2000.

Figure 6.6. From the west entry door of the Roofless Church, a domed canopy comes into diagonal view. It protects the bronze sculpture by Jacques Lipchitz. Photograph courtesy of Christine Gorby, 2000.

Figure 6.7. Adjacent to the hackberry tree group Philip Johnson planned a vista, creating an interplay between open and enclosed space. This balcony view looks toward an area of native Wabash River bottom grasses beyond. Photograph courtesy of Christine Gorby, 2000.

Many Western, Christian, Asian, and other religious emblems were placed in the forecourt of the garden and added to over time by Owen, making it a continually evolving symbolic interplay of elements.

HISTORICAL CONSCIOUSNESS AND UNCONSCIOUSNESS

In recounting her conception of the Roofless Church, Owen said it was "my life-long conviction that only one roof was wide enough to cover all worshippers: the sky. Hence, the walls without a roof, which I had asked Philip Johnson to build."[33] Late in life she reflected again on this thought: "The largest common denominator, beside the earth that bears us, is the sky over all of us"; the sky was a metaphor for Owen and, she hoped for others, to reconsider the "inter-relatedness of all humanity."[34] Helen Duprey Bullock, an early trustee of the Blaffer Trust, said the name Roofless Church reflected the purpose of this place to serve as "an invitation to people of all faiths to enter."[35]

HISTORY, TIME, AND NATURE

Along the east–west axis beyond the hedge wall is a smaller forecourt containing more intimately scaled spaces marked by sculptures and memorials and punctuated by golden rain trees. Personal meditation and reflection can occur at points along the wall. Vegetation was left to grow wild, contrasting with the trimmed lawn of the adjacent space.

237

Figure 6.8. Philip Johnson designed this smaller forecourt as a segment of the Roofless Church. A south view of the subgarden illustrates how Jane Blaffer Owen later added artworks and memorials and encouraged nature to grow wild, thus imparting new possible experiences and meanings of this garden over time. Photograph courtesy of Christine Gorby, 2000.

Architect Evans Woollen was asked by Owen circa 1986 to alter the Roofless Church.[36] He took up most of the limestone paving in the courtyard and replaced it with grass; the paved enclosure became so hot in summer that it was unusable. The lawn added even more to the garden-like effect of the enclosure.

Paul Tillich Park (Dedicated 1963)

Tillich Park is a garden commemorating the Evangelical Lutheran theologian and philosopher; Paul Tillich's ashes are interred there. Five carved granite stones with quotations by Tillich were placed in the park amid a grove of conifer trees planted on earthen mounds.

CHRISTINE GORBY

Figure 6.9. From this Main Street view, Tillich Park, designed by landscape architects Zion & Breen Associates, appears as a dense, small conifer forest. Jane Blaffer Owen commissioned this grove as a memorial to theologian Paul Tillich. Photograph courtesy of Christine Gorby, 2000.

Figure 6.10. Ralph Beyer, a British letter-cutter, carved several epitaph stones for Tillich Park that feature quotations from the theologian's writings. Photograph courtesy of Christine Gorby, 2000.

GARDEN ARCHETYPES:
GROVE, MOUND, GROTTO, LABYRINTH, AND PAVILION

The oldest sacred places in Germany are naturally occurring evergreen forests, likely sites of pre-Christian tree worship.[37] Although the Harmonists came from Germany, they did not worship trees or other natural elements. Harmonists were well-known plantsmen and seedsmen and cultivators of pears and apples.[38] One way they connected with plants was through their domestic viticulture practices. They trained grape vines for winemaking on trellises attached to wood and brick buildings, which evolved into arrangements that were aesthetic and visually appealing.[39] In some cases grape trellises formed an almost continuous line of shaded, landscaped walls down the street. Beauty, utility, and spirituality became inseparable convictions for the Harmonists.

Tillich Park is on a tract known by New Harmony residents in 1962 as "the park."[40] Although Owen owned the property, she encouraged townspeople at that time to use it for picnicking and relaxation.[41]

The initial conception of the park was quite simple. A crèche, displayed during Christmas 1961 in a temporary "stable," would be its defining element. In 1962 Owen commissioned Frederick J. Kiesler to design a permanent cave or grotto in which the crèche figures would be housed; however, by 1965 the project was canceled.[42] The Blaffer Trust planned to build it on a site adjacent to and just to the east of present-day Tillich Park.

When Tillich learned that difficulties had arisen with Kiesler over *The Cave of the New Being,* as the project was called, he outlined his ideas of what the park might become in a letter to Owen in March 1965:

> Plant some beautiful trees, among them two cryptomarias in memory of my trip to Japan and two birch trees under which I read Schelling's philosophy of nature. And perhaps a chestnut tree and some lilac bushes and one Xmas fir tree. Unfortunately, there are no linden trees in this country, otherwise, I would add it to the others, because of memories and poems connected with linden trees.[43]

In the same letter, Tillich confessed he was a "half-pagan adorer of trees."[44] He continued with the suggestion to "make a stone with either a relief of me or some words you choose from one of my books or both."[45] Other scholars have noted that Tillich's romantic ideas of nature were informed by Schelling.[46]

The essence of what Tillich requested was respected. Bullock described it in 1966: "The new park will be in the naturalistic setting Tillich so admired, and will include a few quotations from his writings, and, at his request, some linden trees."[47] Tillich Park is hidden and must be discovered, as is also true of Carol's Garden. The design was inspired by two garden archetypes: the grove and the mound. Johnson served as "architectural consultant," and New York City landscape architects Robert Zion and Harold Breen were "site planners" for the project.[48]

Like the Roofless Church, Tillich Park lies between the realms of landscape architecture and architecture. In August 1965 Johnson defined the project as a "mound building," a reference to the four curving walls of packed earth that form one spatial element of the park.[49] A grove of trees was planted on the earthen mounds. At the low point between the mounds and trees, a flattened, continuously winding, tunnel-like mulched pathway was formed. Of the four earthen mounds, the two on the perimeter are longer, broader, and taller, with a height of about eight feet. The height of the mounds and trees contribute to the sense of enclosure when in the garden.

In the plan the two outer mounds resemble two curving arms positioned symmetrically in relation to each other, but each has a slightly different shape, taking inspiration from Kiesler's design. At an opening to the north where the two outer mounds almost converge, a bronze bust of Tillich by sculptor James Rosati was installed on May 14, 1967.[50] Beyond the bust is a view of a large human-made pond. Owen originally hoped Lipchitz would create this piece, and he welcomed the project, but, because of scheduling difficulties, the commission went to Rosati instead.[51]

Nested inside the two larger, outer earthen mounds are two smaller mounds also in the shape of curving arms. The height of the interior mounds is slightly lower than that of an average person.

Three hundred Norway spruce trees, six feet high, were planted five to ten feet apart on the rising slopes of each mound.[52] Hemlock trees were later intermixed

Figure 6.11. Zion & Breen Associates called for three hundred spruce trees to create Tillich Park, shown here newly planted on shaped mounds in 1966. Coniferous trees held personal memories and special meanings for the theologian. Photograph by James K. Mellow. Courtesy of the photographer and the Robert Lee Blaffer Foundation.

with spruces on the two smaller, inner mounds. By escalating the planting of the trees upward along the earthen banks, the foliage at the lower level of a person's view appeared denser, enhancing the illusion of being hidden deep within nature. By "lifting" the trees vertically as they crept up the mounds, views are directed outward to the thick foliage and upward to the sky between the openings in the forest canopy. The garden directs one outward toward nature and water, downward to the earth, and upward to the sky, symbolizing life, death, and eternity.

HISTORICAL CONSCIOUSNESS AND UNCONSCIOUSNESS

The forested grove, separated from civilization, was made to feel like part of the unconscious, and therefore beyond reasoning.[53] The spiritual can be apprehended in the landscape of Tillich Park through the elements of trees, rocks, and carpets of pine needles leading down to water.

HISTORY, TIME, AND NATURE

Five large glacial boulders were placed at low points beside the mounds along the winding path to the pond. Each boulder was chosen based on size, shape, and geologic origin, a quiet affirmation of the number of important geologists who had lived in New Harmony. Upon the boulders, Ralph Beyer inscribed Tillich's cautionary and uplifting words in 1966. Notable was the use of stone instead of wood. Beyer, a German-born letterer living in England, traveled to New Harmony and stayed there from May to June 1966 to hand-cut and sandblast the stones in situ.[54] When selecting the passages to use for the inscriptions, Owen read "Nature Mourns for a Lost God."[55] This was Tillich's best-known published sermon on the human–nature–religion relationship.[56]

Johnson and Zion & Breen employed a key spatial component of Kiesler's *Cave of the New Being* in the design of Tillich Park: the pair of curving, arm-like earth mounds that protect the center. Kiesler had proposed constructing a negative space for his cave/grotto by excavating below the ground plane. The crèche was to be placed on a pedestal in the hollow of the grotto. Above, Kiesler planned to build a curving earth ridge in the shape of a dolphin to shelter the crèche. Johnson and Zion & Breen used the earth mounds to shape positive space. The tunnel-like path between the mounds is reminiscent of a labyrinth.

Johnson's use of the earth mound may explain his silence about his work on Tillich Park and why the design of the project is attributed solely to Zion & Breen. Johnson spoke little about his New Harmony projects and his involvement with the Blaffer Trust. Johnson may not have wanted to engage in conflict with Kiesler's widow over translating a key element from Kiesler's design after his death in December

1965. Although Johnson frequently called attention to his appropriation of historical architectural elements, he was sensitive to claims that he reworked design ideas first advanced by his peers.

In addition to the connections that could be made between Tillich Park and the Harmonist Labyrinth are the connections between Tillich Park and the prehistoric mounds constructed in and around New Harmony. Native American mounds can be found throughout southern Indiana. Caves are also regionally prominent. Kiesler's mound-like formation in the shape of a dolphin was reminiscent of the Ohio mound builders who shaped landforms into the figures of animals. Johnson and Zion & Breen made no such referential associations in their mounds.[57]

The park reflected Tillich's desire that it be simple and direct. The inscription on the epitaph boulder is from Psalm 1:3 of the Bible and is the most revealing statement linking the design and the setting of this garden to Tillich.[58]

PAUL JOHANNES

TILLICH

1886–1965

AND HE SHALL BE LIKE A TREE

PLANTED BY THE RIVERS OF WATER

THAT BRINGETH FORTH HIS FRUIT

FOR HIS SEASON. HIS LEAF

ALSO SHALL NOT WITHER.

AND WHATSOEVER HE DOETH

SHALL PROSPER.

Owen explained her reason for commemorating Tillich with a garden: "It appeared appropriate that a town, founded by refugees from German militarism, should honor a living person who had come to this country, also an opponent of German aggression, and bearing great gifts for us."[59] Tillich's abhorrence of war and conflict were part of the personal message Owen hoped to impart in Tillich Park. "Civil and world wars—all world wars in fact—begin within our divided human hearts. He [Tillich] had witnessed the worst that people and nations can do to one another; yet, in spite of it all, hope remained."[60] In the talk he gave at the dedication of Tillich Park in 1963, titled "Estranged and Reunited: The New Being," Tillich spoke of this place as a "renewed" place, "not conserved, not removed, but transformed into a new reality."[61]

The experience of Tillich Park today is much changed, a reminder of the fragility and temporality of gardens. When first planted, the Norwegian spruce trees in the lower garden and the eastern hemlocks in the upper area were solid to the ground, creating a dense, green mantle of foliage. With time, the trees have fully matured. The underside of the canopy is well above the height of a person, creating a clear view of exposed tree trunks through the garden. Erosion of the earth banks over time has reduced their height. The element of discovery, part of the mysterious, experiential quality of the grove, has been lost to these changes, which weaken the personal reaction, the spiritual encounters, that occur in the garden.

Carol's Garden and the **Fountain of Life** *(1982)*

The English landscape architect Edward Gilbert recommended during the 1960s that Jane Owen plant Bradford pear trees (Pyrus calleryana "Bradford") on the parcel of land on North Street that became Carol's Garden.[62] Owen reworked the grove of Bradford pear trees to create a hidden forested garden in memory of her daughter, Carol Owen Coleman, after her death in 1979. Jane Owen laid out the paths for Carol's Garden with one helper, Pee Wee York. "I was moved," she wrote, "to create a garden and a fountain which would echo the vitality of her spirit."[63] Spatial and symbolic relationships were created between this garden and the Roofless Church across North Street, Owen's own house next door, and the Harmonist Cemetery nearby.

GARDEN ARCHETYPES:
WALLED GARDEN, GROVE, CEMETERY, LABYRINTH

The plan of Carol's Garden, a circle with radiating paths, evokes archetypal patterns that symbolize the "ritual constructions of a 'Centre,'" including the Celtic cross, the mystic mill, and the mandala.[64] The center held particular meaning for Owen, especially when used symbolically in a cross. In an article exploring the prehistoric origins and uses of crosses, Owen wrote of Celtic Christians who, in their crosses, bound "this intersection with a circle." In addition to the Celtic cross, she included the "circular mandalas, often within a square," "where the converging lines of existence can meet and give peace.[65] Owen said she was "thinking of a mandala" when she conceived Carol's Garden.[66] The twentieth-century historian of religion and symbols Mircea Eliade defined the mandala as "a circle," but in practice its translations vary.[67] Tibetans, for example, emphasize either the physical perimeter of a circle or its center.[68] Owen conceived of the mandala as a physical construction in which the perimeter and center of a circle are given equal weight. Eliade associated ritual use of the mandala with a search for "integral reality—sacredness" to reach the "Centre of the World" or "Heaven."[69]

An eight-foot wooden fence was built to surround four sides of the garden, which is 135 by 114 feet in size, about one-third of an acre.[70] The fence along North Street, where the entry to the garden is located, is set back a few feet from the sidewalk. Lawrence Halprin, a San Francisco landscape architect who was visiting New Harmony at the time this garden was being planned, suggested that Owen recess the fence just enough to allow for a narrow planting bed. She heeded his advice, later planting lilies of the valley along the entire edge of this boundary.[71] Woollen, architect of the New Harmony Inn, also at this meeting, recalled that Halprin additionally made a sketch of the fence surrounding the garden. A slightly lower, more screen-like fence was constructed on the rear (south) side, open to daylight and the lawn of Rawlings House, adjacent to the southeast corner of the garden, where Owen lived.

Kane, who worked for both Owen and Historic New Harmony, designed many similar screen walls, trellises, and fences throughout the northwest quadrant of the town. Kane's permeable fences frame vistas and make visual connections and symbolic associations between places. Rather than delimit space, Kane's fences often make the spatial boundaries between places more ambiguous. The result is the feeling of being in a continuous, almost limitless, garden. The fences are all made of wood, which implies impermanence and the connection of this place with nature and transience. Ralph Schwarz, the first president of Historic New Harmony, described Owen's affinity for wood as a form of "spirituality."[72]

Only one entry leads into Carol's Garden, and the gate is kept closed but not locked, enhancing the feeling of entering a place of mysterious significance. A bronze plaque with an excerpt from the mystic poet Robert Lax was mounted on the fence just to the left of the entry gate and sets the tone of the garden (Plate 17).[73] Verse was a device used by Owen to cross the boundary between life and death.

> And in the beginning was love. Love made a sphere:
> all things grew within it; the sphere then encompassed
> beginnings and endings, beginning and end. Love
> had a compass whose whirling dance traced out a
> sphere of love in the void: in the center thereof
> rose a fountain.[74]

What visitors are likely to experience is a sensation of serenity in almost total shadow, punctuated by fragments of light and sound.

The garden could be interpreted as Carol Coleman's figural grave, although no image of her or information about Carol's life is presented.[75] From the entry gate, movement through Carol's Garden begins along a short, straight path. Dark shade, created by the arching Bradford pear trees, is the only natural effect that hints at the garden's somber origin. Their shadows induce a reflective frame of mind and contrast with the life force implied by the sound of water. The entry path joins a circular path from which passageways, stationed on the cardinal points, lead to a fountain at the center of the circle. Two limestone benches are placed at the ends of the east–west axis marking the limits of the garden. David Rogers, an artist from Bloomington, Indiana, was commissioned in 1982 to craft the benches and limestone fountain.

At the end of the armature, Owen created a small path. This "outside path," in her words, "embraces the whole."[76] Hidden deep in the garden's southwest corner is a small bronze sculpture in the shape of a rectangular box raised on a small pedestal. It poetically evokes the multiple readings this garden yields. The Houston-based artist Carroll Harris Simms for this sculpture wrote to Owen that the meaning of this work, called *Arms,* was "the belief in the return of the seasons: the resurrection, continuity, and the rebirth of life."[77] Animal life thrives in miniature abundance on all sides of this work, each creature evoking some aspect of religious belief. The fish (symbolizing "the miracle of sustaining life"), beetle ("symbolic of resurrection"), coil forms (to give a "quality of energy"), and finally the presence of geese (sacred to the Celts) are used to "spiritually: redundantly: orchestrate the concept of 'Arms.'"[78]

HISTORICAL CONSCIOUSNESS AND UNCONSCIOUSNESS

From the beginning, as one walks through the garden, parables, elegies, and sayings on small signs are "planted" amid the garden, just like another hosta or periwinkle plant:

> Raise the stone and
> you shall find me split
> the wood and I am there

The ethical, religious, and sometimes mournful sayings console and give ethical and religious direction, but they do not literally interpret the meaning of Carol's Garden. They are evocations that enable meditative, spiritual, and prayerful actions to occur. This approach contrasts with the more academic, curatorial approach toward historical buildings and landscapes found elsewhere in New Harmony.

HISTORY, TIME, AND NATURE

Although the darkness of the forested grove is "largely associated with death and destruction," the grove also has connections with the "female principle or of the Great Mother."[79] Hence, it is also a place where death and life thrive. Darkness contrasts with light throughout the garden. The gloss on the leaves of the ivy and the water that bubbles up from the fountain reflect light, creating an impression of brightness and hopefulness. This is the only garden where fall leaves are allowed to wither and decay back into the soil. The dead, decaying leaves nourish and regenerate the soil. The canopy of trees or "veil" formed over the entire garden room protects the space in a way that is similar to the dome of the Roofless Church. The Bradford pear trees, which would normally develop thick, bushy tops, were planted more closely together than convention would dictate. This caused the thin branches to overlap and become tightly knit. Wires are woven into the tree canopies to bend the branches and keep them from breaking. Poetically, this has the effect of shrouding the entire garden.

As in Tillich Park, the natural elements in Carol's Garden—trees, rocks, and water—imbue this setting with spiritual, mystical, and unnamable nuance.

The placement of Carol's Garden on a site once containing houses dating from the Harmonist and Owen periods does not seek to assert a historical connection (although Carol Coleman was the great-great-great-granddaughter of Robert Owen). What is compelling are the symbolic connections made with New Harmony's other gardens, especially the dome of the Roofless Church, visible to those exiting the garden. The dome symbolically reconnects Carol Coleman to the legacy of the Owen family.

Figure 6.12. The north view of Carol's Garden with the fountain and entry gate is shown in close visual relationship with the domed canopy of the Roofless Church, just beyond. Photograph courtesy of Christine Gorby, 2000.

The Cathedral Labyrinth (1997)

Jane Owen commissioned the Cathedral Labyrinth garden in 1997 to correct the 1941 reconstruction of the 1820s Harmonist Labyrinth, which she believed was a multicursal maze rather than unicursal labyrinth. The Reverend Dr. Lauren Artress, canon of San Francisco's Grace Cathedral, where she created a reconstruction of the Chartres Cathedral labyrinth, describes the difference between a labyrinth and a maze: "A maze creates confusion. But a labyrinth has only one path, and, once we make the choice to enter into it, the path becomes a metaphor for our own journey through life, sending us to the center and then back again to the same edge of the path."[80]

Rather than interpret historical texts or attempt another hypothetical reconstruction of the Harmonist Labyrinth, Owen chose to re-create a near replica of the twelfth-century Chartres Cathedral labyrinth, located at the crossing of the cathedral's nave and transepts (Plate 20). Carried out by Kenneth A. Schuette Jr. with Rob Sovinski, the forty-two-foot-diameter labyrinth was constructed of polished and thermal-finished Carnelian granite. It is approached through a trellis-like gateway constructed of silver maple. This leads to a space formed by trees planted to evoke the columns of the cathedral. A fountain for cleansing one's feet by artist Simon Verity was positioned to the south in alignment with the labyrinth stone.

GARDEN ARCHETYPES: WALLED GARDEN, LABYRINTH

What is compelling about Owen's approach in New Harmony is how modern and historical gardens are more potent in terms of the emotional impact they have on observers because of their associations with each other. Although some of her modern gardens make explicit connections to New Harmony's utopian past, others invent, directing visitors toward new interpretations of place and community.

The labyrinth is a recurring landscape type in New Harmony. Of the three labyrinths constructed by the Harmonists, the one in New Harmony is the only one thought to have had a dual role as both a pleasure garden and a meditative space. As a place of amusement, the labyrinth offered a distraction from the arduous spiritual and work lives of Society members. The network of paths leading to a central structure symbolized the difficult path each member would travel on to achieve "harmony" in life.

In the *American Gardener's Calendar*, the first and most important book on agriculture in the United States, Bernard M'Mahon helps situate the meaning of *labyrinth* as it was understood during the Harmonist period.[81] Christoph Muller, a Harmonist doctor and pharmacist, owned a copy of this book when he lived in New Harmony, and it is still in the collection of Old Economy in Pennsylvania.[82] On the meaning of the labyrinth M'Mahon wrote:

Figure 6.13. An interpretive reconstruction from the 1930s of a labyrinth the Harmonist Society built near this location. Photograph courtesy of Christine Gorby, 2000.

Figure 6.14. The Cathedral Labyrinth, carried out by Kenneth Schuette with Rob W. Sovinski, reproduced a medieval labyrinth from Chartres Cathedral, France. Photograph courtesy of Christine Gorby, 2000.

A Labyrinth, is a maze or sort of intricate wilderness-plantation, abounding with hedges and walks, formed into many windings and turnings, leading to one common center, extremely difficult to find out; designed in the large pleasure-grounds by way of amusement. It is generally formed with hedges, commonly in double rows, leading in various intricate turnings, backward and forward, with intervening plantations, and gravel-walks alternately between hedge and hedge; the great aim is to have the walk contrived in so many mazy, intricate windings, to and fro, that a person may have much difficulty in finding out the center.[83]

HISTORICAL CONSCIOUSNESS AND UNCONSCIOUSNESS

In blessing Owen's Labyrinth, the Reverend Canon François Legaux, rector of Chartres Cathedral, echoed her interpretation of the labyrinth, calling it "a spiritual exercise" that tries "to capture inner communion between body and soul, between the physical and spiritual, between the movement of the body and the most serene inner space."[84]

Of New Harmony's Chartres Cathedral Labyrinth, Owen said, "The labyrinth has been a misunderstood tool that has been disrespected from the original intention of the single path. No one gets lost in the labyrinth if you follow it. In the sacred labyrinth no one is lost. The Christian interpretation gave it one path. For the path that leads to life has no dead end. A maze creates confusion, but a labyrinth does not."[85] Owen also cited Tillich's call, which she said parallels the need for the labyrinth: "We are estranged from ourselves. We have too many options, and distractions."[86]

HISTORY, TIME, AND NATURE

Through Owen's vision, New Harmony became a community where tourist attractions and spiritual retreats subtly coexist. Owen drew on themes, particularly from the Harmonist period, that originally had different meanings and reinterpreted them according to her own mystical theology. She did not reject history but employed it, as in the Cathedral Labyrinth, as a means of *spiritual community* building, where

Figure 6.15. A formal entrance gateway of the Cathedral Labyrinth guides visitors along a path to a fountain and the labyrinth beyond. Photograph courtesy of Christine Gorby, 2000.

participants were invited to make connections with the past but were not instructed on what those interpretations should be. Ultimate meaning or enlightenment was for each person to be derived individually.

Conclusion

Depending on one's source, Jane Owen is represented as either an eccentric Texan oil heiress or as a benevolent supporter of creative artists. She often referred to herself as the "town gardener" when tourists stopped her to ask directions as she careened around New Harmony in an electric golf cart wearing a big-brimmed hat and work clothes. She belongs among a diverse group of spiritual women whose projects grow out of their social concerns.[87] If, as Joanne Leonard states, "spirituality denotes experience," then the modern gardens Jane Owen developed were about "creating relationships, participation, awareness and understanding in the life of the individual."[88] Of these key associations, Jane Owen, writing on behalf of the Blaffer Trust, was cognizant of the relation between the present and past. Paul Tillich, she writes, best articulates this aim in an excerpt from his book *The Religious Situation*:

To understand the present means to see it in its inner tension toward the future. In this field, also there is such a thing as spiritual perspective and the possibility of finding amid all the infinite aspirations and tensions which conserve the past but also those which are CREATIVELY NEW AND PREGNANT WITH THE FUTURE.[89]

Owen's contributions to landscape design in New Harmony reinterpret and contrast with the places and ideologies of the historic past. New Harmony is a rare instance in the United States where one can experience an evolving, place-based interpretation of the spiritual within a rich historical context. Her work is a reminder of how gardens and environments, at their most basic and meaningful, can materialize such human qualities and concerns as community relationships, spirituality, mourning, and remembrance. Her work is also a reminder of how gardens can demonstrate profound human emotions—loss, remembrance, and comfort of community—yet quietly become part of the everyday world.

Interpreters of New Harmony, beginning at the turn of the twentieth century, relayed their historical interpretations through a variety of forms, including historical pageants, guidebooks, novels, maps, and preserved or reconstructed architecture and gardens. In contrast, Owen used modern gardens, art, and architecture to develop an alternative narrative of New Harmony as a place of spiritual pilgrimage and retreat. By recognizing the value of historical unconsciousness, she addressed Eliade's powerful cautionary statement about overreliance on historical consciousness to guarantee the "authenticity of an existence."[90] Her gardens can be experienced both inside and outside historical time. She did not insistently impress her historical interpretations or her aspirations for the future on others; instead, she provided implicit cues through poetic texts, works of art, shrubbery, trees, and built structures. These settings were created to induce a *historical consciousness* and also prompt a deeper meditative state, *a historical unconsciousness,* among visitors open to such experiences.

Notes

In addition to receiving a grant from the Institute for the Arts and Humanities at Penn State, the author thanks the following for their assistance with the preparation of this chapter: Ralph Schwarz; Mrs. Owen; Evans Woollen; Jim Sanders and Chris Laughbaum, Robert Lee Blaffer Foundation; Sherry Graves, Margaret Scherzinger, and Ryan Rokicki, Working Men's Institute; Connie Weinzapfel, Historic New Harmony; Amanda Bryden, Indiana State Museum and Historic Sites; Raymond V. Shepherd Jr., Old Economy Village, Pennsylvania; Jennifer Greene, University of Southern Indiana, Evansville; the contributors to this book, Cammie McAtee, Michelangelo Sabatino, Ben Nicholson, Stephen Fox, William R. Crout, and Nancy Mangum McCaslin; and my spouse, Malcolm Woollen.

1. For an overview of the landscape architectural history of New Harmony, Indiana, see Christine Gorby, "Jane Blaffer Owen: Her Modern Spiritual Landscapes of New Harmony, Indiana,"

Landscape Architecture: The Magazine of the American Society of Landscape Architects, June 2004, 36, 38, 40–44; and Gorby, "Jane Blaffer Owen: Her Modern Spiritual Landscapes of New Harmony, Indiana," in *Critique of Built Works of Landscape Architecture,* vol. 8 (Baton Rouge: Louisiana State University, 2003).

2. Owen initially developed Carol's Garden using her private funds, but she later transferred ownership to the Blaffer Trust. Two important landscapes also created by Owen but not discussed here are Our Lord's Woods, developed by the Red Geranium Enterprises in the 1970s, and Fragrant Farms, developed privately by Jane Owen in 1998. The Red Geranium Enterprises is a for-profit group of businesses Owen started. The New Harmony Inn and Conference Center and the Red Geranium Restaurant are part of this business group. Our Lord's Woods is developed as a sprawling forest with walking paths, a large pond, and sculptures. Designed by architect Thomas Kane as part of the New Harmony Inn development, Our Lord's Woods was bounded to the north by the Wabash River, to the south by the New Harmony Inn, to the east by the Barn Abbey, and to the west near the Atheneum. Pines, the dominant tree type in Our Lord's Woods, turned into a stand of red oaks near the Barn Abbey, a Blaffer Trust project. Fragrant Farms (1998) is a for-profit organic farm founded by Jane Owen at the southwest edge of New Harmony. Here, peonies (one of her favorite flowers) are grown for both individual orders and commercial resale to florists, fragrantfarms.com. Grapes suitable for winemaking are also grown. The local community is invited to harvest this small crop, which is sold to an Indiana winery. The cultivation of grapes was a historic nod to the Harmonists, who were well known for their viniculture practice. They grew grapes in the town on trellises mounted on buildings and on the surrounding hillsides of New Harmony. The Harmonists both consumed and sold the wine they produced. This project was a culmination and affirmation of Owen's environmentalism, a passion that began in the 1970s with her interest in the back-to-the-land movement.

3. Robert Lee Blaffer Trust, "Draft Open Letter to Be Printed," n.d. [circa 1960s], p. 2, TS, bMS 649 Paul Tillich Papers, Andover-Harvard Theological Library, Harvard Divinity School, Cambridge, Mass. (hereafter cited as AHTL, Harvard); Paul Tillich, *The Religious Situation,* translated by H. Richard Niebuhr (Cleveland: Meridian Books, 1956), 33–34.

4. Owen traced her connections to New Harmony back to 1941, shortly after her marriage to Kenneth Owen, a direct descendent of Robert Owen, who founded an important nineteenth-century communitarian society in New Harmony. During the 1950s and 1960s Jane Owen, along with state and federal agencies and nonprofit organizations, began to buy land and to renovate historic buildings from the Harmonist period throughout the northwest quadrant of the town. In 1958, through the Robert Lee Blaffer Trust she founded, Owen shifted her efforts away from preserving vernacular architecture toward the commissioning of new modern architecture and gardens.

5. Helen Bullock, "Letter to Mrs. Ora V. Howton," August 2, 1960, TS, box 6 Roofless Church Legal Papers, folder National Trust for Historic Preservation–Mrs. Helen D. Bullock, Robert Lee Blaffer Trust Archives, Robert Lee Blaffer Foundation, New Harmony, Ind. Hereafter cited as Blaffer Trust Archives. Reprinted by courtesy of the Robert Lee Blaffer Foundation.

6. Archetypal forms in use in Owen's gardens included the walled garden (Roofless Church, Carol's Garden, Cathedral Labyrinth, and Sacred Garden), grove (Tillich Park, Carol's Garden, Our Lord's Woods), grotto (Tillich Park—early stage), cemetery (Roofless Church, Carol's Garden, Tillich Park), mound (Tillich Park), and labyrinth (Carol's Garden, Tillich Park, Cathedral Labyrinth, and Sacred Garden).

7. Becky Boyer, "New Labyrinth Planned for New Harmony," *Mount Vernon Democrat,* November 27, 1996.

8. Joanne Leonard, "Teaching Introductory Feminist Spirituality: Tracing the Trajectory through

Women Writers," *Journal of Feminist Studies in Religion* 6, no. 2 (1990): 131; Dorothee Sölle, "Mysticism, Liberation, and the Names of God: A Feminist Reflection," *Christianity and Crisis* 41, no. 11 (June 22, 1981): 179; *ATLA Religion Database with ATLASerials,* EBSCO*host* (accessed July 14, 2013).

9. Jane Blaffer Owen, letter to author, June 23, 2007. Courtesy of the Kenneth Dale and Jane Blaffer Owen Family and Christine Gorby.

10. Connie Weinzapfel (director of Historic New Harmony), in discussion with the author, July 2, 2002.

11. Boyer, "New Labyrinth Planned for New Harmony."

12. See Mircea Eliade, *Images and Symbols: Studies in Religious Symbolism* (Princeton, N.J.: Princeton University Press, 1991), 33. Eliade cited many other everyday ways in which "consciousness is awakened" to surpass "its own historicity." Eliade cited many other "everyday" ways to exist outside "historical time." These included "the state of dreaming, or of the waking dream, or of melancholy, or of detachment, or of aesthetic bliss, or of escape."

13. Paul Tillich, *The Shaking of the Foundations* (New York: Charles Scribner's Sons, 1948), 81.

14. Ibid., 86. The first documentation in which Jane Owen acknowledged Tillich's influence on her thinking was in an unsigned letter she wrote to him on May 19, 1955. Her first direct encounter with Tillich, as Owen recounted, was when she attended his evening lectures at the Union Theological Seminary in New York in about 1953. See Jane Owen, "Letter to Dr. Tillich [unsigned, page(s) missing]," May 19, 1959, transcript, File Cabinet One, folder—Tillich Park-Building and Design, Tillich Archive, Robert Lee Blaffer Foundation, New Harmony, Ind., n.p. Hereafter cited as Tillich Archive, New Harmony.

15. Tillich, *Shaking of the Foundations,* 85. Tillich did not include landscape architecture as one of the arts or the sciences, although he did address nature in his theological writings. Until recently, nature was an understudied dimension of his work by scholars. See Gert Hummel, "Natural Theology versus Theology of Nature? Tillich's Thinking as Impetus for a Discourse among Theology, Philosophy, and Natural Sciences," *Proceedings of the IV International Paul Tillich Symposium, Held in Frankfurt/main, 1992,* edited by Gert Hummel (Berlin: W. de Gruyter, 1994). Unlike Tillich, who called for a reconciliation of people with nature, distancing and exploiting nature was part of the Christian tradition. It stemmed from a Christian belief that Man was created in the image of God and was thereby separated from nature. See Robin Attfield, "Christian Attitudes to Nature," *Journal of the History of Ideas* 44, no. 3 (1983): 369–86, http://www.jstor.org/stable/2709172.

16. Jane Blaffer Owen, interview by Sandra Curtis, March 12, 1980, p. 6, transcript, Archives of American Art, Smithsonian Institution, Washington, D.C., 6.

17. Ibid., 6–10.

18. Ibid., 11–12.

19. Jane Blaffer Owen, "Untitled," July 16, 1974, p. 2, transcript, box 12, folder Blaffer Trust, Blaffer Trust Archives.

20. Ibid., 2. Reprinted by courtesy of the Kenneth Dale and Jane Blaffer Owen Family.

21. Owen, "Untitled," 2. Jane Owen cited Richard Wilhelm's "Golden Flower" that explored the "circular Mandolas" and "other eastern motifs from the writings of Carl Jung," Thomas Merton's "Asian Journals," and Paul Tillich's "last writings [that] dealt largely with religions of the Orient." Reprinted by courtesy of the Kenneth Dale and Jane Blaffer Owen Family.

22. Nobutaka Inoue, "From Religious Conformity to Innovative New Ideas of Religious Journey and Holy Place," *Social Compass* 47, no. 1 (2000): 25.

23. Philip Johnson, *The Philip Johnson Tapes: Interviews by Robert A. M. Stern,* edited by Kazys Varnelis (New York: Monacelli, 2008), 169.

24. Jane Owen, "Letter to Dr. Tillich [unsigned, page(s) missing]," May 19, 1959, transcript, File Cabinet One, folder—Tillich Park–Building and Design, Tillich Archive, New Harmony, n.p. Reprinted by courtesy of the Kenneth Dale and Jane Blaffer Owen Family.

25. Johnson, *Philip Johnson Tapes: Interviews,* 170. Johnson used the walled garden as a formal spatial concept in many of his projects. Most notable among these was the courtyard garden of the Museum of Modern Art. Historians have most often compared the Roofless Church to Johnson's Nuclear Reactor project both for its formal likeness and because this project was designed in a similar time period.

26. The first documented reference in the West to a spiritual walled garden before the medieval period was in the Bible. Found in the Song of Songs 4:12, this passage reads: "My sister [the Church], my spouse, is a garden enclosed, a garden enclosed, a fountain sealed up." See Jean Delumeau, *History of Paradise: The Garden of Eden in Myth and Tradition,* translated by Matthew O'Connell (New York: Continuum, 1995), 121.

27. Before medievalism, "Eden" was viewed differently. It was understood as part of an open, unbounded landscape. With the advent of the medieval period an interpretive shift of "Eden" began. This occurred after vegetable and medicinal gardens began to be walled or "cloistered," against inclement weather and animals, and they also began to be used for meditation. From this new spiritual use, a new association between the walled garden and "earthly paradise" emerged.

28. Delumeau, *History of Paradise,* 122; Herrad of Landsberg (or Hottenburg), *Hortus deliciarum,* 2 vols. (London: Brill, 1979), 1:38.

29. William Pickering, *A plan of the town of Harmonie in Posey County, Indiana. The property of Frederic Rapp* (1824).

30. When the Harmonists left their settlement in 1825, the cemetery was not yet enclosed. It was not until 1874, almost fifty years later, that member Jonathan Lenz was sent back to buy and raze their original cruciform church. The Harmonists believed it had been blasphemed by the Owenites and successor generations. Since the Harmonist's departure the church had been used as a theater, dance and lecture hall, and pork-packing plant. Bricks from the church were used to construct a five-foot wall around their burial area. This wall partially collapsed by the 1960s and was later restored by the Indiana Department of Natural Resources in 1977.

31. John Boyd, "New Shrine at New Harmony is Architectural Pace-Setter," *Evansville Press,* May 1, 1959.

32. Originally the "interior" of the Roofless Church was almost entirely paved in limestone except for four planting areas. These included the hackberry tree group and two geranium flowerbeds in the main courtyard area and a golden rain tree group in the forecourt area. In the 1980s architect Evans Woollen was asked to redesign and remove much of the paving in the main courtyard area. This change enhanced the garden-like quality of this space. Movement now through the courtyard is more axially directed. As to why the change was made, Owen said that "we softened it up" because the limestone was so hard that you could not walk and the red geranium beds burned up in the summer. Jane Blaffer Owen, interview with author, May 2010. Courtesy of the Kenneth Dale and Jane Blaffer Owen Family and Christine Gorby.

33. Jane Owen, "Foreword," Tillich Conference, New Harmony, June 17–20, 1993, edited by Frederick J. Parella (Berlin: Walter de Gruyter, 1995), ix.

34. Jane Owen, interview by Judy O'Bannon, *Communities Building Community,* interview 307 transcript, WFYI Indianapolis (public television and radio station), October 5, 2006, 7.

35. Bullock, "Letter to Mrs. Ora V. Howton," August 2, 1960, Blaffer Trust Archives. Reprinted by courtesy of the Robert Lee Blaffer Foundation.

36. Evans Woollen, telephone interview with author, November 4, 2013.

37. Arnold H. Price, "The Germanic Forest: Taboo and Economic Growth," *Vierteljahrschrift für Sozial-und Wirtschaftsgeschichte* 52, no. 3 (1965): 368, 372–73. http://www.jstor.org/stable/20729190.

38. Ray Shephard (historian, Old Economy Village), in discussion with the author, August 14, 2002.

39. Ralph Schwarz (former president of Historic New Harmony, Inc.), in discussion with the author, August 5, 2002.

40. Camilla A. Corbin, "Minutes, Meeting of Trustees Robert Lee Blaffer Trust," September 14, 1962, transcript, box 12, folder 1960s Robert Lee Blaffer Trust Report, Blaffer Trust Archives.

41. Ibid.

42. Ben Nicholson writes about this commission in his chapter "Frederick Kiesler's Grotto: A Promethean Spirit in New Harmony."

43. Paul Tillich, "Letter to Mrs. Jane Owen," n.d., p. 1, transcript, Cabinet One, folder Tillich-Correspondence, Tillich Archive, New Harmony. Reprinted by courtesy of Ted Farris as representative of the Estates of Paul and Hannah Tillich.

44. Ibid., 1. Reprinted by courtesy of Ted Farris as representative of the Estates of Paul and Hannah Tillich.

45. Ibid., 1–2. Reprinted by courtesy of Ted Farris as representative of the Estates of Paul and Hannah Tillich.

46. Hummel, "Natural Theology versus Theology of Nature?"; Pan-cui Lai, "Paul Tillich and Ecological Theology," *Journal of Religion* 79, no. 2 (1999): 233–49, http://www.jstor.org/stable/1206631.

47. Helen Duprey Bullock, "Letter to Mrs. Clifton Couch," March 3, 1966, p. 2, transcript, box 12, folder 1 Blaffer Trust, Blaffer Trust Archives. Reprinted by courtesy of the Robert Lee Blaffer Foundation.

48. "Service in Homage to Paul Tillich Pentecost, 1966," 1966, transcript, File Cabinet One, folder Service In Homage Paul Tillich Pentecost, Tillich Archive, New Harmony, Ind. Only two drawings of the Tillich Park project have been located and are in the Philip Johnson Architectural Drawings collection, drawer 311, in the Avery Drawings and Archives, part of the Columbia University Libraries, New York City. One drawing, a site plan, pencil on vellum, dated August 11, 1965, scale 1/10 inch =1 foot -0 inches, has "Philip Johnson Architect, 375 Park Avenue New York" written in the bottom corner. The second drawing, a trace overlay sketch site plan, also dated August 11, 1965, is unsigned.

49. Philip Johnson, "Letter to Mr. James Brown [Robert Lee Blaffer Trust]," August 19, 1965, transcript, File Cabinet One, folder Tillich Park–Building and Design, Tillich Archive, New Harmony, Ind. Printed by permission of the Estate of Philip Johnson; courtesy of the Glass House, a site of The National Trust for Historic Preservation.

50. "Robert Lee Blaffer Trust Report Fiscal Year Ending February 29, 1968," February 29, 1968, transcript, box 12, folder 2 1960s RLBT Report, Blaffer Trust Archives.

51. Mrs. Kenneth D. Owen, "Letter to Mr. and Mrs. Paul Tillich," April 15, 1965, transcript, File Cabinet One, folder Tillich Park–Building and Design, Tillich Archive, New Harmony, Ind.

52. David C. Klauba and Reuben K. Verkamp, "Dr. Paul Tillich Park New Harmony Indiana Landscape Regeneration Concept," April 2004, transcript, File Cabinet One, Tillich Park–Building and Design, Tillich Archive, New Harmony, Ind.

53. J. E. Cirlot, *A Dictionary of Symbols,* translated by Jack Sage (London: Routledge, 1962), 112.

54. Ralph Beyer, "Letter to Mrs. Owen," June 6, 1966, transcript, File Cabinet One, folder Tillich Park–Ralph Beyer, Tillich Archive, New Harmony, Ind. Beyer's other most important work in New Harmony commissioned by Owen was ten tablets he lettered for the outside of Waddam's Chapel. Each tablet was hand-cut by Beyer with one of the Ten Commandments (completed 1975). The chapel was

dedicated to Herbert Waddam, former canon of Canterbury Cathedral, who was involved in the World Council of Churches, an important ecumenical organization organized in 1948. The chapel is a small circular room to the back of the Entry House of the New Harmony Inn. Beyer considered this project and his Tillich Park work in New Harmony among his most important public works.

55. Jane B. Owen, "Letter to Prof. Paul Tillich," March 5, 1965, transcript, File Cabinet One, folder Tillich Park–Building and Design, Tillich Archive, New Harmony, Ind.

56. Tillich, *Shaking of the Foundations*, 76–86.

57. Effigy mounds were constructed to resemble various creatures during the Late Woodland Period (1400–750 BP). The bear, bird, turtle, and panther were the most common forms. Effigy mounds were created in what is now the area from northeast Iowa to southwest Wisconsin. Archaeologists believe that these earth mounds may be related to constellations, but no data exist to confirm this or other uses. Burials took place in geometric-shaped mounds. The two most important mound-building cultures of the Woodland Period were the Adena Culture and the Hopewell. The Adena Culture of the Early Woodland Period (000–200 BCE) made a structure built of logs and poles covered with bark and soil for the dead body and objects. This structure was then burned, and a geometric earth mound was constructed over this structure. The pattern was repeated for successive burials. Hopewell mounds, also of a geometric shape, were centered in what is now the Ohio Valley, but they were as far east as what is now Pennsylvania. While some earth mounds are found in and around New Harmony, the nearest most important group were constructed at the Angel Site Mound on the Ohio River near present-day Evansville, Indiana. The over-one-hundred-acre site has eleven individual geometric mounds in a conical shape from the Middle Mississippian Age. The largest earthwork among the group, Mound A, was constructed between 750 and 520 BP. See G. W. Monaghan and C. S. Peebles, "The Construction, Use, and Abandonment of Angel Site Mound A: Tracing the History of a Middle Mississippian Town through Its Earthworks," *American Antiquity* 75, no. 4 (2010): 935–36.

58. Whitfield H. Marshall, "Letter to Jane Owen," March 15, 1966, transcript, File Cabinet One, folder Tillich Park–Ralph Beyer, Tillich Archive, New Harmony, n.p.

59. Owen, "Foreword," x.

60. Ibid., xi.

61. Paul Tillich, "Estranged and Reunited: The New Being [Tillich Park Dedication Address]," June 2, 1963, p. 2, transcript, bMS 649 Paul Tillich Papers, AHTL, Harvard, Cambridge, Mass. Reprinted by courtesy of Ted Farris as representative of the Estates of Paul and Hannah Tillich; the Paul Tillich Papers bMS 649, Andover–Harvard Theological Library, Harvard Divinity School, Harvard University; and the Robert Lee Blaffer Foundation. Paul Tillich's address is reprinted later in this book.

62. Jane Blaffer Owen, letter to author, May 4, 2004, 2. While developing the idea to plant a large grouping of Bradford pear trees on a lot behind Owen's private residence, Rawlings House, Gilbert also designed "an outdoor dining room" for Owen in back of her house. Gilbert was already in the United States on another commission when he came to New Harmony at Owen's request to design these two projects.

63. Ibid., 2. Reprinted by courtesy of the Kenneth Dale and Jane Blaffer Owen Family and Christine Gorby.

64. Eliade, *Images and Symbols*, 52.

65. Jane Blaffer Owen, "Untitled," July 16, 1974, p. 2, transcript, box 12, folder Blaffer Trust, Blaffer Trust Archives. Reprinted by courtesy of the Kenneth Dale and Jane Blaffer Owen Family.

66. Owen, letter to author. Reprinted by courtesy of the Kenneth Dale and Jane Blaffer Owen Family and Christine Gorby.

67. Eliade, *Images and Symbols*, 52.

68. Ibid.

69. Ibid., 53–54. In India a large number of circles were inscribed within a square.

70. Steven E. Hann, "Legal Description [Carol's Garden]," June 19, 1986, MS, box 2 Robert Lee Blaffer Foundation Deeds, folder Pfister–Carol's Garden, Blaffer Trust Archives.

71. Owen, letter to author, 2; Evans Woollen, in discussion with the author, August 2002.

72. Schwarz, in discussion with the author, August 5, 2002.

73. Robert Lax, *The Circus of the Sun* (New York: Journeyman Books, 1959), n.p.

74. This excerpt is reprinted as it was originally published. See Lax, *Circus of the Sun*, n.p. Reprinted by courtesy of Journeyman Books and Robert Lax Literary Trust.

75. Carol Campbell Owen Coleman is interred at Maple Hill Cemetery just south of town. The graves of her parents, Kenneth Dale and Jane Blaffer Owen, are nearby.

76. See note 64.

77. Carroll Harris Simms, letter to Jane Owen, July 30, 1983, p. 3, transcript, Jane B. Owen and Robert Blaffer Trust [Papers], box Jane B. Owen and Robert Blaffer Trust, Folder Carol's Garden, Working Men's Institute (hereafter cited as WMI), New Harmony, Ind. Reprinted by courtesy of Working Men's Institute.

78. Ibid.

79. Juan Eduardo Cirlot, *A Dictionary of Symbols,* translated by Jack Sage (London: Routledge, 1971), 112.

80. Boyer, "New Labyrinth Planned for New Harmony."

81. Bernard M'Mahon, *American Gardener's Calendar; adapted to the Climates and seasons of the United States* (Philadelphia: B. Graves, 1806).

82. Raymond Shephard (historian, Old Economy Village), in discussion with the author, July 12, 2002.

83. M'Mahon, *American Gardener's Calendar,* 67–68.

84. Canon François Legaux, "Dedication of Cathedral Labyrinth," translated by Liliane Krasean, 1997, p. 2, transcript, Jane B. Owen and Robert Blaffer Trust Papers, folder Labyrinth, WMI. Reprinted by courtesy of the Robert Lee Blaffer Foundation.

85. Boyer, "New Labyrinth Planned for New Harmony."

86. Ibid.

87. Leonard, "Teaching Introductory Feminist Spirituality," 126.

88. Ibid., 124–25; Dermot Lane, *The Experience of God: An Invitation to Do Theology* (New York: Paulist, 1981), 6–7.

89. Robert Lee Blaffer Trust, "Draft Open Letter to Be Printed," 2. Reprinted by courtesy of the Paul Tillich Papers bMS 649, Andover–Harvard Theological Library, Harvard Divinity School, Harvard University, and the Robert Lee Blaffer Foundation.

90. Eliade, *Images and Symbols,* 33.

Figure 7.1. The Franklin Court, Philadelphia, historical site and museum complex, with Ghost House structures representing Benjamin Franklin's log cabin. Venturi & Rauch, Philadelphia, 1976. The camp postmodern metaphor of the "Grays" is distinct from the neo-Corbusian forms chosen by the New York "Whites." Photograph courtesy of Michelangelo Sabatino, 2013.

7

The New Harmony Atheneum

White Collage

BEN NICHOLSON

BY THE MID-1970S, New Harmony had firmly established itself as a place of innovative modernist architecture and landscape. The Roofless Church and Paul Tillich Park had been completed and the *Grotto for Meditation* and St. Stephen's Church had been left as projects. The sprawling complex of the New Harmony Inn (1974) and Conference Center (1986) would be completed a decade later. The town's vibrant program of historic preservation was well under way, supported at the highest levels of state, corporate, and private patronage. There still remained one thing to do: the past and the future needed to be brought into an articulate and integrated vision. In a perfect storm of talent, timing, and money, the Atheneum came into being, rising out of the muddy banks of the Wabash River like the incongruent phoenix that it is.

Ralph G. Schwarz Commissions the Atheneum

The Atheneum was inaugurated in 1979, almost twenty years after the Roofless Church was finished. The Atheneum's deconstructed form is a vivid reminder that New Harmony has always been a place of dynamic thought and intellectual inquiry. While it is possible to appreciate the building from the vantage of aesthetics, the logic of the building begins to unfold when the vision and leadership of Ralph G. Schwarz is understood.[1] In 1972 Schwarz met Jane Blaffer Owen, who asked him to become a trustee of the Robert Lee Blaffer Trust. She then hired him to plan and develop the New Harmony Inn, seeing the potential in New Harmony's history as a site of pilgrimage. Schwarz was the first president of Historic New Harmony Inc., an organization founded in 1974 to develop public interest in New Harmony and preserve its historic buildings. At the time of his arrival, New Harmony was in a holding pattern from the tail end of an oil boom. Only some of the historic preservation plans proposed by the earlier Memorial Commission in the 1940s and 1950s had been implemented, in addition to a handful of Owen's private initiatives. Schwarz believed that the role of the past as a component of the present was an important cultural asset. As president of Historic New Harmony, he set out to amalgamate the best of the earlier preservation and tourist planning. He wanted a radical building to exemplify his point of view.

Schwarz had experience and education that gave him a broad view of the world. He was a veteran of the Battle of the Bulge during the Second World War and, after the war ended, was assigned to General Mark Clark's office, where he became involved with the war crimes trials. His postwar education took him on a path through Europe that included studies at the Sorbonne and attending lectures by Le Corbusier, followed by undergraduate studies in mechanical engineering and international relations (1948) and an M.A. in British history (1951) at Lehigh University.[2] From 1949 to 1961 Schwarz worked for the Bethlehem Steel Company in Lehigh, serving as the special representative, legal and real estate, during which time he founded Historic Bethlehem, Inc. in 1957. Between 1961 and 1963 he became assistant to the publisher and president of the *New York Herald Tribune.* He joined the Ford Foundation in 1963 as director of Building Planning and Construction, and in this capacity he worked with Kevin Roche, John Dinkeloo & Associates to reassess the programming of the Ford Foundation Building, designed in 1963 and completed in 1968.[3] The Ford Foundation broke new ground with its massive plant-filled glass atrium, so Schwarz would have known the power of public foundational architecture. He served as president of the Fund for Area Planning and Development and was involved with planning activities for expanding the UN Headquarters before coming to New Harmony in 1972.[4] With a résumé such as this, it was to be expected that whatever he turned his hand to in New Harmony would be groundbreaking.

Schwarz clarifies his decision to push for an iconic building to champion his interpretation of New Harmony's past, present, and future. What he helped create for the Ford Foundation on East Forty-second Street in Manhattan would now be repeated on North Street in New Harmony. Historic New Harmony's building would signify the power of philanthropy to accelerate and reassert a cosmopolitan vision for which this midwestern town was famous. Schwarz's access to leaders in architecture, media, and philanthropy in New York and Washington, D.C., enabled him to tap into Indiana's political resources and match the impetus of Owen through force of persuasiveness.

The form of historic preservation that Schwarz advocated, during his tenure from 1974 to 1984, was to show how New Harmony has changed over time and provide lessons for contemporary society. He envisioned a series of small museums in houses and public buildings throughout the town, each one dedicated to a theme or personality, several of which were completed before he left. To bring this about, Schwarz made a wholesale chiropractic adjustment to the town, which some might call invasive surgery. The process involved relocating houses to their original locations, when known, and reestablishing the townscape to give it interpretable periods of historic relevance.[5] It would enable a choreographed route, visiting sites throughout the town that would elicit the several themes of New Harmony's distinguished past and reinforce its nineteenth-century reputation as the Athens of the West.

Schwarz was working in a context of tourist and heritage communities as various as Colonial Williamsburg (1928) and Kentucky's Shaker Village at Pleasant Hill (1961) at a time when Americans were visiting Disneyland (1955). With the explosion of automobile tourism during the 1960s, Schwarz envisioned that visitors to New Harmony would leave their cars on the edge of town in a three-hundred-space parking lot, be oriented, and then set off on foot or in a golf cart to relive history in real time. Schwarz needed a building to serve as a dynamic gateway to New Harmony without any pretense of being a museum or conventional visitor center. It needed to have the inventive power of Venturi & Rauch's Franklin Court (1976) in Philadelphia, with its controversial Ghost House sculptures for Benjamin Franklin, or Gwathmey Siegel's Whig Hall (1972) on Princeton's Gothic Revival campus, that recycled a fire-damaged classical temple by inserting a bulging modernist form inside it. Both the "Grays" and "Whites," the ideological camps working to challenge canonical modernism, which Venturi & Rauch and Gwathmey Siegel were representing, had stepped into the arena of dramatically reinterpreting historic buildings and sites.

Schwarz's edifice became the Atheneum, referring with classical rhetoric to "A Place of Learning."[6] But in his mind, it was actually a *propylaeum,* a gateway to the classical city. In the context of New Harmony, the name Atheneum derived from Robert Owen's renaming of George Rapp's Harmonie Church, in 1825, to make it clear that religion was being supplanted by reason. Following the English lead in Liverpool and London, the Atheneum was a vital part of early nineteenth-century urban culture in America, whose purpose was to introduce the wealthy and powerful to men of letters, as well as being a place to discuss the latest political news, science, art, literature, and public service.[7] The Philadelphia Athenaeum, which would have been the most directly associated with New Harmony through William Maclure, was founded in 1814 to collect materials "connected with the history and antiquities of America, and the useful arts, and generally to disseminate useful knowledge" for public benefit.

Schwarz tasked the building with providing visitors with the conceptual oversight that would bring the town into a continuous, cohesive whole: it would display maps, models, and a seventeen-minute film substantiated by views through expansive windows and balconies across the landscape and town. In this respect, the Atheneum is less a building than a three-dimensional telescope aligned to reveal the culture of New Harmony.[8] With this vision in place, it was possible to develop a program that could be conveyed to an architect.

Finding an architect to bring about Schwarz's vision required a leap of faith, as the protagonists of late modernism's vision of the past did not necessarily fit with the multivalent interpretation of history Schwarz believed in. Schwarz was looking for a post-structuralist thinker, someone whose philosophy and aesthetic would reveal how the internal mechanisms of thought and action could be opened up and made available for all to see. No architect had yet designed a public building of this nature, and Schwarz had the audacity to believe that one could do so.

Artistic and Conceptual Origins of the New Harmony Atheneum

In the early 1970s there was a controversy brewing that involved the emerging generation of New York and Philadelphia architects: the Whites and Grays, who had radically different approaches to the interpretation of history. Knowingly or unknowingly, Schwarz found himself in the middle of it.[9] On one side were the Whites, aligned with the Purist white architecture of Le Corbusier, to which they added a practice of aggressive collage making associated with Kurt Schwitters, Georges Braque, Pablo Picasso, and Juan Gris.[10] On the other side were the Grays, an eclectic band of contextualists, who believed that American Pop culture could cure the aridity of corporate modern architecture.[11] The Whites had the intellectual support of teacher and critic Colin Rowe and painter Robert Slutzky, coauthors of the essay "Transparency: Literal and Phenomenal," published in *Perspecta* in 1963.[12] The article was later printed as a book titled *Transparenz*, edited by Bernard Hoesli, who advocated for collage as a viable urban planning tool.[13] Rowe, with coauthor Fred Koetter, produced the equally important text *Collage City* (1978) that served as the Whites' manifesto on urbanism.[14]

The Whites and the Grays came of age in 1969, after *in camera* meetings and an exhibition at MIT of the Conference of Architects for the Study of the Environment (CASE).[15] The 1969 CASE meeting was hosted by Arthur Drexler at the Museum of Modern Art in New York and was the basis for the seminal book *Five Architects* of 1972, with essays by Rowe and Kenneth Frampton. The youthful White group, also dubbed the New York Five, was made up of Peter Eisenman (b. 1932), Michael Graves (1934–2015), Charles Gwathmey (1938–2009), John Hejduk (1929–2000), and Richard Meier (b. 1934). Under close scrutiny, they were architects whose differences varied considerably, despite the group's moniker.

The leader of the Grays was Philadelphia architect Robert Venturi, with Yale University's architectural historian Vincent Scully standing beside him as the intellectual counterpart of Rowe. Venturi wrote the seminal book *Complexity and Contradiction in Architecture* (1966), which he and his wife and partner, Denise Scott-Brown, followed with the no less provocative *Learning from Las Vegas,* written in 1972 with Steven Izenour. New York–based Robert A. M. Stern served as the voice of the Grays and organized a counterattack against the New York Five.[16]

Schwarz was familiar with the struggle between the two groups but made a counterintuitive move in not selecting an established architect in the Grays camp who was inspired by historic interpretation. In consultation with Kevin Roche, architect of the Ford Foundation Building, Schwarz chose an almost clean slate of young Whites to interview.[17] The Lilly Endowment Inc., an Indianapolis foundation supporting programs in religion, education, and community development, provided most of the funds for the New Harmony Visitor's Center. The Endowment did not require an architectural selection committee, so Schwarz had a relatively free hand in picking an architect.[18] He could have chosen any of the New York Five to design the Atheneum, for all of them became superstars in their own right, but he selected Meier because "he was so good at form" and was an energetic young architect who matched Schwarz's vision. Meier had made his name with startling white houses, built on steel frames and clad in glass and wood, and was just beginning to move to corporate and housing design projects.

Figure 7.2. Richard Meier with Ralph Schwarz in the Atheneum in 1978 or 1979. Schwarz sided with the "Whites" (New York Five architects) over the "Grays," architects representing postmodernism. Courtesy of Richard Meier & Partners Architects.

Despite the fact that Meier did not have a lot of experience with large buildings, choosing him was smart; he was a perfectionist who would also get the Atheneum built near budget.[19] The Atheneum would bring Meier enormous acclaim as his first large-scale cultural commission and set the tone for the Whites, museum architecture for the next quarter century.[20] Meier's combination of being a reflective craftsman as well as a deft politician would be key to getting the project financed and realized.

Taking a cue from Le Corbusier, who "painted in the morning, did architecture in the afternoon, and wrote at night," Meier was to master two of these three disciplines. Beginning as a painter on the periphery of the New York School, he shared a studio with Graves and later with artist Frank Stella, and from 1959 on he has regularly practiced collage making.[21] In a feature article that the Tokyo architectural journal *Global Architecture* published on the Atheneum, Meier writes about collage:

> The collage seeks paradoxically to reconcile the opposed conditions of order and disorder through a play of combined "found" and drawn elements. A single collage is not begun and finished by itself; on the contrary, works in various stages of development are left in notebooks and on the shelves of my studio, left sometimes for months or even years to their own period of development. A collage is often the result of many revisions. Each must be seen as an element in my total work; the collages are, for me, an adjunct and a passion related to my life as an architect.[22]

There is nothing groundbreaking about Meier's collage techniques or vision. They are a mix of Schwitters' Mertzbau, Braque, Picasso, Robert Rauschenberg, and especially Gris, whose collages were enormously influential for the Cooper Union community, where Meier taught between 1963 and 1973.[23] Apart from Schwitters, there is not much evidence of influence from the "bad boy" collagists (Marcel Duchamp, Francis Picabia, Max Ernst), who worked subversively with collage to overturn social or political mores by confronting the subject with humor and sexual innuendo. That sort of irreverence would have been much more appealing to the Grays. Meier's collages are more painterly, and the lineage he chose concerns form and the delight of a daily conversation with his world, as manifest by crumpled Air France luggage tags, crinkled cigar wrappers, a liberal quantity of public transportation tickets, and the occasional image of a naked woman. He even downplays the politically charged use of a picture of Che Guevara with his explanation: "The photograph of Che that I used was taken by a friend of mine, René Burri, so it is as much about René Burri as it is about Che" (Plate 25).[24] Paper collage was one influence, but he also "collaged" the technological and communication events of the period that influenced the design. In the talk "The Atheneum of New Harmony: Its Precedents and Impact on Preservation" given by Bernhard Karpf from Meier's office in April 2010, slides were shown of the Spacelab Station, Cunard's *Queen Elizabeth II* megaship, a maritime oil-drilling platform, a First World War German observation device, a wooden stereoscope, and a drive-in movie showing Charlton Heston in *The Ten Commandments*.

Designing the Building: Collage Writ Large

Meier began design of the Visitor's Center on July 15, 1975. Schwarz had selected a site on a rise at the northwest corner of town, a hundred yards from the Wabash River, adjacent to the mythologized landing site of the *Philanthropist* keelboat, which brought intellectuals to New Harmony on January 26, 1826.[25] It was clear from the beginning that this building's express purpose was to welcome the world and show that something new was happening in New Harmony, but it was not clear what the program for the building would be, for it evolved in a constant state of expansion and contraction during the design process.

During discussions over three weeks with media consultants, program consultants, and exhibition designers, Schwarz visited Meier's Fifty-seventh Street office in New York, where the design quickly took form. Schwarz formulated the program of the building but did not discuss the architectural idiom with Meier. The conceptual phase of the commission was open and conversational in response to Schwarz's vision; a restaurant was considered, as was a conference center and amphitheater, but these were later deleted so that these parts of Schwarz's concept for New Harmony could exist elsewhere in town. When asked to reflect on the Atheneum, Schwarz had this to say:

I never thought of the Atheneum as a building, which would provide space for offices, museum collections, major interpretative exhibitions in detail, food, or a gift shop. There was, however, one exception, a discrete desk for ticketing. Not unlike the Lincoln Memorial, the Atheneum is an Icon, an inspired place of arrival, introduction, reflection, circulation to elevated planes and over-views, a gateway down the ramp into the historic community, where the contribution of two utopian societies can still be appreciated. When Thomas Jefferson designed the Rotunda at the University of Virginia, there was no question as to what it would be used for. It was to be used as a Rotunda. The Atheneum is an end in itself. It delivers its own inspired utopian message.[26]

Once the conceptual phase was over, Meier generated freehand plans and cardboard models for three schematic designs for the Visitor's Center in various states of spatial undress. The plans and models went from being a cluster of buildings and an assemblage of objects to a singular building reaching into the landscape. The first study model was more of a compound than an object. As it turned out, the building was to become a compound-object, instilled with both categories of spatial representation. The most expansive version spread the building into half a dozen components scattered across the site. Meier was assembling deconstructivist architecture before the phrase had been coined.[27] Schwarz chose the most compact design, and Meier's office produced a schematic design for the Visitor's Center on August 18, 1975 (Figure 7.5). The site plan of the design was figurative in a cubist sort of way.[28] The composition appeared to be a cross between one of Mondrian's diamond paintings and a Gris collage-painting of a guitar. The orientation center formed the torso, beneath which was the rounded bottom of the amphitheater. On a long extruded neck to the north were a conference center and food facility. To the left and right, skinny arms extended toward the Wabash River and the town. A big, flat foot made up the transport component of the program, which included car parking, bicycle racks, and golf cart rental. A generous reflecting pool was set to the west, whose northern part was in the form of a quarter circle and its southern part, a square. Most of this program would not survive.

The building started with a square plan split in half, with a five-degree wedge, a "shift," as Meier termed it, inserted from below.[29] The right lobe was a serene rectangular form: the theater for state-of-the-art media presentations, which takes on the appearance of a well-proportioned golden rectangle.[30] Meier used geometry to generate open-ended form:

> The Atheneum is not about a singular space but about multiple spaces: there are other considerations, in terms of the vertical dimension, in terms of the height, than the Golden Section. I never check at the end of the design process if I know it [the golden section] is there, but I did start there.[31]

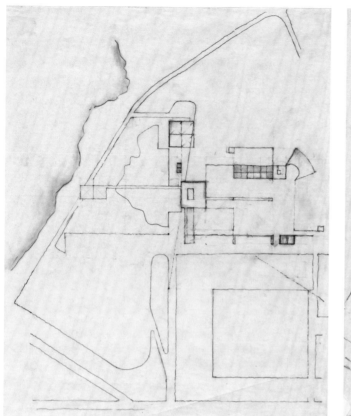
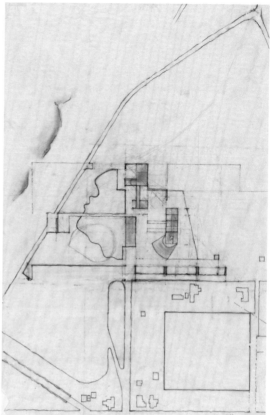

Figure 7.3. Schematic designs of the Visitor's Center, New Harmony, showing programmatic components dispersed in three different configurations, 1975. The forms chosen for the plans make reference to the cubist paintings of Braque, Picasso, and Gris. Drawings courtesy of Richard Meier & Partners Architects. Digital images copyright The Museum of Modern Art. Licensed by SCALA / Art Resource, NY.

To the left of the wedge, on the west, are circulation and the exhibition galleries. The *parti* has all the hallmarks of a 1920s cubist painting of a guitar. In a lower plan there is a voluptuous curve of the guitar shoulder forming the panoramic window; the round hole in the soundboard is the void where a large model of New Harmony was to be placed, and the tapered neck leads north to the restaurant. The plan of the Atheneum was tightened at the second level, where one feels the emergence of the diagonally rotated square that hovers over the west half of the design. The hole is literally a hole in the floor, framing a bird's-eye view of the model of New Harmony below, not unlike the view of New Harmony from the hill to the south known as Indian Mound. Each of the square and diagonal forms is tagged with a scissor staircase leading out of the building. The five-degree wedge has become a three-rise ramp that leads up to the theater on the second level. The third level shows the juxtaposition of the golden rectangle proportion of the theater, adjacent to the diagonally situated room for seminars and contemplation, with a view to the north of the cocktail lounge in the restaurant building.

Figure 7.4. Model of schematic design for the Visitor's Center, studying the sculptural qualities of a dispersed program, 1975. Only the torso of the building would remain, and the program within the limbs was later canceled. Courtesy of Richard Meier & Partners Architects.

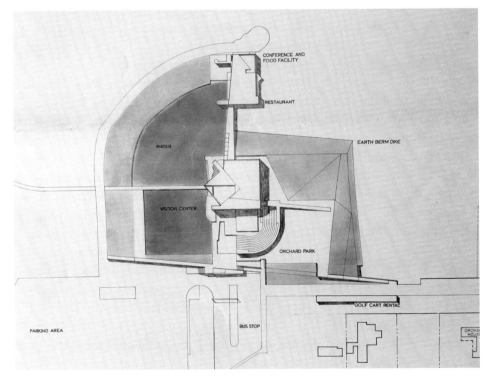

Figure 7.5. Detail of schematic design showing conference center and restaurant to the north, amphitheater and park to the south, reflecting pools and pavilion on Wabash River to the west, and the Visitor's Center at the midpoint, August 18, 1975. Drawing courtesy of Richard Meier & Partners Architects. Image from the Collections of Historic New Harmony / University of Southern Indiana.

A door from the theater leads out to a long step-ramp descending to ground level and the town beyond.

The history of architecture is full of defining moments where a concept is introduced in a drawing and then enters into the canon of built projects. One such moment was the axis shift, "a five-degree wedge" as Meier termed it, which jolts the orthogonal plan a few degrees, creating an overlay akin to double vision and an opening ripe for spatial intrigue, a perceptual mechanism that resonated with the Whites. The Atheneum was one of the first public buildings in which this spatial device was used to great effect, but it was not a design methodology that originated in Meier's studio. During the mid-1970s the Princeton School of Architecture, where Graves held sway, produced student thesis projects that included the axis shift, and the fewer degrees that the shift made, the more daring the digression. Princeton graduates were in demand in New York, and their work and sensibility can be felt in this scheme. Where else would the chalky white sections drawn in high relief on orange card stock have come from, or design concepts such as the axis shift? (Plate 26). They were certainly not a part of Meier's Cornell education. Buildings that emanate from an architecture office reflect the vision of the principal, but they are also subject to the creative energy of the young people who work on the schemes and the new concepts they bring from the cosmopolitan architecture schools in the vanguard.

The schematic design for the Visitor's Center was Meier's response to Schwarz's program for a three-story building that would function as both an internal and an external promenade. It was a place of circulation that shattered walls by using ramps and stairs to explore multiple views from the many surfaces. The scheme would not have a roof per se, but an extensive series of terraces and balconies from which visitors could survey the town. The building is in a state of rotation, which blurs the conventions of inside and outside, yet is still connected to the river and the town.[32] Schwarz envisioned that the path from the town, through the Atheneum to the river, would lead to a boat ramp for river tours on the Wabash, no doubt recalling the arrival of the *Philanthropist* keelboat in 1826.[33]

Meier made a set of preliminary plans for the Visitor's Center on September 2, 1975. This version places the restaurant in the floodplain to the west, attached to the orientation center by a raised boardwalk. It was rejected, but, had it been built, it would have made for an especially dramatic site for the restaurant, as every few years the building would be standing in the floodwaters of the Wabash River. An executive decision was then made to keep the restaurant out of the floodplain and to expand the project to the east, toward the town. On September 23, 1975, the Lilly Endowment approved the schematic design concept and awarded preliminary funding. The project was now good to go.

Once Meier's exploratory designs were approved, the building dropped its title of Visitor's Center and was now called the Atheneum. The next iteration of the design

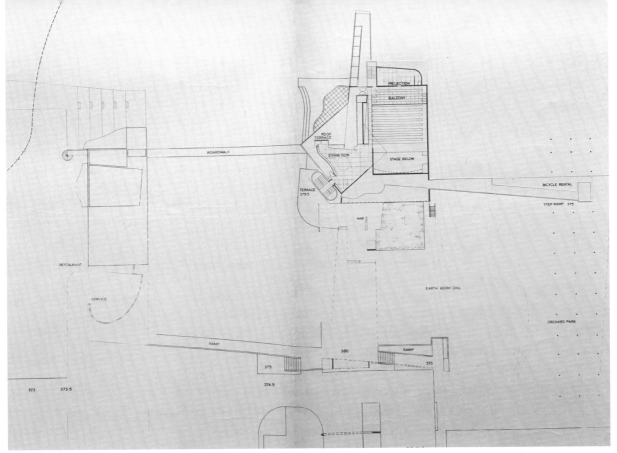

Labels visible in the plan: PROJECTION, BALCONY, ROOF TERRACE, BOARDWALK, EXHIBITION, STAGE BELOW, BICYCLE RENTAL, STEP RAMP 375, TERRACE 379.5, MAP, EARTH BERM DIKE, ORCHARD PARK, RESTAURANT, SERVICE, RAMP, RAMP, 380, 375, 375, 374.5, 373, 373.5

Figure 7.6. Preliminary plan of the Visitor's Center ground floor, with restaurant to the west in the Wabash floodplain, September 2, 1975. The building becomes criss-crossed with ramps and stairs within which the exhibits and views of the landscape are intermingled. Drawing courtesy of Richard Meier & Partners Architects. Image from the Collections of Historic New Harmony / University of Southern Indiana.

was named Scheme I, and sketches show a large secondary building for cultural and intellectual pursuits landscaped into the raised plinth of the building. A ramp leads out of the Atheneum and cuts through a long box called the Theatrum, set above an amphitheater holding the restaurant and conference center. The panoply of circulation systems in the Atheneum was supplemented by an elevator, which was later abandoned.

A fourth group of design drawings was prepared on October 16, 1975, that shed the painterly collage origins of the scheme. The drawings addressed the difficult task of making things fit while not losing sight of the conceptual origins of the design. A study model gives the sense of the architect walking around a corner, seeing light from above or off to one side. The whole three-dimensional construct is now in Meier's head. He need only draw what he envisions internally to make the spaces come to life. From the detritus of the drafting room floor only one or two sections and axonometric drawings remain, hastily drawn on skinny tracing paper.[34] The orientation center was a design that pushed the methodological limits of hand-drawn plans, sections, elevations, and axonometrics, prior to the use of computers. In the experience of walking through the building today, one still senses the graphic techniques of the 1970s. Scheme I was drawn up on November 10, 1975.

Meier focused on resolving the complexities of the Atheneum, with a nod to the Modern Masters. The circulation systems likely took cues from Le Corbusier's

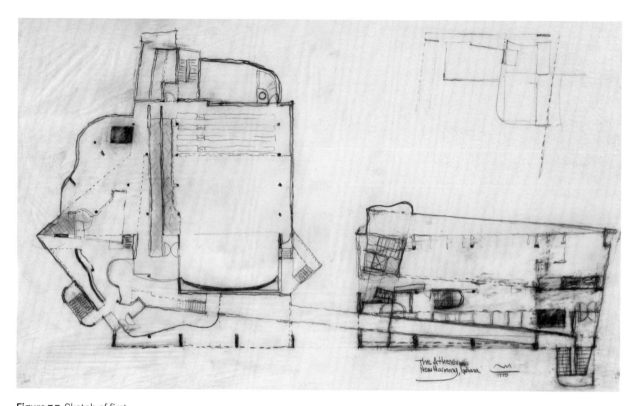

Figure 7.7. Sketch of first floor for scheme I of the Visitor's Center, now named the Atheneum, Fall 1975. A ramp connects to a conference center and restaurant toward the east. All the major elements of the Atheneum are now in place, but the conference center and restaurant were later abandoned. Drawing courtesy of Richard Meier & Partners Architects.

promenade architecturale at the Carpenter Center at Harvard University, completed in 1962, as well as the spiraling routes of Wright's Guggenheim Museum in New York, finished in 1959. Elements of the Whites' lodestone, Le Corbusier's Villa Savoie, are in evidence as well. The intricacies of the program were fit into every nook and cranny of the colliding, shifting forms of diagonal, orthogonal, and curved lines, and lifts the building out of the reach of Mies van der Rohe's orthogonality. Another aspect of Le Corbusier's work, to which Meier paid homage, was the metaphor of the building-as-ship. Not only is the Atheneum surrounded on three sides by water in the irregular spring flood cycle of the Wabash, but the metal stair gantries and railings would take their cue from ship-building detailing of the 1920s and 1930s.

In a pencil drawing from this period, which shows Meier's thoughts on his buildings fitting into an urban context, Meier draws a site plan that shows the Atheneum in the context of the Wabash River and town of New Harmony. Prominently drawn is the curve of the river, the stark square walls of the Harmonist cemetery, Johnson's Roofless Church, Meier's own design for the Sarah Campbell Blaffer Potter's House, and Zion's landscape interpretation of Frederick Kiesler's Paul Tillich Park. The whole composition is a procession of connections, mediated by curves and straight lines, that passes from the wildness of the uncontrollable river to the Cartesian grid structure of the town.

Much like the relationship between the British architectural group Archigram

Figure 7.8, left. Study model with interior view of theater, oriented toward the south (and later oriented to the north), Fall 1975. The theater plan is proportioned with the golden mean, around which the circulation and exhibit space are ordered on fractured grids. Courtesy of Richard Meier & Partners Architects.

Figure 7.9, below. Scheme I, second-level plan of the Atheneum, with conference center, restaurant, and amphi-theater to the east, November 10, 1975. Components of the building are collaged together, around shifting axes and grids. Drawing courtesy of Richard Meier & Partners Architects. From the Collections of Historic New Harmony / University of Southern Indiana.

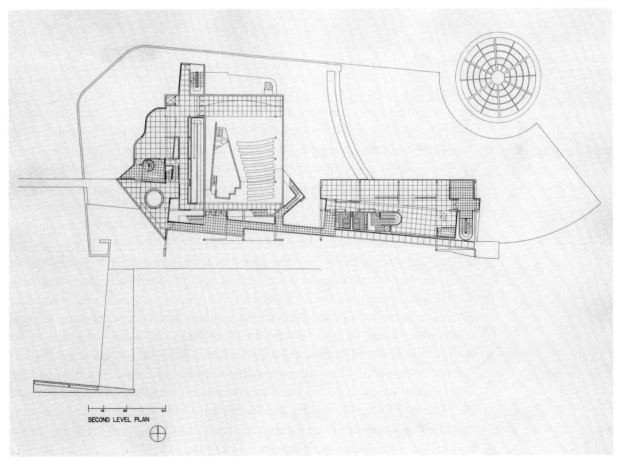

SECOND LEVEL PLAN

Figure 7.10. The ship metaphor of Le Corbusier is reflected in the decks, stairs, and rails of the Atheneum, especially during regular flooding of the Wabash River. Photograph courtesy of Ben Nicholson, 2008.

and the architectural team of Piano & Rogers, who solidified Archigram's hypothetical designs in the Pompidou Centre in Paris in 1977, Meier might have had difficulty visualizing this design had he not been privy to the *Nine Square Problem* developed by Hejduk at Cooper Union's architecture school and Slutzky's *Two Dimensional / Color Exercises* in collage. Meier occasionally taught at the Cooper Union architecture school[35] and was building Hejduk's academic *Nine Square Problem* in the round and for real, enriched by Slutzky's collage *Exercises* in a feat of spatial imagination and gymnastics that few have equaled.[36]

The Whites were known for their use of three-dimensional axonometric or isometric drawings. The beauty of the axonometric drawing is that it has no vanishing points. Consequentially, the Atheneum sits in a papery lacuna tenuously attached to the landscape by skinny paths, with nothing but itself and its articulate internal mechanisms to suggest a new spatial direction. The axonometric drawing belongs to the canon of technical drawings associated with Citroën motorcars and Messerschmitt fighter planes. It had no truck with the engineering diagrams of the Miesians or the vibrant splashes of color favored by the postmodern Grays. Some of the Grays did work with axonometric, but historically grounded perspective drawing, with its graduated vanishing points leading off into classical pastoral and postindustrial landscapes, was more their medium.[37]

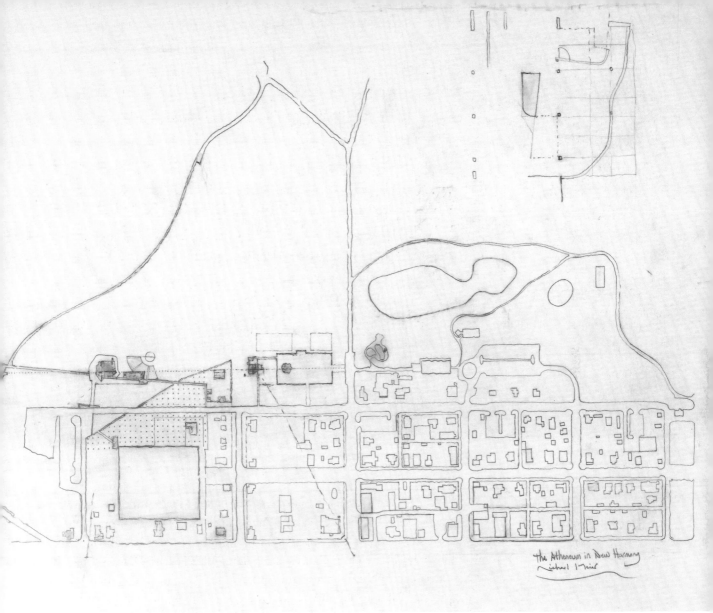

The Atheneum in New Harmony

Figure 7.11. Site plan, September 1975. The Wabash River, boat landing, Harmonist Cemetery, Atheneum, Potter's House, Roofless Church, Tillich Park, and New Harmony Inn are connected by a dynamic series of curves and straight lines along North Street. Drawing courtesy of Richard Meier & Partners Architects.

Late in 1975, a fifth group of presentation drawings of the unbuilt design were prepared in ink to be published in Meier's first monograph.[38] These included a highly crafted axonometric drawing, a view from the south, and for the first time a representation showing the connections of the interior spaces and the layered overlapping of the facade planes. The measured spatial complexity of the building could now be clearly understood. The drawing showed a scissor-form seating plan, later abandoned, arranged in front of a curved screen-wall in the theater that is now oriented to the north. Had it been kept, the seated audience would have experienced the dramatic grid shifts that permeate the rest of the building. The as-built solution for the theater offers a respite from the drama of the entrance ramps. On the west facade, the outside stair of the earlier solution was abandoned. In its place was a

275

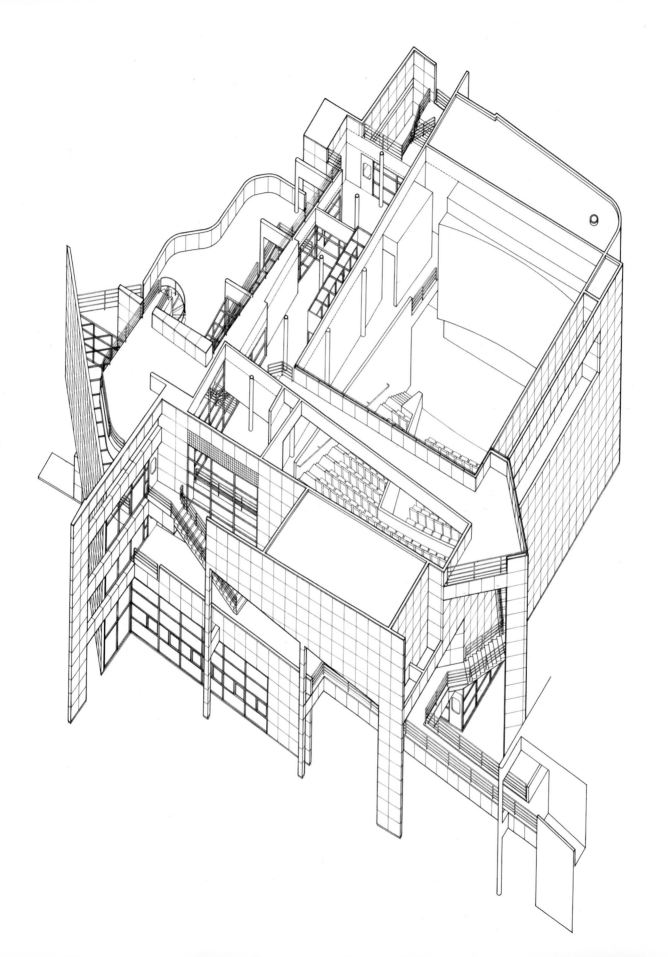

Figure 7.12. Axonometric drawing of the Visitor's Center, highlighting the two lobes of the design, 1976. The exhibition galleries are in the left lobe, and the south-facing theater is in the right lobe. Perspective drawing was eschewed for axonometric drawing, which preferences a homogenized hierarchy of building components that better reflects the neo-Purist vision. Drawing courtesy of Richard Meier & Partners Architects.

diagonal facade pierced by the pillbox doorway in the northwest corner. The set of drawings was complemented by an immaculate white model, now in the collection of the Museum of Modern Art (Plate 27).[39] The schematic design phase was coming to a close, but it happened too slowly to keep up with the initial timetable. The September 2, 1975, schedule called for completion of construction documents by December 12, 1975, yet only Scheme I, a set of fifteen plans, sections, and elevations at a quarter inch to one foot, had been finished by December 16, 1975.

Over the new year of 1976, a major reassessment occurred. The amphitheater, restaurant, and conference center were abandoned.[40] Meier was left with a stand-alone "object" building into which he could pack a multidimensional spatial construct, where the object and the cluster of volumes became united. Throughout the design process Meier and Schwarz's program had been kept in flux.[41] The drawings now confirmed the extent of the building's program, and it was time for its logic to be announced in public. Meier's first scheme was published in the Italian magazine *Parametro* and then in the monograph *Richard Meier Architect: Buildings and Projects, 1966–76*.[42] In stilted, self-conscious prose, Meier tells his story about the meaning of the project, now called the Atheneum.[43] In the first paragraph he refers to Stedman Whitwell's design for the "Community" in New Harmony, sometimes referred to as the "Phalanstery," a model town for two thousand workers dropped into the forest in the guise of a Georgian London square (Figure 7.13; Plate 8).[44] Meier was intrigued by the utopian dimension of Whitwell's tabula rasa project for Robert Owen, and he was just as impressed by an 1835 bird's-eye view of New Harmony, attributed to French naturalist artist Charles-Alexandre Lesueur, showing the square, gridded town set in the pristine wilderness (Figure I.6).[45] Meier found contextual justifications for his design that was a departure from orthodox modernism. His stance would have impressed Venturi's Grays in Philadelphia, where, coincidentally, much of the intellectual backbone of Robert Owen's New Harmony had come from, through William Maclure and the Academy of Natural Sciences.[46]

Meier summarized the Atheneum in this way:

> The Atheneum (the term means a literary or scientific association) is intended as a center for visitor orientation and community cultural events. It will be a public gathering place in physical and visual proximity to the Wabash River, an "event" by the water's edge. Building in the flood plain is not without problems, as the Wabash

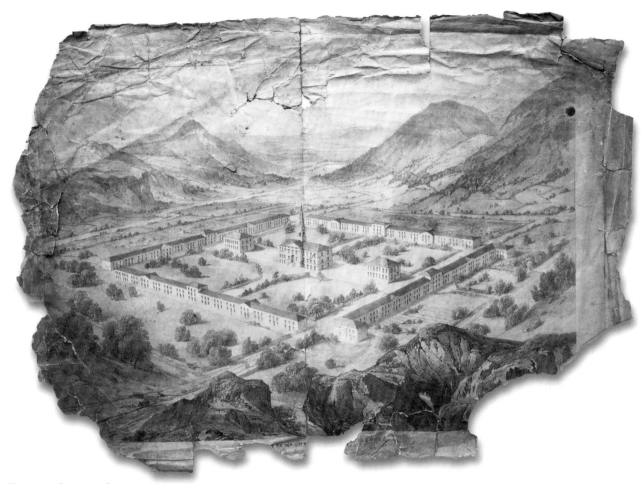

Figure 7.13. "View . . . of Mr. Owen's . . . Villages." The print fragment shows a stripped-down version of Stedman Whitwell's Gothic-inspired "Design for a Community of 2000 Persons" that was an inspiration for Meier's Atheneum. Whitwell's project was known as the "Phalanstery" in the 1970s, drawing from Fourier's "Phalanstères." Drawing courtesy of Caroline Dale Lewis, New Harmony.

floods to varying heights every year. These natural problems influenced the planning throughout the design process for this project, and the siting has been determined as a response to the threat of annual floods. The new building maintains the existing street grid, and yet the public gathering spaces relate to the water.

The Atheneum is a place of arrival, an interpretation and orientation center, and the beginning of circulation for the tour of the town. Movement spaces can be places of initiation: this is the beginning of a route. The intention of the design solution is to function as a transitional element, a link between two different worlds—even a link between the past and the present. The entire movement system is a continuous experience, in which the building is a place of social interaction that is linked finally with the town of New Harmony itself.

Meier goes on to discuss the way the building is organized conceptually and physically:

The building complex has two dispositions. Its predominant order is orthogonal in response to the existing street grid of the town, as every new structure should respect the presence of this grid of the landscape. But the form of the building is influenced by the diagonal random edge of the town. The organization of the plan ultimately draws

BEN NICHOLSON

everyone to the center of the building, to an interior ramped space that becomes the building's armature, with the major spaces arranged around it. This ramped circulation spine, as it leads from the entry-orientation level up through the exhibition and lounge spaces to the film center, serves as a key to the comprehension of the building.

The restaurant is located adjacent to The Atheneum, reinforcing the function of the other, externalized, circulatory route as a major orienting feature. The amphitheater provides an outdoor background for events, with vistas to the open country and the water. The exterior ramp links the building complex with the site, thus dramatizing the continuity between the present and the past.[47]

Finally, he states his "evolutionary" attitude toward placing a building, a quite different approach than the Modern Masters of the recent past.

The task being addressed here is that of conceiving a building as an extension of a single place, as a foreshadowing of the experience the visitor will have, and offering an evolutionary experience within an historic context. In my view, there are two ways in which a building may be related to its site: one is to make it textually similar, to imitate what is already there; the other is to allow the building to acknowledge the more general aspects of the context, to order it in such a way that it recognizes and responds to its surroundings, and invites a reciprocal involvement. The design approach here was to express this latter attitude toward the pre-existing physical context, differentiating architecturally between public and private spaces, between individual activity and communal activity.

Figure 7.14. Erection of steelwork and decks of the Atheneum, 1977. The raw forms of colliding floor plates and circulation patterns are on full display. Photographer unknown. From the Collections of Historic New Harmony / University of Southern Indiana.

279

With the design phase concluded, Meier concentrated on getting everything into a single building envelope. Subsequent design changes were minor: the major change being to extend the promenade out over the top of the building to a much larger viewing platform overlooking the town to the east. The building was a labyrinth of circulation patterns, an encyclopedia of ways of moving through space. A programmatic decision was made to move the "1825 Model" of New Harmony from the ground floor to a dedicated balcony on the second level. The scale model is a realistic depiction of central New Harmony in 1825, at the transition of the Harmonist and Owen-Maclurean eras. Like a precious jewel, it is placed in a voluptuous display case that seems to be suspended in thin air.[48] Meier translated the former cubist hole-in-the-floor into something of substance. The model was to be top lit by daylight leaking down the west wall from a long gap in the third floor, supplemented by light from the adjacent glazed exterior "room," where a sculptural spiral stair curls up to the skies above. The design phase concluded on March 25, 1976, when Meier sent out the forty-four contract drawings for construction bids. The Evansville contractor Peyronnin Construction Company won the contract and during the next three and a half years constructed the building.

The Sarah Campbell Blaffer Potter's House (1975)

With the design of the Atheneum finished, Meier was invited by Jane Owen to design a pottery studio. Since she had not financed the Atheneum, the commission would keep her in the loop of Schwarz's relationship with Meier. The studio was completed in 1978, a year before the Atheneum, and was dedicated to her mother, who believed in both fine art and the crafts. This two-pronged interest was not lost on Owen, whose own taste in art leaned toward the passionate rather than the intellectual. The dedication plaque reads:

> As Sarah Campbell Blaffer believed that creative crafts deserve the instruction, support, and honor accorded the fine arts, this studio for pottery is dedicated to this philosophy and to the quest for quality: the mainspring of her life.[49]

Owen asked Meier for a humble building by a great architect. Meier listened to her vision, and they decided on a site between the Atheneum and the Roofless Church for the low, one-story building, which would not reach higher than the twelve-foot walls of the Roofless Church (Plate 24). Owen liked to think of the Atheneum and the Potter's House as shining white Greek marble figures, representing the mind and the hand, each speaking Greek to the other.[50] The Sarah Campbell Blaffer Potter's House lasted twenty-five years before it failed structurally and climatically.[51] The wood roof rotted in the humid atmosphere of the moist river bottoms. The operable windows to foster cross breezes in the studio had jammed, and the pristine white walls were constantly getting dirty from smears of clay and clouds of dust. After Owen's exhausting fight with Johnson over the crumbling walls of the Roofless Church in the mid-1970s, as well as her difficulties with Frederick Kiesler in the 1960s, she took direction and ordered Meier's building to be demolished in 2002. A vernacular shed designed by the local builder was put up in its place, painted the color of clay and laid out according to the needs of the resident potter.[52]

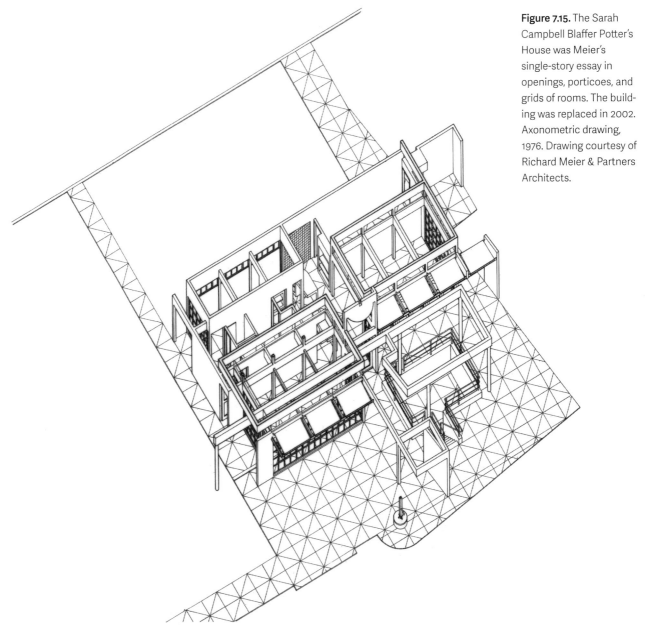

Figure 7.15. The Sarah Campbell Blaffer Potter's House was Meier's single-story essay in openings, porticoes, and grids of rooms. The building was replaced in 2002. Axonometric drawing, 1976. Drawing courtesy of Richard Meier & Partners Architects.

Critics and Photographers Form the Image of the Atheneum

The Atheneum took much longer to build than the anticipated nine months allocated in the 1975 schedule, but it was constructed close to its budget of $1,600,000.[53] Schwarz had wanted the building's dedication to occur on the two-hundredth anniversary of the Declaration of Independence on July 4, 1976, but that did not happen.[54] When the Atheneum was completed in 1979, an enthusiastic reaction from the press made up for the disappointing delays. The project graced the cover of the first issue of *Global Architecture Document 1*.[55] Ada Louise Huxtable hailed it in the *New York Times* as "the kind of development that has always marked the change from one period of art to another; it is the way Mannerism and the Baroque grew out of the Renaissance."[56] The only reservations, in an otherwise glowing review, were voiced by Kenneth Frampton, who cautioned it is "a building bereft of its need, like a thing to be visited, not to be used"—a penetrating observation that has been vindicated by the experiences of successive executive directors, who still wonder what the purpose of the building is.[57] Since its inauguration, unusual exhibition and performance solutions have been held in the space.[58]

Figure 7.16. Cover of *Global Architecture* 60, featuring Yukio Futagawa's color photograph of the south facade of the Atheneum. The Atheneum was photographed by both modernist and postmodernist photographers, who projected markedly different sensibilities of the same structure. Photograph courtesy of Ben Nicholson, 2015.

Richard Meier & Associates
The Atheneum, New Harmony, Indiana. 1975-79
Edited and Photographed by Yukio Futagawa
Text by Paul Goldberger

The dedication of the Atheneum was accompanied by the exhibition *Richard Meier: Collages and Architectural Drawings* at the New Harmony Gallery of Contemporary Art. The show included seven Atheneum drawings, two Pottery Shed drawings, fourteen collages, six unspecified framed items, and a black wooden bench and lectern.[59] Meier also worked with the print-making department of the University of Evansville to produce a lithograph of the Atheneum in an edition of seventy-five copies. It is revealing that there were so many collages in the exhibition and that one of them, *Collage Che—New Harmony Exhibit* (1977), has all the markings of the Atheneum's spaces (Plate 25). The collage is composed of a large green square set down in a blood-red field. Along the top edge is a string of colored panels that lead to nowhere. The middle is a flickering compote of bus tickets, and a dominant photograph of Che Guevara stares out from the void. He shares with the public his parallel artistic practice to his design process of building, without committing to a one-to-one transfer.

Apart from incisive initial critiques, the building was depicted in different ways.[60] The black-and-white

photographs made in 1979 by Ezra Stoller show the Atheneum's spaces in highly articulated light, full of graphic contrast and from dizzying angles made possible by the high level of camera lens design of the time. Futagawa's photographs, made for the first issue of his *Global Architecture* (1980), show the building in a blaze of color, demonstrating Meier's proposition that his white building is full of hued light reflected from the verdant landscape.[61] Futagawa's photographs clearly make the relationship between Meier's vibrantly colored collages and his articulate white buildings: they see them as one and the same production. The Atheneum was one of the first buildings involved in the transition from black-and-white to color photography in architectural publishing. Stoller's stark photographs of the building serve as the grand finale of modernist black-and-white photography. Stoller did make color photographs of the Atheneum, but they appear awkward. Futagawa caught the energy of the place.[62]

Building as Collage: Walking In and Out and Around and About

Having established that the design of the Atheneum was driven by collage, one might ask how, when walking about the building, does two-dimensional collage translate to bodily experience? Meier applied pictorial planar collage to the three plans of the building; how does that technique translate when stretched out into three dimensions, when the three composed plans come into each other's realm?[63] Meier made extensive use of the section to resolve the collision of the three plans. Each section has a well-tempered orthogonality, composed of rectangles punctuated by spiral or scissor stairs. Some of his sections have the graceful hand strokes and geometric machinations of the collage-driven plans, but these were made for exhibition purposes after the design process. There is only a hint that the *intellect* of the building was worked through in section. The section was no more than a *tool* that brought the plans into reconciliation with each other. The fallout of this is that when the building is visited, it is hard to find those moments of sublimity where the thoughtfulness of the plans and the labor of the section feel comfortable together.

The technique of using two different drawing methodologies has consequences. Axonometric representation introduces such a spatial distortion to the junction of the z axis to the x and y axes that it does not help clarify what is going on spatially. Meier supplemented the spatial maelstrom with hand-drawn perspectives to be able to figure out what the spaces were going to be like when built. Had Meier designed the sections in a technique of painterly collage, rather than through conventional section cuts, the building may well have had the roundedness he was after. Nevertheless, with this building he broke through the conceptual barrier of the rectangular modernist plan.[64] The outcome of this experimentation with drawing convention is that the Atheneum is a collection of discrete moments, many of which are masterful.

A circumambulation of the building displays radically different facades clad in large sheets of glass and thirty-inch square and curved white-enameled steel panels.[65] Numerologists and proportion disciples might hope that the tiled walls pay homage to the architectural past, but no such luck. The walls are proportioned with a scatter of ratios without an overriding logic. The one or two standard architectural proportions that Meier used might as well be put down to happenstance rather than erudition.[66] The southwest side, facing the parking lot, forms a big white wall that feels like a negation of the building, the white canvas of the painter. It has a huge chunk cut out of the lower left corner into which the entrance box is inserted. Walking to the right in a counterclockwise direction, the building displays itself through big plate-glass windows that enable one to peer into all three levels. The facade is lanced from the east by a long step-ramp leading down to the town. Walking beneath the ramp or around it, visitors amble into a meadow. Looking back at the building, one sees its least photogenic aspect. It is big and plain and has a menacing feel, like confronting the majestic Moby Dick for the first time but beached on the banks of the Wabash. In all likelihood, the blank wall was the result of a large chunk of the program being removed during the design process and left unresolved. The second half of the circumambulation rolls around to the northeast, and the building comes back into view and returns to life. A double recurve wall, responding to the bends in the river, is nestled between the stair tower to the north and the wall, set at forty-five degrees, that hangs over the entrance box. From this view you see the entrails of the building, and it is deeply satisfying to look at.

Now visitors are ready to go into the building through the main door. But before doing so, one should remember that there are about a dozen doors into the building, a few situated at every level. The pillbox west entrance is set among the protruding,

Figure 7.18. The curved wall of the Atheneum, recalling the cubist and neo-Purist iconic guitar form and the meanders of the Wabash River. Northwest elevation, 1979. Photographer unknown. From the Collections of Historic New Harmony / University of Southern Indiana.

angular upper decks, simultaneously welcoming the visitors and keeping them at arm's length. In the lobby, the ramp to the upper levels hangs dangerously out into the space.[67] The ramp turns back and forth three times, and one can feel how difficult it must have been to fit in, as the angle of inclination requires so much space. Once you begin your pilgrimage up the ramp, you come face-to-face with the magnificent, often-photographed white branching column in the center of the building. It has the appearance of a native sycamore tree, with a firm trunk and a tangle of cantilevered white horizontal branches. You get the sense that this is the structure of the building from which everything hangs. The column stands at the place where the five-degree shift becomes a wedge driven into the building between the rectangular theater and the contortions of the circulation. The presence of the five-degree angle of the wedge is almost impossible to perceive in the building, for the white tree-column blocks it. It reveals itself as a misshapen square at the base of an indented column by the door leading to the step-ramp, in a witty homage to Mies's indented corner. The five-degree shift is also acknowledged in the trapezoid footprint of the exterior standing column to the south. In moments such as these, the vivacious building confirms its architectural heritage and affords glimpses of the sublime. The aroma of ineffable space is present and heralds the majestic power that Meier's later buildings accrue.

Figure 7.19, right. The main entrance of the Atheneum, set beneath pointed walls that both welcome visitors and put them on guard. Parts of the building's form anticipated deconstructivist architecture. West elevation, 1979. Photograph courtesy of Ben Nicholson, 2017.

Figure 7.20, opposite. Section through interior corner column, showing the junction of the two main lobes of the Atheneum, meeting at a five-degree angle. This small detail is the hinge around which the building's design rotates. Drawing courtesy of Richard Meier & Partners Architects. From the Collections of Historic New Harmony / University of Southern Indiana.

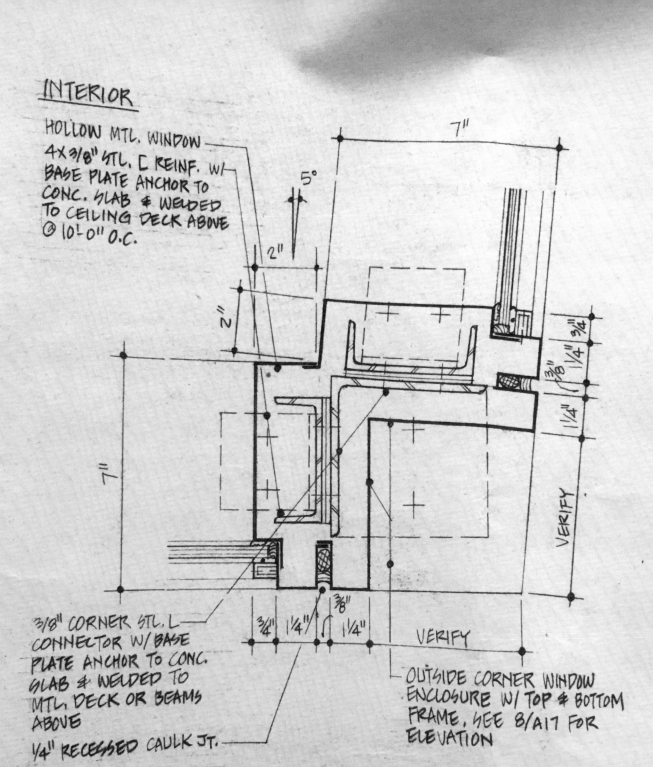

INTERIOR

HOLLOW MTL. WINDOW
4 X 3/8" STL. L REINF. W/
BASE PLATE ANCHOR TO
CONC. SLAB & WELDED
TO CEILING DECK ABOVE
@ 10'-0" O.C.

7"

5°

2"

2"

7"

3/8"
1/4"
3/4"
1/4"

VERIFY

3/4" 1 1/4" 3/8" 1 1/4"

VERIFY

3/8" CORNER STL. L
CONNECTOR W/ BASE
PLATE ANCHOR TO CONC.
SLAB & WELDED TO
MTL. DECK OR BEAMS
ABOVE

1/4" RECESSED CAULK JT.

OUTSIDE CORNER WINDOW
ENCLOSURE W/ TOP & BOTTOM
FRAME, SEE 8/A17 FOR
ELEVATION

EXTERIOR

(11 / A 17) **OUTSIDE CORNER**

When visitors walk into the Atheneum, it is rare to hear gasps of incredulity. Breathtaking beauty escapes eager visitors. Instead, one has the feeling of being in the presence of an accomplished virtuoso who has hit almost all the notes in a newly invented composition. The Atheneum has the quality of cocky adolescence, necessary to the evolution of architecture and an enormous contribution, but not yet transcendent.[68]

A note that reaches the desired pitch is the model vitrine on the second-level mezzanine. As you walk around the form, it changes radically. At one moment it has a meteor-like stability; then it lifts up and rapturously ascends through the skylights. This oversized object both defies and embraces gravity. One side of the mezzanine looks onto a glass light-well filled with the spiral stair that joins the terraces above. A door leads visitors into this remarkable space, which feels like a secret garden of light in which you are surrounded by three glass walls and the fourth, set at a forty-five-degree angle, is a pointed balcony with an expansive vista across the floodplain to the river. From this vantage point you understand that the building's elevations are as valuable when seen *from* as they are when *looked at*: the Atheneum moves and you move with it.[69]

Another great moment in the building is the theater. Here the east wall pulls away from itself; the building's inner rotation of five degrees separates the layers of the wall, and it exfoliates spatially, in a searing display of draftsmanship. The windows are smartly located. One skinny window is set at ninety degrees to the main ply of the wall and has an operable cloth-blind to close out the light. When opened, the light rakes across the wall's surface; when closed, it brings the space of the wall to a full stop in a dark shadow. In this room Meier's remark that natural light is his favorite building material makes sense.[70] The other window, to the north, is a big square with a cross in its center, reminiscent of a Russian constructivist painting. Inside it, a massive door lumbers across the window plane to the tune of electric servomotors to shut out the light when the orientation film is running. As the show closes, the door slides open to reveal the projected landscapes in the film to seamlessly morph into the real landscape outside the window.

An enormous, free-floating movie screen, pushed out from the wall with a generous shadow around its edges, takes up the north wall, and an acoustical plane hovers beneath the black ceiling, suspended in thin air above theatergoers' heads. All the surfaces of the theater seem to exfoliate. Visitors are on their toes in expectation because the room breathes an atmosphere of imminent inward collapse. Meier's

Figure 7.21. The vitrine for the 1825 Model of New Harmony, seemingly suspended between two floors of the Atheneum. In Meier's early design drawings, this form had been a hole in the floor, which in turn had reflected a cubist painting of the body of a guitar. Photograph courtesy of Ben Nicholson, 2015.

other accomplishment in the auditorium is the unusual seating, onto which he deftly rolled his signature gray carpet over every surface: seats, stage, and all. It appears as if the seating has pushed up through a membrane of carpet and the floor plane is rippled with waves of gray seats that run all the way through the space.

Caretaking, Preserving, and Curating the Atheneum Forty Years On

After a major renovation in 2001–2 to prolong the life of the building before it rusts away and is swept down the Wabash, the Atheneum still stands as testament to the moment when American design culture challenged its own newly invented public modernist architecture of the postwar period. Today the Atheneum is not the same as it once was because Schwarz's vision of its use has grown faint. Attempts over the years have been made to insert exhibitions or upgrade the facility by administrators and designers who struggle to understand the conceptual and programmatic underpinning of the project. In retrofits, exhibition cases were positioned so that they marred sight lines and consequentially diminish the building's awkward poetry.[71] In 2001 a design was commissioned to install the massive stone doorway from Rapp's church, the original Atheneum. Fortunately, the plans were abandoned. It would have required cutting a deep rhomboid hole into the maple floor, and the stone doorway would have leaned against the frail white wall set on the diagonal, the only spare form in the building. By doing this, the large interior white wall, Meier's gesture to bounded normalcy, would have been annulled.

State-of-the-art media were of crucial importance to the original design, and the theater was to be a showpiece of technology. A 35-mm film was commissioned by Schwarz to tell the story of New Harmony, shot in Kodachrome, and run on a six-foot-high Century MSA projector, which is now standing in the projection booth collecting dust. As each decade passes and each generation of digital transfers is made, the film has lost its former impact.[72] Today it is so washed out that visitors have to sit in the back rows in order to focus on the pixilated images projected by a brand-new data projector. The question here is not whether the film should be replaced but how, in a historic building, is electronic media that was so crucial to the original architectural program being respected? Should electronic media presentations be given the same status as a fresco in a church? Schwarz considered Meier's Atheneum building, *The New Harmony Experience* film, and the exhibited model of New Harmony to be three parts of the same thing. Conceptually the ideas of architecture, cinema, and model were different modes of expression of the same idea, and addressed a conundrum concerning spatial representation that had been dogging twentieth-century architects since the invention of cinema.[73]

The single most problematic change, made immediately after the building opened,

BEN NICHOLSON

was to close the roof decks to general visitors because of the perceived dangers.[74] Meier's design, opening up the building to the public, so that the rooms inside and decks outside are of equal consequence, was groundbreaking. But almost from the beginning, the building could not be experienced as a play on circulation in which every kind of stair and ramp, and every kind of relationship between inside and outside, is tested. While doors to the outside can be opened by special permission, the fear of liability litigation has foreclosed one of the most basic of human experiences, the visceral sensation of multiple perspectives.[75] In the architect's eye, moviegoers had the option to leave the theater by an upper door to the outside and either walk up to a viewing deck or walk slowly down the ramp to town, moving from a cinematic re-creation of the past to the embodied presence of the past. Today, the audience for the orientation film returns down the interior ramps to the front entrance, clogging the circulation with an uncomfortable counterflow on the narrow one-way ramp and neglecting to see the building and the landscapes in their full glory from the roof. Without access to all the doors in the building, the space loses meaning. Were they to be opened once more, the building would reassert the ambulatory experience that takes you to the edge—literally. As in so many public spaces today, Americans are no longer trusted to walk their own walk and given the right to roam through space, for fear of litigation.

Another critical programmatic change has been to mothball the third-floor exhibition space. Planned as an office and conference room, the third floor was subsequently programmed to become the Lilly Rare Book Room. It is impossible to imagine a less appropriate space for the storage and perusal of rare books, as the scorching sunlight would turn the volumes to dust in months. When the Atheneum opened, the room was graced with a magnificent, long black table designed by Meier and designated as an exhibition space, complete with a low, sinuous vitrine, forming a parapet adjacent to the wall behind.[76] Meier is an accomplished furniture designer, and his furniture relates closely to his architectural vision. He placed a number of his pieces in the Atheneum and designed a lecture podium especially for the building. The black table and its twelve accompanying chairs have been moved from the third-floor gallery and restored, after having deteriorated in the searing sunlight. Rather than find another location for them in the Atheneum, they have been transplanted to the Schnee–Ribeyre–Elliott House, a Victorian home decorated with reproduction furniture and frilly window treatments that now serves as the headquarters office of Historic New Harmony.

It is not too late to pay tribute to the idea of a Lilly Rare Book Room. Since 1979 many of the pivotal texts of the Robert Owen scientific and educational period have been reproduced in facsimile, so it would be possible to reconstruct the space as a pre–digital age reading room with the Meier table and chairs, which are a significant part of New Harmony's intellectual and artistic legacy. To it could be added the many splendid commentaries and new volumes on art and science that have been written about New Harmony since then.[77]

These are small issues. Each one can be countered with care and by understanding the fullness of the Atheneum's poetry. Overall, the building has been well maintained. In the meantime, New Harmony is fortunate enough to have a pivotal building of the twentieth century, not bad for a town of 788 people. The building has been awarded both the American Institute of Architects' Honor Award in 1985 and its highest honor, the Twenty-five Year Award in 2008, which recognizes enduring architectural significance.[78] Despite this, New Harmony is still confronted with the task of breathing life into its historic past and finding a way for the Atheneum to play its part in that process. Meier is well aware of the difficulties the building presents and, in an interview with the author, suggests new uses.

> MEIER Well, I think that the building is going to have a difficult time standing on its own. It has to be attached to some program in New Harmony for which this building becomes used as a center for studies for whatever that may be . . .[79]

> *Do you imply that the building can respond to the activities of the town?*
> MEIER It's a building in search [of] a home. It still could be used by a university as a place for scholars to go for research and special studies of some sort.

> *It's as if the town is blaming the building for its own sense of lack of direction.*
> MEIER It's not the building's fault. But the town itself never really had any real direction.

> *It is both the tragedy and beauty of Utopia, and is still that way.*[80]

To have a building of the caliber of the Atheneum in a small town brings both gratification and difficulty. Thirty-five years old in New Harmony's bicentennial year, 2014, the Atheneum is no longer new, but it does represent newness by adding the next chapter in New Harmony's lexicon of distinctive architecture and historic preservation. In 2001 the Atheneum was restored, thereby joining the pantheon of New Harmony buildings that are part of the preservation movement. It has the potential to be the 1970s poster child for the International Committee for the Documentation and Conservation of Buildings, Sites, and Neighborhoods of the Modern Movement (Docomomo), but it is a little too soon for the building to gain a position in the pantheon of architectural masterworks and be protected as such.[81] Two thousand nineteen is its fortieth anniversary, and questionable architectural changes have already been made by Historic New Harmony / University of Southern Indiana. With funding now being sought for ADA compliance, it is essential to have input from both Meier Associates and Docomomo US for further changes.

Modern buildings become vulnerable when, by about the age of forty, they have outlived the ways they were designed to be used. Because the Atheneum was built with a specific program to interpret New Harmony in a particular way, the building finds itself high and dry once the interpretive program becomes out of sync. To fill the programmatic void, artists move in to imagine what the place could be.

The great gift of the Atheneum to New Harmony is that it is a singular work of architecture that makes explicit the multidimensional relationships between history, landscape, and civic engagement (Plate 28). When experienced emotionally and viscerally by those who visit the building through manifold ways of seeing, being, and feeling, the architecture still maintains its power. Completed in 1979, the Atheneum might be the last analog building, not only in the drawing technique Meier's office used and the way it was assembled but also in its demands on the body. Even though the Atheneum still has no elevator, the experience of walking slowly on the long ramps continues to work for all.

Buildings of this nature cannot be evaluated solely on their practicality, usefulness, and economic efficiency. Their responsibility is to touch both visceral and emotional qualities in us that we do not know we have, and for that we are eternally grateful.

Figure 7.22. Artist Tom Williams repurposes the Atheneum as an Intergalactic Recycling Station, 2011. Richard Meier encourages the program of the Atheneum to creatively develop with the times. Courtesy of Tom Williams.

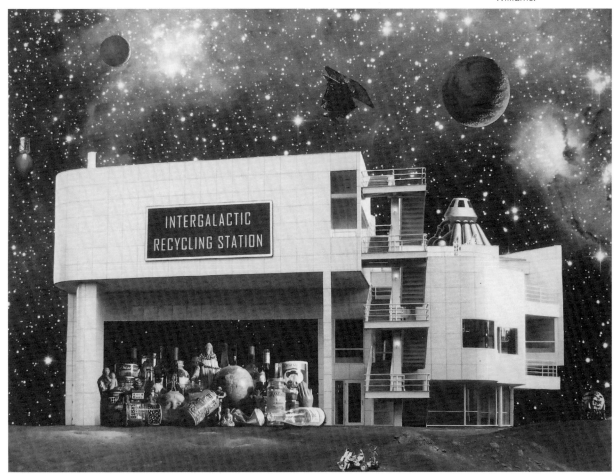

Notes

1. Ralph G. Schwarz was interviewed for this chapter by the author on December 31, 2009. At that meeting he mentioned that the main archive of his papers relating to the New Harmony Atheneum is in Southport, Connecticut, with architect David Parker, who at one time worked for Richard Meier. An account of Schwarz's early career is in the *Lehigh University Music Festival 1949,* Special Collections, Lehigh University, Penn.

2. Schwarz received an honorary Doctor of Humanities from Indiana State University in 1974.

3. According to Schwarz, "When I was appointed Director of Building Planning and Construction for the Ford Foundation, I reviewed the earlier programming initiatives of the Board which had already selected Kevin Roche to be the architect. The project had been proposed along conventional lines, however, there was one fundamental desire expressed by the Board. They believed that the new building provided the opportunity to bring a renewed focus on the Foundation as an entity, not a shell in which there were many departmental grant-making 'empires.' Obviously, Kevin and I ran with the ball. The challenge was extraordinary, and so was the building. The Chairman of the Board Building Committee was J. Erwin Miller of Columbus Indiana." Ralph Schwarz, correspondence with author, September 20, 2013. Printed by courtesy of Ralph G. Schwarz.

4. "AIA Intensifies Urban Involvement," *Preservation News* 9, no. 2 (February 1, 1969).

5. Schwarz, correspondence with author, September 20, 2013.

6. "The term Atheneum was always used by me [Schwarz] for the building. The correct translation for it is 'A Place of Learning.' References to visitor center, orientation center, information center were used informally as functional descriptions." Schwarz, correspondence with author, September 20, 2013. The first record of the term *Atheneum* in New Harmony was by Alexander Maclure, who renamed the 1816 Harmonist Church the "Mechanic's Atheneum." See Nora C. Fretageot and W. V. Mangrum, *Historic New Harmony Official Guide,* centennial ed. (Evansville, Ind.: Kellor Crescent, 1914), 11, archive.org.

7. Atheneums, each with its own independent agenda, were established in Liverpool (1797), Boston (1807), Salem (1810), Philadelphia (1813), and London (1824).

8. Cammie McAtee notes that Bernard Tchumi's Acropolis Museum has a program and *promenade architecturale* that are heirs to the New Harmony Atheneum. The building has a complex program that involves revealing the archaeological site beneath the building, exhibiting the artifacts that have survived, providing a visual connection between the remaining pediment sculptures and the actual Acropolis, and being a viewing platform for the same. Along the way there are spaces for restaurants, shops, and watching propagandistic films about the history of the monument.

9. In 1981 Tom Wolfe wrote a satire in which he critiques modernism and describes the standoff between the Whites and the Grays. See Wolfe, *From Bauhaus to Our House* (New York: Farrar, Straus and Giroux, 1981), 125–43.

10. The founders of the Whites included Peter Eisenman, Michael Graves, Richard Meier, Charles Gwathmey, and John Hejduk.

11. The core Gray architects included Robert Stern, Robert Venturi, and Charles Moore. In an interesting move for New Harmony, Peter Zweig, one of Moore's posse of "Texas Grays," designed a Japanese tea house for Jane Owen, which remained on the drafting table.

12. Colin Rowe and Robert Slutzky, "Transparency: Literal and Phenomenal," *Perspecta* 8 (1963): 45–54.

13. Hoesli was one of the "Texas Rangers," with Rowe and Slutzky, and was a consummate practitioner of collage. See Colin Rowe and Robert Slutzky, *Transparency: With a commentary by Bernhard Hoesli* (Basel: Birkhauser, 1997).

14. Colin Rowe and Fred Koetter, *Collage City* (Cambridge, Mass.: MIT Press, 1978). The generative manuscript *Collage City* from 1973 is reprinted, with an introductory essay, in K. Michael Hays, *Architecture Theory since 1968* (Cambridge, Mass.: MIT Press, 1998), 88–90.

15. The CASE group included Eisenman, Rowe, Michael Graves, Hank Millon, Robert Venturi, and Stanford Anderson. See Suzanne S. Frank, *IAUS: An Insider's Memoir* (Bloomington: Indiana University Press, 2011), 211–12.

16. Stern organized the conference *5 on 5*, held at the Museum of Modern Art, that served as the Grays' counterattack against the Whites. See "Five on Five," *Architecture Forum* 137 (May 1973): 46–57; and Robert A. M. Stern, "Gray Architecture as Post-modernism, or, Up, and Down from Orthodoxy," *L'Architecture d'Aujourd'hui* 186 (August–September 1976), reprinted with an introductory essay in K. Michael Hays, *Architecture Theory*, 240–45.

17. "It was inevitable that when I had the opportunity to interview architects for the Atheneum, I would turn to Kevin (Roche) for advice. Because the budget was modest, the building was not large, and I had set my sights on building an Icon, I turned to the slate of architects we have already discussed (Charles Gwathmey, Michael Graves, Richard Meier, and Jaquelin Robertson). Kevin offered advice carefully and objectively. He shared my enthusiasm for the architects I wanted to consider. When I finally told him of my desire to select Richard Meier, he concurred." Schwarz, correspondence with author, September 20, 2013.

18. Although the Lilly Foundation paid for the building, it would ultimately be handed over to the State of Indiana, whose Governor Otis R. Bowen was a good friend to New Harmony. Another influence on the project was Herman B Wells, chancellor of Indiana University at Bloomington, who served on the boards of Historic New Harmony Inc. and the Robert Lee Blaffer Foundation. He was a supporter of the project and desired to intellectualize the New Harmony community. Ralph Schwarz, conversation with author, December 31, 2009.

19. In the postscript to *Five Architects*, written on April Fools' Day 1974, Philip Johnson describes Meier thus: "Richard Meier, the most traditional of our five youngsters, makes the most 'acceptable houses.' . . . Meier knows his history best of the five, studies it most, learns from it most. His recent designs for Olivetti USA give great promise, but life (for an architect) begins at 45. The new (non-Corbusier) direction has begun? Is beginning?" Peter Eisenman et al., *Five Architects: Eisenman, Graves, Gwathmey, Hejduk, Meier* (New York: Oxford University Press, 1972), 138.

20. Schwarz later became a partner of Meier and worked with him on the Getty Center project. Schwarz, conversation with author, December 31, 2009.

21. In 1980 Meier was invited to exhibit at the Wadsworth Atheneum in *Richard Meier MATRIX 58*. The MATRIX exhibits were a sign of arrival in the art world and included the most influential artists of that time. About sharing his studio with Stella, Meier said, "I worked in a small apartment where I slept in one room and had a table where I could do architecture in the other half. I couldn't paint because there was no space, so I started doing collages because that was the amount of space that I had to work on. I did the first collages in 1959 and then continued in 1963. Doing collages was sporadic, at one time I would do it, and I would do other things. When I started work on the Getty in 1976, each month I would spend a week in New York, a week in California, and two weeks moving around and so I was on the airplane a lot. I had a box that fit between the arms of the seat where I would carry my material and do collages in books. In that way I would sit on the airplane for four, five, or six hours and have something to do. I have been doing that ever since, so I now have 150 books of collages." Richard Meier, interview with author, March 25, 2010. Printed by courtesy of Richard Meier & Partners Architects and Ben Nicholson. See full interview at http://archinect.com/features/article/102847. See David Shapiro, "Richard's Almanac: Scissors Pleasure Plane Paper," in *Richard Meier Collages*, exhibition catalog

(Beverly Hills, Calif.: Gagosian Gallery, 2005). Printed by courtesy of Richard Meier & Partners Architects and Ben Nicholson.

22. Richard Meier, "A Collage and Study Sketches for the Atheneum," in *Global Architecture Document 1* (Tokyo: GA Publications, 1981), 25.

23. Bernhard Karpf, representing Meier's office, gave a slide lecture in New Harmony on April 8, 2010, in which he juxtaposed Meier's sketch plan for the Atheneum with Gris's 1914 painting *Guitar*. The lecture includes a rich trove of source materials that influenced Meier's building. Meier had been given an early draft of this chapter in 2009, prior to the March 2010 interview. Karpf generously responded to several sources cited and went on to propose several more, in particular, the events that were happening in the 1960s to which Meier referred. The lecture, "The Atheneum of New Harmony: Its Precedents and Impact on Preservation," was part of Indiana's Statewide Preservation Conference called "Preserving Historic Places."

24. Meier, interview with author, March 25, 2010. Printed by courtesy of Richard Meier & Partners Architects and Ben Nicholson.

25. Donald E. Pitzer, "William Maclure's Boatload of Knowledge: Science and Education into the Midwest," *Indiana Magazine of History* 94 (1998): 110–35.

26. Schwarz, correspondence with author, September 20, 2013. Printed by courtesy of Ralph G. Schwarz.

27. In 1988 the Museum of Modern Art staged the exhibition "Deconstructivist Architecture." See Philip Johnson and Mark Wigley, *Deconstructivist Architecture* (New York: MoMA, 1988).

28. Meier's close relationship with Rowe permitted him to reflect Rowe's provocative ability to be both an advocate for the aesthetic Purism of Le Corbusier as well as a historical contextualist. Meier had been a student of Rowe at Cornell and extended that friendship into his professional career.

29. "Whenever you start a project you look at the program, the location, the site and the siting, and it seemed to me that the building had a responsibility both to the world outside New Harmony and to historic New Harmony as well. The five-degree shift made that transition from what one saw as the edge of the Wabash River (it is really not straight, but one saw it that way) from the bridge, and the location of the historic houses that one passes through as you go from the Orientation Center to the town. So the shift really is a device to say that we are not relating to New Harmony in only one way, but relating in two ways: both to the present as well as the past." Meier, interview with author, March 25, 2010. Printed by courtesy of Richard Meier & Partners Architects and Ben Nicholson.

30. Kenneth A. "Kent" Scheutte proposes that the ratio for the theater plan is the golden ratio, and that the five-degree angle is generated from a sight line that meets the northeast corner of the original grid of the town. (Schuette's unpublished paper was presented to Meier in New York on April 9, 1996. At the meeting, Meier acknowledged that the auditorium was a golden rectangle in plan.) The building's main grid is "straight with the world," an Indiana farming term used to describe the N, S, E, W axes of the Jeffersonian grid. (Thanks to Sarah Brown for pointing this out.)

31. Meier, interview with author, March 25, 2010. Printed by courtesy of Richard Meier & Partners Architects and Ben Nicholson.

32. Meier describes the relationship between inside and outside as quintessentially different from Frank Lloyd Wright's vision. Meier, interview with author, March 25, 2010. Reprinted by courtesy of Richard Meier & Partners Architects and Ben Nicholson.

> *How do you see the contribution of your building in coming to terms with the inside and the outside, an issue that the twentieth century has spent such a lot of time working through?*
>
> **MEIER** It is antithetical to Frank Lloyd Wright's vision, in terms of the relationship of interior and exterior space. Wright always thought about the extension of space to the exterior from the

interior, this is not about the *extension* of space; it's about the *relationship* of spaces, between exterior and interior.

How would you characterize that relationship?

MEIER It is a distinction between the man-made and the natural. It's a clear distinction rather than attempt, in the Wrightian sense, to say that the building is organic and therefore spatially continuous.

It's like there is a one-way omnipotence in Wright's vision, you're in the ship looking out, whereas with your building you never know whether the landscape is coming in or you are going out to the landscape.

MEIER Right. It's different.

It's a beautiful ambiguity in every respect. And so if there was ever a way to be situated within a three-dimensional collage, then the New Harmony Atheneum has to be that project.

MEIER Good!

33. "We designed the path, I don't know if it's still there, that leads from the river to the building, as the theoretical entry. Of course the riverboats are no longer there, but it serves as a reference to what once was there." Meier, interview with author, March 25, 2010. Reprinted by courtesy of Richard Meier & Partners Architects and Ben Nicholson.

34. Yellow trace was the preferred paper of the Grays; the Whites used white trace.

35. John Hejduk, *Education of an Architect: A Point of View* (New York: Monacelli, 1999).

36. Meier has the head for cutting out chiseled spaces that are then molded by hand with a putty knife: something that fellow White Eisenman's buildings have never accomplished, as his buildings are too intellectually brittle to have quite the same artistic grace.

37. Some of the finest axonometric drawings made are found in Auguste Choisy, *L'art de bâtir chez les Romain* (Paris: Ducher, 1873). The Roman buildings were drawn brick by brick, from a worm's-eye view. Philadelphia's well-known Victorian brickwork is exemplified by architects such as Frank Furness and Louis Kahn, in Venturi's hometown.

38. Richard Meier, *Richard Meier Architect: Buildings and Projects, 1966–76* (New York: Oxford University Press, 1976).

39. Stanley Abercrombie, "A Vision Continued," *AIA Journal,* mid-May 1980, 126–37.

40. There was a scheme to tuck a Theatrum, beneath the crown of Indian Mound, overlooking the Wabash River to the west, in the manner of a Greek amphitheater on the slope of a hill.

41. The working affiliation between Meier and Schwarz did not end with the Atheneum. It was to continue during the creation process of the Getty Center in Los Angeles.

42. Silvio Cassara, "Intrinsic Qualities of Remembrances: The Atheneum at New Harmony, Indiana," *Parametro* (July–August 1976): 16–19, 59.

43. The project has been given various names since its inception. Design drawings from August 18, 1975, are titled Visitor's Center, but by November 10, 1975, the drawings are titled The Atheneum. Once the project was built, a 1980 brochure distributed by Historic New Harmony names the building The New Harmony Atheneum. Currently Historic New Harmony / University of Southern Indiana refers to the building as Atheneum Visitors Center (without the apostrophe).

44. Stedman Whitwell was an English architect who designed the utopian project "Southville" at Leamington Spire before designing Robert Owen's "Community," for New Harmony, neither of which was built. The "Community" is thought to have been designed circa 1824: a pamphlet about the design was published in *Description of an Architectural Model From a Design by Stedman Whitwell, Esq. for a Community Upon a Principle of United Interests, as Advocated by Robert Owen, Esq.* (London: Hurst Chance, 1830). Whitwell lived in New Harmony 1825–26, and he invented a naming system for a new

town based on its longitude and latitude. New Harmony would have been renamed "Ipba Veinul." *New Harmony Gazette,* vol. 1, 1826, 226–27. New Harmony's "Community" project is generally referred to as the "Phalanstery" by architects, based on Charles Fourier's concept of a Phalanstère. See Fourier, *Fourier: The Theory of the Four Movements,* Cambridge Texts in the History of Political Thought, edited by Gareth Stedman Jones and Ian Patterson (Cambridge: Cambridge University Press, 1996.)

45. It is not known who prepared this drawing, but Meier attributes it to Lesueur. Meier, *Richard Meier Architect,* 194.

46. Leonard Warren, *Maclure of New Harmony: Scientist, Progressive Educator, Radical Philanthropist* (Bloomington: Indiana University Press, 2009).

47. Meier, *Richard Meier Architect,* 198–202.

48. One of the change orders not approved April 2, 1979, was the building of a model of the Phalanstery. A drawing of it was included in Meier, *Richard Meier Architect,* 195. Note that Robert Owen referred to his model town as "Agricultural and Manufacturing Villages of Unity and Mutual Co-operation" and sometimes simply "Quadrangles," nomenclature in use by historians and communal studies scholars. While neither Owen nor Whitwell used the term *Phalanstery,* it would have appealed to architects of the 1970s, who were well aware of Fourier's utopian city of that name.

49. Printed by courtesy of the Robert Lee Blaffer Foundation.

50. Jane Blaffer Owen, personal conversation with author, 2009.

51. "That was a disaster from the beginning! Jane felt that while I was there I should do something. . . . It was a temporary structure. It was to keep the sun off the students as they worked in the yard." Meier, interview with author, March 25, 2010. Reprinted by courtesy of Richard Meier & Partners Architects and Ben Nicholson.

52. The potter was Les Miley, professor emeritus of art at University of Evansville.

53. Peyronnin Construction submitted the final bill for $1,693,625.99 to Historic New Harmony, Inc. on December 12, 1979, a sum that was not too far over the $1,600,000 budgeted in 1975. An inkling of the difficulty of attending to the myriad of details required to achieve the quality of the design is reflected in the 153 change orders, amounting to $362,509.11, which caused friction between the architect and contractor.

54. "As you know, among other things, when this job was originally bid, the plans were so incomplete as to detailing that it required many change orders not only to modify the plans, as such, but to further detail those matters which were not originally set forth in the plans initially. To date we have in excess of 130 change orders dealing with additional detailing, modifications, as well as clarification of the original general plans upon which the original bid was made." E. G. Schmitt of Peyronnin Construction Company to Richard Meier, March 3, 1979, Richard Meier Archive, Historic New Harmony, University of Southern Indiana.

55. Yukio Futagawa, ed., "Collage and Study Sketches for the Atheneum"; Kenneth Frampton, "Meier's Atheneum"; Arthur Cohen, "Richard Meier, An American Architect"; "The Atheneum, New Harmony, Ind. (First Scheme)"; "The Atheneum (Executed Scheme)," in *Global Architecture Document 1* (Tokyo: GA Publications, 1981). The project was also published in a second format as *Global Architecture 60: Richard Meier & Associates* (Tokyo: GA Publications, 1981).

56. Ada Louise Huxtable, "A Radical Addition for Mid-America," *New York Times,* September 30, 1979.

57. Futagawa, *Global Architecture Document 1,* 33.
    Meier remarks on the relationship between the building and the exhibits:
    MEIER Well, for me that's what it's about: movement internally to experience the external setting. The exhibits that we had, I don't know what there is now, were pretty insignificant.

Right, there were small models, and very few of them too.

MEIER I mean, they hardly justify a building of that scale. So therefore the *exhibit* is really the *place*. That's what it's about.

Meier, interview with author, March 25, 2010. Reprinted by courtesy of Richard Meier & Partners Architects and Ben Nicholson.

58. In the first period of the Atheneum, a dramatic exhibition was staged. Before he left in 1982, Schwarz mounted a large exhibition celebrating the hundredth anniversary of New York's Metropolitan Opera, showing the collection of Marcella Sembric. The difficulty of the building as an exhibition space is that it has only two short walls on which to mount anything, and the display cases beneath the windows are a climatic disaster.

59. The list of items to be included in the exhibition was sent in a letter of September 21, 1979, from Meier's office to Historic New Harmony Inc. Meier Archive HNH/USI.

60. In 1989 an educational film *Atheneum: Analysis of Form* was made by an architectural team that dissects the space of the building using early computer animation with a narration overlaid in the deadpan analytic manner of Rowe, but without his humor. *Atheneum: Analysis of Form* was produced by Gordon Brooks III, AIA, and written and presented by Geoffrey Baker RIBA, for the University of California Extension Center for Media and Independent Learning, Berkeley, California, in 1989. The twenty-eight-minute film was later distributed by the University of Arkansas in 1997.

61. "The whiteness of the architecture is all color. The color changes because it reflects its surroundings, because of the whiteness of the building. It is the color of nature that gives the color into architecture. The color of nature doesn't do much for the collage! The changing light of the day doesn't necessarily affect the collage. Collage is, sort of, inert, whereas the architecture is alive and constantly changing." Meier, interview with author, March 25, 2010.

62. "I loved Ezra, and I loved working with Ezra. I would tell him, 'Now let's move the camera over here because the light is coming in.' . . . Ezra was great in that respect. Futagawa worked on his own. I remember when I received the first photographs that he took, they were small black & white photographs, it was like a different building, totally different. You can't imagine how the two great photographers were more different from one another. I have been with Futagawa when he photographs: he goes click-click, click-click, click-click, voom! He would move like hell!" Meier, interview with author, March 25, 2010. Reprinted by courtesy of Richard Meier & Partners Architects and Ben Nicholson.

63. "Collage is a two dimensional medium. You are dealing with two-dimensional elements and there is no illusion to a third dimension. Architecture is about making space that we move in, live in and use; architecture is related to human scale. Collage is related to human scale only in [as] much as the scale of the element that you are holding in your hand. I think that they are completely separate and one is not related to the other. . . . When I'm working on a collage, or doing a collage, it's only afterwards that I think about the three dimensionality of it, not during the making of it. . . . I think models sometimes are useful, but very rarely do models indicate a need for change." Meier, interview with author, March, 25, 2010. Reprinted by courtesy of Richard Meier & Partners Architects and Ben Nicholson.

64. It would take Daniel Libeskind, and his laboratory of students at Cranbrook Academy, to bring this third "sectional" dimension of collage into viable architectural form, but that was the task of the subsequent generation of architectural discourse that took place over the following five years.

65. "I wanted a material that would age well. But also enable us to deal with rectilinear and curvilinear forms, and a metal panel has that ability." Meier, interview with author, March 25, 2010. Reprinted by courtesy of Richard Meier & Partners Architects and Ben Nicholson.

66. The following walls have these ratios. The southwest wall is 21:15 (7:5) with a 9:5 (Fibbonacci)

hole cut out of its lower left corner. The south facade has a 16:20 (4:5 is a musical fifth) with a rhomboid hole to accommodate the ramp whose top hole is 7 panels from the top to the east and 3 and a half panels to the top to the west; it is a nice try at tidying up a messy situation, but it comes without precedent. The column on the south facade is 1:8 parts high, the Vitruvian proportion for an Ionic column. The east stair wall is 17:4: no precedent there. The east and north walls meet at a quarter round corner, and Meier started to cut panels and make odd-sized panels to cope with the plan within the building.

67. The ramp wobbled to such an extent after the building opened, the cantilever was hastily welded to the steel frame of the building by the addition of two crude pipe columns, visible in Stoller's photographs of 1979.

68. In car talk, what we have here is the Bugatti 35B: all racing and adolescently beautiful, but a design beholden to the mechanic's wrench to make it go faster whatever the cost to its looks. The Atheneum is like this: it is not the sister to Bugatti's ravishing Coupe Napoleon.

69. Schwarz lent this insight into the way the building's facades work.

70. Thanks to Bernhard Karpf for pointing this out in his lecture "The Atheneum of New Harmony: Its Precedents and Impact on Preservation," given at the Atheneum, April 7–9, 2010.

71. Happily, the exhibitions were removed in 2010, and the view through the serpentine window reestablishes a connection with the river.

72. "The film should be remastered and shown utilizing today's advanced digital technology. The original has high quality and excellent sound. When we made the film, I consulted with the producers and writers of *Voice of a Patriot* at Colonial Williamsburg. Their film had gotten so bad that they had to spend millions to remaster it digitally. It is fabulous and continues to be shown in two theaters every twenty minutes, every day. After sixty years, it is credited with being the longest film in continuous use in America. *The New Harmony Experience* would be hard to replicate. Many local citizens participated in its production. In pristine condition, it is excellent and a great asset. Perhaps funding its remastering and a superior projection system should be a target for the 2014 Events." Schwarz, correspondence with author, September 20, 2013. Reprinted by courtesy of Ralph G. Schwarz.

73. The Philips Pavilion was built in 1958 by Le Corbusier and the composer Iannis Xenakis. It integrated film, projected slides, colored lights, and the musical score *Poème électronique* by Edgar Varèse.

74. Low metal gates to the ramps and staircases were installed by 1979 to control walking up to the roof. Historic New Harmony does allow walking through the multiple doorways onto the roof with permission, and parties are permitted on the upper decks.

75. The gates to the ramps still have the original enameled plaques with the words "Unlawful to proceed beyond this point."

76. Meier developed the design for this table for the Guggenheim Museum's Conference Room. The New Harmony table is wider and lacquered black rather than unfinished natural maple. It was around this table that the committee sat in the New Harmony Atheneum to select the architect for the Getty Center. They loved the building and subsequently hired Meier. Schwarz, conversation with author, December 31, 2009.

77. Upon reflecting on the current use of the building, Schwarz feels that the bookstore belongs in the center of town, as he originally had it, and that this space would be ideal to exhibit a model of the "Phalanstery" or an exhibition of the history of the *Atheneum*. He also mentioned that a model was made of the Harmonist Church that the visitor could peer into. Schwarz, conversation with author, December 31, 2009.

78. The Twenty-five Year Award was presented on February 22, 2008, by Marshall Purnell, FAIA. He had this to say about the building: "For centuries, the seekers have crossed the waters of the Wabash, urged on by the hope of a better world. A memorial to this passage and a gleaming gateway between

what is and what might be, The Atheneum draws the visitor in a tight embrace, then after yielding a vision of the promised land, teases the imagination by its own perfection to dream again dreams as old as those who first gazed back and saw an angel who shut fast the gate of Paradise."

79. The management of Historic New Harmony, Inc. was transferred to the University of Southern Indiana in 1985. In 2010 Historic New Harmony created a Vision Plan, part of which calls for New Harmony to be an off-site campus for academic programs and outreach of the University of Southern Indiana, located twenty-five miles away. In 2013 the Vision Plan included multiple academic programs involving students.

80. Meier, interview with author, March 25, 2010. Reprinted by courtesy of Richard Meier & Partners Architects and Ben Nicholson. See also note 16.

81. It would become eligible to join New Harmony's National Historic Landmark District in 2029. Age can be trumped by exceptional significance if the National Park Service so desires, as was done multiple times in Columbus, Indiana.

Three Voices in New Harmony

Estranged and Reunited

The New Being

PAUL TILLICH

Paul Tillich visited New Harmony for the dedication
of Paul Tillich Park and *Cave of the New Being*
at Pentecost, June 2, 1963.

Address in the Roofless Church, Pentecost, 1963

Dear friends, let us concentrate on the words that will be the words of dedication of
the cave: "Estranged and Reunited: The New Being." Consecrating the cave reminds
us of many great symbols connected with the word "cave," symbols of the new reality: the mother's womb, which brings forth the child; and a child, perhaps, who is
a saving power in the world; or the tomb, which is the tomb of burial, and perhaps
one of resurrection; or the cave of darkness to which we are all bound, in which we
only see shadows of the things that are true; and our longing for the full light liberated from the darkness of the cave. In all this, the saving power is expressed in this
one great symbol. "Saving" means healing, making whole what is split and what is
disrupted.

The name of this community indicates this symbol. "Reunited" can be translated
by a "new harmony" [that] has been lost. This is both history and symbol—in all
places, in all mankind.

From the many lectures I gave in my academic career I remember the nature
and the characteristic of that great period in Western history, which we call "The
Enlightenment," when the central concept was harmony—"harmony" in a very definite sense, namely harmony in spite of disharmony. In this the people of enlightenment believed: that if everybody pursues happiness, pursues his ideas, then a unity
will come into existence. To a certain extent, they were right. The man who is one
of the founders of this community, Robert Owen, was one of the first who observed
that this principle does not hold true, that when everybody follows his own interests, not hidden harmony, but open disharmony is the consequence. He saw the

Dr. Paul Tillich, pho-
tographed by Archie
Lieberman, 1966. Tillich
was Jane Owen's spiritual
mentor, and she created
Paul Tillich Park in his
honor. His ashes are
interred there. Courtesy
of the Estate of Archie
Lieberman.

victims of this belief in a direct, immediate harmony. He believed that through our action, through historical action, we would reach a harmony of another kind. But he believed only in historical action, and this is not enough.

Man's estrangement from his true being demands more than historical action. Reliance on mere progress leads to Utopian ideas and this leads to disappointment. The history of this community is one of enumerable witnesses to the fact that reliance exclusively on historical action, on action of men in history, is not enough to produce harmony. But there is a power above history, which breaks into history and produces a new harmony after the catastrophe of the old one, which was merely historical. I call this power the *Spiritual Presence,* namely the presence of God in our spirit, of the divine spirit in the human spirit. And on this Pentecost morning this Spiritual Presence is the image toward which millions of people all over the world are looking.

Now what is the estrangement, which requires a new reunion, a new harmony? It is the estrangement of man from his true being in a threefold way: the estrangement from the ground of being, the estrangement from himself, and the estrangement from those with whom he lives. All religions, all social action, all healing attempts, and all forms of healing have tried to overcome these estrangements. Universal healing as envisaged in our great religions and personal healing have become so important. We have realized in our century, perhaps more than ever before, the estrangement of every person from himself and his true being. The healing of nations, social healing and political healing within the nation and between the nations[,] has become our deepest concern.

In Germany after the First World War when I studied the history of religiously founded Socialism, I first met the name of Robert Owen. In all of these studies it was said that the combination of the socialist transformation of society and the religious dimension moving toward the ultimate started with this man. So it is very moving to be in this place, and to speak in this community where he worked.

Nevertheless, it was a first harmony. It was a harmony by mere acting and working in history. Therefore, it was somehow Utopian and broke down. We need a harmony that originates beyond the split of the different parts of our being. This is the meaning of every religion—to point to, and to actualize, the Spiritual Presence within personal life and the life of society. The spirit creates within individuals and in groups something which is both reality and anticipation. It is not only reality which we have, but it is also what we do not have. We hope for it, we expect it. And I think this is the situation of all human beings: there is a unity of *reality* (something which is given, something which we have) and *anticipation* (something for which we hope, for which we are longing). It is not the certainty which says, "Here is salvation!" And it is not the uncertainty which says, "There is no salvation." But it is this inner tension of the spirit, having and not having at the same time.

This Roofless Church into which the divine spirit descends is, therefore, an adequate and necessary symbol in the context of a new reality. The new being is a creation of the spirit wherever it happens. But let us not forget the other side. It is hidden in a cave—another meaning of this great symbol. Out of the cave, out of hiddenness, it radiates. It is never a thing that we can grasp, and of which we can say, "Here it is! We have it." It is always both hidden and manifest.

A week or two weeks ago when I had time to speak to a very large group of leading people in this country at the *Time* magazine anniversary about the human condition, I asked myself, "Where is such new reality developing? To what can I point?" Then, an experience of the last years came to mind. It was the surprising experience that in many places where I was asked to speak[,] I was told that there are small groups which center around an important book. These people struggle with it in the depths of their spiritual life, week by week, forgetting all the superficial forms which are half-necessary, half-dangerous, which are communicated by the easy means of communication in our day. And I believe that this group here, around this wonderful symbol, and these wonderful different symbols, is such a group. And I want to say personally that I am glad to become a part of this small group in which the elements of reunion are manifest, hidden and manifest, real and expected.

Here is a small group in which what once was created is now being renewed—not conserved, not removed, but transformed into a new reality. This is exactly what the Spirit does who is present in our human spirit, not denying it, not denying our total being, body and mind, not removing it and putting something else in its stead, not affirming it as it is; but transforming it. By the act of dedication to which we shall proceed, we express the hope of a transformation of the old into a new being, here and everywhere in the universe. So may it be with our work as far as it can go, always in the power of the Spiritual Presence. Amen.

The Act of Dedication of the Ground of Paul Tillich Park and the Cave of the New Being

I, Paul Tillich, give my name to this place, and dedicate the ground of this park and the *Cave of the New Being* to a new reality, conquering what is estranged and reuniting what belongs to each other, in the power of the Spiritual Presence.

Professor Tillich's Response to a Community Reception, Sunday Afternoon, June 2, 1963

When I was asked to come here this weekend for the dedication of Paul Tillich Park and the *Cave,* I felt more than the usual amount of what Kierkegaard calls "fear and trembling." I have learned from my psychological friends that fear is something which has to do with the unknown. And if it is entirely unknown, then anxiety is produced. So I can translate Kierkegaard's words as "anxiety and trembling." Now what was the anxiety? Anxiety always arises when you imagine something which is not really there. You cannot be courageous about it. It is unknown, and anything may happen. As long as there is real fear, you can be courageous, and I wrote some time ago a book about Courage. But the things of which nothing is known produce this terrible feeling of anxiety. As you all know from your own being, the greatest anxiety is the anxiety of having to die, because there the absolutely unknown stands against us.

Now I came yesterday in a plane which served nobody else but Mrs. Tillich and myself. This was the first step toward overcoming a little bit of anxiety. And it went like this. In the evening before going to bed, Mrs. Tillich and I confessed to each other that we had the feeling here of a reality into which we were taken without particular words, without any trick, without any method, simply by the most important thing in the world—namely being itself.

The being of this place, the being of this group, was the power which overcame anxiety. And, as I said this morning, the new being overcomes the estrangement and strangeness of beings to beings. This was just what happened when we came into this group. Strangeness was overcome in an almost miraculous way. It was overcome by the landscape which brought me back sixty and more years of my life into places in Eastern Germany where I grew up in surroundings very much like this, and Mrs. Tillich was reminded of Western Germany, which is not much different. She also was immediately taken in by the landscape.

When we met a few people and had dinner with them, something else, beyond the landscape, took us in, the reality of a community which has one thing in contrast to most small communities—it does not suffer from narrowness. It is wide open in all directions, toward India as well as toward Europe and toward all the other sections of the world. And it is open not only geographically, but it is open also in terms of new ideas. And I cannot avoid saying that this is largely due to Mrs. Owen, who has done many things which are very bold and very adequate to our century.

When last night we walked through the Roofless Church, I said to her (I will repeat it here) that this alone justifies the century in which we are living—that our century is not only able to produce bad imitations of former centuries, but that it is able to create something born in our time, understandable to our time, and great in the symbolic power it has in all directions.

I have seen the model of the new park and the *Cave* in it. It was sent to me in bronze, a very heavy package, and was immediately powerful in its symbolic character, even in the diminished form of a model. So I look forward to one day when Mrs. Tillich and I might be here again, to see the work as it is finished. In any case, my impression of this place is an impression of something astonishing, surprising, great in itself, in its past, and in its present. And my wish is that it may remain great also in its future.

Ralph Grayson Schwarz directed Historic New Harmony between 1973 and 1985 and became its president. He commissioned the New Harmony Atheneum, dedicated on October 10, 1979. Most of the tours he created for multiple exhibitions of the historic personalities and structures throughout New Harmony remain in place today. Photograph courtesy of Ralph G. Schwarz.

Reflections on New Harmony

RALPH GRAYSON SCHWARZ

DURING THE LATE 1940S AND THE 1950S, the toll taken on American cities and towns, which had been in decline from the Great Depression and the deprivations of the wartime economy, gave way to a renewed belief in the American dream. Urban centers slowly began to reassess the task of rebuilding their infrastructures, housing needs, and cultural assets. There was a resurgence of the desire for American progress, reinforced by pride in American history. Emerging federal guidelines for redevelopment as a function of urban renewal, as well as the legalization of well-defined Historic Districts to protect and enhance historic sites and buildings, were gaining public favor. Three early examples for establishing Historic Districts are Cambridge, Massachusetts; Alexandria, Virginia; and Bethlehem, Pennsylvania. Jane Owen was aware of the role that I and her dear friends Helen Duprey Bullock of Colonial Williamsburg and Walter Whitehill of Boston had played in advancing the historic renewal of Bethlehem, Pennsylvania.

I had known Jane Owen for twenty-five years prior to her inviting me to New Harmony in 1972, at the suggestion of Helen Bullock, to serve on the board of her foundation, the Robert Lee Blaffer Trust, which had been created to support Jane Owen's philanthropic endeavors in New Harmony. She had a growing concern that preserving and enhancing the historic environment and improving the economy of the total community of New Harmony necessitated comprehensive involvement on a broader scale. Through her contacts at the state level and with the involvement of community leaders, the Indiana State Legislature created a second New Harmony Commission in April 1973. By August, Governor Otis Bowen had named Lieutenant Governor Robert D. Orr of Evansville and twenty others to the Commission to plan legislation to aid in developing New Harmony as a historic site. Lieutenant Governor Orr served as chairman, and I served as vice chairman.

An initial step toward advancing interaction with the Board of the Town of New Harmony proceeded when a representative of the Indiana Planning and Research Department, Indianapolis, discussed revising and updating the earlier plans for New Harmony, which were set up in 1969. With a challenge grant made by Betty Couch, in memory of her late husband, Clifton Couch, former chairman of the Board of Trustees, the Town of New Harmony paid one-third of the cost and the state paid two-thirds. These actions catalyzed the planning process. While this was proceeding,

311

I was asked by Jane Owen in 1973 to serve as a consultant to review the current status of the community and its ability to apply for federal, state, and philanthropic assistance. In order to avoid a conflict of interest, I asked to be removed from the board of the Blaffer Trust when I began to receive compensation from Jane Owen Enterprises as a paid consultant. The Red Geranium Bookstore, the Mews, and the New Harmony Inn were for-profit activities, not philanthropic.

I was also prepared to study the physical history of the historic settlement. After reviewing available documentary materials, I created overlay maps for the years 1810, 1824, 1843, 1887, 1907, 1929, 1943, and 1972 (and later 1981). I was greatly assisted in this endeavor by Karl Arndt, noted scholar of the Harmony Society, and Josephine Elliott, respected authority of the Robert Owen / William Maclure years. My experience, as an official of the Ford Foundation, the Fund for Area Planning and Development (the United Nations), the Urban Design and Development Corporation (the American Institute of Architects), and the National Trust for Historic Preservation, had provided experimental opportunities for me to develop new methods for approaching historic preservation. This was a challenging time: the field was developing, new legislation was being explored, and the Historic American Building Survey was being enthusiastically advanced. The Department of Interior was preparing technical bulletins.

A few qualified scholars were writing books, and related professional disciplines were just being explored at some universities. There was a change in attitude toward the preservation process: for it to be considered successful, the historical process now required community participation and education. The process of new construction—enlarging, layering, relocating, and dismantling—is endemic to architecture. It is continuous and ever changing, and an awareness of these changes is an essential consideration for understanding the richness of the preservation process.

At this opportune time, New Harmony was seen as a new model for public and private participation in the resurgence of a small rural community. New Harmony was, however, also unique as the site of two successive Utopian communities. In April 1973 the Town of New Harmony enacted a zoning ordinance for the first time in its history. The Comprehensive Plan initiated in 1973 was completed in May 1974, with Implementation Procedures. While I was directly involved in these tasks, special recognition should be given to the planning firm of Kane and Carruth, under contract to the Indiana State Planning Services Agency. Tom Kane was a remarkable and talented professional who, during his career, pioneered many outstanding preservation and restoration landscape initiatives across the nation. He was highly respected by Jane Owen and Robert Webb, the new president of the New Harmony Plan Commission.

With direction from Jane Owen, I was given the opportunity to orchestrate, with her manager Gary Gerard, key projects that she personally advanced at that time: a new forty-five-room inn; the restoration and adaptive reuse of a five-store complex in the business area; and a "Mews" to be dominated by a bookstore, specializing in books related to Indiana history, with particular emphasis on literature related to New Harmony history. The Red Geranium Bookstore also provided the opportunity for me to assemble all available preservation and restoration literature and essential background materials in architecture and planning. It was an immediate success. Herman B Wells, University Chancellor, Indiana University, declared it "unsurpassed in the Mid-West."

Concurrently, in January 1974 the New Harmony Commission voted to create a not-for-profit corporation to "carry out the work of the organization and to raise funds." I was elected president. Jane Owen preferred not to serve on the Commission or the board of the new not-for-profit corporation, Historic New Harmony Inc., in order to avoid any possible conflict of interest. Historic New Harmony and the Atheneum were funded, in part, by the Lilly Endowment, and it was necessary to keep Jane Owen's for-profit and philanthropic activities, and direct involvement, totally separate.

Even so, her opinions were solicited because she was admired, respected, and always well informed—traits that continued throughout her life. I was in communication with her until a few months before her death in June 2010. In February she had written, "I hope that we can continue our dialogue with mutual joy." Jane was loved and has left her legacy in her beloved New Harmony. Her vision, energetic activity, and personal philanthropy were major forces in the restoration movement.

Historic New Harmony Inc. was created to help implement the Town of New Harmony's planned objectives: (1) restoration of one of America's unique historic sites; (2) economic revitalization of a rural community; and (3) development of an international cultural and education center. Historic New Harmony Inc. sought to bring together resources from public and private sectors for the common good. Because of the interest and support of the Lilly Endowment, Historic New Harmony Inc. was, as progress justified them, the beneficiary of significant incremental grants. Three men were especially supportive: Herman Wells, Richard Ristine, and Will Hays Jr. They caught the vision and, in their various capacities, engaged the support of others. The acquisition of strategic sites would not have been achieved without local cooperation. Two men stand out as indispensable leaders, Gary Gerard and Donald Parker.

During the next five years, from 1974 to 1978, the New Harmony Plan was implemented. Three architects played key roles: Evans Woollen and LeRoy Troyer, both Indiana architects, and Robert Hatch, an architect from Connecticut. The entire staff of Historic New Harmony Inc. were dedicated and tireless workers, and two were outstanding: Neil Pagano and Doris Manning.

In the spring of 1975 the enthusiastic support of the Lilly Endowment enabled me to proceed with the selection of an architect to design and build a new building that would introduce the New Harmony legacy; the community of historical personalities and the sites they were associated with would reveal the story. The new building would not only be a place of arrival but also a place of learning, an Atheneum. The end of the twentieth century signaled a shift in architectural paradigm away from modernism's International Style: the building had to add the dimension of continuity and architectural evolution, inspired by the past but with internal circulation to provide an overlook and dramatic entry into both the historic and living community. I believed that in order to fulfill this extraordinary legacy of innovative ideas, we had to be as lively and vital today as Rapp, Owen, and Maclure had been in their time. Finding the right architect was a challenge. The contract would not appeal to any of the large firms because the size of the project was comparatively modest, both in scale and in budget.

The process by which I finally selected Richard Meier as the architect is discussed by Ben Nicholson in this volume in the chapter "The New Harmony Atheneum: White Collage." Time has vindicated the decision, for the building achieved formidable recognition and even today, in the second decade of the twenty-first century, remains highly praised. Adding to Nicholson's commentary, I would like to make several observations.

The building was sited at the edge of the Town of New Harmony near the Wabash River. Its location respected the town's grid and was situated as a place of arrival, far enough away that it did not impose a confusing addition to the original town plan. Its scale and volume were intentionally restrained and further reduced during the design process. One of the obvious programmatic reasons for the Atheneum is for the parking, reception, ticketing, and introduction (overview) of visitors to New Harmony. The name Atheneum (a place of learning), rather than Visitor Center, was selected to create the opportunity for other learning experiences as well. The conference or seminar facility (with the impressive conference table and chairs designed by Meier), together with the theater, on upper levels, can be readily available for scheduled educational functions in coordination with other venues within the community. Combined, they create a unique, significant, and spectacular intellectual setting for conferences, seminars, and forums.

The Atheneum is more than just a functional structure. It is an icon, dramatically set apart on its own podium above the floodplain, challenging and inspiring twenty-first-century scholars. Its simple but architecturally complex interior is also designed to circulate the visitor or student from the reception level up to the observation platform, with its ramp system descending directly into the beautiful and meaningful village.

Galleries in the interior of the building were planned to subtly contain features reflected in Meier's design. A model was planned, but not executed, for Gallery I of

Robert Owen's proposed Phalanstery, designed by Stedman Whitwell, which was to have been located outside the Harmonist town. The Phalanstery presented architecture as an agent of social change. Meier's building, too, was conceived to have iconic significance in its design. Like the Phalanstery, the Atheneum was planned to be an isolated building, placed on a podium in a natural landscape. Gallery III was designed around a dramatic, large-scale, realistic model of New Harmony in 1824. Because only eight Harmonist sites and fifteen Harmonist buildings are identifiable today in central New Harmony, the model was conceived as the best possible means of relating these sites and buildings to their original context. The model was housed in a specially engineered environment that Meier created. Aligned with the present town grid, the model was situated so that key features of the present-day landscape, viewed through the gallery's windows, would be oriented to features of the model itself. The gallery also exhibited the nine overlay maps that I prepared to document the changes that, over time, altered and/or enhanced the landscape of New Harmony. Finally, *The New Harmony Experience,* a film produced by Historic New Harmony Inc. to be shown daily on the large screen in the Clowes Theater, continues to provide the ultimate opportunity for visitor orientation, motivation, and inspiration. Composer/conductor Richard Wetzel, a scholar of Harmonist and Owen/Maclure period music, wrote the score for the film. The New Harmony model, used extensively in the film, shows the original Rapp mansion with its belvedere above the roof that provided an overview of the town. Rapp's belvedere was captured by Meier with his building circulation that moves across the roof and culminates in a great overview. The important point here is that the Atheneum, the models, and the film were created to relate together and inform the visitor.

My role in New Harmony was never intended to be permanent. Neither could the initial support of the Lilly Endowment be expected to continue beyond the early years in which we were generating promising ideas, preserving, and stabilizing the local economy, although the Lilly Endowment did provide substantial support for the renovation of the Rapp–Owen Granary. As William Marlin reported in "Revitalizing the Architectural Legacy of an American 'Camelot,'" published in the *Christian Science Monitor* on April 16, 1976: "The tree-textured town of New Harmony, during the last few years, has been engineering a refurbished place for itself in the nation's intellectual sunshine."

After my departure, the decision to affiliate the interests of Historic New Harmony Inc. with the University of Southern Indiana in 1985 appears to have been very promising, since the third objective (noted above) for its creation by the New Harmony Commission was "development of an international cultural and education center." The proximity of the university is ideal. Undoubtedly, Dr. David Rice, president emeritus of the University of Southern Indiana, who maintained an office in New Harmony, and Donald Pitzer, New Harmony scholar and professor emeritus of history and director emeritus of the Center for Communal Studies at the University of Southern Indiana, and the current USI administration could provide initial thoughts. Institutions change as their leadership moves on. A concerted effort with aggressive leadership could turn New Harmony into a midwestern Aspen, a think tank, and bring new distinction to the University of Southern Indiana.

Near the end of my decade in New Harmony, I obviously had thoughts about the future. The New Harmony Plan was in place. Buildings had been restored; new buildings had been added. A tour plan, emanating from the Atheneum, provided the visitor an opportunity to proceed to selected destinations. This remarkable perspective plan was drawn by David Parker. Born in New Harmony, he was in his final years in high school when the Atheneum was under construction. Parker met Meier at that time and was inspired by all that was happening in New Harmony to proceed with a career in architecture, later graduating from the University of Virginia and then Harvard University. Today Parker is a highly respected architect with a national reputation. While an undergraduate at the University of Virginia, he returned home for summer vacations and would volunteer to work with us at Historic New Harmony Inc. In preparing the perspective tour plan, Parker developed a new concept that, I believe, is unique to New Harmony: that of telling the story in the historic environment in segments, at locations where specific actions or events occurred. Obviously the Harmonist and Owen/Maclure communities provided the original physical plan. Their contributions and subsequent events reveal a much greater story. These related but individual diverse segments that act as mini-museums are what make the New Harmony tour unforgettable and relevant. Parker's perspective map did not address all the possible segment destinations, but it does illustrate alternative routes of visitor circulation, achieving some chronology, that would climax in Jane Owen's twentieth-century section before returning to the Atheneum parking lot.

The miracle is that New Harmony is clustered in the toe of Indiana, a rural, quiet, beautiful area. It is the kind of destination people long for. All they need is the incentive to visit. All the support facilities are here: wonderful accommodations, great food, superb conference facilities, theaters, a dynamic and intellectual environment, and isolation from the busy world, perfect for relaxation, a think tank, or the stimulation of new ideas. The future holds great promise for New Harmony.

My response to the following question, posed to me by the editor of this book, seems a fitting conclusion: "Jane Blaffer Owen repeatedly cited Paul Tillich's *The Religious Situation,* in which he declares that 'to understand the present means to see it in its inner tension toward the future.' How do you feel about this relationship in terms of your work in New Harmony?" I believe that if we are to preserve that history which is most precious to us, we must not isolate it from contemporary life. In New Harmony now, we are intent on integrating a distinguished history with a proud present and an exciting and successful future. For we have found that history is continuous. We are discovering that only by living with the past in a contemporary sense can we give lasting impact and real meaning to our most venerated ideals and institutions.

Architect Kenneth A. Schuette Jr. created the Cathedral Labyrinth in 2000 and began development of the Jane Blaffer Owen Sanctuary Plan in 2013. He has restored and developed plans for Jane Owen's landscape and building designs for the Blaffer Foundation. Courtesy of Griffin Norman.

The Jane Blaffer Owen Sanctuary Plan within Her Vision for New Harmony

KENNETH A. SCHUETTE JR.

The Vision

Jane Owen believed that sacred space came about by imparting spiritual energy into a domain. For her, landscape design was capable of changing the natural sphere into a spiritual landscape, as if transubstantiation had taken place within the earth. She was inspired by the writings of the Reverend George MacLeod of Iona Abbey, Scotland. In 1976 she dedicated a guest room to Jane Watson in the Orchard House in New Harmony, which has the dedication document. MacLeod's blessing at the dedication of the house contained the following:

> Lord Christ, with you there is no distance or space or time. You are above us and beneath us. So, we ask further to build this house so that its very atmosphere inspires faith in its changing residents, engenders hope and its fellowship breeds love. We ask You to build a community round it, a city that is obedient, courageous, co-operative and vibrant with the sound of a New Harmony: where the old may find comfort, the middle-aged recover vision, and the young find courage.

The Sanctuary Landscape

The creation of the Jane Blaffer Owen Sanctuary in 2013 by a unanimous vote of the board of directors is a permanent program of the Robert Lee Blaffer Foundation. A support organization, the Friends of the Jane Blaffer Owen Sanctuary, was also approved in 2013. The Sanctuary calls for a unified landscape in which the concept of regeneration is at the core. Living landscapes are in a perpetual cycle of life, death, and rebirth. In respect to this grand cycle, of which we are all an integral part, the Sanctuary is envisioned as a unified landscape of gardens consisting of seven structures, eight gardens, six fountains and pools, and twenty-one outdoor sculptures that Jane Owen, with her husband, Kenneth Owen, created or restored over sixty years to be one indivisible landscape. The unified plan proposes a planting strategy for species that ensures a continuous blooming period of trees, shrubs, and perennials, taking into account the scent, color, and form of the flowers that the Harmonists, Maclurian naturalists, and Jane Owen worked with. (George Rapp's plant list is in the State Archive, Harrisburg, Pennsylvania.) In 2015 the landscapes of the Roofless Church, Carol's Garden, and Paul Tillich Park were extensively restored by replanting trees, flowers, and groundcover.

The Future Plan

Historic gardens associated with the vision of personalities, such as Victoria (Vita) Sackville-West and her husband, Harold Nicolson, at Sissinghurst, England, have become vital centers of contemplation and ecotourism. The spiritual landscapes and sacred spaces Jane Owen left to the community are ripe for renewed leadership in order to be sustainable, protected, enhanced, and moved forward into the next century. The future could envision a dedicated curatorial and gardening staff akin to that established for Thomas Jefferson's Thousand Foot Garden at Monticello, Virginia.

The Sanctuary plan follows the sixteen Articles of *The Venice Charter for the Conservation and Restoration of Monuments and Sites,* established in 1964. The Jane Blaffer Owen Sanctuary in New Harmony would take a position on landscape preservation, opening the gardens to an agenda of engagement, which includes participation *in* the landscape rather than solely wandering *through* it. Contemplation would have an active and practical aspect of working the land, planting and maintaining flowers, and considering preservation to be a form of participatory ecotourism in the Midwest United States. It would be a meditative practice, reflecting the Benedictine motto *ora et labora* (prayer and work), which Jane Owen followed as she labored in her gardens throughout her life.

Structures, Gardens, Fountains and Pools, and Sculptures Commissioned or Restored by Jane Owen Included in the Jane Blaffer Owen Sanctuary Plan (2013)

The following catalog includes the name, date of completion, and architect or sculptor of landscape elements and artworks in the Jane Blaffer Owen Sanctuary Plan. The author and editors do not claim to know of past or current ownership of these works. Dates and names of some buildings (in parentheses) are taken from *Posey County Interim Report, Indiana Historic Sites and Structures Inventory,* Historic Landmarks Foundation of Indiana, 2004. This catalog does not include art within the interior of buildings. Items marked (RLBF) belong to the Robert Lee Blaffer Foundation.

STRUCTURES

1. Barrett–Gate House, 1814, 1960 renovation by Robert Hatch (RLBF).
2. Mother Superior House (attached to Kilbinger House, 1820), circa 1965 renovation by James Associates, Rose Aimee Broz (RLBF).
3. Poet's House (George Frank House), 1822, 1988 renovation by James Associates, Rose Aimee Broz (RLBF).
4. Owen Community House, circa 1840, 2013 addition by Kenneth A. Schuette Jr. (RLBF).
5. The Roofless Church Shrine, including Solomon's Women's Porch, 1960, Philip Johnson (RLBF).
6. The George MacLeod Barn Abbey, 1976, Robert Hatch (RLBF).
7. Sarah Campbell Blaffer Pottery Studio (site of Rose Bank House), 1978, Richard Meier, 2000 reconstruction by Koester Construction (RLBF).
8. Our Lady Queen of Peace Shrine, honoring Thomas Merton, placed in 1986, French carver, antiquity artist and date unknown, sited by Thomas J. Kane (RLBF).
9. Chapel of the Little Portion (St. Francis Chapel), 1988, Stephen De Staebler (RLBF).
10. Cathedral Labyrinth and Sacred Garden Gate, 1996, Kenneth A. Schuette Jr. (RLBF).
11. Mark Hampton Court Gate, 1998, Kenneth A. Schuette Jr. (RLBF).

GARDENS

1. The Roofless Church Garden, 1965, Philip Johnson; garden revision, date unknown, Thomas J. Kane, landscape architect (RLBF).
2. Paul Tillich Park, 1965, Robert L. Zion, landscape architect (RLBF).
3. Carol's Garden of Life, orchard design by Edward Gilbert, 1969; garden plan by Jane Blaffer Owen, 1979; in process of restoration, 2017 (RLBF).
4. Cathedral Labyrinth and Sacred Garden, 1996, Kenneth A. Schuette Jr. (RLBF).
5. Mark Hampton's Court, 1998, Jane Owen, garden design unfinished (RLBF).
6. The Poet's House Garden, landscape design by Jane Blaffer Owen (RLBF).

FOUNTAINS AND POOLS

1. Carol's Garden: *Fountain of Life,* 1982, David Rogers (RLBF).
2. Roofless Church: *Grandparents' Baptismal Fountain,* 1995, William Schickel (RLBF).

3. Cathedral Labyrinth and Sacred Garden: *Orpheus Fountain,* 1998, Simon Verity (RLBF).

4. *The Crucible,* 2002, Theodore Prescott (RLBF).

SCULPTURES

1. Roofless Church: *Descent of the Holy Spirit (Notre Dame de Liesse),* 1960, Jacques Lipchitz (RLBF).

2. Roofless Church: *Suzanne Glémet Memorial Gates,* 1962, Jacques Lipchitz (RLBF).

3. *Meditation,* 1965, John Chase Lewis (RLBF).

4. Tillich Park: *Bust of Tillich,* 1964–65, James Rosati (RLBF).

5. Tillich Park: five stones, 1966, Ralph Beyer, letterer (RLBF).

6. *The Prophet and the Shepherd,* 1967–68, Herold Witherspoon (RLBF).

7. Roofless Church: *Polish Memorial,* 1968, Ewa Żygulska (RLBF).

8. *Peace Arch,* 1971, Bruno La Verdiere (RLBF).

9. Carol's Garden: two benches, 1982, David Rogers (RLBF).

10. Roofless Church: *As the Clay . . .* (tablets), 1983, Gail Russell (RLBF).

11. Carol's Garden: *Mother–Daughter Bench,* 1983, Carroll Harris Simms (RLBF).

12. Roofless Church: *Pietà,* 1988, Stephen De Staebler (RLBF).

13. Roofless Church: *Beauvais* and bench (whereabouts unknown), 1988, Mark Mennin (RLBF).

14. *St. Francis and the Angel of the Sixth Seal* (on the mound), 1989, Brother David Kocka.

15. Granite stone next to St. Francis with carved seats, 1990, William P. Duffy (RLBF).

16. *Shalev, or Angel of Compassion,* 1993, Toby Kahn (RLBF).

17. Roofless Church wall: *Scent of Memory* (plaque, *God's Breath*), 1994, Mark Mennin (RLBF).

18. Mark Hampton's Court: three benches, 1998, Simon Verity (RLBF).

19. *Angel of the Annunciation,* 1999, Stephen De Staebler (RLBF).

20. *Saint Francis and the Birds,* 2006, Frederick Frank.

21. Roofless Church wall: *Canterbury Cross,* date and artist unknown, gift of Herbert Waddams (RLBF).

22. *St. Francis Cross at Chapel,* date unknown, Allen Ditson (RLBF).

Structures, Gardens, Fountains and Pools, and Exterior Sculptures Commissioned or Worked on by Jane Blaffer Owen Not Included in the Jane Blaffer Owen Sanctuary Plan (2013)

STRUCTURES

1. Rapp–Maclure–Owen House, 1814, Frederick Rapp; 1844, Alexander Maclure, in the style of Benjamin Latrobe; 1989, restored by Kenneth Dale and Jane Blaffer Owen.
2. Rawlings House, 1815.
3. Rapp–Owen Granary, 1818, Frederick Rapp; 1890; 1999, restoration and renovation by Hafer and Associates.
4. No. 5, a.k.a. No. V (Hornle House), 1822.
5. Studio House (Johannes Stahl House), 1822.
6. 1840 House (John Wheatcroft House), 1841; restoration by James Associates, Rose Aimee Broz, Roll McLaughlin.
7. Duclos House, circa 1840; renovation, architect unknown.
8. David Dale Owen Laboratory, 1859, architectural design attributed to (but unproved) Dr. David Dale Owen and James Renwick Jr.; circa 1941–44, Kenneth Dale Owen supervised the renovation by Fred E. Cook, with historical assessment from Earl H. Reed, FAIA.
9. Green Gothic (Pelham House), 1860, 1960 renovation by James Associates, Rose Aimee Broz.
10. Orchard House (Lichtenberger House), 1867, 1970s renovation by Robert Hatch with interior design by Mark Hampton.
11. Earth Care (Railway Depot), circa 1881.
12. The Mews, 1880, 1970s renovation by Robert Hatch.
13. The Red Geranium Restaurant, circa 1960, builder unknown.
14. The New Harmony Inn, 1974, Evans Woollen, architect.
15. Inn Entry House, 1974, Evans Woollen, architect.
16. Tree of Life Clinic, 1975, James Associates Architects (demolished 2013).
17. Lanark Green Townhouses, circa 1982.
18. Pleasure Boat, circa 1960–85, Edward Gilbert, artist.
19. The House of Tomorrow, circa 1997, Roger Rasbach, architectural designer.

GARDENS

1. Byzantine Islamic Arbor, dedicated to Afsaneh K. Ettehadieh, 1997, Robin Brent Davis, constructed by Thomas Helfrich.

2. Lenz Garden, 2002, history-inspired design by Horticulture and Landscape Architecture Department, Purdue University.
3. Our Lord's Woods sign, date unknown, constructed by Thomas Helfrich.
4. Church Park, 1997, Storrow Kinsella, landscape architect; reinterpreted by Jane Blaffer Owen, James E. Parrent Jr., and Connie Weinzapfel.
5. Our Lord's Woods, date unknown, Thomas J. Kane, landscape architect.
6. St. Benedict Garden, date unknown, Evans Woollen, architect, and Thomas J. Kane, landscape architect.
7. Marshall Rose Garden [Mary Jane ("Maisie") and Whitfield H. ("Pat") Marshall], late 1970s until mid-1980s, artist unknown.
8. Fragrant Farms, 1995, South Street.
9. Ricky's Garden, date and designer unknown.

FOUNTAINS AND POOLS

1. Swan Lake and Waterfall, 1983, D. K. Parker Company, Inc.
2. Byzantine Islamic Garden (arbor, fountain, and mosaic), 1990, Robin Brent Davis.
3. Fountain of Commitment, Church Park, 2001, Donald Gummer.

SCULPTURES

1. *Ten Commandments,* around Waddams Chapel, 1975, Ralph Beyer, sculptor.
2. *Sky Dance,* 1985, Larry Reising, fabricated by Thomas and Elmer Helfrich.
3. *St. Louis,* 1988, Robin Brent Davis, case designed by Evans Woollen.
4. Canterbury Gate, 1989, designed by Robin Brent Davis, built by Thomas Helfrich.
5. Peace Pole, 2010, peacepoleproject.org.
6. Monet Bridge, date unknown, built by D. K. Parker Company, Inc.
7. Bench, date unknown, William Duffy.
8. Our Lord's Woods: two ceramics, date and artist unknown.

Acknowledgments

AVANT-GARDE IN THE CORNFIELDS serves as a scholarly complement to Jane Blaffer Owen's posthumously published *New Harmony, Indiana: Like a River, Not a Lake: A Memoir* (Bloomington: Indiana University Press, 2015). Our book's gestation was facilitated by a host of generous individuals and institutions in the Midwest (Chicago and New Harmony) and the Southwest (Houston). The relationship that Jane Owen held between the small rural town of New Harmony, where she spent four months of the year, and the cosmopolitan metropolis of Houston, her family's base, is what makes this story particularly intriguing. We thank all who have made a contribution.

The roots of the book reach back to 2005, and its genesis is indebted to academic institutions in both Chicago and Houston. Our thanks go to all those who catalyzed the process. In his role of director of the Chicago-based Archeworks, Stanley Tigerman invited Ben Nicholson to publish "New Harmony: The Hands Can't Do What the Mind Can't See" in *The Archeworks Papers* 1, no. 3 (2006). Donna Robertson, then dean of the College of Architecture, Illinois Institute of Technology, supported a New Harmony Option Studio in 2006. Joseph Mashburn, then dean of the Gerald D. Hines College of Architecture and Design at the University of Houston (UH), celebrated the New Harmony and Houston dialogue with an exhibition he curated with architectural historian Stephen James, *Jane Blaffer Owen and the Legacy of New Harmony* (Spring 2007). UH faculty Andrew Vrana and Joe Meppelink worked with Ben Nicholson, who directed the 2008 Kiesler Studio, on realizing Jane Owen's last built project, *The New Harmony Grotto,* which now stands on a site adjacent to the Gerald D. Hines College of Architecture and Design.

In 2010 the symposium "Frederick Kiesler—From New Harmony to Houston" was curated by Michelangelo Sabatino and held at the University of Houston. Our thanks go to Beatriz Colomina and Jane Owen for their significant contributions. In the summer of 2016 the Eighth Annual Architecture, Culture, and Spirituality Symposium came to New Harmony with the theme of Utopia, Architecture, and Spirituality. We are indebted to the participants' insights.

Throughout the past decade, our thanks go to the students from the Illinois Institute of Technology, University of Houston, School of the Art Institute of Chicago, University of Michigan, and Purdue University who completed various projects related to this book. In their inquisitive manner, akin to a pack of bloodhounds, they opened up questions that the authors would never have been able to see by themselves.

Initially, this book was titled *Forms of Spirituality,* and its center of gravity was Frederick Kiesler's unbuilt cave/grotto project in New Harmony. After Owen's death in 2010, it became clear that the book's trajectory should address the wide cultural impact of New Harmony on a number of fronts, including architecture, gardens and landscape, and preservation. We are especially grateful to Laura McGuire, Joe Meppelink, John Philip Newell, Monika Pessler, Kenneth A. Schuette Jr., and Andrew Vrana, who worked on texts that were sacrificed for this critical change of direction. We are glad that some of these chapters have been published elsewhere.

From the beginning, Jane Owen supported the project and the independence of its scholarship. Anne Dale Owen continued family interest in the book with access to archival material and photographs of the Blaffer Owen family. We are grateful to Barrie Scardino Bradley, former executive director of the Architecture Center, who arranged funding from the Architecture Houston Foundation, and to Joseph Mashburn, professor emeritus and former dean of the Gerald D. Hines College of Architecture and Design, for matching funds.

In New Harmony, Gerry Gerard and Erik Arneberg of the Robert Lee Blaffer Foundation gave us access to the Robert Lee Blaffer Trust Archives and the Tillich Archive and, together with Docey Lewis, ensured that anything that would help the book's passage would be made available to us. We thank the Robert Lee Blaffer Foundation for its permission to publish archival materials. Clement Penrose VII, director of the New Harmony Artists' Guild, gave advice and succor throughout. Connie Weinzapfel, director emerita of Historic New Harmony, Inc., has been a constant friend and adviser to this project. She introduced us to Jennifer Greene, the reference and archives librarian at the David L. Rice Library, University of Southern Indiana. Donald E. Pitzer, professor and director emeritus of the Center for Communal Studies at the University of Southern Indiana, kindly shared his wisdom and knowledge.

Amanda Bryden, State Historic Sites Collections Manager, Indiana State Museum and Historic Sites, has an encyclopedic knowledge of all things in New Harmony and worked tirelessly on our behalf with her collections assistant, Meagan Patterson. Calligrapher Janet Lorence, a longtime resident of New Harmony, drew a fine map of New Harmony for this book and generously devoted time to research questions related to public works of art. Thanks also go to Historic New Harmony's team over the past twelve years, including Christine Crews, Marlene Huffaker, Jan Kahle, Erin McCracken Merris, Jacque Nodell, Sarah Talley, and Linda Warrum. Ryan Rokicki, director of the New Harmony Working Men's Institute, along with his predecessors, has been a fount of information. Judy Alsop, formerly of the New Harmony Inn, and Chris Laughbaum of the Robert Lee Blaffer Foundation have been champions of logistics.

We owe thanks to all the authors who contributed chapters to this book. Inevitably, working with a group of individuals spread across the country presents challenges in terms of logistics and scheduling, and we thank them for their immense patience.

William R. Crout, founder and curator of the Paul Tillich Lectures, the Memorial Church, Harvard University, died before the book was published and, with great courage and fortitude, worked on his contribution right up to the end. Through his treasured friendship with Dr. Mutie Tillich Farris, we thank her son, Ted Farris, for permission to include unpublished archival materials related to Paul and Hannah Tillich to enhance our book.

We appreciate and thank the staff at the many archives we worked with in the United States and Europe. Sarah Buffington, curator of Old Economy Village in Pennsylvania, helped us on issues relating to George Rapp, and Jane Masters, heritage manager of the New Lanark Trust, helped us with matters concerning Robert Owen. Dieter Bogner, director, and Monika Pessler, former director, of the Austrian Frederick and Lillian Kiesler Private Foundation were generous collaborators from the start, and Jill Meissner made available to us every aspect of the Foundation's archive. We thank the Austrian Frederick and Lillian Kiesler Private Foundation for its permission to publish archival materials. Stephen M. Cadwalader, vice president of the Jason McCoy Gallery that houses many of Kiesler's works, has been enormously generous to the project. Our thanks go to Richard Meier with Bernhard Karpf of Richard Meier & Partners Architects, who gave interviews on every aspect of the New Harmony Atheneum as well as opened their archive.

A number of anonymous readers for the University of Chicago Press offered insightful advice at various stages of the review process. Although we did not publish with the University of Chicago Press, executive editor Susan Bielstein was a champion of the book and a tireless critic from whom we learned much. To Margaret Grubiak goes a very special mention for suggesting that we contact the University of Minnesota Press, whose senior acquisitions editor Pieter Martin and Anne Carter have been incredibly efficient and supportive. Nancy Mangum McCaslin, resident of both New Harmony and Houston, and editor of Jane Owen's memoir, has given herself tirelessly at every stage of the writing, research, and editorial process.

To those not named who have nevertheless shared their knowledge and time with us during this labyrinthine journey, we thank you for your collective contributions. Finally, we are humbled by the inimitable town of New Harmony that sets the strains of cosmopolitan, provincial, and vernacular culture into high relief. As a living laboratory, where the urban and rural converge while mediated by an unknowable spirit, it continues to inspire all those who pass through it.

Ben Nicholson and Michelangelo Sabatino

Contributors

WILLIAM R. CROUT (1929–2015) was founder and curator of the Paul Tillich Lectures at the Memorial Church, Harvard University, and a former graduate student, editorial assistant, and friend of Paul Tillich. He worked with the Office of the University Marshal, Harvard University. He established and led the Cambridge Writers Group for more than twenty years.

STEPHEN FOX is an architectural historian and a fellow of the Anchorage Foundation of Texas. He teaches at Rice University School of Architecture and the Gerald D. Hines College of Architecture and Design at the University of Houston.

CHRISTINE GORBY is an architect, historian, and associate professor of architecture at The Pennsylvania State University.

CAMMIE MCATEE is an architectural and design historian and curator. She is coeditor of *The Politics of Furniture: Identity, Diplomacy, and Persuasion in Post-War Interiors* and editor of *Montreal's Geodesic Dreams: Jeffrey Lindsay and the Fuller Research Foundation Canadian Division.*

NANCY MANGUM MCCASLIN is an editor and writer who divides her time between Houston and New Harmony. She edited Jane Blaffer Owen's memoir *New Harmony, Indiana: Like a River, Not a Lake*. She is a member of the advisory board of Historic New Harmony, a unified program of the University of Southern Indiana and the Indiana State Museum and Historic Sites.

BEN NICHOLSON is professor at the School of the Art Institute of Chicago. He is the author of *Appliance House, Thinking the Unthinkable House,* and *The World: Who Wants It?* as well as guest editor of *CLOG + GUNS.*

MICHELANGELO SABATINO is professor and former dean of the College of Architecture of the Illinois Institute of Technology. He is the author of *Pride in Modesty: Modernist Architecture and the Vernacular Tradition in Italy* and coauthor of *Canada: Modern Architectures in History.*

KENNETH A. SCHUETTE JR. is an architect and professor in the Purdue University Landscape Architecture program. He was commissioned by Jane Blaffer Owen to replicate the Chartres Cathedral labyrinth in a Sacred Garden in New Harmony. He is on the board of directors of the Robert Lee Blaffer Foundation in New Harmony.

RALPH GRAYSON SCHWARZ (1925–2018) was a foundation executive, planner, architect, and historian. He authored *Bethlehem on the Lehigh, Bach in Bethlehem,* and *Saucon Valley Country Club: An American Legacy, 1920–2000,* and coauthored *Southport: The Architectural Legacy of a Connecticut Village.*

PAUL TILLICH (1886–1965) was an influential twentieth-century Protestant theologian and philosopher who reached a broad audience with his popular books *The Courage to Be* and *The Dynamics of Faith.* His three-volume *Systematic Theology* was also a classic. He emigrated with his family from Nazi Germany and began teaching at Union Theological Seminary before accepting an appointment in 1954 as University Professor at Harvard; his final position was at the University of Chicago.

Index

Massachusetts Institute of Technology (MIT) Chapel, xxviii, 113, *114*, 115

mathematics, 140–41; aesthetics and, 167n121

Matisse, Henri, 40

Maximilian-Bodmer Collection, 91

Maximilian of Wied-Neuwied, Prince, xv

May, Rollo, 206, 207

May Day, 110, 131, 192

McAuliffe, Martin L., Jr., 21

McCarthy, Joseph, 60n50

McCaslin, Nancy Mangum, xxii, xxxvn12, 30n31, 58n32, 60n50, 63n72, 155n10

McGuire, Laura M., 56n20

McLaughlin, Harry Roll, 79

"Mechanic's Atheneum," 294n6

media, 59n35; electronic, 290; high culture and, 57n27

Meditation (Lewis), 322

Meier, Richard, xii, 26–27, 59n35, 60n46, 93, 264, 266, 272, 274, 283, 291, 294n1, 294n10, 295n17, 295n19, 295n21, 296n23, 296n28, 296n30, 296n32, 298n45, 298n48, 298n57, 300n76, 315, 316; Atheneum and, xxx, xxxi, 105, 265, 277–78, 278–79, 280, 284, 286, 288, 290, 292, 293; Blaffer Owen and, 21, 280–81; design process and, xxx, 277; exhibition by, *plate 25*; five-degree wedge and, 270; influences on, 272, 278; monograph by, 275; plan of, xxx; Potter's House and, 280–81; Schwarz and, 266, 267, 270, 295n20, 297n41; selection of, 314; Visitor's Center and, 81, 266, 270–71

Meier Associates, 292

Mellow, James K.: photo by, *241*

Menil, Dominique Schlumberger de, 19, 41, 46, 50, 54, 56n19, 57n22, 62n67, 110, 158n36; ecumenical movement and, 48, 50; Johnson and, 115; patronage of, xxii, 48, 51

Menil, John de, 19, 41, 43, 50, 52, 54, 56n19, 56n20, 57n22, 110, 116, 158n36, 159n39; career of, 62n62; death of, 50, 51; Johnson and, 42, 115; media attention for, 62n6; patronage of, xxii, 48, 51; segregation and, 62n62; University of St. Thomas and, 44

Menil Collection, 51, 62n67

Menil House, 51

Mennin, Mark, 322

Meppelink, Joe, 210, 212, 225n141

Merton, Thomas, 96, 231, 255n21

Mertzbau, 265

Mews, The, 312, 313, 323

Mies van der Rohe, Ludwig, xxviii, 58n34, 108, 113, 162n70, 164n91, 179, 186, *188*, 210, 272, 274, 286; Farnsworth House and, 60n50

Miley, Les, 298n52

Mili, Gjon, 186; photo by, *188*

Miller, J. Irwin, 41, 42, 46, 49, 50, 51, 52, 61n57, 61n58, 294n3; March on Washington and, xxxviin27; patronage of, xxii, 48

Miller, Will, 61n58

Miller, Xenia S., 49

Miller House, 49

Mill Number 1, 2, 3 buildings, *xxi*

Milton, Hank, 295n15

Minerva Society Pageant, 68, 71

Ministry of Education and Health Building, 220n90

Mitchell, Cynthia, 27n4

Mitchell, George, 27n4

M'Mahon, Bernard, 248

modern architecture, 42–44, 46, 47, 53, 58n34, 213n4, 261; critique of, 58n28; superiority of, 58n29

modern art, 12, 13, 14, 40, 42, 43, 46, 53, 58n29, 110, 116, 229; secular, 20, 23

modernism, xii, xxii, xxvii, xxviii, 19–21, 35n90, 39, 42, 49, 52, 57n21, 210; history and, 53, 57n21; metropolitan, 43; myths of, 54; populist aversion to, 47; propagation of, 42

"Modernism in New Harmony" (conference session), 26

Modern Masters, 271, 279

Modulor, theory of, 144

Moholy-Nagy, Hattula, 158n28

Moholy-Nagy, Sibyl, 113, 135–36, 138, 144, 147, 149, 158n28

Mondrian, Piet, 267

Monet Bridge, 324

Mongan, Agnes, 14, 35n90

Moore, Charles, 294n11

Moore, Robin, 163n77

Morton, W. Brown, III, 85

Mother–Daughter Bench (Simms), 322